Iberian Military Politics

Iberian Military Politics

Controlling the Armed Forces during Dictatorship and Democratisation

José Javier Olivas Osuna

Fellow, The London School of Economics and Political Science, United Kingdom

palgrave
macmillan

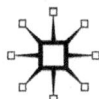

First published 2014 by
PALGRAVE MACMILLAN

Palgrave Macmillan in the UK is an imprint of Macmillan Publishers Limited, registered in England, company number 785998, of Houndmills, Basingstoke, Hampshire RG21 6XS.

Palgrave Macmillan in the US is a division of St Martin's Press LLC, 175 Fifth Avenue, New York, NY 10010.

Palgrave Macmillan is the global academic imprint of the above companies and has companies and representatives throughout the world.

Palgrave® and Macmillan® are registered trademarks in the United States, the United Kingdom, Europe and other countries.

ISBN: 978–1–137–32537–2

This book is printed on paper suitable for recycling and made from fully managed and sustained forest sources. Logging, pulping and manufacturing processes are expected to conform to the environmental regulations of the country of origin.

A catalogue record for this book is available from the British Library.

Library of Congress Cataloging-in-Publication Data

Olivas Osuna, José Javier, 1976–
    Iberian military politics : controlling the armed forces during dictatorship and democratisation / José Javier Olivas Osuna.
      pages cm
    ISBN 978–1–137–32537–2 (hardback)
    1. Civil military relations – Portugal – History – 20th century. 2. Civil-military relations – Spain – History – 20th century. 3. Portugal – Armed Forces – Political activity – History – 20th century. 4. Spain – Armed Forces – Political activity – History – 20th century. 5. Dictatorship – Portugal – History – 20th century. 6. Dictatorship – Spain – History – 20th century. 7. Democratization – Portugal. 8. Democratization – Spain. I. Title.

JN8514.O55 2014
322'.50946—dc23   2014024478

For Mariana, Victoria, and Martín

Contents

List of Figures

List of Tables

Acknowledgements

There are many people I want to thank for their support and contribution to this book.

It is difficult to find words to express my gratitude to Martin Lodge for his detailed and unfailing support at the Department of Government of the London School of Economics and Political Science. He provided a constructive source of challenge throughout the years of my research. I am also indebted to José Antonio Olmeda for his extremely helpful feedback and guidance on Spanish civil-military relations. He and Salvador Parrado were incredibly hospitable during my time at UNED in Madrid. Stefan Bauchowitz (LSE) has my gratitude for his excellent suggestions and editorial support. To Rafael Vázquez, Miguel Jerez Mir (Universidad de Granada), and Jonathan Hopkin (LSE), I owe much for their very useful comments and practical advice in the later stages of this project. To Eduardo Martins and Pedro Aires de Oliveira (Universidade Nova de Lisboa), I am thankful for their help concerning Portuguese history; as well as Vassilis Paipais (University of St Andrews) and Anar Ahmadov (Universiteit Leiden) for the clarifications and long discussions on theory and methodology. Next, I want to express my gratitude to Sebastian Balfour whose course in Spanish politics at the LSE became a source of inspiration for this research. I also want to thank my colleagues and friends from the LSE100 and the Department of Government at the LSE for all the comments and debates that helped me rethink and polish several aspects of this book.

This book would not have been possible without the financial support of the *Fundación Ramón Areces, Fundación Caja Madrid, Abbey/Santander* Travel Research Fund, *University of London* Central Research Fund, *LSE* Postgraduate Research Scholarships, and the *Becas Talentia* of the Andalusian Regional Government.

This book is dedicated to my wife Mariana whose love, patience, and support have been fundamental all these years. It is also thanks to Mariana that I had extra sources of joy and motivation to write this book: my children Victoria and Martín.

Lastly, I wish to thank my parents, Mari and José; my brother, Santiago (also the designer of the cover) and his wife, Esther; and my nephews Santi and Javier, my aunt, Isabel, and my grandmother Adela. Despite the distance, I always had very present their love and care. All the people above have made this long journey much more meaningful and enjoyable.

List of Acronyms and Abbreviations

ALEMI   Altos Estudios Militares (Advanced military training programme organised by CESEDEN)

AMI   Agrupamento Militar de Intervenção (Portuguese Military Intervention Group)

AP   Alianza Popular (Spanish right-wing political party)

BMI   Brigada Mista Independente (Independent Mixed Brigade. Portuguese elite brigade established in Santa Margarida)

CDS   Centro Democrático Social (Portuguese Social Democratic Centre Party)

CEME   Chefe de Estado-Maior do Exército (Chief of Staff of the Portuguese Army)

CEMGFA   Chefe de Estado-Maior-General das Forças Armadas (Chief of the Joint Staff of the Portuguese Armed Forces)

CESEDEN   Centro Superior de Estudios de la Defensa Nacional (Centre of National Defence High Studies)

CESID   Centro Superior de Información de la Defensa (Higher Centre of Defence Information)

CODICE   Comissão Dinamizadora Central (Central Dynamising Committee)

COPCON   Comando Operacional do Continente (Continent Operational Command). Special forces unit active during Portuguese transition

CR   Conselho da Revolução (Council of the Revolution)

CSDN   Conselho Superior de Defesa Nacional (Portuguese Higher Council of National Defence)

DAC   Division Acorazada (Armored Division of the Spanish Army established in Brunete, near Madrid)

DGS   Direcção-Geral de Segurança (Portuguese Security General Directorate). Portuguese secret police previously called PIDE

DRISDE   Dirección de Relaciones Informativas y Sociales de la Defensa (General Directorate of Information and Social Relations of Defence, Spain)

DSC   Direcção dos Serviços de Censura (Portuguese Directorate for Censorship Services)

EMACOM   Estado Mayor Conjunto (Joint High Staff). Spanish senior military training programme organised by CESEDEN

EME	Estado-Maior do Exército (Portuguese Army Staff Office)
EMGFA	Estado-Maior-General das Forças Armadas (Portuguese Joint Chiefs of Staff Board)
ETA	Euskadi Ta Askatasuna (Basque Homeland and Freedom). Basque separatist terrorist group
FNFF	Fundación Nacional Francisco Franco (Franco's Foundation which hosts his personal archive)
FOG	Fundación Ortega y Gasset (Spanish Foundation that hosts an audio archive with interviews about Spanish transition)
GNR	Guarda Nacional Republicana (Portuguese Republican National Guard)
GRAPO	Grupos de Resistencia Antifascista Primero de Octubre (First of October Anti-Fascist Resistance Groups). Spanish Maoist terrorist group
IDN	Instituto de Defesa Nacional (Portuguese National Defence Institute)
INI	Instituto Nacional de Industria (Spanish State-Owned Industrial Holding)
ISFAS	Instituto Social de las Fuerzas Armadas (Social Institute of the Armed Forces, Spain)
JEMAD	Jefe Estado Mayor de la Defensa (Chief of the Joint Staff of the Spanish Armed Forces)
JEME	Jefe de Estado Mayor del Ejercito (Chief of Staff of the Spanish Army)
JSN	Junta de Salvação Nacional (Junta of National Salvation)
JUJEM	Junta de Jefes de Estado Mayor (Spanish Joint Chiefs of Staff)
MAAG	US Military Assistance Advisory Group
MFA	Movimento das Forças Armadas (Armed Forces Movement)
PCE	Partido Comunista Español (Spanish Communist Party)
PCP	Partido Comunista Português (Portuguese Communist Party)
PIDE	Polícia Internacional e de Defesa do Estado (State Defence International Police). Portuguese secret police, previously called PVDE. Later known as DGS
PJM	Polícia Judiciária Militar (Portuguese Military Judiciary Police)
PPD	Partido Popular Democrático (Portuguese Democratic Popular Party)
PPM	Partido Popular Monárquico (Portuguese Monarchist Popular Party)
PRP	Partido Revolucionário do Proletariado (Revolutionary Party of the Proletariat)
PS	Partido Socialista (Portuguese Socialist Party)

PSD	Partido Social Democrata (Social Democratic Party). Successor to PPD
PSOE	Partido Socialista Obrero Español (Spanish Socialist Party)
PSP	Polícia de Segurança Pública (Portuguese Public Security Police)
PVDE	Polícia de Vigilância e de Defesa do Estado (State Defence and Surveillance Police). Portuguese secret police, later transformed into PIDE
SDCI	Serviço de Detecção e Coordenação de Informações (Information Detection and Coordination Services)
SECED	Servicio Central de Documentación (Central Documentation Service)
SIED	Serviço de Informações Estratégicas de Defesa (Portuguese Defense Strategic Information Service)
SIFNE	Servicios de Información del Nordeste del España (Service of Information of the North-East Frontier). Francoist information services active during the Civil War
SIME	Serviço de Informações Militares do Exército (Military Information Service of the Portuguese Army)
SIP	Servicio de Información de Personal (Personnel Information Service)
SIPM	Servicio de Información y Policía Militar (Service of Information and Military Police)
SNI	Secretariado Nacional de Informação (National Information Secretariat)
SPN	Secretariado de Propaganda Nacional (Portuguese National Propaganda Secretariat)
UCD	Unión de Centro Democrático (Democratic Centre Union, Spanish centre-right political party)
UDP	União Democrática Popular (Popular Democratic Union)
UMD	Unión Democrática Militar (Spanish Democratic Military Union)

Part 1
Ambitions and Choices

1
Civil-Military Relations and Policy Instruments

The civil-military relations of Portugal and Spain have taken different trajectories during the twentieth century, in particular during the periods of authoritarian rule of Salazar and Franco and the transitions to democracy that followed. In Portugal, the military, which had overthrown the First Republic in 1926 and peacefully handed power over to a civilian dictator, António Oliveira Salazar, became a threat to the regime and ended up causing the downfall of the authoritarian Estado Novo with the Carnations revolution of 1974. In Spain, the military, which had helped Francisco Franco defeat the Republic in 1939, remained loyal to the dictator's principles and continued to pose a threat to democracy, culminating in the 23-F coup attempt on 23 February 1981.

This monograph analyses and compares the policy instruments that governments used to control the military throughout two stages of Portuguese and Spanish contemporary history: first, Salazar's and Franco's dictatorships and, second, the transitions during the early democratic periods (until 1986). It applies Christopher Hood's (1983) 'NATO' (*nodality, authority, treasure,* and *organisation*) framework for the study of the tools of government in order to identify trajectories and establish comparisons across time and across countries. This book shows that there was no one single 'Iberian' government style or model of civil-military relations nor a constant country-specific style throughout the period analysed. Authoritarian as well as transitional governments adopted different military policies and combinations of control tools in Portugal and Spain. Only from 1982 onwards can a clear process of convergence be observed in both countries. Finally, this book draws on neo-institutional theory to interpret the evolution of tool choices and civil-military relations. It explains that macro-historical events, such as

3

regime formation periods and wars, generated junctures and new trajectories in the control toolkit and that these trajectories were also shaped by institutional factors and the ideational environment.

This book combines extensive primary and secondary historical research with a political analytical framework. In addition to new facts, it provides – through the systematic application of the NATO framework – an innovative angle on preexisting empirical evidence and an alternative narrative about the evolution of civil-military relations in Portugal and Spain.

1.1   Why study civil-military relations?

The military is an essential instrument in the creation and maintenance of social communities and consequently in the building of nation-states (Finer 1975:84–103). However, history shows that militaries have also used their strength to influence, blackmail, displace, or even supplant governments (Finer 1988 [1962]:127). The interest in studying civil-military relations derived from the special institutional features of the armed forces and in the paradox that the organisation created to protect the polity is granted enough power to overthrow it (Feaver 1999:214).

Even in the twenty-first century, the tensions between the political and military spheres are more than evident in many contexts. The coups in the Central African Republic (2003), Fiji (2006), Guinea (2008), Mauritania (2008), Madagascar (2009), Honduras (2009), Niger (2010), Guinea-Bissau (2012), Egypt (2013), and Thailand (2014) are the latest evidence on how the military can successfully overturn the government of a country.[1] The problems experienced in countries currently trying to consolidate a democratic system, and in particular those belonging to the so-called 'Arab Spring', have brought concerns about civil-military relations back to the policy-making and research agendas. For instance, military intervention has been a crucial factor in overthrowing Ben Ali in Tunisia, Mubarak in Egypt, and Gaddafi in Libya. In Tunisia, the military that helped Ben Ali reach power via a coup in 1987 has exerted pressure on him to leave office (Brooks 2013). Once he had left the country, they judged and sentenced some of the leaders of the former regime and then retreated from the political arena during the transition process. Similarly, in Egypt, the military withdrew its support from the dictator provoking his downfall. However, in Egypt, the military has since actively intervened in the transition process. The Supreme Council of the Armed Forces granted itself extensive political powers and was criticised for resisting the electoral results and trying to condition the transitional outcome (Frisch 2013). The civil-military relations remained so tense that one year after the first democratic elections, the military removed President Mohamed Morsi and suspended the new Constitution. In Libya, Islamist militias, NATO airstrikes, and military defectors were instrumental in the defeat of Gaddafi's regime. Libya now faces the challenge of creating a unified national army to secure the government's monopoly of violence in order to facilitate democratisation (Gaub 2013).

Since there has been a longstanding normative consensus on the necessity of military subordination, the central question is not *whether* the military should be controlled but *how* the military should be controlled. Historians, sociologists, and political scientists have studied the military, their relations with the political power and society at large, as well as the mechanisms or strategies to control them. These concerns that were already present in classical military studies[2] have been expanded by a substantial body of modern literature which emerged in the twentieth century. Four waves of literature on civil-military relations can be distinguished.[3] The first wave appeared before the Second World War and supported the idea of demilitarisation.[4] The second one emerged during the early Cold War period and discusses the need for a permanent army given the threat to liberty that such an arrangement could pose.[5] The third wave that began in the 1960s may be divided into two streams: one favouring a sociological examination of the military,[6] and another focusing on an institutionally oriented examination of civil-military relations in developing countries with a special focus on the problem of military coups.[7] Finally, after the end of the Cold War, a new wave of civil-military literature has arisen focusing on the new challenges faced by democratic governments and following an approach closer to mainstream political science.[8]

Despite the interesting lessons that all of these works have provided, the underlying concerns and debates in the civil-military relations literature have not evolved greatly. As Forster (2006:11) argues, the literature on civil-military relations has been excessively self-referential and backward looking which has resulted in the slow evolution of the discussion and approaches to the field.[9] The traditional sociological debates in civil-military relations centred around the concept of professionalisation, the political or apolitical ethos of the military, the need for insulation or integration, and the military's autonomy remain well entrenched in the literature.[10] These debates, after having dominated the field for several decades, seem to have reached a dead end and have exhausted their capacities of theory generation (Feaver 1999:213). The lack of consensus has hindered cumulative progress. There is enough empirical evidence to challenge the best known theories in the field and more fine-grained analyses and theories are required (Staniland 2008:329)

1.2　Why a 'tool' or 'policy instrument' approach on civil–military relations?

This book marks a clear departure from the discussions that have dominated the literature and further connects the study of civil-military relations to public policy analysis. Rather than developing a general explanation of military control,[11] it focuses on the 'tools of control' or 'policy instruments' that governments choose. The goal is to contribute to a more fine-grained analysis and nuanced understanding of this complex phenomenon of military control.[12]

This monograph assumes that governments are concerned about military subordination but does not focus on measuring the degree of control over the military.[13] Instead, it seeks a better understanding about *what* is actually done to control the military and *why*. In particular, it explores *what* instruments were used by the governments to achive military subordination and *why* they were chosen. This exploration entails moving the focal point back along the causal chain aiming to provide some less divisive common ground of knowledge and a more stable basis for further academic attempts to assess the degree of civilian control and its implications.

Most definitions of the policy instruments and the tools of government stress their role as a means of social control that governments have at their disposal.[14] For instance, Salamon calls them 'techniques of social intervention' (1981:256). For Vedung they are 'techniques by which governmental authorities...wield their power in attempting to ensure support and effect social change' (1998:50). Landry and Varone define tools as a 'means of intervention by which governments attempt to induce individuals and groups to make decisions and take actions compatible with public policies' (2005:107–8). According to Lascoumes and Le Galès, a policy instrument 'constitutes a condensed form of knowledge about social control and ways of exercising it' (2007:3). In sum, policy instruments are the manifestation of the government's power and consequently, its instrument choices reflect different government strategies or styles. Since an understanding of governments and the way they exercise their power is important for civil-military relations, taking a closer look at the tools that the government employ seems a logical endeavour.[15]

The tools can also be considered the building blocks of policies (Linder and Peters 1989:42; Salamon 2002:20). The deconstruction of multi-faceted entities, such as policy programmes, into their basic components, tools, allows making sense of the growing complexity involved in modern government action.[16] In this case, the deconstruction of the governments' strategies to control the military into different and 'smaller' instruments helps to identify trends, to establish comparisons, and to trace policy change (Lascoumes and Le Galès 2007:18). Therefore, the dissection of complex military policies into a set of basic policy instruments paves the way for further cumulative research.

Focusing on the the tools used rather than on decision-making processes or on the evaluation of outcomes, reduces subjectivity and simplifies the analysis. Focusing on 'what government does' rather than on 'how it is decided' or 'what are its ultimate goals' diminishes the room for speculation and misunderstandings in the analysis of civil-military relations.[17]

Besides, it is interesting to observe the contribution of this book against the backdrop of the still not very well-developed literature on policy instruments.[18] So far, policy instruments have not been sufficiently studied (Vedung 1998:50) nor considered central in political science (Lascoumes and Le Galès 2007:1). Some recent works indicate a revival of the scholarly interest in policy instruments.[19] Despite this revitalisation, empirical studies are still scarce and their comparability is limited in the literature about policy instruments (Landry and Varone 2005:108). Too much attention continues to be devoted to single instrument studies, ignoring that the action of the government in practice always involves a mixture of the whole range of types of tools available (Hood 1983:154; Ringeling 2005:192; Howlett 2005:33). Moreover, the existing literature has failed to address the interplay of explanations based on historical legacies and contextual factors in policy choices. On the whole the policy instrument literature remains somewhat idiosyncratic and fragmented.

This book fills some of these gaps. It provides new empirical evidence drawn from comparative cases showing that governments generally employ combinations of several different types of tools.[20] In this endeavour, Hood's (1983) 'NATO scheme' for the study of the tools of government is adapted and used as a framework to deconstruct and compare military policies. NATO is an acronym that refers to the four basic resources that governments possess (*nodality, authority, treasure, and organisation*) and from which policy instruments draw their power. The analysis in this book shows that Hood's NATO framewok has the capacity to become a standard framework for future comparative studies in the field of civil-military relations and beyond. Moreover this book explores historical and contextual explanations for tool choice.

In sum, a policy instrument approach to the study of civil-military relations is justified by a series of theoretical considerations and the opportunity to contribute to a developing body of literature. First, policy instruments are manifestations of the government's power and their stance on social control, which makes them relevant objects of study. Second, the dissection of policies into their basic components, that is, policy instruments, facilitates and strengthens the analysis because it helps make sense of the growing complexity in policy issues by identifying trends, tracing policy change, and establishing comparisons. Third, by focusing on 'what government does', a tool approach reduces the room for speculation and subjectivity in the analysis. Fourth, the many questions unresolved and the very few empirical comparative works in the incipient policy instrument literature create an invitation for further research and theoretical contributions. This book grasps that opportunity.

1.3   Puzzling Iberian civil-military relations

As explained earlier, militaries continue to shape political outcomes and provoke changes in political regimes. In order to better understand the current challenges of the lessons from civil-military relations, comparable processes in the past should be examined. Portugal and Spain are two different paradigmatic cases of transitions from authoritarianism to democratic consolidations.[21] The new wave of democratisation that the Arab world is experiencing today makes the study of these Southern European countries increasingly relevant.[22] Spain and Portugal successfully implemented civilian control of their militaries and developed new democratic political systems. However the processes were not easy and straightforward. These cases help in the understanding of the complexities and some of the problems currently faced at the level of civil-military relations by many countries, including those belonging to the so-called 'Arab Spring'.

When observing civil-military relations in both contries, we quickly encounter an empirical puzzle: very similar countries experiencing similar political regimes and transformations developed very different civil-military relations and levels of control over the military.

In Portugal, a military coup ended the First Republic in 1926. Salazar, a former university professor, was appointed finance minister in 1928. Thanks to his success in dealing with economic problems, the military handed political power over to Salazar. In 1932, he became prime minister and inaugurated the civilianised dictatorship with fascist features: the Estado Novo (Porch 1977:21; Nataf 1995:23). The military did not exercise direct control of the regime but maintained important prerogatives. The armed forces were autonomous with little interference from civilian oversight organs, there was important military presence in the government and regime administration, and diverse political views were tolerated among the ranks. Although Salazar experienced many military coup attempts (at least 15 between 1931 and 1965), overall the military remained subordinate to his regime (Ferreira 1992:329–30). Salazar used the Spanish Civil War, the Second World War, and the cooperation with NATO allies during the Cold War to reinforce his sway on the military. However, the Colonial Wars (1961–75) emerged as an important source of disagreement between the government and the military. Civil-military tensions were aggravated during Caetano's rule (1968–74). Caetano's ability to implement policies was undermined by the very strong pressures exerted by hard liners.

A military coup put an end to the Estado Novo on 25 April 1974. The so-called Carnations Revolution opened a transitional process which, from the civil-military perspective, was very convoluted. The Portuguese transition can be divided into two different phases. During the period of provisional governments (1974–6), the military controlled not only the armed forces but also all of the governing institutions. During the period of constitutional governments (from 1976), the military influence gradually dwindled. The dissolution in 1982 of the Council of the Revolution, a military institution with far-reaching political powers, was a milestone in Portuguese civil-military relations. Portugal's EEC membership in 1986 marks the conclusion of the process of democratic consolidation.

In Spain, the socio-political situation was very unstable during the Second Republic (1931–9) (Jackson 1965). On 17 July 1936, important sectors of the military with the support of conservative political forces and the Church rebelled against the left coalition 'Frente Popular'. The uprising failed in many zones and a civil war began dividing Spain into two camps: the loyalist Republicans and the rebel Nationalists who – led by General Franco – won the war in 1939. This war affected the life of Spain for the next four decades. Similar to the Estado Novo, the Francoist regime was for the most part a civilianised regime (Linz et al. 1995). Nonetheless, the military became the backbone of the dictatorship. Franco enjoyed the loyalty of the military who gained important privileges and high levels of prestige (Payne 1967:445; Preston 1990:103–4).

Franco thoroughly purged the armies, established personal ties with the military leadership, promoted a mythical image of the armed forces, and granted the military a central role in the fight against the 'internal enemy'. The military also became important as a vehicle to disseminate the 'new' values and the Castilian language in multicultural Spain (Olmeda 1988:120–1). Thus, Franco did not have to face any major threat from the military, which remained loyal and perceived themselves as guardians of its traditions and values even after his death.

The death of Franco in 1975 initiated a transition process extensively studied and considered an example of success (Preston 1986; Linz 1996; Gunther et al. 2004). Many factors contributed to the process of democratisation, such as economic growth, industrialisation, urbanisation, and skilful elite leadership; however, it is very difficult to understand it fully without examining civil-military relations. The military played a prominent role during the dictatorship and the early stages of democracy, jeopardising and conditioning the transition. The coup attempt on the 23 February 1981 (23-F) has caught the attention of many scholars but it was only one among at least six military plots against the democracy between 1978 and 1985, including a plan for the assassination of the King and the Government in Coruña in June 1985 (Gilmour 1985:230–48; Preston 1990:175–202; Díaz Fernández 2005:221–4).

In sum, whereas in Spain the armed forces remained the bastion of authoritarianism and loyal to Franco, in Portugal the military overthrew the dictatorial Estado Novo. The attitude of the armed forces during the transitions in both countries may be considered almost diametrically opposed. In Portugal, a left-wing revolutionary military led the transition. In Spain, a right-wing reactionary military was obstructing democratisation.

This book throws light on this empirical puzzle by showing that the Portuguese and Spanish governments used different tools to subordinate the military and by explaining why the choices of tools diverged or converged.

Similarly, this book explores the existence of well-defined styles for governing the military and whether these styles were contingent upon geopolitical features or type of political regime.[23]

Historians and political scientists have debated the existence of some underlying Iberian ethos (Herr and Polt 1989; Telo and Torre 2000; Wiarda 1988; Magone 1996). The existence of academic publications such as the 'International Journal of Iberian Studies' and the 'Journal of Iberian and Latin American Research' as well as several research institutes and groups devoted to 'Iberian Studies' implicitly support this assumption. However, the evidence collected in this study suggests that there was no one single 'Iberian style of government' or 'Iberian model of civil-military relations', nor a constant country-specific style throughout the period analysed.

Is it at least possible to link the type of political regime – authoritarian, transitional or democratic – with a specific style for governing the military? Many political scientists have studied the regime type as an explanatory factor for economic and political outcomes (Przeworski and Limongi 1993; Olson 1993; Linz 1994; Cheibub 1998; Geddes 1999; Lijphart 1999). This book shows that in Portugal and Spain, the strategies and means for the subordination of the military within each type of regime varied across time and that it therefore is not accurate to refer to a single 'authoritarian' or 'transitional' style. However, there was a clear convergence in tools and civil-military relations from 1982 onwards, implying that the existence of a 'democratic' model of control cannot be rejected.

Inspired by neo-institutionalist literature,[24] this monograph also explores to what extent the evolution of civil-military relations in these countries was the result of 'historical causes' and/or 'constant causes' (Stinchcombe 1968). The policy instrument literature suggests both the capacity of past events to trigger institutional change and create inertias (Doern and Phidd 1983:322; Hood 1983; Linder and Peters 1989:42; Howlett 1991) and the impact of the context in the selection of tools (Anderson 1971; Hall 1993; Woodside 1986; Linder and Peters 1989; Bressers and O'Toole 1998). This book analyses the legacy of macro-historical events such as the rise of Fascism, the Spanish Civil and Second World Wars, NATO membership, colonial conflicts, and transitional political processes as 'historical causes'. It also assesses some ideational features, such as perceptions and ideologies, organisational and systemic institutional aspects, and the impact of international actors that show that these 'constant causes' altered the desirability and availability of the tools of control.

1.4 Outline of the book

This monograph is divided into four parts: Part 1 (Chapters 1 and 2) outlines the ambition and choices of the book. Chapter 1 justifies the study of civil-military relations and the policy instrument approach. Next, it shows that Portugal and Spain civil-military relations are interesting and idiosyncratic enough so that their comparison elicits a rich analytical outcome. Academics and practitioners concerned with the role of the military in regime change and democratisation should therefore consider their experiences. Chapter 2 outlines its fundamental analytical choices. It introduces the refined version of Hood's NATO framework employed in this book to compare the military policy of Iberian governments and briefly presents the historical and contextual factors used later to explain the trajectories in control instruments and civil-military relations.

Part 2 (Chapters 3, 4, and 5) and Part 3 (Chapters 6, 7, and 8) are comparative historical analyses based on primary and secondary sources of civil-military relations in Portugal and Spain, respectively. Chapters 3 and 6 explore chronologically the contemporary history of civil-military relations in Portugal and Spain from the inception of Salazar's and Franco's dictatorial regimes up to 1986. These chapters introduce the historical processes and contextual factors that conditioned the evolution of the governments' approaches to military subordination. For comparative purposes Chapters 4, 5, 7, and 8 all follow the same structure and classify, according to the refined NATO framework, the tools that the Portuguese and Spanish governments used for the subordination of the military. Chapter 4 covers the period of the Estado Novo (1932–74), Chapter 7 the Francoist regime (1936–75), and Chapters 5 and 8 the transition and early democratic stages in Portugal (1974–86) and Spain (1975–86).

Part 4 (Chapters 9 and 10) compares and explains the trajectories in the choices of control tools. Building on the previous empirical chapters, Chapter 9 contrasts the most striking features in terms of trajectories in both countries and explains how macro-historical events, such as the Spanish Civil War, the Second World War, the Colonial Wars, and the political transitions from authoritarianism, impacted the choices of control tools and the civil-military dynamics. Chapter 9 also examines the continuing action of the context on the trajectories of tool choice by focusing on three sets of environmental factors: ideas, political institutional structure, and the international environment. Chapter 10 summarises the main findings and contributions to wider methodological and meta-theoretical debates. It argues that no clear 'Iberian style' or 'Iberian path' can be identified. No common trajectories can be associated with their 'authoritarian' and 'transitional' periods either. Both historical legacies and the continuing effects of the ideational, institutional, and international contexts explain the different trajectories in military politics. Chapter 10 emphasises that a policy instruments framework helps in developing a better understanding of civil-military relations. The NATO scheme provides a different angle and a solid ground for orderly comparisons between the two countries that enables the identification of previously unrecognised patterns in their civil-military relations.

2
An Interdisciplinary Analytical Framework

This monograph is a comparative analysis of Portugal and Spain based on the historical examination of their civil-military relations and the application of a refined version of Hood's (1983) NATO framework. This chapter briefly describes the historical sources that were investigated as well as the comparative and explanatory frameworks utilised. Then, it presents Hood's original NATO resource-based typology for the classification of tools of government (1983) and some adaptations made to operationalise it in the context of civil-military relations. This chapter also introduces as an explanatory framework two alternative neo-institutionalist approaches to the evolution of civil-military relations and control tools: one based on the legacies of past historical events and the other based on the continuing action of environmental factors such as ideas, the political institutional structure, and the international environment.

2.1 Comparative historical analysis

Most civil-military studies have either focused on one single country[1] or compared many countries.[2] This book seeks a nuanced position between the virtues of inference and those of complexity. It studies two countries but through different periods in their history. The utilisation of Hood's resource-based framework involves a bias towards qualitative analysis and away from rational choice paradigms that have dominated comparative political science recently. Historical and interpretative analysis can elicit not only descriptions but also explanations and generalisations and therefore contribute to a coherent and rigorous body of research (Adler 1997:348; Wendt 1998:115–18). Although some of the policy tools are numerically measured here – in particular, military expenditure and budgets – a purely quantitative template fails to capture the salience of some of the instruments of control and the impact of the historical legacies and contextual factors on their choices.

The analysis presented in this book is grounded on the historical research of primary and secondary sources concerning civil-military relations in Portugal and Spain from the early 1930s to 1986: from their right-wing authoritarian regimes until their membership in the European Economic Community. All narratives about tool choices are constructed by combining several different authors and resources in order to increase the level of confidence in the accounts.

The primary research focuses on the examination of defence and military internal reports, laws, decrees, budgets, speeches, interviews, and letters. In the case of Portugal, the main primary resources scrutinised were the personal archives of António Oliveira Salazar and Marcello Caetano as well as the Council of the Revolution and the Portuguese Military History archives. These historical archives provide valuable information on Spanish political transformations and the relationships between the Iberian countries, which for the most part have not been explored in previous analyses of Spain.

For Spain, the most important sources used were Franco's personal archives and the extensive audio collection of the 'Fundación Ortega y Gasset', which contains interviews with political and military leaders as well as recordings of the conferences on military issues held during the early years of democracy. These archives have hitherto been underutilised by researchers of Spain's public policy and civil-military relations.

Portuguese and Spanish legislations on defence have served as another fundamental base of evidentiary support. Newspapers and military magazines as well as books and correspondence written by some of the most relevant actors (such as Salazar, Caetano, Franco, General Spínola, General Gutierrez Mellado, and Narcís Serra) are used in this book.

Finally, due to the length of the periods covered, the complexity of the subjects analysed, and the existing gaps in the primary resources available,[3] this research also covers a wide range of secondary sources, including extensive history, sociology, and political science bibliographies related to defence, military affairs, international relations, and politics as well as biographies of political and military leaders.

2.2   Developing a tools perspective: a revised NATO framework

Hood's (1983) NATO framework sums up the four basic resources that governments possess as policy instruments: *nodality, authority, treasure,* and *organisation*. Instruments are categorised according to the main resource from which they draw their power.[4]

Nodality is the 'property of being in the middle of an information or social network' (Hood 1983:4). Governments use their nodal situation, that is, their location in relation with the formal and informal network of communication channels to transmit and receive information. *Nodality* is used through messages, such as notifications, public announcements or propaganda, as well as by means of information gathering and management.

Authority refers to the 'possession of legal or official power...to demand, forbid, guarantee, adjudicate' (*ibid.*:5). By definition, governments are granted the power or the right to give orders or make decisions concerning others. *Authority* is used through tokens such as certificates, laws, and sanctions.

Treasure indicates 'the possession of a stock of moneys or fungible chattels' (*ibid.*:4). Governments can spend their financial resources to attain policy goals. *Treasure* is spent in salary, rewards, materials, and other equipment.

Organisation denotes 'the possession of a stock of people...land, buildings, materials and equipment somehow arranged' (*ibid.*:6). Governments can utilise the structure or machinery of the state as an instrument. *Organisation* as a resource is employed in what Hood calls 'treatments', namely the use of people's efforts and other material capabilities of the organisation.

These resources can be organised according to the criteria of 'depletability' and 'constraint' (Hood and Margetts 2007:152–6). *Treasure* and *organisation* are considered 'immanently depletable'. The financial and material capabilities of a government are depleted as they are used. *Authority* and *nodality* are 'contingently depletable' because the utilisation of these resources does not necessarily diminish them; it may even augment or strengthen them.[5] On the other hand, *organisation* and *authority* are considered to have the potential to set high constraints on the actions of policy subjects while *nodality* and *treasure* are usually less restraining.

Since this book adapts the NATO framework to the context of civil-military relations, some clarifications are important for understanding how this framework is operationalised. While Hood's study focuses on the relationship between the government and the society at large, here the military constitute the subject or 'problem' addressed by the government tools. Moreover, this book does not evaluate whether tools were successfully or intelligently designed and implemented,[6] nor does it provide a comprehensive typology of government policy styles. A systematic assessment of the historical success of military subordination policies involves great subjectivity at two levels: the selection of the evaluation criteria and the collection of evidence.

Most importantly, this book introduces new subcategories to the NATO framework (Table 2.1). Hood's basic fourfold typology is parsimonious and flexible enough to be used in the context of civil-military relations. However, the fact that there is a large degree of variance within each of these four categories is problematic (Linder and Peters 1989:40). Each of them can capture very dissimilar approaches to military subordination. For instance, armed paramilitary forces, military education, and the provision of jobs in the administration are three common *organisation* control instruments. Legal limitations and the prohibition of military unionism, as well as promotions and privileges rewarding obedience are all *authority* tools. The acquisition of military materials and weaponry, salary raises and individual economic incentives are *treasure* tools. In the *nodality* category, too, there are disparate tools ranging from information and disinformation campaigns to the collection of information through official internal reports or the actions of secret services.

To overcome this problem, Hood divides each of the four categories of tools into two subcategories: 'detectors' and 'effectors'.[7] However, the extension of the concept of 'detectors' beyond *nodality* becomes problematic.[8] *Nodality* seems to be indissolubly linked to the capacity to use information as a means of control (Hood 1983:6). In contrast, Hood's definitions of the other three basic resources do not mention their function as detectors of information and their role seems to be circumscribed to that of 'effectors'. Thus, in this book as in most interpretations of Hood's framework (Linder and Peters 1989:40; Vedung 1998:38; Howlett and Ramesh 2003:90), *nodality* is equated to 'information' tools and the subdivision between 'effectors' and 'detectors' is not extended to the other three basic resources.

Organisation tools are divided into 'coercive' and 'non-coercive' tools according to whether control is to be achieved by force or threat or by other means that do not entail violence or physical power.[9]

Nodality tools, as explained above, are classified into 'information effectors' that serve to disseminate information and 'information detectors' that enable the government to gather information.

Authority tools are divided into 'rewards and incentives' on the one hand and 'sanctions and constraints' on the other. The former are those that enable or stimulate specific behaviours and the latter to discourage them.[10]

Further, *treasure* tools are divided into 'staff' and 'equipment expenditure'. Staff expenditure denotes the utilisation of a government's financial resources spent directly to pay salaries, pensions and other types of benefits to the target group. 'Equipment expenditure' refers to the money spent to acquire goods, in this case essentially materials and weapons, with the aim to create some conditions that reinforce certain behaviours. These subcategories also capture the distinction between money being transferred directly to the target group or resources spent in a way that shapes the target group's actions indirectly (Table 2.1).

Finally, analytical reasons suggest the utilisation of the NATO framework to compare civil-military relations in the Iberian Peninsula. Resource-based classifications, such as Hood's, offer an important advantage. Concentrating on the basic resources from which instruments obtain their power, rather than on intentions, capacities, or

Table 2.1 Revised NATO framework

Hood's Tools of Government	Subcategory Examples of the tools in the context of military subordination
Organisation	*Coercive:* utilisation of the stock of people, buildings and equipment in order to directly impose a desired behaviour (or deter by force a non-desired one)
	Examples: paramilitary or police forces, special military units, disciplinary and political tribunals, penitentiary system
	Non-coercive: utilisation of the stock of people, buildings and equipment in order to persuade or stimulate behaviour without the direct use of force
	Examples: military education and training; exploitation of the organisational design and geographical deployment; provision of services, goods, and jobs
Nodality	*Information effectors*: utilisation of the government's central position to disseminate, modify, or omit information in order to induce a desired behaviour
	Examples: posters, publications, public speeches, mass media; organisations in charge of propaganda and censorship
	Information detectors: utilisation of the government's central position to gather information about observance or deviance from the desired behaviour
	Examples: action of intelligence services, informants, and official reports

Continued

Table 2.1   Continued

Authority	*Rewards and incentives*: utilisation of the government's legal power to enable and stimulate actions in accordance with the desired behaviour
	Examples: promotions, appointments, and privileges granted to loyal officers; functions granted to the military (e.g., participation in public order and justice)
	Sanctions and constraints: utilisation of the government's legal powers to punish, forbid, or hinder actions in disagreement with the desired behaviour
	Examples: limitations, prohibitions, removal of officers from crucial positions
Treasure	*Staff expenditure*: utilisation of the government's financial resources by transferring money directly to the target of the policy as a means to 'buy their will' and follow government wishes
	Examples: salary raises, pensions, and economic incentives
	Equipment expenditure: utilisation of the government's financial resources on the acquisition of materials as means to increase the satisfaction of individuals and their compliance.
	Examples: acquisition of modern equipment and weapons and better facilities

degrees, simplifies the categorisation and reduces the impact of subjectivity.[11] Moreover the NATO framework fits the empirical evidence on civil-military relations better than any other generic classification. The analysis of the tools employed to subordinate the military in Portugal and Spain provides several examples for each of the categories and subcategories; all instruments scrutinised can be easily identified with (at least) one of them.[12] This is not always the case with other frameworks.[13]

2.3   Explaining choices and change in military politics: history and context

As explained above, Hood's NATO framework provides a good basis for identifying patterns in civil-military relations and establishing cross-country and cross-temporal comparisons. However, its capacity as an explanatory framework for the evolution of tool choice is much more limited (Linder and Peters 1989:40–1). To escape this shortcoming, this book decouples the comparative from the explanatory framework. Hence, it restricts the role of the NATO scheme to that of a 'marker' or 'indicator' of distinct patterns and relies on neo-institutional theory to explain choices and changes in military politics.

The choice of policies, including those that aim at controlling the military, is rarely the result of simple rational calculations. Economics has explored technical or rational choice explanations for policy instruments (Posner 1974; Stokey and Zeckhauser 1978; Mitnick 1980; Wolf 1987; Weimer and Vining 1992). Nonetheless, the generalisability of their findings remains limited and most studies in political science agree that tool choices are not merely a matter of rational or technical deliberation. For instance, political scientists have argued that policy instruments are not neutral and that they are not selected on the bases of an optimal relationship between policy goals and means (Nispen and Ringeling 1998:211–12; Ringeling 2005:192–3; Trebilcock 2005). There is no best or most efficient instrument; the values and normative considerations need to be examined in policy-making (Doern and Phidd 1983:321–2; Macdonald 2005:222). Moreover, the cognitive limitations and millions of possible combinations of instruments hinder decision-makers' ability to evaluate systematically all of the options, as proponents of rational choice explanations assume (Hood and Margetts 2007:147; Weyland 2008:291).

Most authors adopting a policy instrument approach in political science defend the explanatory value of both history and context. Decision-makers do not always pick the same instrument for the same problem; policy choices are made according to the possibilities in a given historical and cultural context (Anderson 1971:122; Linder and Peters 1989:38, 48–53). Instrument choice is rarely a matter of neutral deliberation; choices are shaped by politics, ideology, and culture (Woodside 1986; Hood 2007:137). The emergence of new instruments, the intervention of international actors and other developments in the national or international context make some instruments more popular while other fall into disgrace (Ringeling 2005:202).

The tools of control can be considered the *institutions* that structure the relationship between the governments and the military.[14] Neo-institutional theory provides an alternative to pure technical and rational-choice angles on the choices of control tools. The trajectories of tool choice and civil-military relations in the Iberian Peninsula are explained here by drawing from two different but largely complementary approaches to neo-institutionalism:[15] the first one is based on 'historical causes' which refers to the impact of previous events in inhibiting or stimulating present choices. The second type of explanation focuses on the continuous impact of environmental factors – 'constant causes'.

In reality both approaches overlap. While history matters, it does not explain the whole picture of the evolution in the governments' control toolkit. The analysis of the contextual factors fills the gaps left by explanations based exclusively on past legacies.

2.3.1 Historical legacies on civil-military relations

One of the fundamental ideas in neo-institutional theory is the importance of history and its legacy. Many of the classical figures in social sciences such as Tocqueville, Marx, or Weber adopt historical approaches and stress the importance of temporality (Pierson 2004:2). Past events and choices leave 'policy legacies' that shape decision-makers' ideas and interests (Skocpol and Weir 1985:119). Social scientists have shown that in order to understand policies and institutions it is necessary to look at earlier choices and formation periods (Heclo 1974; Hall 1986; Skocpol 1992; King 1995; Lodge 2002). The analysis of large-scale processes, such as the evolution of civil-military relations and the control toolkit, requires sufficient perspective and attention to how events unfold over time (Mahoney and Rueschemeyer 2003:7).

Stinchcombe originally introduced the concept of 'historical causation' which refers to where the '*effect* created by causes at some previous period *becomes a cause of that same effect*' (Stinchcombe 1968:103). Inspired by this concept, neo-institutional social scientists[16] have developed explanations on why 'history matters' in the context of institutional change by using the notion of 'path dependence'. Path dependence refers to the fact that historical events can trigger some institutional changes and self-reinforcing mechanisms that contribute to establishing certain trajectories or patterns that persist even in the absence of the original event. Path-dependence explanations identify and explore 'critical junctures' in history. The concept of a critical juncture, first introduced by Lipset and Rokkan (1967:37), refers to 'a period of significant change, which typically occurs in distinct ways in different countries (or other units of analysis) and which is hypothesised to produce distinct legacies' (Collier and Collier 1991:29). These critical junctures entail some specific paths of action, inertias, or historical legacies that may have a continuing effect on tool choice and civil-military relations. Institutional change and stability can thus be explained as the result of reinforcing (or self-undermining) mechanisms triggered by past exogenous shocks.

The works influenced by path-dependence accounts often focus on the impact of small random events, but insufficient attention is devoted to macro-historical processes (Katznelson 2003:292). In contrast, this book examines the legacies of four macro-historical events that the literature has continuously associated with changes in civil-military relations and the patterns in the utilisation of control tools: the Spanish Civil War, the Second World War, the Colonial Wars, and the political transitions from authoritarianism. All of these events left a profound imprint on Iberian military politics which stimulated some changes in the governments' strategy of control which often created or truncated trends on tool choice.

2.3.2   Environmental factors

In addition to the impact of previous historical events, it is necessary to assess the continuing effect of some contextual mechanisms or 'constant causes' (Stinchcombe 1968:101–29; Collier and Collier 1991:35–9; Thelen 2003:214–17) on civil-military relations. Context can be defined as the set of cognitive and material factors and circumstances that surround a particular episode at a specific time.[17] Three sets of factors are examined here: ideas, the political institutional structure, and the international environment. The goal is to acknowledge the role of the specific institutional and ideological settings in which decisions are made which deterministic interpretations based on historical legacies often ignore. The selection of these categories is justified by theoretical considerations deriving from the public policy and policy instrument literature and by their heuristic value.[18]

'Ideas', the first category studied, points to the relevance of a cognitive dimension of the context which influences the decision-makers' preferences concerning military policy. The independent role of ideas in determining the course of events has been sufficiently demonstrated in public policy in the last three decades.[19] The study of policy instruments also emphasises the role of ideas (Linder and Peters 1989; Salamon 2002/ ed.:602; Ringeling 2005:186). Different sets of principles or worldviews may lead to different approaches to governance (Doern and Phidd 1983; Hood 1983). Ideas and perceptions influence decisions by specifying the nature of the problem, the policy goals, and the instruments considered available in a given situation (Hall 1993:279; Hall and Taylor 1996:948).

As cognitive psychology shows, the rationality of decision-makers is bounded (Weyland 2008). Roles or functions normally carry embedded norms of behaviour. In order to understand the choices of policy tools and the responses to them, it is necessary to consider the interpretations that the individuals in the government and the military make of their roles and responsibilities (Bressers and O'Toole 2005:134; Bruijn and Hufen 1998:26). Several comparable theoretical perspectives such as the 'logic of appropriateness' (March and Olsen 1989, 2006), 'isomorphism' (Meyer and Rowan 1977; DiMaggio and Powell 1983), and 'search for legitimacy' (Beetham 1991; Tyler 2006:63) can be used to link the cognitive dimension of the context to the choice of policy tools. Actors are both socialised and strategic, and therefore their actions are not merely a direct reflection of material interests.[20] The perceptions or ideas that individuals have of their own material interests define their choices.[21]

The second factor, 'political institutional structure' captures how the political and administrative setting within a country stimulates or constrains not only the availability of the government's basic resources but also the capacity to introduce changes in the utilisation of policy instruments (Doern and Phidd 1983:132; Ringeling 2005:192; Jennings and Lodge 2011). The underlying theoretical assumption is that the political and administrative structures shape political action and reform (Immergut 1992; Thelen and Steinmo 1992; Huber et al. 1993; Knill 1999; Pollit and Bouckaert 2000). In order to understand the evolution of military politics, it is important to examine the configuration and transformations of the executive's and the legislature's powers as well as on the administrative state apparatus throughout the dictatorship, transition, and democratic periods. Centralisation or fragmentation, symmetrical or asymmetrical relations of power; the administrative entrenchment and veto power of some actors and institutions helps to elucidate some changes and inertias in civil-military relations.

The last factor, the 'international environment' aims to capture how actors and institutions outside the national context affected tool choice in Portugal and Spain. This divide between 'national' and 'international' illustrates that apparently even the much closed Salazar and Franco regimes were not impervious to external influence. This impact can be captured by the three mechanisms of institutional isomorphism proposed by DiMaggio and Powell (1983): 'coercive', 'normative', and 'mimetic'.[22] First, foreign countries and international bodies may impose a certain structure, standard, or operating procedure on domestic public policy, including military issues. The international community can exert control through 'coercive' mechanisms such as direct demands, edicts, sanctions, and formal requirements. For instance, the international embargo and sanctions against Spain and the requirements for NATO membership imposed on Portugal are examples of coercive mechanisms. Second, international actors can exert influence through 'normative' pressures by seeking voluntary adherence to some principles or international standards (Radaelli 2000; Sahlin-Andersson 2002; Halpern and Le Galès 2011). Portugal and Spain were searching for legitimacy and resources and became sensitive to the normative influence of international organisations. Third, the international environment can unintentionally or passively condition tool choice. Under conditions of high uncertainty, governments tend to mimic choices made by other governments. Mimetic isomorphism was common in Spain and Portugal. These countries often imitated each other as well as other Western European countries. The impact of the 'international environment' is circumscribed to the analysis of the coercive and normative processes. The mimetic processes linked to uncertainty but not directly associated to planned foreign action are dealt with in the 'ideas' section.

2.4 An innovative stance on civil-military relations

This chapter has introduced the sources and analytical process that makes this monograph a unique work in the field of civil-military relations. The following chapters classify and compare a large body of historical evidence on Iberian civil-military relations according to a revised version of Hood's NATO framework and draw on neo-institutionalist theory to explain the choices and evolution of military politics.

The NATO scheme is a resource-based framework that classifies the tools of government alongside four categories: *nodality, authority, treasure,* and *organisation,* each of which has been here divided into two subcategories (Table 2.2).

Alongside the NATO comparative framework, this book contrasts two alternative neo-institutionalist explanations. One is based on the impact of history and links the evolution of the Spanish and Portuguese military politics with the legacies of the Spanish Civil War, the Second World

Table 2.2 Subcategories in the revised NATO framework

Basic resources	Subcategories
Organisation	Coercive/non-coercive
Nodality	Information effectors/information detectors
Authority	Rewards and incentives/sanctions and constraints
Treasure	Staff expenditure/equipment expenditure

War, the Colonial Wars, and their political transitions. The other angle emphasises the role of context and studies three sets of environmental factors (ideas, the political institutional structure, and the international environment) that act as constant causes shaping their trajectories. Both approaches have their advantages and limitations. This book illustrates the complementarity of the two views and, more importantly, demonstrates that neo-institutionalism can be productively integrated into the analysis of civil-military relations and tool choice.

The following chapters analyse and compare the contemporary history of civil-military relations in Portugal and Spain.

Part 2
Portugal

3
History of Contemporary Civil-Military Relations in Portugal

Civil-military relations were very turbulent from the Napoleonic Wars and the fall of absolutism to the end of the First Portuguese Republic. During this convoluted period of over a 100 years, the military took a leading role in the process of redefining political power (Mascarenhas 1982; Gallagher 1983; Caeiro 1997). The level of military participation in politics is reflected in the number of military uprisings or 'pronunciamentos', by their involvement in the enactment and modification of constitutions and fundamental laws, and by the fact that most Portuguese governments were led by military men. Military participation in politics became a tradition entrenched in the ideational and institutional setting.[1] The military, who often threatened Salazar's governments, provoked the fall of Caetano in 1974 and later shaped the democratisation process. Many officers, as well as politicians and other societal actors in Portugal, understood the recourse to force as a legitimate instrument to reach power or achieve certain political goals. Thus, the control of the military was a top priority for any Portuguese government.

This chapter scrutinises the history of civil-military relations in Section 3.1. This section deals with the emergence of Salazar and the Estado Novo, the political institutional setting of the regime, the Estado Novo's international relations, the impact of NATO membership, the ethos and views of the Portuguese military, and the downfall of the regime during Caetano's rule. Then, Section 3.2 analyses the transition and initial stages of democracy in Portugal by distinguishing between the period of provisional governments (1974–6) and that of the constitutional governments (1976–86). During the first, the revolutionary bodies selected governments and the military controlled policy and politics, and during the second, they were gradually disentangled from politics.

This chapter explains the context in which the government operated and introduces most of the factors and forces that conditioned the government's policies and tools. The analysis of the tools of control according to the revised NATO framework is developed in Chapter 4 for the dictatorial period and in Chapter 5 for the transitional one.

3.1   Estado Novo

3.1.1   Salazar and the inception of the Estado Novo

Military infighting, financial problems, and civilian political pressures weakened the military dictatorship that had replaced the First Republic in 1926 (Antunes 1978; Ferreira 1992:145; Caeiro 1997). In 1928, António de Oliveira Salazar, a former university professor, was appointed minister of finance and granted special powers to tackle the economic crisis. The initial success of the economic reforms consolidated Salazar as the political leader of Portugal. In 1932, he was appointed prime minister and launched a constitutional project to create a civilian-led dictatorship: the Estado Novo (New State).[2] The Estado Novo should not be considered an extension of the military dictatorship established in 1926 nor a radical depart from it.[3] Although the military continued to occupy crucial positions in the government and administration, the Estado Novo became a civilianised authoritarian regime (Linz and Stepan 1996:117). The Estado Novo developed an autarkic and corporatist model based on a complex system of equilibriums between the interests of elite groups, with an important level of dependence on the colonies as source of commodities and as a market for Portuguese manufactured products. Conservatism, traditionalism, Catholicism, ruralism, and paternalism were the markers of its identity (Rosas 1989; Medina 2000:42).

The autocratic ideologies that emerged in Europe in the 1920s and 1930s shaped the regime from its beginning (Campinos 1975). Salazar strongly believed that authoritarianism was not a transient trend but the political model of the future (Salazar 1935:345–6). In 1936, he wrote: '[w]e are anti-parliamentarians, anti-democrats, anti-liberal, and we are determined to establish a Corporatist State' (Salazar 1939:29). Salazar despised the liberal concept of citizenship which he considered as being against the common interest.[4] Social and economic rights were above individual rights. Everything was subordinated to the 'national interest'.[5] This autocratic and interventionist ideology explains some of the choices made concerning information control and the use of coercive force to deter contestation.

Salazar defined the Portuguese Republic as a corporatist state (Salazar 1939:21). According to him, the sovereignty rested with the nation and the nation was composed of 'natural organs', amongst which the military was one of the most important.[6] The ideology of the Estado Novo was an amalgamation of different conservative doctrines. The Estado Novo was designed to enhance the cohabitation amongst different ideological groups within the ruling elite (Porch 1977:19; Pinto 1994:67–75; Azevedo 1999). The birth of the single party National Union aimed at the reconciliation of the different political streams of the Portuguese right. Like Franco, Salazar did not endorse any particular doctrine or political stream. He used them to counterbalance each other avoiding the concentration of power in a single faction and thus enhance his own personal power.[7] Thus, the longevity of the Estado Novo can be attributed to a great extent to Salazar's skilfull management of the elites' equilibria (Rosas 1986, 1989).

The Estado Novo was a system of limited pluralism, with a less well-defined guiding ideology than the totalitarian regimes and a less relevant role of the single party and paramilitary forces (Linz 1970 [1964]:255–6; Lucena 1976, 1984). Due to his strong religious beliefs and law education, Salazar rejected totalitarianism (Salazar 1935:336–7; Braga da Cruz 1988:49). In 1934, Salazar banned the extremist National-Syndicalist party,[8] also known as 'camisas azuis' (blue shirts) that imitated Italian Fascism and German Nazism (Pinto 1994). The government's strategy was to minimise the use of terror (Martins 1969:263). Compared to Franco's regime, the Estado Novo had a low level of political imprisonment and violence (Pimlott and Seaton 1983:45). Punishments applied to military insurgents were also generally soft during the regime.

Salazar was concerned by the political activity of the military and insisted that they should be detached from politics and subordinated to the government. He believed that if the military became used to civilian life they would gradually lose their esprit de corps and sense of discipline. Salazar publicly advocated the professionalisation and improvement of the material conditions of the military as means to disengage it from politics (Ferro 2003 [1932–38]:21–3; Salazar 1935:103). However, the evidence suggests that in practical terms, Salazar was less concerned with developing military professionalism and modernisation than with co-opting their leadership so they remained subordinated (Wheeler 1979; Faria 2000). Moreover, he did not succeed in establishing strong and clear boundaries between politics and the military, which periodically threatened his government. The numerous coup attempts that Salazar faced show that Salazar was in a weaker position vis-à-vis the military than Franco, who was essentially unchallenged. This discrepancy in the relative strength of each dictator is also reflected in the type control mechanisms utilised by each.

3.1.2   Political power in the Estado Novo

The Estado Novo was highly centralised, and Salazar retained extensive powers which he used to gradually offset the sway of the military that had previously helped install him (Almeida and Pinto 2003:12–14). Since his appointment as finance minister in 1928, Salazar was granted special powers over the rest of the ministries;[9] to the extent that he became known as the 'Finance Dictator' (Nunes 1930). Within a year, he managed to balance the budget and stabilise the Portuguese currency (Gallagher 1983:48). The positive economic results in 1928–9 increased his personal prestige enormously (Antunes 1994:16–17). Finally, in 1932 he was appointed prime minister. During the 1930s, Salazar's influence and powers grew. The Spanish Civil War and Second World War accelerated the process of personal empowerment. On top of being prime minister (1932–68), Salazar accumulated other positions in the government, such as finance minister (1928–40), war minister (1936–44), minister of foreign affairs (1936–49), defence minister (1961–2), and even the interim president of the republic (in 1951).

The Estado Novo had an elected president but the executive power was de facto held by the prime minister (Graham 1975; Campinos 1978). Officially, the prime minister was appointed by the president of the republic, who in turn was elected by the people in often unfair elections. However, Salazar effectively had the upper hand in the power relationship because he controlled the Central Commission of the National Union which nominated the presidential candidates.[10] The centralisation of powers in the hands of Salazar was so evident that Caetano referred to the Estado Novo as a system of 'prime-minister presidentialism' (Caetano 1957:67).

Salazar strengthened his executive power and repeatedly rejected parliamentarism, which he feared.[11] The chambers of the Portuguese parliament, the National Assembly, and the Corporative Chamber merely had symbolic roles. The legislative power of the chambers was very limited. Salazar and Caetano used them as 'divide-and-rule' devices and sources of internal and external legitimacy (Schmitter 1999:81–90). The National Assembly was an institution inherited from the First Republic. It had more autonomy than the Francoist *Cortes* (Fernandes 2006:154–8) but did not control the actions of the government or the military. Caetano referred to it as the organisation where the 'little political activity' in Portugal took place.[12] The Corporative Chamber was comparable to an upper chamber where the productive sectors and institutions such as the Church, the universities, and the military were represented. There was a National Defence Section in the Corporative Chamber but the military was also represented amongst other corporative or interest groups. Such was the extent of military representation that 15.2 per cent of its members had a military education (Ferreira 2009:345).

The absence of a strong party system empowered Salazar. The single party National Union was founded in 1930, inspired by the Spanish Patriotic Union of Miguel Primo de Rivera (Antunes 1994:20).[13] It was defined officially as a non-partisan organisation which was independent from the state and had voluntary membership (SPN 1943:15). It did not interfere in the government's actions and had very little influence in the selection of the members of the government and senior officials. The National Union was less autonomous than the Spanish Falange (Moore 1970:52) and did not have any significant influence on the strategy of control of the military.

In sum, the concentration of executive and legislative powers and the absence of political actors with veto powers increased the resources at Salazar's disposal and placed him in a position to impose his personal preferences in terms of policy choices.

The military institution was very prominent during the Estado Novo and held much political influence. Due to the general weakness of civil institutions and especially the political ones, the military acquired a stronger role. Especially during the initial years of the Estado Novo, the army was granted a large degree of autonomy as a means to incentivise its support for the regime (Ferro 2003 [1932–38]:22–3). However, later Salazar, concerned with military subordination, took direct control of the War Ministry during critical periods such as the Spanish Civil War, the Second World War, and the beginning of the Colonial Wars. Moreover, Salazar surrounded himself with trusted officers in order to strengthen his control on the military. Fernando Santos Costa provides the best example: in 1936, the army captain and former Salazar student became undersecretary of state and, in 1944, war minister. For 22 years, until 1958, when he was replaced by Botelho Moniz as national defence minister, Santos Costa's power in the state apparatus was second only to that of Salazar (Antunes 2000:58).

Salazar awarded his military supporters with important positions in the state apparatus. Although slightly lower than in Spain, the participation of the military was always important in Estado Novo's governments:

Table 3.1   Military ministers as a percentage of total number of ministers

Cabinets (% of military)	Jun. 1926	Apr. 1933	Feb. 1938	May. 1941	Jul. 1945	Jul. 1951	Feb. 1957	Jul. 1962	Oct. 1969	Mar. 1975
Spain			41.6	46.1	50	37.5	44.4	42.1	26.3	15.8
Portugal	37.5	22.2	22.2	11.1	33.3	35.7	21.4	13.3	18.2	33.3

Sources: Agüero (1995:46) and Antunes (1994:409–14). Author's own analysis.

26.2 per cent of the ministers had a military occupational background (Almeida and Pinto 2003:25, Table 3.1). Many officers were also members of the chambers and occupied high-level positions in the administration. For instance, from 1934 to 1939, 16.7 per cent of the members of the Assembly and 9.3 per cent of the Corporative Chamber were military officers. From 1934 to 1942, the representation of the military in the top political-administrative positions was only inferior to that of the groups of 'professors and educators' and to that of 'lawyers and judges' and much higher than the representation of landowners, industrialists, engineers, physicians, or workers (Schmitter 1979:12–19). The military was also very well-represented in the Censorship Services, the Republican National Guard (GNR), and the paramilitary Portuguese Legion. In sum, the military had a privileged position in the Estado Novo from which they could influence politics and civil-military relations.

3.1.3 Portugal and the foreign powers

The Estado Novo's civil-military relations must be examined against the backdrop of Portuguese international relations. Portugal due to its historical alliance with the United Kingdom, its colonial possessions, as well as its fear of its larger neighbour always sought to be more actively involved in international affairs than Spain (Ferreira 1980:48, 1989, 2006; Oliveira 2007). The strategic importance placed by the United Kingdom and its allies on the Portuguese Atlantic isles and the longstanding Anglo-Portuguese treaties enabled Portugal to play an important role in the complex system of international relations during both World Wars. The international environment constrained some of the choices of policy instruments but also provided opportunities to strengthen government control over the military. Salazar's foreign policy aimed to consolidate internally the Estado Novo regime (Ferreira 2006).

The special nature of the Portuguese-Spanish relations can be considered the main factor that shaped Portuguese foreign policy (Ferreira 1989:51–3). During the Spanish Civil War, the Portuguese government sided with Franco's camp in order to reinforce and legitimise the authoritarian Estado Novo. Salazar could not completely refuse the British pressures for an embargo but delayed its application (Rosas 1988:44). Especially during the initial months of the war, material support to the Francoist troops was very important (Oliveira 1987:154–5). Salazar and the military were extremely concerned about the possibility of a Spanish invasion by either the Republican or Francoist camps.[14] Salazar took advantage of the threat of the Spanish Civil War to take over the War Ministry in 1936 and strengthen his personal leadership.

Salazar and Franco signed the Iberian Pact of Defence (1939) and the Additional Protocol (1940) in order to seal the collaboration and friendship between the two regimes. However, despite the good relations between the neighbouring regimes, the fear of Spain remained entrenched amongst the Portuguese military and political elites (Gallagher 1983:150).[15] Thus, during the Second World War, Salazar campaigned for Spanish neutrality (Nogueira 2000:210; Beirôco 2003:67–8) and later for Spain's integration into NATO (Vicente 1996:303–7).[16] Salazar considered the Iberian Peninsula as the last bastion of a Christian and conservative Europe, with Spain acting as a gatekeeper that helped maintain stability in Portugal and protect its borders against a communist attack (Telo 1996:27, 64).

Nazi Germany also had an important impact on Portugal and its civil-military relations. Germany understood the strategic value of Portugal in the context of an eventual war and tried to gain its support. On the other hand, Salazar sought recognition and material support from them. Portugal became the target of intensive Nazi propaganda which stressed the similarities between the German Nazi government and the Estado Novo and attacked the United Kingdom and communism.[17] Germany collaborated with the Portuguese secret services and helped developing institutions such as the paramilitary Portuguese Legion and 'Mocidade' (Stone 2005:208). The use of censorship and propaganda, as well as paramilitary forces as instruments to control the military was directly inspired by Germany. Morever, seeking to counterbalance British influence, Germany became the main supplier of armaments in the late 1930s until 1944 (Telo 1996:171–2).

Notwithstanding, Salazar also feared German expansionist ambitions and opted for declaring neutrality during the Second World War, adopting a nonbelligerent stance but facilitating the action of the Allies. Portuguese military material capabilities were clearly insufficient to undertake an active role in the war (Ferreira 1992:203). Moreover, this strategy allowed Salazar to honour the historical Anglo-Portuguese alliance and gain support amongst the senior ranks, which were predominantly anglophile.[18]

Salazar, who initially showed some anti-American preconceptions did not fully realise that, after the Second World War, the United States was to occupy the traditional role of the United Kingdom as the main power in the Western world (Oliveira 1989:83). He rejected the first stage of the Marshall Plan (1948–9) missing the opportunity to use US economic support to increase military expenditures. Later, Salazar changed his views. Portugal requested participation in the second stage of the Marshall Plan (1949–50), agreed to the American use of the Lajes military base in the Azores (1948), became a founding member of NATO (1949), and signed a Defence Agreement with the United States (1951) (Beirôco 2003:72–3; Ferreira 2006:90–1). The alliance with the United States and other major Western powers reinforced most of the Estado Novo's basic resources and influenced its tool choice.

3.1.4   The NATO 'revolution'

Portugal was offered to become a founding member of NATO mainly due to the strategic value of some of its overseas ports. The position of the military was clearly in favour of NATO membership (Nogueira 1980:142–4). Salazar saw an opportunity to finally consolidate the subordination of the military and was also supportive of NATO membership. Although the Portuguese government was genuinely worried about the defence of its territory, the main reason for joining NATO was to increase the prestige of the regime (Crollen 1973:45–8).

The integration into the alliance in 1949 had special relevance in terms of civil-military relations. NATO, and in particular the United States through the Military Assistance Advisory Group (MAAG), pushed the regime to adapt its defence structures and multiply the contacts with members of other more modern militaries at different levels. NATO introduced a new doctrine, procedures, organisational techniques, and methods of action (Ferreira 1992:257; Telo 1999:71) and contributed to the idea that civilians should monitor military and defence issues.[19] NATO experts, after evaluating the Portuguese military, considered the organisation too complex and with inadequate military training, including the preparation of the generals (Matos 2004:170). They suggested reorganising the military to enhace coordination, to reinforce the instruction of Portuguese officers, to concentrate efforts on the preparation of one modern division, and to eliminate the elitist Corps of High Staff. Many of NATO's recommendations were implemented. The government created the National Defence Ministry and restructured the military;[20] many officers were trained by US military staff and others went to American academies; the Santa Margarida division became the first truly modern one; and although the Corps of High Staff was not eliminated, its entry requirements were broadened (Matos 2004:170). Furthermore, NATO advised Salazar to increase military salaries and equipment expenditure. NATO allies, in particular the United States, supplied weapons and materials and contributed to the development of a Portuguese defence industry. Overall, the reforms imposed by NATO in the late 1940s and 1950s improved the coordination and the operational capacity of the Portuguese military.

The officers that in the 1950s were sent abroad to be trained in other NATO member states became known as the 'NATO generation'. Through their international experiences, many of these officers changed their negative opinions of Western democracies. They soon occupied high positions in the hierarchy and influenced successive generations of officers supporting the introduction of the NATO doctrine and templates (Telo 1999:84–5). The hundreds of officers trained in the United States later trained thousands of other Portuguese military. Owing to the influence of NATO, they developed a new understanding of their profession as well as new preoccupations and claims (Carrilho 1992). Many of these officers opposed the regime and participated in conspiracies, which started in the early 1960s.

Portugal remained the sole non-democratic member of NATO, perceived as a strategic ally but also as an inconvenient colonial power. The path of the transformations induced by NATO slowed down when the Colonial Wars erupted. NATO excluded the Portuguese colonies from its scope even though the United States and some of its European members benefitted from the overseas Portuguese ports. The dictatorial character and methods of the Estado Novo were not seriously contested until 1958, partly due to the country's declared anti-communism. The disagreements around the Portuguese colonial policy made the United States reduce the number of Portuguese officers in American schools, especially after 1958. In 1961, allegedly the United States was supportive of the Defence Minister Botelho Moniz's plot against Salazar. However, the loyal military with the aid of the GNR and the Portuguese Legion kept the situation under control (Maxwell 1995:47–51; Rodrigues 1996; Ferreira 2006:110). Salazar, aware of the American collaboration with the plotters and the independence movements in Africa (Mahoney 1983:187–222; Antunes 1991), decided to distance the Portuguese military from the United States and NATO and reduce the military cooperation and exchange with them.[21] This departure had an important impact on military politics; the government abandoned most of the NATO-sponsored reforms introduced.

Salazar, however, did not manage to reverse the impact NATO had had on the on the way the military perceived their profession and government policies. The contacts with NATO had produced profound changes in the mentality of many officers. The military demanded better training and instruction programmes; a new territorial organisation; provision of housing, health care, and education for the families; as well as better equipment and material facilities.[22] NATO had served as a yardstick to diagnose the deficiencies of the Portuguese military.[23] Many young officers lost some of their respect for their older superiors and the government that maintained a more traditional or outdated vision of the military. This damaged the level of discipline within the ranks. Many of those involved in Botelho Moniz's coup belonged to the 'NATO generation'. The influence of NATO can be traced up to the military that led the Carnation Revolution in 1974. In sum, NATO produced a 'quiet revolution' in the military (Telo 1996:201, 246, 329–30). This revolution had a direct impact on the level of professionalism in the military but also an indirect one, raising awareness of the problems of the Estado Novo and the Portuguese military. Ultimately, it became one of the triggers for the overthrow of the regime in 1974.[24]

3.1.5 Politicisation and discontent in the ranks

Throughout the Estado Novo period, the Portuguese military held more political power and were more prone to intervene in politics than their Spanish counterparts (Gunther 1995:74). The rebellions in Madeira (1931), in Marinha Grande (1934), in the river Tagus (1936), in Mealhada (1946), the 'Abrilada' revolutionary plot (1947), the rebellion of Sé (1959), the Botelho Moniz's coup (1961), the rebellion in Beja (1962), and the Carnation Revolution (1974) are probably the best known expressions of military discontent and opposition but not the sole ones. The sheer number of plots and coup attempts, up to 20 between 1926 and 1974 (Manuel 1995), shows that military subordination was not fully achieved. Senior officers led most political opposition movements in the Estado Novo.[25] Moreover the poor working conditions and some unpopular reforms undertaken by the government fuelled the resentment against the regime, in particular amongst the lower ranks. There were frequent complaints about the policies of retirement and promotion[26] as well as abouth the material and working conditions.[27]

The Portuguese military had developed a strong interest in politics partly due to the discouraging fact that its military power was very low compared to that of other European countries. The Portuguese military was corporatist and very bureaucratic and did not value internal competition or innovation. Patriotism took precedence over technical skills (Telo 1996:230–1). The military's lack of material, preparation, and discipline was revealed during its participation in the First World War (Ferreira 1992; Marques 2004). Portugal did not have the capacity to guarantee the defence of its territory through military means and the colonial map did not allow further conquests. These factors contributed to the redefinition of the role of the military to one of acting as guardians of the internal order, a sort of police that dealt with radical political opposition movements and revolts. Their role as guarantors of law and order made them more prone to intervening in politics (Welch 1987:22).

The government and many young officers were highly concerned with the politicisation of the military.[28] Most military reforms during the regime aimed to diminish the military's involvement in politics and to subordinate them to civilian power. However, they did not manage to radically change the perception of the military as responsible for maintaining order in the metropole and in the overseas territories. The type of involvement of the military in the colonial conflicts later reinforced this perception.

The military conception of discipline and authority was another important factor in the civil-military relations. The supreme authority they had historically obeyed, the monarch, was ousted in 1910. Discipline in the Portuguese military was based on the perceived capacity of leadership rather than on a strict legal-rational authority (Carrilho 1985:453). Salazar had earned a reputation as a skilled leader especially during the times of instability and crisis in the military dictatorship. In the 1930s, the young officers that had participated in the 1926 coup were those that more strongly supported Salazar. These young military had seen their careers obstructed by the inherited excess of officers from the First World War and had blamed the senior ranks for the poor situation in the military. Salazar decided to introduce a set of reforms aimed mainly at subordinating the military to his civilian authority (Faria 2000). The senior ranks wanted to maintain greater autonomy but did not manage to block the reforms (Telo 1996:172–3). In the process, many of the old officers were forced into retirement and replaced by younger military officers whose allegiance to Salazar and his government was reinforced.

The emphasis on leadership rather than on hierarchical rank was accentuated during the Colonial Wars, albeit not to the advantage of the government. The Colonial Wars were fought in small units, and in most of the field operations, there was no officer above the rank of captain. Loyal senior officers mainly stayed in Lisbon, far from the conflict zones, devoting themselves to administrative tasks. They lost prestige and authority in comparison with the middle-rank officers that had created a reputation by fighting. Moreover, some military leaders in the colonies, such as Spínola in Guinea, Kaúlza in Mozambique, and Luiz Cunha in Angola, exhibited caudillistic traits and did not follow a strategy that was fully coherent with government policies.[29] The government also lost part of its authority with the substitution of Salazar by Caetano, who did not enjoy the popularity or legitimacy of his predecessor. Contrary to Franco, Salazar did not make any effort to groom a successor. In the eyes of the military, this resulted in a lack of legitimacy for Caetano.

The composition of the Portuguese military, more heterogeneous than that of Spain, also impacted the civil-military relations. In Portugal, the military was not as ideologically homogeneous and monolithically supportive of the government as in Francoist Spain. Different ideological factions existed within the military (Fernandes 2006:164). The sociological composition of the military was also diverse (Carrilho 1985). The Second World War entailed massive recruitment which stimulated an influx of young militia officers with diverse backgrounds (many from urban areas) and political ideas (liberals, monarchists, integralists, and socialists). Despite the process of de-mobilisation after the war,[30] the Portuguese military further diversified after the late 1950s due to NATO and the Colonial Wars. Recruitment patterns changed when Salazar, following NATO advice, abolished the tuition fees in the Military Academy and offered salaries to cadets in 1958 (Schmitter 1975:16). Most of the officers that later plotted against Caetano graduated after 1958 and their socioeconomic backgrounds were modest (Porch 1977:68).

The Colonial Wars resulted in an extension of the period of service and made a military career a less attractive means of social mobility for middle and upper-middle class youths. At the same time, the incorporation of middle to lower class officers contributed to the introduction of less conservative ideas clashed with the ideology of the regime and the senior ranks.[31] Moreover, the wars forced the government to launch regulations seeking to attract and to keep in service the militia officers ('milicianos').[32] The numbers of militia officers in service increased rapidly, many of them were former university students who had been actively involved in left-wing organisations and who did not endorse the government (Maxwell 1995:37).

The Colonial Wars exacerbated the military unrest. In 1961, Portugal surrendered Goa, Damao, and Diu to the Indian army and an independence war broke out in Angola. The wars, in particular after the extension of the conflict to Guinea (1963) and Mozambique (1964), drained the government's resources and legitimacy. The military considered the government plans of maintaining all the overseas territories by sheer force as unrealistic.[33] There were many complaints about the insufficient material conditions, lack of expertise, and about the negative treatment that the regime's propaganda machinery was giving the military, especially after the loss of the possessions in India.[34] The military insurrection in 1961 was also stimulated by the perception that the international community was greatly in favour of the position of self-determination of the colonies.[35] In the colonies, the discontent was amplified by the large gap between the military's and the white settlers' salaries and by the difficulties working outside the barracks.[36] The dissatisfaction originating in the economic disparities led most of the military to detach themselves from the government's policies as well as from the white colonial elites, internalising leftist and revolutionary ideologies and in some cases even sympathising with the African insurgents. The Colonial Wars that were initially exploited by the government to consolidate the Estado Novo regime, ended up becoming one of the main causes of military contestation and ultimately of the fall of the regime (Ferreira 2006:60).

3.1.6 Caetano and the downfall of the regime

In 1968, Marcello Caetano, a former professor and a politician, was appointed prime minister after a domestic accident left Salazar disabled.[37] Caetano's reform plan 'Renovation within Continuity' ('Renovacão na Continuidade') aimed at limited liberalisation and revitalisation of the Estado Novo (Sánchez Cervelló 1993:22–31; González Hernández 1999:34–5). Caetano legalised some opposition movements; increased the powers of the National Assembly; and, emulating the Spanish government, gave preference to civilian technocrats over the military in his government. Thus, in 1971, Caetano recruited a new generation of technocrats ('a camada nova') in order to reform the economy and move closer to Europe. Policy-making became a more collective responsibility and the Council of Ministers gained relevance (Graham 1983:224). However, these reforms were superficial and did not substantially modify the regime (Lucena 1976:185; Graham 1993:15). They faced the resistance of part of the military and the conservative President Américo Tomás, two institutional barriers that held back the evolution of the regime. The power struggles between different political streams weakened Caetano's power and his government's control instruments (Rebelo de Sousa 1990:66; Fernandes 2006:169–70). The half-hearted reforms only served to stress the latent contradictions of the Estado Novo, and the radical substitution of the regime as the only solution to the institutional crisis (González Hernández 1999:39).

The attitude of the government vis-à-vis the colonial conflict was especially controversial. Thirteen years of expensive Colonial Wars in Africa undermined the support for the Estado Novo from the Church and business and intellectual elites (Sánchez Cervelló 1993:20–1; Manuel 1995:29–32). However, for Caetano, the most difficult challenge was to keep the military under control (Antunes 1985:27). During his rule the corporatist claims and discontent grew drastically. The military requested rights of association, salaries and pensions raises, earlier passage to the reserve, free public transportation, longer holidays, better conditions for the veterans disabled during the Colonial Wars, pensions for children and widows, elimination of the High Staff Corps (which was perceived as a cast system), and a better selection process in the Military Academy. The military realised that their material means were often inferior to those of the insurgents.[38] Many of them, such as the influential Generals Costa Gomes and Spínola,[39] tried to transform the foreseeable military defeat into a political victory and requested a political solution along the lines of the British and French decolonisation processes.[40] That solution may have reduced the levels of discontent in the military and prevented the coup. However, Caetano chose to remain close to the most conservative political and military figures and discharged the reformist officers (Manuel 1995:28).

An increasing number of episodes of military indiscipline due to disagreements with the Colonial Wars and corporate grievances took place during Caetano's rule. The enactment of Decree-Law 353/73 (13 July 1973), which aimed to enhance the control of the military to grant privileges to the conscript officers, became a landmark in the deterioration of the civil-military relations.[41] The decree fostered the academy officers' discontent and internal fragmentation. A month later Decree-Law 409/73 (20 August 1973) amended Decree-Law 353/73, but due to the continuation of protests, it had to be finally revoked shortly afterwards (12 October 1973).[42] This incident revealed Caetano's weakness. The government's legitimacy was questioned and the loss of control was evident. Decree-Law 353/73 became an excuse for the organisation of career officers' reunions in which the scenario of a military coup to terminate the dictatorship gradually became salient.[43]

The Armed Forces Movement (MFA), constituted in September 1973, was a clandestine progressive movement of junior officers that conspired against the regime and triggered the events of the Carnations

Revolution. Initially, the MFA demanded that Caetano revoke the Decree-Laws 353/73 and 409/73, increase military salaries, and reconsider colonialist positions. However, after December 1973, the MFA began to discuss a military intervention. Captains Vasco Lourenço and Otelo Saraiva de Carvalho were assigned the preliminary preparations for a hypothetical coup. On 5 March 1974, 200 MFA members met in Cascais and approved Major Ernesto Melo Antunes' document 'O Movimento, as Forças Armadas e a Nação'. The manifesto stated a 'three d's political programme': democracy, development, and decolonisation. Caetano's government failed to satisfy their claims. Changes in the military strategy were constrained by the highly legalistic and institutional framework that slowed down any reform and precluded more energetic actions to counter the imminent upheaval (Maxwell 1995:44). On 16 March, some soldiers rebelled in Caldas da Rainha and as a result 150 soldiers were imprisoned. On 24 March, the MFA decided to attempt a coup. Caetano underestimated the capacity of the rebels and tried to use them as a threat to counterbalance the influence of the reactionary groups that had held up almost any type of change in policies.[44]

The coup eventually took place on 25 April 1974. Captain Otelo led an operation carried out exclusively by junior officers. He took control of Lisbon's airport and its radio and television broadcast centres. He also took control of the military headquarters in Lisbon and Oporto. He moved troops all over the Portuguese territory to give the sensation of a general uprising and sealed the borders with Spain to avoid any kind of intervention from Francoist troops. This well-planned operation became a success quickly. Caetano surrendered to General Spínola at the GNR Headquarters.[45] Many people went to the streets to celebrate the fall of the regime. There were some clashes between police and youths. On the morning of the 26 April, the secret police DGS headquarters, the last focus of resistance to the rebellion, surrendered. Five people died from DGS fire, these were the sole victims of this otherwise peaceful revolution (Porch 1977:90–3; Robinson 1979:191–3). The Estado Novo was defeated by the same element that created it: the military.

3.2 Transition and democracy

3.2.1 Provisional governments (1974–6)

After the 25 April coup, the process of design and development of the new democratic institutions was launched. Political parties were legalised and decolonisation initiated. During the Portuguese transition, the military and in particular the MFA shaped the process of institutional change. Military and government affairs were extremely intertwined during this period of instability. The militarisation of politics accelerated the politicisation of the military. Military structures proliferated and overlapped with the political system. This was a period of instability; six different provisional governments and two military coups took place between the Carnations Revolution and the enactment of the new Constitution in 1976, which officially opened the period of democratically elected governments. A failed military coup in November 1975 served to consolidate the moderate reformist agenda and to reduce the power of those who demanded more radical political transformations. But, at the same time, the coup signalled a turning point in the government strategy vis-à-vis military subordination.

The period of provisional or pre-constitutional governments may be subdivided into four distinct stages each of them with distinct features in terms of civil-military relations (Manuel 1995). First, from April to September 1974, the new President of the Republic Spínola and the First Provisional Government headed by Adelino da Palma Carlos tried to moderate the MFA's revolutionary programme. They attempted to increase the powers of the executive at the expense of the military, to slow down the devolution of the colonies, and to re-establish a traditional hierarchical conception of the military. They failed to impose their views over those of the MFA Coordination Committee and were obliged to resign. Palma Carlos was substituted by General Vasco Gonçalves in July and Spínola by General Costa Gomes in September following important social mobilisations orchestrated by the left.

The second period, from September 1974 to March 1975, was characterised by the disputes amongst different factions within the MFA: the MFA-Moderates, MFA-Radicals, and the MFA-Populists.[46] The MFA-Moderates, headed by Majors Melo Antunes and Vasco Lourenço, were linked to the Socialist Party, PS. This group gradually attracted many of the conservative officers and dominated most of the military regions. The MFA-Radicals or 'gonçalvistas', led by Vasco Gonçalves, were close to the Portuguese Communist Party (PCP) and controlled the information services, the Fifth Division, and the navy. Finally, the MFA-Populists, led by Otelo, were inspired by the third world liberation movements, were linked to left-wing parties such as the Revolutionary Party of the Proletariat (PRP) and the Popular Democratic Union (UDP), and controlled the Special Forces Unit COPCON. Moreover, outside the MFA, the military was in favour of change but in less abrupt terms than their counterparts. Many of these officers were close to the centrist

Democratic Popular Party (PPD) and the centre-right Social Democratic Centre Party (CDS). The most prominent figure of this group was General Antonio Spínola (Manuel 1995:34–5; González Hernández 1999:52).

After the crisis of September 1974, the MFA tried to reinforce its position by purging non-revolutionary officers (Porch 1977:141–3) and by institutionalising its power (Robinson 1979:232). The creation of the Higher Council of the MFA, the MFA Assembly, and the first pact between the MFA and the political parties were examples of this effort. The Pact MFA-Political Parties granted the MFA the surveillance and control of the constituent process and a decisive role in the election of the president. The political parties approached the MFA to acquire influence on the government, in exchange providing legitimacy to the military.[47]

The third stage of the period of provisional governments began on 12 March 1975 with the failure of the right-wing coup, which strengthened the MFA-Radicals. The revolutionary agenda gained momentum. Some of the most important revolutionary measures were land seizures from rich proprietors and the nationalisation of big companies. The Council of the Revolution (CR) was established to promote the objectives of the MFA Programme and to guarantee security during the process of transition.[48] The first elections after the fall of the regime took place on 25 April 1975 to form a Constituent Assembly. The level of social tensions increased especially within the left. This tension happened not only at the political level where there were struggles between the PCP and the PS, but also at the military level between the MFA-Radicals that controlled the government and the the MFA-Moderates and Populists.[49] Pressures from the MFA-Moderates and social mass mobilisations forced the resignation of Gonçalves as prime minister in September 1975, marking the end of the third stage.

During these first three stages, the decentralisation of decision-making power (with the emergence of many actors with veto power), and the political instability contributed to freezing many aspects of the government's strategy towards the military. The tools of control used were very similar to those in place during the dictatorship.

The fourth stage, from September 1975 to July 1976, coincided with the sixth provisional government. The new Prime Minister Admiral Pinheiro de Azevedo tried to reverse the revolutionary transformations which attracted the criticism from the MFA-Radicals, the MFA-Populists, and the left-wing political parties, except for the PS. At least 58 protests and acts of indiscipline took place in the Portuguese military between September and November 1975 (Carrilho 1994:67). The rising tensions culminated in a left-wing military coup on 25 November 1975. The moderate Lieutenant-Colonel António Ramalho Eanes successfully led the military operations to control the putsch.[50] The failure of the coup contributed to discrediting the most radical revolutionary theses and consolidating the hegemony of the MFA-Moderates.

The November coup was a tipping point in the political transformations and in the strategy and tools to control the military. Many political and military figures understood then that the role of the military in politics should be reduced. The second pact between the MFA and the political parties in February 1976 reflected this changing trajectory.[51] The new Constitution, approved on 2 April 1976, confirmed the process of military disengagement from politics and the new trajectory in tool choice.

3.2.2   Constitutional governments (1976–86)

The transformations in civil-military relations from 1976 to 1986 were crucial for the consolidation of democracy in Portugal (Graham 1993:37–8). Although the Constitution established that the governments should take steps towards the construction of a 'socialist state', electoral legitimacy substituted the revolutionary legitimacy and the political parties were emancipated from the MFA (González Hernández 1999:26). The Constitution restricted the participation of the military in politics to the CR. Eanes, the candidate of the MFA-Moderates, became the president after the elections on 27 June 1976; and Mario Soares, leader of the PS, was elected prime minister of first constitutional government after the general elections on 25 April 1976 (Manuel 1996). These political developments reinforced the process of military detachment from politics and the new trend in the control toolkit.

However, the political instability continued due to the fact that the elections produced minority governments, the fragmentation of the political spectrum, and the continual tactical changes in political alliances.[52] From the legislative elections in 1976 to the interim elections in 1979, Portugal had five brief constitutional governments.[53] These governments had to deal with numerous socioeconomic issues, such as the normalisation of relations with the former colonies, absorption of 500,000 refugees ('retornados'), the reactivation of Portuguese participation in NATO, negotiations for EEC membership, high levels of inflation, unemployment, and budget deficits. All these problems diverted resources and attention away from the policy for military subordination, slowing down some reforms.

The participation of the military in politics remained higher than in most Western democracies. The functions and scope of the CR, although delimited by the Constitution, were still far-reaching. The CR held complete control over the military and veto power over important political decisions. The CR was guarantor of the constitutional institutions with capacity to enact military laws and control military promotions. Many politicians, including the president, were military men and they did not consider the CR as an anti-democratic institution. Even the moderate military officers who had controlled the rightist and leftist military upheavals were considered too interventionist for a European style democracy (Maxwell 1995:2–3). The 1976 Constitution also granted the CR with a legitimacy superior to that of the Assembly. This was problematic because part of the military leadership still championed the spirit of the revolution and a socialist type of democracy which contradicted the ideas held by the mainstream political parties that represented the majority of Portuguese voters (Gallagher 1983:230–9; Manuel 1996:3–11; González Hernández 1999).

The Social Democratic Party, PSD (previously the PPD), and the CDS became the main opposition to the power of the CR (Manuel 1996:37–8). In the 1979 interim elections and 1980 legislative elections, the centre-right coalition Democratic Alliance[54] obtained the majority of the seats in the Assembly. Prime Minister Francisco Sá Carneiro and, after his death, Prime Minister Francisco Pinto Balsemão[55] gave priority to the relations with the EEC and NATO and declared the will to reform the Constitution, reverse the agrarian reform, enhance the private sector, and limit the powers of the president and military. Finally, Balsemão even obtained the support of the PS, the main party in the opposition, in order to get two thirds of the Assembly seats required to circumvent President Eanes' veto and launch the 1982 Constitutional Reform.[56] This reform eliminated all references to the goal of achieving a 'socialist democracy', sensibly reduced the powers of the president of the republic and, most fundamentally, abolished the CR and reduced the role of the military.

NATO became the model and driving force for the reforms in the military initiated by the Law of National Defence and the Armed Forces of 1982.[57] This new law, approved despite the initial opposition of Eanes, was crucial in the redefinition of Portuguese civil-military relations and was the result of an agreement between the different political parties (Silva 1986:11). It passed the control of the military and defence decisions from the president to the prime minister and the government, charging the defence minister with managing day to day military affairs. The organisational reform became an important mechanism of civilian control. President Eanes and his supporters eventually understood that in order to build a democratic regime and enter the EEC, the military should disengage completely from politics, undertake a process of professionalisation, reform their structure, and participate more actively in NATO (Graham 1993:41). The gradual process of the transfer of powers from President Eanes and the military to the civilians in the government and parliament continued during Soares' coalition government PS/PSD (1983–5) and later with Cavaco Silva's PSD governments (from 1985). By the time Soares won the 1986 presidential elections, replaced General Eanes, and Portugal joined the EEC, the reorganisation of the military that consolidated a democratic Western type of civil-military relations had been launched, and the principle of civilian supremacy was uncontested. Portuguese civil-military relations and the government's control tools were finally converging with those of its Western allies, including Spain.

3.3   Conclusions

The military had a central role in most major political transformations in Portugal during the twentieth century. They were not submissive vis-à-vis the civilian power and remained a source of concern for governments and political elites throughout the dictatorship and transition to democracy. The façade of stability and endurance of the Estado Novo (1933–74) conceals the much more volatile civil-military relations during that period. The military had initially appointed Salazar and granted him extensive powers. However, they never completely accepted a subordinated role and frequently threatened his rule. Later they provoked the fall of his successor, Caetano, in 1974 and became central political actors shaping the transitional process. This chapter also highlights the political and institutional context as well as several historical junctures such as the Spanish War, the Second World War, the Colonial Wars and the transition to democracy that had important impacts on military attitudes and on civil-military relations.

4
The Estado Novo's Tools of Government

This chapter analyses the Estado Novo's strategy for military subordination according to Hood's four basic resources (*organisation, nodality, authority,* and *treasure*) and the subcategories introduced in Chapter 2. It outlines the most significant tools and the main trajectories observed in their usage from 1933 to 1974. Although there is evidence of the utilisation of all categories and subcategories of policy instruments, the relative magnitude in which they were employed clearly differed.

In order to guide the reader throughout this chapter, Table 4.1 summarises some of the most important features concerning *what* the government did to keep the military under control. For instance, Salazar used coercive *organisation* tools such as security forces, the paramilitary Portuguese Legion, and loyal military units to prevent and neutralise military plots throughout all of the period analysed (Section 4.1.1). Non-coercive *organisation* instruments, such as military education, training, and the capacity of the government to shape the organisational design of the defence institutions became central to the control strategy during 1950s, mainly due to the influence of NATO and the Western allies (Section 4.1.2). *Nodality* effectors, such as propaganda and censorship, were central in the 1930s and early 1940s but gradually lost relevance later (Section 4.2.1). Conversely, information detectors such as the secret police PIDE (later DGS) and the network of informants grew in salience (Section 4.2.2). *Authority* incentives and rewards were very important, particularly from 1938 to 1945, when the regulations that introduced the system of ministerial approval, 'escolha', made possible the substitution of all senior officers by young loyal officers. The regime also granted great autonomy and prerogatives to the military (Section 4.3.1). Sanctions and legal constraints were not very severe (Section 4.3.2). Finally, the use of *treasure* tools was very limited, the military's

Table 4.1 Summary of tools of government during the Estado Novo (1933–1974)

	Tools	Trajectory
Organisation	*Coercive* (Section 4.1.1): Loyal army units, security forces (GNR, PSP, PVDE/PIDE/DGS), and the Portuguese Legion helped counter military plots. Martial courts, imprisonments, and executions were avoided	Stable
	Non-coercive (Section 4.1.2): Formal military education and training. NATO and MAAG support. Training periods abroad	Low intensity although some actions from the late 1930s. Very important during 1950s. Abandoned during the Colonial Wars
	Organisation design: introduction of coordination bodies, centralisation of decision-making, inter-branch competition, geographical deployment of troops	Important reforms in the mid-1930s and in the 1950s (instilled by NATO). The Colonial Wars forced changes in the organisation design, hampering military control
	Provision of goods, services and jobs	Provision of services and goods grew during the Colonial Wars
Nodality	*Information effectors* (Section 4.2.1): Propaganda (via public speeches, cinema, pamphlets, books, military magazines, premilitary training in Mocidade) The SPN/SNI coordinated the action	Very strong during the 1930s and The first half of 1940s, then declining
	Censorship. DSC, PVDE/PIDE/DGS, Portuguese Legion	Very strong during Spanish Civil War and Second World War. The Colonial Wars hindered the capacity to censor the information within the ranks
	Information detectors (Section 4.2.2): PVDE/PIDE/DGS, SIME, Network of informants ('bufos'), letters and internal communications	Increasing utilisation

Authority	*Rewards and incentives* (Section 4.3.1): System of ministerial approval and appointment ('escolha') for military promotions and membership in the High Staff Corps	Introduced in 1937. Very important during Salazar's rule. Caetano relied less on military promotions and appointments
	Appointments of officers loyal to the government and top positions in the administration	Important representation of the military in all the regime institutions. Declining from 1960s on
	Wide powers and responsibilities granted to the military in the maintenance of public order. Military led the security forces, judged political crimes, worked in prisons and censorship	Stable
	Other privileges conceded: autonomy, tolerance with secondary jobs, guarantees and military awards	Autonomy reduced after the Second World War. Rights and decorations increased during the Colonial Wars
	Sanctions and constraints (Section 4.3.2): Reduction of retirement age and limitations to the size of the armed forces	Introduced in 1937. Important after the Second World War. Decreasing during Colonial Wars
	Punishment of officers involved in conspiracies (expulsions, demotions)	Stable. In general punishments were not severe
	Prohibitions in order to enhance a distinct esprit de corps and detach the military from politics	Stable
Treasure	*Staff expenditure* (Section 4.4.2): General salary rises (fundamentally to compensate inflation). Salary differentials to get support from some groups. Pensions and benefits	Overall low intensity. The most significant salary raises occurred in 1938 and 1945
	Equipment expenditure (Section 4.4.3): Successive efforts of rearmament and modernisation of military materials insufficient. Dependence on foreign suppliers such as Britain, Germany, and later the United States	Overall very low intensity. The most significant rearmament and modernisation attempts were undertaken during the mid-1930s, the Second World War and 1950s

living and working conditions were never good enough to contribute positively to military subordination (Section 4.4). As Table 4.1 also shows, many important changes in the trajectories of tool choice can be linked to the Spanish Civil War, the Second World War, NATO membership, and to the Colonial Wars.

4.1 Organisation

Salazarist governments used the *organisation* capacity of the state to achieve military subordination both through coercive and non-coercive means. Loyal units of the military were the main deterrent against military plots; although police and paramilitary organisations such as the PIDE, PSP, GNR, and the Portuguese Legion also contributed to this task. The use of these coercive *organisation* instruments remained stable throughout the regime. More variability can be captured amongst the non-coercive *organisation* tools. The utilisation of education and training acquired special salience during the 1950s. With the Colonial Wars, this salience was reduced and the provision of good services was fostered.

4.1.1   Coercive organisation

The utilisation of coercive *organisation* tools was not very intense or systematic. Salazar did not reach power by violent means and in general the oppression in the Estado Novo was more subtle than in the Francoist regime (Rosas 1989:27–9). Even during the late 1930s, when Salazar was at the height of his power and the regime was more repressive than ever against the leftist political movements, there was no strong systematic pattern of coercive *organisation* tools of control on an insubordinate military. This lack does not mean that coercion was absent from the control toolkit but that it was not as central as for the Francoist regime in the late 1930s and early 1940s.

The government mainly used loyal military units as coercive tools to neutralise other mutinous military units, as in the cases of the rebellions in 1927, 1928, 1931, 1935, 1936, 1946, and 1962. However, Salazar also used the GNR and PSP security forces as well as new organisations, such as the powerful secret police PVDE (later called PIDE and eventually DGS)[1] and the civilian paramilitary Portuguese Legion,[2] to control and deter military insubordination. The surveillance of and later the arrest of military officers in September 1935 and April 1938 are examples of how these organisations combined their forces to avert plots against Salazar (Pinto 1994:281–7).

Although their fighting capacity was very small compared to that of the army, the PSP, GNR, and PVDE/PIDE/DGS,[3] actively helped loyal army units neutralise many of the plots against the regime. The GNR and the PVDE were especially well-trained police forces and very loyal to Salazar (Medina 2000:157–8). In addition to the military and police forces, the Portuguese Legion could be considered as a means to challenge the monopoly of violence to the military.[4] The Legion maintained its character of an armed militia and its loyalty to the government throughout the Estado Novo. However, in terms of military subordination its overall importance remained relatively low. The Legion was a lightly armed organisation and did not have the power that similar paramilitary organisations such as the Blackshirts (*Camicie Nere*) and SA (*Sturm Abteilung*) had acquired in Italy and Germany.[5] Quickly it became obvious that the Legion was not in real competition with the military (Gallagher 1983:122). The Legion remained subordinated to the military, independent from any political party, and acted as an organisation of second line and civil defence linked to the state (Caetano 2000 [1975]:177).

In case of rebellion, all of the armed entities, Legion, GNR, PSP, PVDE and military, were placed under direct command of the government through the war minister (Telo 1996:169–70). Insubordinate military sometimes suffered torture, exile, and harsh conditions in Salazarist prisons.[6] However summary executions, court martials, or long-term imprisonments were generally avoided. Prison confinement was usually for short periods; *authority* instruments such as exile or expulsion from the military were preferred. For instance, Captain Mendes Norton's coup attempt planned for 20 May 1935 was quickly neutralised by the military and the police. The officers involved were arrested, but released soon afterwards.[7] Only after a second attempt on 10 September 1935 did the government decide to deport Norton and the rest of the plotters to the Azores (Faria 2000:84). The reaction to the rebellion in Beja in 1962 is the main exception to the general absence of imprisonments. There were 65 prison sentences, including a six-year-sentence for Captain João Varela Gomes the military leader (Wheeler 1979:214). The assassination of the regime opponent General Humberto Delgado in Spain in 1965, apparently by agents of PIDE, is probably one of the darkest examples of the use of a coercive *organisation* instrument.[8] Although some deaths of military men have been attributed to PIDE,[9] there is no solid evidence of a strategy of extra-judiciary executions of military officers in any period of the regime.

Caetano, like his predecessor, trusted his secret police (DGS), the Legion, and the paramilitary security forces GNR and PSP with the task of defending the regime (Porch 1977:22–3). The real deterrent capacity of these organs of control and repression vis-à-vis the military was, nonetheless, very limited and drastically reduced in the last years of the regime. In general, army officers led all security forces. The heavier weapons, better training, and the experience fighting the insurgency in the Colonial Wars gave the military a coercive superiority. Moreover, the geographical dispersion of the troops made it more difficult to control them. The detention by the DGS of 200 soldiers and officers following an uprising in March 1974 did not suffice to prevent the April revolution. During the military coup on 25 April 1974, the loyal DGS, GNR, and Legion showed a complete incapacity to defend the regime against army units.

4.1.2 Non-coercive organisation

The *organisation* power of the state was also used in a non-coercive fashion in three ways. First, through education and training so that the military could improve their professional skills and learn the necessity of remaining separated from politics and subordinated to the government. Second, the government used its capacity to shape the structure of the military (including changes to the hierarchy, attribution of functions, and the deployment of the troops) to enhance the subordination of the military. And third, the government used the provision of goods, services, and even employment to the military and their families as a means to improve their living standards and levels of satisfaction with the governments.

Salazar believed that if the military were concentrated on their professional duties they would be less prone to intervene in politics. Military education and training had to be reinforced in order to increase military professionalisation and as well as to correct the serious deficiencies of the Portuguese military.[10] Thus, in the late 1930s and 1940s, some reforms were launched which aimed to introduce a more technical approach in military education and training.[11] The Military School was transformed into the Army School in 1939, and in 1940 a reform of military education was launched to eliminate all content related to political science and sociology (Ferreira 1976:146). The High Military Studies Institute was created in 1937 and the Naval High Institute of War in 1948. Salazar's concern with military education and subordination was portrayed by his personal involvement in the reforms.[12] These reforms, however, were insufficient and the general level of instruction and professional preparation remained deficient.[13] Salazar was afraid that the military that had government skills could challenge him. Thus, the education that officers received was outdated and ignored politics, sociology, and, at least partially, economics, administration, and modern management (Wiarda 1988:128).

Training and education were improved in the 1950s thanks to NATO's influence. From 1951, many Portuguese officers travelled to the United States to undertake military training. In parallel, the MAAG, examined the command, logistics, training, and maintenance systems in Portugal. As a result of these exchanges, a series of reforms were launched in the 1950s.[14] From 1951 to 1957, many regulations inspired by the US military were approved. The education programme for senior officers, the High Staff Course, was reformed.[15] New courses were offered which were often run by those in the military that had been previously sent abroad. Logistics and operational methods and military exercises were improved following American assistance (Duarte 2010:258).

From 1958 to 1961, the government introduced another set of NATO inspired reforms related to military education, training, territorial organisation, and support services.[16] Nonetheless, from the outbreak of the Colonial Wars, the collaboration with the United States and the emphasis on military instruction were reduced. The Colonial Wars negatively impacted formal military education, which at the end of the regime remained deficient both in tactical-technical terms and in terms of socioeconomic and political instruction.[17] Moreover, the NATO-led advances in education and training ended up being counter-productive for the subordination of the military to the regime. The new approach to their profession brought new preoccupations and claims. The officers that participated in the exchanges with NATO allies realised the qualitative gap that separated them from other Western militaries and became more critical with the state of the Portuguese military and with the government (Telo 1996:213–4). They led the opposition movements against the regime from the late 1950s onwards.

Second, in addition to the efforts on military training and education, some changes in the organisational design of the military were employed to achieve its subordination. The reforms in the 1930s constitute the best example.[18] With these reforms Salazar sought to centralise the decision-making power by creating several coordinating bodies under his control. The Higher Council of National Defence (CSDN), the Higher Council of War Planning, and the Mixed Commission of the High Staff were all created in 1935. Other important changes were the diminution of the size of the army, the creation of the exclusive and loyal High Staff

Corps, the direct subordination of the chief of staff of the army (CEME) to the war minister, and the reduction in powers of the Higher Council of the Army and the army major general.[19]

By 1935, the head of the army Major General Morais Sarmentos expressed opposition to the reorganisation project because it withdrew an important part of the political powers and autonomy that the army held.[20] Later, in 1936, a letter exchange between Salazar and the war minister, General Passos e Sousa, shows that the reorganisation of the army was not made following the dictate of the CSDN but that of the Council of Ministers in which Salazar had the upper hand.[21] Salazar was in a strong position vis-à-vis the military and pushed forward his idea of creating a smaller military under civilian control.

The opposition of many senior officers, who wanted to preserve the autonomy of the military, did not halt Salazar's reorganisation (Telo 1996:150). In 1936, he took over the War Ministry and in 1937 launched some further reforms which aimed for higher levels of political control.[22] The fundamental change was that instead of the War Ministry being subordinated to the army, the metropolitan army became subordinated to the War Ministry (Duarte 2010:114–20). In the new structure the undersecretary of state, Santos Costa, became a crucial figure leading many of the reforms and shielding Salazar from many internal problems (Faria 2000).

The new organisation also preserved the separation between the continental and colonial forces and the separation of the branches in different ministries which reduced the internal cohesion of the military and the likelihood of a coordinated conspiracy while enhancing inter-branch competition and oversight. This seems to confirm the hypothesis of a divide-and-rule tactic (Wheeler 1979:199).

After the Second World War, the army was reorganised and downsized (Ferreira 1992:189, 192–3), the CSDN became a consultative body, and the government took on the responsability of defining defence policies.[23] Nonetheless, the most important changes followed the signing of the North Atlantic Treaty in 1949. In 1950, a National Defence Ministry and a chief of the Joint Staff (CEMGFA) were introduced.[24] Their functions were to coordinate the military branches (which still maintained distinct ministries). In 1956, following the NATO doctrine, the government redefined the bases for the organisation of the military to consolidate the subordination of the defence structures and policies in the government.[25] The CEMGFA, which was subordinated to the defence minister, was reinforced and the participation of military in the CSDN reduced (Duarte 2010:272–5). Finally the adaptation to the NATO model culminated in 1959 with a reorganisation of the army and a reinforcement of the army information services, SIME.[26] The new organisational design was a NATO requirement but was perceived by the government as an opportunity to reduce the autonomy of the branches. Moreover, in the new integrated structure, the air force, army, and navy had to compete for resources from a limited budget, which introduced competition and mutual oversight amongst the branches.

The geographical distribution of troops also served a control purpose as a means to neutralise of the military's attempts against the government. Loyal and elite units, such as the 'Hunters' and the 'Machine Guns' battalions and the brigades of cavalry, were strategically located in the territory to defend the regime (Teixeira 2004:42). The decision-making power was fundamentally located in Lisbon and centralised under Salazar and a few loyal officers. Even the armed forces in the colonies were deployed such that they could support the metropolitan troops in a possible war in the peninsula.[27] However, after 1958, the defence of the overseas territories became the main goal, which required new geographical organisation and operating procedures. The military grew from 40,000 men in 1961 to 217,000 in 1974.[28] The command structure adapted to this growth.[29] The new war techniques and the bigger and decentralised structure weakened the authority of the senior officers and the government. Top ranking officers were rarely in the theatre of operations. Many lower ranking officers felt far from the centres of decisions and became alienated. Thus, the new organisational design launched by the government with a specific defence purpose indirectly contributed to undermining their control over the military.

Third, the government used its organisational resources to provide and subsidise services and goods for the military and their families in order to increase satisfaction with the government and compensate for low salaries. This use of the state's capacity acquired relevance in the late 1950s.[30] The Social Services of the Armed Forces was created in 1958 to assist military families with housing and health problems.[31] The government also created a supermarket that offered credit and low prices for the military. After 1960, the acquisition of housing was also financed by the government (Matos 2004:166). The provision of goods and services was intensified during the Colonial Wars. The Caetano government also tried to increase military satisfaction by providing free transportation to the overseas territories and medical care and housing benefits to the families of the military fighting the war.[32] The public sector served as a source of employment for many officers not only after they retired but also as a second job while in active service. Although salaries in the administration were low, they often provided power, prestige, perks, and facilitated access to better paid positions in the private sector after retirement from active service (Pimentel 2007:71).

4.1.3   (Limited) deterrence and organisational reforms

The Salazarist regime used coercive and non-coercive *organisation* instruments to control the military. The regime used loyal army units; the security forces GNR, PSP, and PVDE/PIDE/DGS; as well as the paramilitary Portuguese Legion to deter and neutralise. Although these tools were primarily used by the regime to control the civilian population, they held some deterrent capacity vis-à-vis military insurrections. The security and paramilitary forces at the service of the regime were a limited deterrent against the military due to their inferior material means and lack of combat readiness. They were primarily used by the regime to control the civilian population. The recourse to these coercive tools was stable throughout the regime. From the military rebellions in the 1930s to the Carnations Revolution in 1974, the government always relied on its coercive power to force subordination or deter further rebellion.

The non-coercive use of the organisation of the state was more varied. The regime used military education and training, the institutional design and the provisions of services, and goods and jobs to keep the military under control.

First, the government believed that better preparation would enhance professionalisation and separate the military from politics. Some initiatives were undertaken in the late 1930s and 1940s but overall education and training remained clearly deficient. NATO membership produced a small revolution intensifying training and military exercises throughout the 1950s. Many officers were trained abroad and new techniques and ideas were introduced. The military became more professional but also more critical of the regime. The Colonial Wars cut short this trend and during the 1960s and 1970s, military education ceased being a priority.

Second, Salazar used the organisational design to control the military. This was especially important in the 1930s and 1950s. In the 1930s, Salazar created coordination organs, such as the CSDN that he could dominate, to exert control over the three branches of the military. In the 1950s, further organisational changes were made following the dictates of NATO to consolidate the civilian supremacy over defence. The most important measures were the creations of the National Defence Ministry and CEMGFA and the reinforcement of the CSDN. There are some signs of the utilisation of the geographical deployment of troops as instruments to prevent internal threats to the regime. However, the Colonial Wars forced the growth and decentralisation of the defence structures which hampered the previous efforts to control the military through the institutional design.

Finally, the government used its organisational capacity to provide services, goods and jobs for the military and their families as a means to increase their support. These became more important during the Colonial Wars.

4.2 Nodality

There is much evidence of the use of *nodality* through both information effectors and detectors. Like other authoritarian regimes, the government intensively manipulated the information available to the military in order to project a positive image of Salazar and to avoid discontent. Thus, the selective production (propaganda) and restriction of information (censorship) became central in the strategy of military subordination. Additionally, the regime employed several mechanisms to retrieve information, such as the secret police and other information services, networks of informants, and the internal communications in the administration, in order to prevent military insurrection. In general, the information effectors reduced their intensity throughout the regime while the detectors grew in salience.

4.2.1 Information effectors

The use of propaganda and censorship was especially important during the 1930s and early 1940s. The control of the information exerted by the Estado Novo was similar to that of other fascist-like regimes such as Franco's. The fall of the Axis, the exchanges with NATO allies, and the Colonial Wars ended up decreasing the utilisation and effectiveness of information effectors upon the military.

In 1932, Salazar, influenced by the journalist António Ferro, launched his 'Política do Espírito' (politics of the spirit) that aimed to strengthen the regime through propaganda and censorship (Ferro 1933; Pimentel 2007:93). The National Propaganda Secretariat (SPN), established in 1933, became the core of the Estado Novo's propaganda machinery. Military speeches, the radio, press, cinema, military publications, pamphlets, and books were the information channels through which the government transmitted the official discourse.[33] The fascist-like youth movement 'Mocidade' also became a *nodality* instrument contributing to the control of the military through the moral and civic indoctrination of future soldiers and officers.[34] The projected representation of Portugal was that of a unitary, rural, religious, and traditional country with a glorious past and a strong leader, very similar to Francoist representations of Spain. Moreover there was an effort to personalise the regime in the figure of Salazar (Paulo 1994:63). Attacking Salazar meant attacking the new regime.

The theme of the military was recurrent in the regime's propaganda. The always positive depiction of the military aimed to increase its professional reputation and self-esteem (Soares 1987:165–6). Since the inception of the Estado Novo, the government discourse emphasised the necessity of keeping the military separate from politics in general and from communism and totalitarian views in particular.[35] The use of nodal effectors was intensified whenever the stability of the regime was threatened. For instance, propaganda was used to counter the effects of leftist navy rebellion in September 1936 (Faria 1995; Freire 1998) and the unrest triggered by the 1937 military reforms (Paulo 1994:86; Faria 2000:184–7). Moreover, the Spanish Civil War and the Second World War were propagandistically used to drive military attention away from internal politics.[36] The specialised military publications that proliferated during the regime[37] tried to stimulate the esprit de corps and introduced technical content as a means to reduce military concerns about politics (Melo 1970).

From the mid-1940s, there was a gradual decline in the utilisation of propaganda. In 1944, the SPN was renamed the National Information Secretariat (SNI) and in 1968 transformed into the Information and Tourism Secretariat. Although with lower intensity, propaganda continued to be used throught the regime. For instance, the propaganda machinery magnified the 'Soviet menace' to maintain the military united;[38] supported Salazar's candidate, Admiral Américo Tomás, against General Humberto Delgado in the 1958 presidential elections;[39] and more importantly used the Colonial Wars to produce a patriotic exaltation and military support for the regime.[40]

Censorship was also widely employed. In 1933, Salazar transferred the responsibility of censorship from the War Ministry to the Interior Ministry[41] and created the Directorate for Censorship Services (DSC).[42] Many different bodies of the administration collaborated in the censorship effort including the Legion and the PVDE/PIDE/DGS (Azevedo 1999:305–14, 345–57; Pimentel 2007:92–4). The elimination or modification of the content of articles related to military affairs became a fundamental control mechanism. News concerning the military were suppressed and the journalists often intimidated by the secret police (Ferreira 1992:233). Expressions of discontent were silenced.[43] Censorship was so entrenched that in an interview in 1938, Salazar declared that censorship 'constitutes the legitimate defence of the free independent States against the big disorientation of the modern thought' (Ferro 2003 [1932–8]:158). The regime tried to limit the exposure of the military to any information that could undermine the morale or raise doubts about the government.

Censorship was very severe in the late 1930s and early 1940s (Azevedo 1999:415–38). Later its intensity diminished until the outbreak of the colonial conflict when Salazar and Caetano used censorship to prevent an open debate on the colonial question (Ferreira 1992:290–1; Ferreira 2006:107). Although Caetano did not abolish the censorship,[44] gradually it became more lax which enabled the media to criticise the government (Pimlott and Seaton 1983:47). The government lost its grip on information, especially in the colonies. The military were exposed to alternative sources of information and to new progressive ideas. The regime ended up being blamed for the conflict and Caetano discredited (Soares 1987:167). The publication of General Spínola's book 'Portugal e Futuro' in 1974 in which he criticised the government exemplifies the regime's loss of control of information.

4.2.2   Information detectors

The Estado Novo also relied on information detectors to subordinate the military. Several state organisations collected information critical to the stability of the regime. The most important was the secret police PVDE/PIDE/DGS. Salazar and Caetano also relied on a wide web of informants and on their central location within the Estado Novo information network. Although the use of information detectors grew throughout the dictatorship, they failed to prevent the military insurrection that precipitated its fall.

The secret police, PVDE, created in 1933, quickly became a fundamental control tool employed not only to counter opposition amongst civilians, usually communist and far-right activists, but also threats from other quarters (Pimentel 2007:498–519). The well-armed secret police was used as a coercive *organisation* tool and as an information effector fundamentally thanks to its role in the Estado Novo's censorship strategy. However, its main contribution to military subordination derives from its function as an information detector. From 1937, the PVDE ran politico-ideological checks on military officers and the candidates for the Military Academy (Carrilho 1985:421). PVDE was notorious for its inquisitive surveillance; techniques learnt from German and Italian police (Gallagher 1983:118). In 1945, it was transformed into PIDE and its powers increased. The interception of letters, tapped phones, interrogations, and even torture were common methods to obtain information. The secret police became notorious internationally especially during the Colonial Wars when its actions were intensified. In 1969, it was renamed DGS. Its personnel increased from 521 in 1949 to 3,472 in 1972 (Pimentel 2007:52–3). Rather than the use of violence, the key to success for the secret police was maintaining an important network of informants ('bufos') (Gallagher 1983:117–20). In 1974, there were 20,000 informants working for DGS (Pimentel 2007:308–37). The information collected by the secret police served to neutralise several military plots.

The government also used other information detectors to prevent military conspiracies such as the SNP, the DSC, and the Legion.[45] There is also evidence that Salazar relied on personal informants in order to assess what units in the military should be suspected of anti-Salazarist views.[46] However, since the military strongly disliked being scrutinised by external bodies, and especially by the secret police, the utilisation of non-military information detectors was used with caution.[47] The regime complemented their action with the help some loyal officers and military services, such as the army information services, SIME.[48]

Additionally, Salazar and Caetano used their nodal position within the state apparatus. Letters, internal memos, and reports served to obtain valuable information concerning the military. Salazar and Caetano maintained extensive correspondence with other figures in the administration and the military.[49] Moreover, they constantly received reports and copies of internal communications about military reforms, defence budgets, and discontent within the barracks.[50] To a lesser extent than Franco, Salazar and Caetano used informal friendship networks as a tool to control the military. They had no military background themselves and maintained a more distant rapport with their entourage. Despite those efforts, the coup attempt in 1961 by the Defence Minister Botelho Moniz and the inadequate assessment of the risks of military plots against Caetano shows the deterioration of the information detection mechanisms.[51]

4.2.3 Propaganda, censorship, and spies

Information control was a very important aspect of the regime's military subordination strategy. On the one hand, Salazar and Caetano manipulated the information available for and about the military through information effectors. On the other, they closely monitored the military to anticipate discontent and insurrection through information detectors.

The government's propaganda was very intense and involved many different means of communication. The government projected an idealised image of Salazar, Portugal, and the military. The very powerful SNP/SNI was in charge of coordinating the propaganda action. Additionally, several organisations exerted censorship in the Estado Novo, such as the DSC, the PVDE/PIDE/DGS, and the Legion. The goal was to eliminat any information that could cause concern or raise discontent amongst the military. Both propaganda and censorship were very strong during the Spanish Civil and the Second World Wars. Later, they gradually declined. After the fall of the Axis, the type of information manipulation used by the Estado Novo became questionable in the Western sphere. During the Colonial Wars, the new, larger, and more decentralised organisation of the military as well as its more heterogeneous composition undermined the effectiveness of the government's information effectors.

Conversely, the utilisation of information detectors grew continuously throughout the regime. Most of the institutions involved in propagating and censoring information were also employed to detect threats. Amongst them, the PVDE/PIDE/DGS was the most important. Its inquisitive surveillance helped to neutralise many military plots. The government also relied on a wide network of informants as well as on Salazar's and Caetano's priviledged position vis-à-vis the information flows within the Estado Novo's administration. Letters, internal communications, and reports received from senior officers and civil servants contributed to the assessment and prevention of risks coming from the military.

4.3 Authority

The *authority*-based rewards and incentives were another pillar in the military control strategy. The capacity of the government to shape military promotions, the appointment to top positions in the state apparatus, and the functions and privileges granted to the military were used to increase loyalty within the ranks. The Salazarist regime also used *authority* sanctions and constraints as control mechanisms. The government limited the retirement age and size of the military, punished disloyal military, and sought to enhance the esprit de corps and detach them from political activities. Overall, the utilisation of *authority* tools was very important and slightly more stable than that of the *organisation* and *nodality* tools. However, an important peak in the use of authority tools can be observed in the late 1930s, when Salazar managed to substitute all of the top senior officers by loyal younger ones through a combination of *authority* tokens. Later, a progressive decline in the centrality of these tools can be observed during the 1960s forward, mainly linked to the Colonial Wars and the loss of legitimacy of the government.

4.3.1   Rewards and incentives

First, military promotions became control tools. Most of the young officers that had participated in the 28 May 1926 coup were supportive of Salazar. Salazar gradually replaced senior officers, who in general kept a more critical attitude towards his reforms, with young, loyal ones. The use of promotions and military appointments intensified after 1936, when Salazar became self-appointed war minister.[52] Salazar took advantage of the ongoing military reforms to institutionalise a mechanism of political appointment and ministerial approval, 'escolha', for the senior ranks (Matos 2004:160). In 1937, a merit-based system of appointment replaced the traditional seniority principle for military promotions from the rank of captain upwards.[53] Loyalty and subordination became highly rewarded. The political-ideological filter made at the top of the hierarchy was reproduced down to the rank of captain (Carrilho 1985:421). After 1937, ministerial approval also became a condition for the admission to the elite High Staff Corps.[54] This corps was very appealing for most of the military because it involved a higher salary, fast-track promotions, and access to the most desired positions, such as those in the urban centres and embassies. Ambitious officers publicly showed their allegiance to the regime in order to be admitted to the High Staff Corps and be promoted. These authority-based instruments were arguably those with the highest impact on the control of the military during the Estado Novo because they allowed the goverment to replace the top ranks with loyal officers (Pinto 1994:288). The 'escolha' persisted during Caetano's rule but he was less involved in the appointment of military chiefs than Salazar (Matos 2004:175). He did not enjoy the same legitimacy amongst the ranks as his predecessor and was afraid he would create unrest by interfering in the promotion system (Fernandes 2006).

Second, Salazar and Caetano used their capacity to influence appointments in the administration as control tools. They systematically reserved some of the most important positions in the regime for loyal military officers, including many ministerial positions and that of the president of the republic. Although presidents were formally elected, candidates had to be approved by the prime ministers who controlled the single party, National Union.[55] These appointments served to reward allegiance and held important symbolic value for the military. Moreover, many other top positions in the administration were allocated to the military. From 1936 to 1944, about 35 per cent of the civil governors and almost all the colonial governors were military men. The military had significant representation in the National Union, the Corporate Chamber, and the National Assembly (Faria 2000:24–6). There is evidence that the appointment of military personnel to top positions in the state apparatus continued throughout the regime.[56] Only after the late 1950s did their representation in the government and state institutions decline (Schmitter 1975:31–3; Carrilho 1985:446).

Third, some of the the functions entrusted to the military and some of the privileges that the military enjoyed can be considered *authority*-based rewards and incentives. According to the 1933 Constitution, the military were the guarantors of the 'National Revolution' and were charged with the 'maintenance of order and public peace'.[57] The military held important power concerning public order during the Estado Novo. The security forces PIDE, PSP, GNR, and the border and maritime control police Fiscal Guard were always led by senior military officers. Until 1945, the military were in charge of judging political crimes through special military courts, and after 1949, the responsibility of the defence of the empire was transferred from the Overseas Ministry to the military. Military officers also worked in prison services, in the Legion and the Mocidade, in the censorship services, and in the colonial administration (Wheeler 1979:201).

Additionally, there was a tacit agreement between the government and the military according to which the military maintained their autonomy, privileges, and some representation in the administration to compensate for their extrication from politics. For instance, there was a great level of tolerance for holding second jobs,[58] and until 1945, the military were immune from arrest by the civilian police (Wheeler 1979:199–205). In 1947, the first Armed Forces Officer's statutes were launched, introducing new guarantees for the military. During the Colonial Wars, some new privileges were introduced. For instance, in 1961, the Estado Novo reintroduced the right to vote in the legislative elections (eliminated in 1947) and, in 1965, the Armed Forces Officer's Statutes increased officers' rights and guarantees.[59] Moreover, numerous military decorations were awarded every year to combatants, often personally by Salazar.[60] All of these functions, privileges, and formal recognitions aimed to make the military feel empowered and increase their satisfaction.

4.3.2 Sanctions and constraints

Authority tools were also used to restrain the capacity of the military to oppose the government. These can be organised into three groups: limitations to the size of the military and retirement age, punishments to rebellious officers and regulations to enhance their esprit the corps, and separation from politics.

In addition to the 'escolha' system, the 1937 reforms introduced legal limitations to the size of the army,[61] to the length of the military service,[62] and to the retirement age.[63] The oversized army was problematic. The government believed that a smaller military could be better paid, trained, and equipped; thus reducing the risk of military disaffection. The government also aimed to rejuvenate the senior ranks by stimulating early retirement.[64] This measure was enhanced by financial incentives. In some cases the pensions of early retirees became higher than salaries. The measure resulted in the reduction the total number of officers on active duty by 25 per cent and the complete renewal of the top ranks by 1940. This was extremely important from a control point of view because (coupled with the newly introduced 'escolha' system) it gave Salazar the opportunity to promote many loyal military to the top of the hierarchy. From 1938 to 1939, 15 new generals were appointed. This combination of *authority* tools was so effective that in only five years, it produced the retirement of all of the generals that had participated in the reorganisation of the military in 1935 and allowed a generation of young loyal officers to occupy most of the high ranking positions (Carrilho 1985:440; Telo 1996:152; Faria 2000:176, 192–3).

By the end of the Second World War, the government enacted new regulations to reduce the size of the army, which had grown to face a possible invasion. This process included a fast process of de-mobilisation of militia officers ('milicianos') recruited during the war period, amongst which many did not support the regime (Telo 1996:185). The size of the military was reduced by more than 40 per cent from 1944 to 1951 (Matos 2004:162). Later, however, the Colonial Wars again hindered the goal of maintaining a small army.

The government also used its official capacity to discharge or demote officers when their behaviour was disloyal. This served to punish the military involved in the several anti-government plots while creating opportunities for the appointment of loyal officers. There are many examples. For instance, in May 1935, the government dismissed Generals Mendes Ribeiro, Norton de Matos, and Mendes Cabeçadas; Colonel Ferreira Guimarães; and Major Rodirgues Areosa Feio for conspiring against the regime (Matos 2004:161). After the Tagus revolt in 1936, there were purges in the navy (Freire 2003:150–1); and after the revolt of April 1938 Colonels Silva Casqueiro, Lello Portela, and Ferreira Guimarães and Brigadeiro João Almeida were forced into exile (Pinto

1994:281, 287). Captain Henrique Galvão was arrested in 1952 and later forced into retirement for criticising the colonial policy. In April 1961, Botelho Moniz and Costa Gomes were fired and Craveiro Lopes was forced into retirement after their failed coup. In 1963, ten officers were expelled from the army for disobeying government orders to defend Goa against the much larger Indian troops in 1961, including General Vassalo e Silva who was in charge of the colony (Gallagher 1983:152–3). Notwithstanding, overall the government's stance was comparatively soft and often military plotters were reintegrated into the military.[65] The *authority* disciplinary measures were not very stringent and did not have a strong deterrent capacity.

Finally, the government employed restrictive regulations to enhance the military's distinct esprit de corps and detachment from politics. The right of association was restricted and secret societies such as the Freemasons and the Carbonari were prohibited due to their historical connection with republicanism.[66] The government introduced caps for militia officers' careers.[67] The military were not allowed to exercise liberal professions; they needed permission to get married; and could only do so with non-divorced Portuguese women.[68] From 1947 to 1961, they were not even allowed to vote.

4.3.3 Escolha, age limitations, and special functions

Authority tools were probably those with the greatest impact on military subordination during Salazar's rule. The system of appointment and ministerial approval, 'escolha', combined with the limitations to the retirement age introduced in 1937 allowed Salazar to replace completely the often critical senior ranks with younger loyal military officers. Pro-Salazarist officers were appointed to key positions, not only in the military but also in other parts of the regime's administration. The use of the government's capacity to shape appointments and the presence of the military in the state institutions was very important until the mid-1960s, but then it declined. The regime also reserved some special powers for the military concerning the maintenance of public order so that they felt empowered. Moreover, the military enjoyed formal rewards and incentives to increase their satisfaction, such as a high degree of autonomy, tolerance with secondary jobs, immunity to civilian arrest, and military decorations. These rewards were intensified during the Colonial Wars.

In addition to lowering the retirement age that facilitated the renewal of the military hierarchy, there were other *authority*-based sanctions and constraints used to enhance the control over the military. The government established formal limitations to the size of the military. The smaller military could be better paid, trained, and equipped. Moreover, the government wielded its authority to demote or expel those involved in anti-government plots or opposed to the regime's colonial policy. However, in most cases punishments were not severe. Finally, some restrictions were imposed on the military in order to enhance a distinct esprit de corps and to keep them separated from politics.

Overall, the use of *authority* was fundamentally stable with an important peak around the 1937 reforms. Later, with the outbreak of the Colonial Wars (1961) and the arrival of Caetano (1968), most *authority* tools became less important to the government's control toolkit. This development suggests the gradual depletion of *authority* as a government resource, the culmination of which may be observed in the failure of Caetano's *authority*-based attempts to maintain the military on his side.

4.4   Treasure

Salazar and some of the young officers of his entourage regarded the rearmament and modernisation of the military and the salary raises as incentives for the military to develop professionalism and encourage a return to the barracks. However, these ideas collided with the generally very poor economic situation in Portugal and with the austerity measures that Salazar championed and that earned him his reputation. Military budget increases were connected with reforms, such as in the second half of the 1930s and in the 1950s and with external threats, such as the Second World War and the colonial conflicts. These increases had, nonetheless, little impact on military living and working conditions and therefore on their level of subordination.

4.4.1   Evolution of military budgets

The military dictatorship (1926–33) and the Estado Novo did not produce significant growth in military budgets (Figure 4.1). Although the impact of the Great Depression was comparatively lower in Portugal than in other Western countries (Mateus 1998:47–50), Portugal's general economic situation was poor. Portugal's industry was not competitive and had a high dependence on imports and emigrant remittances (Rosas 2000). The Great Depression accentuated the trade deficit and the depreciation of the Escudo. Exports and remittances diminished drastically (Mata and Valerio 1994:190–3). Salazar, influenced by the new totalitarian regimes in Europe, adopted a highly autarkic and austere economic policy which

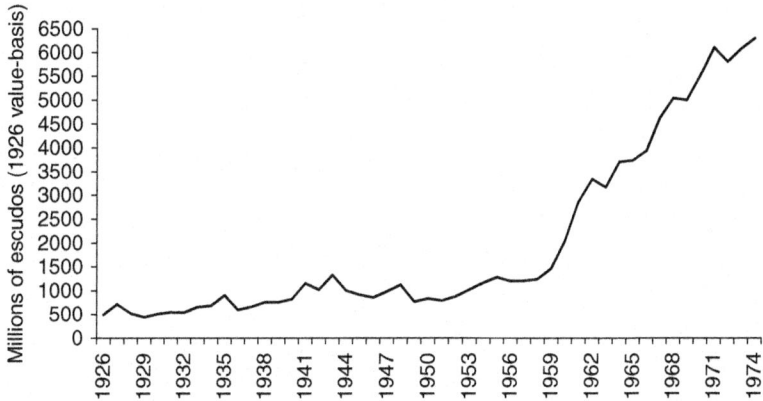

Figure 4.1 Defence expenditure in constant million escudos in 1926 (military dictatorship and Estado Novo)*

Note: *It includes expenditures in the overseas territories.

Source: Based on Mata and Valerio (1994:253–4, 270–1).

served to counter the effects of the international crisis and legitimised his rule in the early 1930s. However, they also hampered the utilisation of *treasure* tools. The salary increases and modernisation of equipment requested by the military in the early 1930s were not approved due to austerity imposed by Salazar.[69] The rearmament plans of the navy and army (1933–5), the reforms of 1937, and the threat of the Spanish Civil War increased military budgets.

During the Second World War, exports grew drastically and temporarily corrected the trade deficit. However, the crisis of supply and an inflationary process linked to the war affected the purchasing power of the military. The increases in defence budgets during the war did not positively affect military satisfaction. Most expenditure was directed to the reinforcement of the garrisons in Cabo Verde, the Azores, and the frontier with Spain and did not contribute to the improvement of the salaries and working conditions of the military.

The Portuguese economy grew without interruption from 1946 to 1974 (Mata and Valerio 1994:200, 254), but this growth was not reflected in the military budgets. Portugal remained the second poorest European country after Greece and suffered some structural deficiencies that made Salazar prioritise other expenditures such as health, education, and infrastructures over defence. In real terms, military expenditure grew slowly until the late 1950s. The weight of defence expenditure vis-à-vis total public expenditure decreased until the membership in NATO and

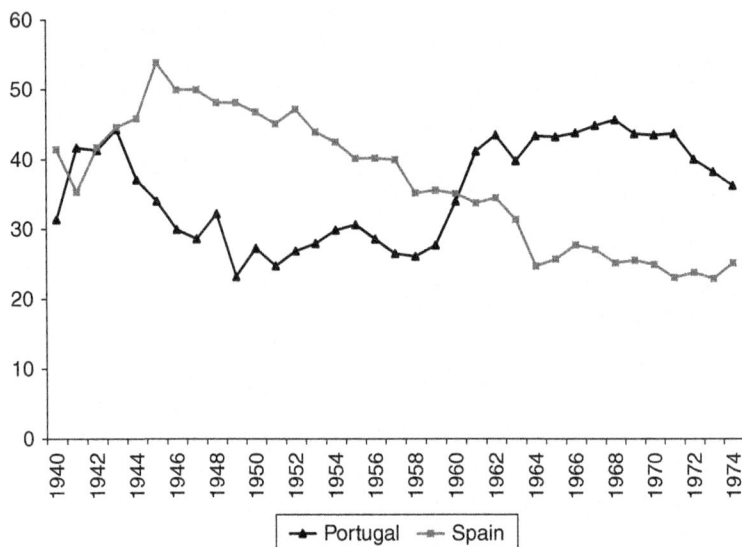

Figure 4.2 Defence expenditure as percentage total public expenditures in Portugal and Spain (1940–74)*

Note: *Portuguese data include expenditure in the overseas territories.

Source: Based on Olmeda (1988:204) and Mata and Valerio (1994:253–4, 270–1).

then remained stable until the colonial conflict (Figure 4.2). During this period, the financial resources devoted to military and defence purposes were comparatively low (Table 4.2).

After 1958, the military budgets quickly soared. The colonial war effort necessitated enormous sums of money, which constrained the capacity of the government to use *treasure* for control purposes.[70] Moreover, emigration and the wars provoked a dramatic shortage of man-power that worsened the state of the Portuguese economy.[71]

4.4.2 Staff expenditure

General salary raises, differentiation in wages, as well as pension and other complementary remunerations were used to keep the military under control. However, the intensity and frequency of their utilisation was very limited due to factors such as the size of the army, economic crises, and the special needs of war periods.

The economic problems coupled with Salazar's austerity doctrine limited military salaries in the early 1930s. The reduction of the size of the armies launched in 1937 made increasing salaries easier for the

Table 4.2 Defence expenditure as a percentage of the GDP (NATO countries + Spain)

	1949	1950	1951	1952	1953	1954	1955	1956
USA	5.7	5.5	10.9	15	14.8	12.9	11.2	10.9
UK	7	7.3	8.9	11.1	11.2	9.8	9.2	8.8
France	6.6	6.8	8.8	10.5	11.4	9.1	7.7	9.5
Canada	2.6	3.1	6.6	9.1	9.2	8.2	7.7	7.3
Greece	7.4	7.6	8.4	8.3	6.4	6.9	6.4	6.8
Netherlands	4.3	5.2	5.6	6.2	6.2	6.7	6.4	6.6
Turkey	6.7	6.4	5.8	5.6	5.6	6.1	5.8	5.2
Norway	2.4	2.6	3.3	4.4	5.7	5.7	4.4	4.1
Italy	4.4	4.7	5.2	5.6	4.7	5	4.4	4.1
Germany						4.8	4.9	4.4
Portugal	3.7	3.5	3.5	3.9	4.4	4.5	4.6	4.4
Belgium	2.5	2.4	3.4	5.2	5.1	4.9	4	3.8
Spain	5.3	4.4	3.7	4.2	4	3.7	3.9	3.7
Denmark	2.1	1.8	2.3	3	3.7	3.6	3.6	3.4
Luxembourg	1	1.5	1.7	2.6	3.2	3.6	3.6	2.1

Sources: Carrilho (1985: 452) and Olmeda (1988: 204).

government. An important general raise was decided on by Salazar in 1937 to bridge the gap between the military and civil servant salaries, increased in 1935, and also to prevent criticism of the other more controversial organisation reforms that the government was launching at the end of the year.[72]

The government also used salary discrimination amongst different ranks and corps to reinforce military loyalty. For instance, raises approved in 1937 were especially high for the senior ranks to maintain their loyalty. Their salaries were higher than those of equivalent positions in the civil service (Faria 1996:32). This salary raise aimed to compensate the military elites for the reduction of their political power (Carrilho 1985:376–7). Membership to the new High Staff Corps also meant higher salaries for equivalent ranks (Table 4.3). Since ministerial approval was a requisite for the senior ranks and for High Staff Corps membership, ambitious officers had strong incentives to show allegiance to the regime.

In addition, there were other economic supplements for critical units like those in Lisbon and Porto, for pilots, and for some especial tasks. By targeting some specific units that could have an important impact in case of an internal uprising, Salazar was securing his position vis-à-vis a potential military threat.

Table 4.3   Military monthly salaries in January 1938 (in escudos)

Ranks	Generals	High Staff Corps	Infantry, Cavalry, Artillery, Engineering, Air Force, Military Administration, Health and Veterinary	Support services, chiefs of military bands
General	4500			
Brigadier			4000	
Colonel		3250	3000	
Lieutenant-Colonel		2750	2500	
Major		2500	2250	2150
Captain		2000	1800	1700
Lieutenant			1400	1300
2nd Lieutenant			1100	1100

Source: Decree 28403 (31/12/1937). Salazar Archives AOS/CO/GR-11, Folder 9, Document 1, Pages 261–262.

Due to the inflation during the Second World War, salaries became insufficient, and the military often needed secondary jobs to sustain their families. The government approved a 15 per cent general salary raise in February 1945 following the military's criticism of the plans intending to freeze military expenditures.[73] Again, salary raises were made possible thanks to the downsizing process launched in 1944. This general raise was, nonetheless, insufficient and did not successfully manage to curb military discontent.[74]

Salazar was asked by NATO to augment military budgets and officers' salaries to incentivise exclusive dedication and attract qualified personnel (Matos 2004:166, 170). Despite NATO's aid, the financial problems persisted and no relevant salary increases were made.[75] In 1958, Portugal was the second European NATO country which devoted the highest percentage of the army budget to staff expenditures: 70.3 per cent.[76] However salaries continued to be insufficient to guarantee exclusive dedication. In 1958, the salary of a colonel covered only 76 per cent of the minimum living expenses for his household, that of a captain between 60 and 73 per cent, and that of a sergeant between 40 and 43 per cent.[77]

To compensate for poor salaries, the government introduced some economic perks. For instance, in 1960 the government created a fund to compensate the families of deceased officers.[78] In 1962, exemptions and reductions in the payment of some services were introduced for the families of the military killed or handicapped during the Colonial Wars, and in 1966 and 1970, military pensions were increased (Matos 2004:177). However, given the complexity of the colonial conflict and the size of the mobilised military[79] the increases in budgets overall did not have a positive impact on military salaries, which remained very low compared to other European militaries (Porch 1977:45–53). Military discontent at the end of the regime supports this lack of impact (Chapter 3, Section 3.1.6).

In sum, although there is evidence of the utilisation of salaries and other economic incentives, the contribution of staff expenditure as a control tool was very limited throughout the regime.

4.4.3 Equipment expenditure

Salazar considered the rearmament and modernisation of the military as an incentive for the military to return to the barracks. However, similar to Spain, most defence expenditure was earmarked for officers' salaries and the living costs of the troops. Salazar's austerity policies contributed to curtailling expenditures in materials and weapons, and the insufficient capacity of the defence industry made Portugal very dependant on foreign aid. The modernisation of the armament and equipment remained very limited during the Estado Novo.

There was a scarcity in terms of equipment, weapons, and ammunition (Faria 2000:39–41). In 1933, Salazar's government approved 200 million escudos in investment for the acquisition of equipment for the military and in particular for the navy.[80] On top of the strategic reasons, such as the defence of the Lisbon port, the maritime communications and the colonies, the consolidation of military subordination was central to the decision. Traditionally, republican ideas had flourished in the navy. Despite some initial purges during the military dictatorship, the opposition to the regime enjoyed important support in the navy. Salazar intended to buy their loyalty. However, shortly after, the army became again the privileged recipient of funds as a means to prevent a land invasion from Spain where growing political instability was alarming the Portuguese military and political elites. The ambitious plan of rearmament of the army initiated in 1935[81] was hindered by Salazar's support to the Francoist camp. The United Kingdom and France limited their sales of weaponry to prevent them from reaching Franco (Telo 1996:155). Germany replaced the United Kingdom and France as the main equipment supplier.[82]

With the outbreak of the Second World War, the supply of weapons and equipment from Germany was quickly reduced. The situation of the military in 1939 was still very unsatisfactory; only one division had modern equipment. All experts agreed that Portugal could not resist an invasion from Spain.[83] Once the 'Operation Felix' for the attack of Gibraltar (which included an eventual occupation of Lisbon) was postponed in 1941, Germany continued to support Portuguese rearmament to counterbalance British influence and remained its main supplier until 1944.[84] In 1943, after an agreement with the allies for the utilisation of the bases in the Azores, the United Kingdom started to provide Portugal with some weaponry considered obsolete but sufficient to improve Portuguese fighting capacity.[85] These rearmament efforts only enabled Portugal to fully equip three infantry divisions and a battalion of artillery and to partially renew the armament of two other divisions at the end of the war (Teixeira 2004:52).

After the end of the Second World War, the government launched a programme of construction of quarters to improve military working conditions, most of which were inaugurated in the 1950s (Matos 2004:161, 171).[86] However, the process of modernisation of weapons and materials continued to be very slow after the war. Portugal benefitted the least amongst the recipients of the Marshall Plan (Rollo 1994). Despite NATO membership, the US military aid received by Portugal was very low.[87] The rearmament of the navy became again a priority following NATO demands and also as a means to compensate for the navy's loss of autonomy and political influence. The navy's budgets were increased at a higher pace than those of the army. However, the economic needs of the navy overseas in order to defend the colonies hindered the modernisation efforts in continental Portugal and did not have a considerable impact on military satisfaction (Telo 1996:212–13, 280–1).

The Colonial Wars produced growth in the military and its budget without a positive impact on military material conditions. There was little flexibility in personnel budgets and the government made clear that salaries were the priority over equipment. For instance, from January to May 1964, 580 million escudos out of the 500 million requested were authorised for staff expenditure while only 150 million out of the 717 million requested were authorised for equipment. The minimal material needs could not be satisfied, to the extent that in 1963 there were only two rifle bullets per man/day.[88] Dissatisfaction grew and corporatist claims multiplied. The use of *treasure* through equipment expenditure continued to be minimal and not considered central to the strategy of military subordination until the end of the regime.

4.4.4 Low salaries and equipment penury

Treasure tools can be used to improve military living and working conditions but did not play a major role during the Estado Novo. The precarious economic situation of Portugal limited *treasure* as a resource. Overall, salaries were comparatively low and more a source of unrest than satisfaction. General salary raises, such as those in 1937 and 1945, served to compensate the effects of inflation and to appease the military when other controversial reforms were launched. These raises were made possible by policies aiming to reduce the size of the army. NATO also pushed the government to improve salaries as a means of professionalisation but the colonial conflict hindered the process. In addition to general salary raises, salary discrimination was used to enhance loyalty of the senior ranks and some key corps and units. During the Colonial Wars, pensions and economic benefits for military families were introduced too.

Equipment expenditure was also very limited. Not only were military budgets low but most of them were earmarked for officers' salaries and the troops' living expenses. Despite the rearmament plans in the 1930s, during the Second World War and in the 1950s, the Portuguese military remained poorly equipped throughout the regime. Salazar's austerity policies and Portugal's dependence on foreign suppliers were limiting factors. The insufficient investment in equipment and the prioritisation of personnel expenses shows that the government was more concerned with keeping the military relatively satisfied than with developing a strong fighting capacity. The financial penuries during the Colonial Wars also limited the capacity to equip the military, which worsened working conditions. In sum, although there is evidence of the utilisation of staff and equipment expenditure for control purposes their intensity and frequency was very low and their overall impact very limited.

4.5 Conclusions

The Estado Novo used many different tools to keep the military subordinated, and their use evolved throughout the regime.

Although the Estado Novo developed *organisation* instruments with coercive capabilities to control the population, such as the police forces PVDE/PIDE/DGS, PSP, GNR, and the paramilitary Portuguese Legion, their overall relevance in the control of the military was limited. These bodies helped deter some military plots, but the action of loyal army units was more decisive in neutralising military coups with force. Non-coercive *organisation* tools were more important. Salazar shaped the organisation of the military following a divide-and-rule logic. During the 1950s, the United States and NATO induced important changes in military education and training as well as in the military's organisational design. These changes were intended not only to improve Portuguese defence capabilities but also to consolidate military subordination. Additionally, the provision of jobs, goods, and services for the military officers and their families proved to be effective tools. The Colonial Wars meant a reduction in the utilisation of non-coercive tools except for the delivery of services and goods.

Nodality tools were very important to the government control strategy too. The government, inspired by the totalitarian Germany and Italy, used several state organisations such as PVDE/PIDE/DGS, SNP, Legion, SIME, and the DSC usually as both information effectors and detectors. Propaganda and censorship were especially intensive from the inception of the regime until the end of the Second World War. Afterwards, information manipulation tools became less acceptable in the West, and the exchanges with NATO allies opened new alternative sources of information for the military. The Colonial Wars and Caetano's timid attempts at liberalisation also helped diminish the effectiveness of information effectors. Conversely, the utilisation of information detectors increased in salience. PVDE/PIDE/DGS acquired more power and growing networks of informants: 'bufos' collected sensible information for the regime. Additionally, internal communications, reports, and correspondence exchanges helped Salazar and Caetano.

The *authority*-based incentives and rewards were extremely relevant. The 'escolha' system of promotions and retirements introduced in 1937 enabled Salazar to completely renew the top tier of the military and placing loyal military in the most important positions. The military had a strong incentive to comply with the government because of its power to approve or veto the appointments to the senior ranks and the elitist High Staff Corps. The appointments to top positions of the administration; the wide powers granted to the military related to the maintenance of public order; and other privileges, such as greater autonomy, tolerance with secondary jobs, and military awards can be also considered relevant *authority*-based incentives for subordination. On the other hand, the *authority*-based sanctions and constraints were less decisive. Restrictions to the size of the armies and to retirement age contributed to facilitate the actions of other types of tools, such as salary raises and promotions of loyal officers. There were sanctions for the military involved in conspiracies and legal restrictions to enhance a distinct esprit de corps and detach officers from any political activity. The contacts with other NATO armies, the Colonial Wars and later the arrival of Caetano gradually depleted the government's *authority* and limited the utilisation of this type of tool.

Finally, *treasure* tools were the least important in the government toolkit largely because this resource was to a great extent depleted. General salary raises were used to counter inflation. Nonetheless, except for the senior ranks, the Portuguese military was poorly paid throughout the regime. Similarly equipment expenditure was insufficient and did not contribute to military subordination. The acquisition of armament and other military materials was constrained by the dependence on foreign suppliers and the austerity policies. NATO demanded increases in military expenditures but the budget did not substantially grow until the beginning of the Colonial Wars. During this conflict, the larger budgets were absorbed by the growth of the armies which worsened the defence effort and material conditions.

Overall, the most relevant tools were: *authority* incentives and rewards (especially in the 1930s and 1940s), non-coercive *organisation* tools (in the 1950s), and *nodality* tools (effectors until 1945 and detectors afterwards). It can be construed, therefore, that the regime relied more on 'carrots' than on 'sticks'. Even at the level of *treasure*, the government emphasised financial rewards over improving working conditions. At the level of trends, it is worth mentioning that the Colonial Wars produced an overall depletion of the government's resources which was manifested by the decline in the utilisation and impact of many of the government's tools, which in turn facilitated the success of the Carnations Revolution and the fall of the Estado Novo in 1974.

5
Tools of Government in the Portuguese Transition to Democracy

The Carnations Revolution in 1974 did not bring immediate, radical changes to the government's control toolkit.[1] However, after the failed military left-wing coup d'etat of November 1975, which marked the consolidation of the MFA-Moderates and the abandonment of the radical revolutionary agenda, the pattern of utilisation of most of the basic resources underwent important transformations. The coercive *organisation* instruments (Section 5.1) and *nodality* tools (Section 5.2) were very important for the initial provisional governments but abandoned after the November coup. Organisational design was used to recentralise the military by eliminating the parallel MFA hierarchical structures that had emerged during the revolution. Military education and training, which had been marginal since the outbreak of the Colonial Wars, gained salience progressively after 1976 (Section 5.1.2). Conversely, after 1976, the use of *authority* tools such as military appointments and demotions decreased. The autonomy and special functions that had been granted to the military were severely curtailed by the constitutional reform and the new defence law in 1982 (Section 5.3). Finally, the utilisation of *treasure* continued to be very low and only after 1985 did military investment and rearmament programmes acquire significance (Section 5.4). Table 5.1 outlines the main tools employed during this period.

5.1 Organisation

The coercive power of the state and a decentralised organisational design aiming at the political control of the military were key tools for the

Table 5.1 Summary of tools of government in Portugal (1974–86)

	Tools	Trajectory
Organisation	*Coercive* (Section 5.1.1): COPCON, AMI, some loyal military units, the security forces, the judiciary, and penitentiary systems. Even civilians were used as coercive tools during the peaks of instability in 1974 and 1975	Increasing salience until November 1975. Almost no evidence of utilisation after 1976
	Non-coercive (Section 5.1.2): Organisational design. The new MFA institutions created a parallel hierarchy. Later a process of recentralisation by eliminating the revolutionary institutions and concentrating power in the civilian government	Decentralisation until 1975, recentralisation afterwards
	Military education through IDN, Military Academies and Institutes and the organisation of joint activities and courses with civilians to improve mutual awareness. Military exercises and exchanges with NATO	Education and training insignificant during the revolutionary period. It grew significantly after 1976 and became a priority after 1985
	Provision of services, goods, and jobs to compensate low salaries. Some new services were provided. The administration employed many military returning from the colonies	Stable
Nodality	*Information effectors* (Section 5.2.1): Propaganda and censorship were used to politicise the military to enhance loyalty to the MFA. Fifth Division, CODICE, Dynamisation Cabinets, and SDCI. Media were instrumentalised and censored. Military ad-hoc committees control the media	Very intensive use until the end of 1975. After 1976, propaganda and censorship were abandoned and the MFA information effectors eliminated
	Public and updated the information about the military and defence to improve mutual awareness of the military and civilian spheres. The media free of censorship campaigned in favour of the complete military subordination	After 1976. Increasing
	Information detectors (Section 5.2.2): SDCI, Fifth Division, CODICE, Second Section of EME and other state institutions collected information concerning the political allegiance to MFA in the ranks and scrutinised the media to avoid information that could create unrest in the ranks	Important until the November 1975 coup. Abandoned in 1976. Use of detectors was extremely low until 1982
	Political oversight mechanisms	After 1982. Increasing
	New integrated secret services SIRP (SIED, SIS, and SIM)	After 1984. Increasing

Continued

Table 5.1 Continued

	Tools	Trajectory
Authority	*Rewards and incentives* (Section 5.3.1): Military promotions and appointments to the government institutions, administration, and MFA institutions within the military	Very important during the revolutionary period. Low intensity from 1976
	Extraordinary level of autonomy of the armed forces	Extremely high until 1982
	Special functions granted to the military in the political arena and internal affairs	Extremely high. Decreased in 1976 and finally eliminated in 1982
	Amnesty laws	Abundant amnesties from 1974 to 1981
	Sanctions and constraints (Section 5.3.2): Expulsions and demotions of the Estado Novo supporters and those that rebelled against the government	Very important in 1974 and 1975, decreasing afterwards
	Abolition of the institutions such as those linked to the Estado Novo control machinery and later of the revolutionary institutions	Very important in the aftermath of the Carnations Revolution and November 1975 coup. Suppression of CR in 1982
	Legal constraints aiming at the depoliticisation and professionalisation (demobilisation of troops, prohibition to political activities, unionism, accumulation of jobs and function)	Low intensity until 1976. Reinforced in 1982
Treasure	*Staff expenditure* (Section 5.4.2): Staff spending prioritised over equipment spending. However, military budgets decreased. Salaries and pensions were updated regularly to compensate for inflation but remained comparatively	Low intensity. Stable
	Equipment expenditure (Section 5.4.3): Re-equipment and modernisation efforts limited due to budget constraints. The BMI was the sole military unit well equipped. Portugal depended on the cooperation with NATO allies for the acquisition of equipment and the reinforcement of Portuguese defence industry	Very low intensity until 1985
	New process for military planning and a general re-armament. These measures contributed to improve the equipment and to establish civilian control on military investment and re-armament programmes	After1985

MFA-controlled provisional governments (1974–6). During this period, political elites only played a secondary role in the government. After the end of the dominance of the MFA-Radicals and the failure of the 25 November leftist coup, coercive *organisation* tools were abandoned and the institutional design reversed. Politicisation and decentralisation were replaced by professionalisation and centralisation. From 1976, political elites gradually recovered their power. The constitutional governments promoted military education and training to keep the military focused on their professional duties and far from politics. The provision of services, goods, and jobs to the military continued to compensate for poor salaries. These were especially important for those returning from the colonies.

5.1.1 Coercive organisation

The provisional governments used coercive *organisation* tools to control the military even more actively than the Estado Novo. The use of loyal military units to prevent and neutralise insurrections was prominent during the peaks of instability in September 1974 and March and November 1975. Additionally, the security forces, the judiciary, and the penitentiary systems as well as some organisations of civil society acted as deterrents against military insubordination. After 1976, coercive *organisation* tools became marginal.

The MFA-controlled government wanted to display a clear break with the past and with the Salazarist control machinery. Immediately after the 25 April Revolution, and due to their identification as repression forces, some of the traditional coercive *organisation* tools of the Estado Novo, such as the DGS and the Legion, were abolished and others, such as the PSP, the Fiscal Guard, and the GNR, were put under public scrutiny. Nonetheless, at the same time, the government created the Continent Operational Command, COPCON. This was a military structure consisting of several units of Special Forces with the function of controlling internal threats to Portugal, including military insurrections.[2] The COPCON was led by Major Otelo and formally subordinated to the Joint Chiefs of Staff Board (EMGFA) but was in fact controlled by the MFA (Rato 2000:138). The COPCON held an ambiguous police-military character depriving the PSP and GNR of some of their traditional functions. COPCON also had access to intelligence.[3] The COPCON participated in the dissolution of the right-wing mobilisations in September 1974 and blocked the entrance to Lisbon in order to prevent a right-wing military counter-coup. The COPCON provided the MFA-controlled government with a military advantage over the right-wing forces during the March 1975 coup (Graham 1979:236; Carrilho 1994; Manuel 1995).

When the MFA-Moderates seized control of the government, the COPCON, which continued to support the revolutionary agenda, became a threat. In September 1975, the prime minister, Admiral Pinheiro de Azevedo, complained about the government's lack of authority especially within the military sphere. The PSP, GNR, and the information services were reinforced and more importantly the Military Intervention Group (AMI) was created.[4] The AMI was a strategic emergency unit under direct orders of the president of the republic established to counter the threat of COPCON. The AMI was a strongly armed, cohesive, and disciplined unit ready to neutralise coups against the government.[5] The AMI was a deterrent for the revolutionary insurrections in October and November 1975. However, as a coercive tool it was formally suppressed on 20 November 1975 as part of a wider strategy to destabilise the most radical revolutionary actors and to justify the elimination of the COPCON on 25 November 1975.[6]

The security forces contributed to deterring military insubordination too. Although there is evidence of the reliance on the PSP, GNR, and the Military Judiciary Police (PJM) to counter military threats, these paramilitary forces lacked human and material means to undertake action against heavily armed organisations.[7]

The judiciary and penitentiary systems were also implicated in the action against military disobedience. After the coup attempts on 11 March 1974 and 25 November 1975, the Higher Councils of Discipline in the three branches (army, navy, and air force) prosecuted many officers for their participation in the plots.[8] A military revolutionary tribunal was set up to judge the March 1975 coup plotters.[9] Military rebels were often imprisoned and subjected to solitary confinement.[10] About 130 officers were arrested and almost a thousand trials were held for the participants in the insurrection of November 1975. Although instability decreased after November 1975, the problems of discipline continued. A permanent committee for military justice and discipline was constituted by the CR.[11] The last significant example of coercive *organisation* was the arrest, trial, and imprisonment in 1985 of Otelo, who was accused of membership to the leftist terrorist group FP-25.

Finally, the civilian population was also employed as coercive *organisation* tools during the revolutionary period. For example, social mobilisation orchestrated by the information service, Fifth Division, helped in countering the coup of March 1975 (Sánchez Cervelló 1993:226). Military units could have easily defeated the civilians that opposed them but a violent action could have produced many civilian casualties which was deemed unacceptable in that context. Although the possession of arms was restricted and civilian militias were forbidden,[12] some civilian institutions linked to political parties also experienced a process of militarisation.[13] Civilians collaborated with soldiers to carry out arrest warrants issued by COPCON (Maxwell 1995:89) and later helped to neutralise the left-wing military coup attempt of November 1975. The main leaders of the PS went to the north and put themselves under the command of General Pires Veloso. The militants of the PPD surrounded the paratrooper unit that had rebelled in Monte Real, and farmers from Rio Maior controlled the accesses to Lisbon. Equally, far-left civilians were mobilised and were ready to follow orders from the military conspirators.[14]

The failure of the November 1975 coup and the suppression of the AMI and COPCON also marked a change in the control toolkit of the government. The end of political instability and overt actions of military rebellion was accompanied by the replacement of coercive *organisation* tools by other less intrusive non-coercive *organisation* approaches.

5.1.2   Non-coercive organisation

The capacity to shape the design of military and political institutions was very important for the Portuguese governments. Two opposite trajectories can be observed: an initial decentralisation process until the end of 1975 introduced by the MFA followed by a reorganisation aiming to recentralise power and avoid fragmentation and infighting.

Immediately after the Carnations Revolution, the MFA, seeking to reassert military power and autonomy, created a military Junta of National Salvation (JSN). The JSN was composed of seven military officers and had the capacity to control the programme of the provisional governments.[15] Later, the MFA undertook a process of 'democratic institutionalisation' ('estruturação democrática') that aimed at the active participation of all of the military in the revolutionary process which insured its cohesion and discipline, controlled the democratisation of the military, and stimulated the information flows from and to the government. In October 1974, the MFA created the Higher Council of the MFA and the Armed Forces Assembly.[16] Political reunions and committees were held at the unit, military region, and branch level.[17] The MFA organisation within the military acted as a parallel and alternative power structure to the traditional military hierarchy and aimed to insure the support within the military to the 6 provisional governments appointed by the MFA.

However, the MFA was not a cohesive organisation. Power was fragmented across not only different institutions but also different factions.[18] The struggles amongst them provoked great institutional instability. After the March 1975 coup attempt, the MFA sought to consolidate its rule with a less fragmented institutional structure that united political and military power. Thus, the JSN, the Higher Council of the MFA, the MFA Coordinating Committee, and the State Council were merged into a single executive authority: the CR.[19] The CR accumulated political and socioeconomic functions. Most importantly, it substituted the Joint Chiefs of Staff Board (EMGFA) as the supreme body of military authority. Moreover the Armed Forces Assembly was replaced by the MFA Assembly that, for the first time, allowed noncommissioned officers and enlisted men amongst its members. This organ was in charge of monitoring the CR.[20]

The military coup of November 1975 revealed the degradation of the MFA revolutionary institutions and their incapacity to rule Portugal. It marked the beginning of a gradual military withdrawal from politics and fostered the process of centralisation of power (González Hernández 1999:26). The MFA apparatus was dismantled.[21] Under the 1976 Constitution, the CR remained the sole military body with political functions. It exerted constitutional review and legislative powers on military issues.[22] The EMGFA was re-established as the supreme military institution. General Ramalho Eanes was elected president of the republic and appointed Chief of the Joint Staff of the Portuguese Armed Forces (CEMGFA). Paradoxically, Eanes' accumulation of political and military functions was positive for the process of military disengagement from politics since he promoted non-partisan and a more professional military (Graham 1993:41; Rato 2000). The traditional military hierarchy, supported by Eanes, used administrative rules to circumvent the formal authority of the CR on military issues. As a result the CR gradually became a secondary player in both the political and military arenas (Rato 2000:154).

Notwithstanding, the government still did not control the military aspects of defence,[23] and the CR and the president interfered in some of its reforms.[24] The constitutional reform in 1982 eliminated the CR, reduced the competences of the president, and concentrated the power in the government.[25] Moreover the new Law of National Defence and Armed Forces transferred the supreme military authority back to the civilian government and integrated the branches in the hierarchy of the Defence Ministry.[26] The organisational design of the political and military institutions thus became comparable to that of most Western NATO allies including Spain and for the first time aimed to guarantee the supremacy of a democratically elected civilian government.

The Portuguese governments also relied on professional education and training to subordinate the military, but only after November 1975. Before this date, the organisational capacity of the state, as well as that of the MFA and some left-wing political parties, was employed to politicise the military and to gain their support for the MFA revolutionary principles. During this period, cooperation with NATO and the Western allies was reduced and there was little emphasis on military training. The politicisation of the military and the overlap of political and traditional military command structures led to the multiplication of acts of insubordination in the ranks (Porch 1977:118, 161; Sánchez Cervelló 1993:247). Politicisation undermined the control of the military and their capacity to carry out their defence functions.

After November 1975, the government, aware that the previous politicisation strategy had created disunity and discontent in the ranks, reversed its approach to *organisation* tools. Through education and training, the government aimed at the depoliticisation of the military and the increase of its operational capacity and professionalism. The government recognised the deficiencies in military instruction, the importance of bridging the gap between the military, and civilian education as a means to consolidate civilian supremacy and the need to further integrate and coordinate the branches (Ferreira 1976; Santos 1980:102–7). Several actions contributed to this new effort. The National Defence Institute (IDN) was created in 1976 as a tool for the professionalisation of the military.[27] The curriculum of the Military Academy was adapted to the new laws, institutions, and values of the constitutional arrangement.[28] The High Military Studies Institute, the Air Force Academy, and the Naval Superior Institute of War contributed to the development of a new unified doctrine in agreement with the new political and military context after 1976 (Ravara 1989:168; Ferreira 1994:238).

These institutions promoted the new conception of national defence, introduced by the IDN in 1979, that went beyond the traditional military approach to defence by encompassing economic, diplomatic, and social efforts and therefore legitimising civilian defence leadership (Correia 1978; Comprido 1979). Since 1979, both civilians and military attended defence courses. The official defence doctrine was again revised by the defence law of 1982. The fundamental change was the elimination of the internal enemy component (Ferreira 1994:236).

In 1985, education became a top priority. The government wanted to encourage a better understanding between the military and civilian spheres as a means to increase military prestige and their voluntary subordination. After 1985, the diplomas and courses of military education were made equivalent to those in civilian higher education and joint research was actively promoted (Almeida 1986:29, 35). Many activities were introduced to promote the culture of defence, coordination amongst the branches, and mutual awareness between the military and society. In addition to the prestigious National Defence Courses, many seminars, conferences, as well as visits to military and political institutions were organised (Lânhoso 1985:19–21).

Military exercises were another tool for professionalisation. During the Colonial Wars and the revolutionary period, these were neglected and collaboration with the Western allies reduced to the minimum. After 1976, the Independent Mixed Brigade (BMI) of the Army stationed in Santa Margarida became a very important *organisation* tool aiming not only at the cooperation and normalisation of the relations with NATO but also training the Portuguese military in the latest operational techniques and professional principles. New military exercises were introduced. In the mid-1980s, many units of the three branches participated regularly in these exercises, many of which were organised by other Western allies or NATO (MDN 1986:96–145). This renewed impulse to military training and exchanges with other militaries helped consolidate the change in the military's mentality by shifting its attention from domestic affairs to defence issues.

Finally, the state capacity to provide services, goods, and jobs to the military and their families was also used. These prerogatives served to compensate the poor salaries and working conditions that had generated widespread support for the 25 April coup. The Social Services of the Armed Forces continued to provide health, housing, and financial services. New concessions to the prices of public transportation were granted,[29] and the support for disabled veterans was reinforced.[30] Moreover the state-owned companies such as the Military Laboratory of Chemical and Pharmaceutical Products and the Military Maintenance provided not only cheap or free products to the military families but also secondary jobs for the officers (Barata 1980). In 1976, the CR finally decided to stop this practice and banned the military in active service from having civilian jobs.[31] Nonetheless, the public sector continued to play a crucial function by absorbing many of the military (and civil servants) who had been forced to return from the colonies to the metropole.[32]

5.1.3   Abandonment of coercion and re-centralisation

Organisation was a very important source of power for the ruling bodies during the transition and consolidation of democracy. The failed

November 1975 coup marked drastic changes in the patterns of utilisation of both coercive and non-coercive tools. On the one hand, the coercive use of the state organisation to neutralise attacks against the governments grew from the Carnations Revolution and reached its peak in 1975. Military units, in particular the COPCON; the security forces; the judiciary; penitentiary services; and even groups of civilians contributed to fight military insurrection. After the failure of the revolutionary coup of November 1975, the coercive component was abandoned.

Non-coercive *organisation* tools were very salient throughout the period. First, the capacity to shape the state institutions was used by the MFA to ensure political loyalty in the ranks. Its fundamental feature was decentralisation of political and military power in multiple institutions. The instability and displays of military indiscipline in 1975 made the governments reverse their approach to organisational design. There was a gradual re-centralisation of power and separation of the military and political spheres. After the coup of November 1975, the MFA apparatus was dismantled. Nonetheless, the military CR continued to oversee political developments until 1982 when the constitutional reform and the new law of national defence abolished military participation in politics and integrated the military into the Defence Ministry.

Second, military education and training that had been neglected since the beginning of the Colonial Wars became again relevant non-coercive control tools after 1976. The IDN and the military academies and institutes worked to inculcate military subordination through a new defence doctrine and the development of mutual awareness between the civilian and military spheres. The new military exercises and exchanges with the NATO allies also contributed to the professionalisation and depoliticisation of the military. Finally, the provision of services, goods, and jobs by the public administration continued to be a source of reward for the military. The end of the Colonial Wars forced a supplementary effort in order to integrate and compensate ex-combatants.

5.2 Nodality

As in the case of *organisation* tools, two different trends can be observed in the utilisation of *nodality*. The turning point was again the failed coup of November 1975. Before the coup, information effectors were central to the government's strategy. The MFA tried to indoctrinate and politicise the military using newly created instruments such as the Fifth Division, the Central Dynamising Committee (CODICE), the Information Detection and Coordination Services (SDCI), and the media. These institutions also contributed to censoring and collecting information relevant to ensure political support. After November 1975, there was a reversal in the government's approach to control. Politicisation was then considered counterproductive for stability and military subordination. The organisations that had conducted the propaganda campaigns and spied on the military were dismantled or transformed into public relation services operating in civil society. The government released its grip on the media, which then became very critical of the military institution. Until 1984, information detectors disappeared from the government's control toolkit.

5.2.1 Information effectors

As soon as the MFA overthrew the regime, it launched an information campaign to win over the military and society for the revolutionary cause. The psychological action on the local population and the enemy had been very important during the Colonial Wars.[33] Many of those who joined the MFA had participated in the propaganda and information action against the rebels. Immediately after the revolution, a strong information effort was required to ensure that the military in the overseas territories endorsed the MFA and provisional governments. There is evidence of communiqués to the local media, internal memos, and speeches to the military for that purpose.[34] Transcripts of important speeches in Lisbon and political manifestos were distributed in the ranks.[35] Given the political and military instability during the transition, the MFA also intensively used information effectors as a means of control in the metropole.

The information services of the EMGFA and the Fifth Division were established in September 1974 and became very active in the propaganda campaign.[36] The Fifth Division aimed to promote the implementation of the MFA Programme and to improve the image of the military in public opinion. It acted as a think tank on civil-military relations, organising consultations, colloquia, debates, and the study of the MFA doctrine (Ferreira 1992:311; Carrilho 1994:45–6). The Fifth Division also coordinated the actions of other important information tools such as the SDCI,[37] CODICE,[38] and the Unit Assemblies and Dynamisation Cabinets.[39] The goal of these *nodality* tools was the cultural and political education of the military following the logic of control through politicisation (Carrilho 1994:60–1).

Although the MFA Programme had officially requested the end of censorship as a means to promote people's freedom, the media continued to be censored and used by the MFA-controlled governments to spread propaganda (Pimlott and Seaton 1980, 1983:50–1). Informing about the acts of indiscipline within the barracks was prohibited by the CR. The infringement of this norm entailed the sequestration of the publication.[40] A Committee for the Control of the Press, Radio, Television, Theatre, and Cinema was established in 1974 to censor reactionary ideas and confidential military issues.[41] Information regarding the process of decolonisation was also censored to avoid agitation.[42] For instance, the CR asked the CEMGFA to undertake judiciary action against the newspaper 'A Capital' due to 'defamatory information' about the military in Angola.[43] There are also examples of journalist arrests for their criticism of the government or a revolutionary agenda such as that of Vera Lagoa, a journalist of the magazine 'O Tempo' in September 1975 by COPCON.[44]

The MFA leadership cultivated good relationships with many journalists and after the 25 April coup, the media intensively praised the new revolutionary institutions, and military figures were often invited to radio and television programmes. Moreover, the action of the Social Communication Ministry and military teams working in the public broadcasting corporation, RTP, ensured the support of the MFA doctrine.[45] The media influenced public opinion and promoted social mobilisation in favour of different factions of the MFA. For instance, during the initial stages of the transition, the press was often criticised for its partiality and pro-communist stance.[46] The notion of the importance of the media was so entrenched amongst the military that the radio and TV stations as well as newspapers headquarters were priority military targets during all of the revolts that occurred from the 25 April 1974 to the 25 November 1976 (Sánchez Cervelló 1993; Manuel 1995).

However, after November 1975, the official revolutionary discourse was replaced by a moderate one that insisted on the necessity of military subordination and warned about military intervention as the main threat to democracy (Santos 1980). In 1976, following a series of severe criticisms for its radical political bias,[47] the Fifth Division was restructured and downsized and later abolished in 1977. The SDCI, CODICE, and the Dynamisation Cabinets were abolished in 1976. The journal 'Nação e Defesa', created in 1976 by the IDN, became an influential information effector that contributed to the evolution of the defence and military doctrine and to mutual awareness between the civilian and military spheres.

The relationship with the media also changed. After the November coup, the CR wanted to counter the ideological influence that the revolutionary left had on the media (Sánchez Cervelló 1993:247). The nationalisation of many publishers and the suspension of many publications due to their previous radical revolutionary stance was decreed. Many newspapers were affected by this measure such as 'O Século', 'A Capital', 'Diario de Noticias', 'Diário de Lisboa', 'Jornal do Comércio', 'Jornal de Noticias', and 'O Comércio do Porto'.[48] After 1976, the media changed their attitude vis-à-vis the military and the CR. They demanded their depoliticisation and subordination to the political power. Publications such as 'O País', 'Liberdade', 'Jounal Novo', 'A Rua', 'Tempo', 'Barricada', and 'O Diabo' directed strong criticism against the members of the CR and published classified information about the military.[49]

The information campaign against the CR can be interpreted as part of the government's strategy to delegitimise the CR and thus pave the way for its dissolution in 1982 (Ferreira 1992:315). It also shows that the CR had lost control of the media and censorship was disappearing.[50] After the dissolution of the CR, the media and society had so clearly embraced the civilian supremacy as a democratic principle that in 1985, the presidential electoral campaign was fundamentally focused on the defence of the idea of civilianisation, and for the first time, there was no military candidate (Ferreira 1994:238).

In sum, from the fall of the regime to the end of 1975, propaganda was an even more salient tool than in the late period of the Estado Novo. Several organisations created by the MFA and most of the media cooperated in an intensive propaganda campaign to promote the MFA's revolutionary agenda. After November 1975, the idea of politicising the military was abandoned. The propaganda apparatus was dismantled. Information campaigns were launched to introduce a new defence doctrine and to raise mutual awareness between the military and society. Censorship disappeared and the media contributed to promote the idea of the depoliticisation of the military and the demilitarisation of politics.

5.2.2 Information detectors

There was less emphasis on information detectors than on information effectors but these still played an important function, especially during the period of provisional governments. Several bodies monitored the military, the political parties, and the media in order to detect threats to the governments. Their actions were fundamental to neutralising the military coups of March 1975 and November 1975 and to weaken the factions that launched them. Afterwards, the use of information detectors decreased drastically until the 1980s. The introduction of parliamentary oversight on military affairs in 1982 and the reorganisation of the information services launched in 1984 marked a new gradual increase in the use of information detectors.

Although all of the information services linked to the Estado Novo had been abolished, new organisations were used to detect information relevant to the control of the military. Most of these bodies were also involved in the propaganda and censorship action. The SDCI, created in May 1974, was the main information detection tool for the CR but not the only one. The PJM was established in September 1975 under the direct supervision of the CR to investigate military crimes and played a central role in the court case against the November 1975 plotters.[51] The bodies in charge of political indoctrination within the military during the provisional governments also collected information related to the political alignment of the military. The Fifth Division was used to detect anti-government movements within the three branches of the military.[52] The CODICE and the Dynamisation Cabinets scrutinised the press and the internal communications on the military[53] and collaborated with the Fifth Division and the government to detect the infiltration of insurgents in the military.[54] The Second Section of the Army Staff Office (EME) was in charge of the army's internal communications and collected information from the GNR, the Fiscal Guard, and the military regions. The information gathered by the EME on political activities outside and within the military was shared with the CR.[55] Furthermore, the Military Committee for the Control of the Press, Radio, Television, Theatre and Cinema[56] and the attorney general of the republic monitored the media and collected information to prevent military unrest.[57]

The intelligence collected about the Spínolist military coup in March 1975 permitted the reversal of its effects. Officers linked to the Fifth Division and the navy decided to allow the military coup to be launched in order to create the fear of returning to the Estado Novo and, therefore, enhancing the revolutionary sentiments in the country (Sánchez Cervelló 1993:225–7). Similarly information detectors were very important in neutralising the coup of November 1975. Although the far-left rebels controlled the Fifth Division and the SDCI, the government prepared a successful counter-offensive based on the information collected by loyal officers. As a result, the coup failed, the MFA-Moderates consolidated their sway on the CR, the moderate political parties were strengthened, and the revolutionary agenda was abandoned.

During the period of the constitutional governments, discipline was gradually restored and the information detectors disappeared from the control toolkit. After the abolishments of the DGS in 1974, the SDCI and CODICE in 1976, and the Fifth Division in 1977, there were no real information detection mechanisms for the control of the military, and the information exchanges between the military and the government were limited (Cardoso 1980a, 1980b; Santos 1980:105–6).

In 1982, the military was formally integrated into the hierarchy of the Defence Ministry, which stimulated the information flows on military issues from and to the government. Parliamentary oversight and other mechanisms of inspection on the military were introduced. Finally, in 1984, three new information services were integrated into the new Information System of the Portuguese Republic (SIRP) that was coordinated by and hierarchically linked to the prime minister: the Service of Strategic Informations of Defence (SIED), the Military Information Service (SIME), and the Security Information Service (SIS).[58] These services imitated those of other European countries. They worked for the defence of democracy and the constitutional order which included ensuring that the military fulfilled their mission (SIS 2010; SIED 2010). Thus, at the end of the period, analysed information detectors acquired new salience.

5.2.3 Intensification and dismantling of information control machinery

Two different trends can be appreciated in the utilisation of *nodality* tools. First, an intensive information campaign was launched in the colonies and continental Portugal to politicise and obtain the endorsement of the military for the MFA. The Fifth Division was the military unit that coordinated the propaganda campaign. Other bodies such as the SDCI, CODICE, and the Dynamisation Cabinets also contributed to political indoctrination. The MFA exerted control on the media to protect the image of the military and MFA. Although *nodality* was primarily used through effectors, the role of detectors should not be understated. Most of the organisations that participated in the revolutionary propaganda and censorship also collected information about political views and sources of unrest in the ranks. This gathered intelligence served to control some insurrections and to neutralise the coups of March and November 1975.

Second, after the failed coup of November 1975, the MFA's propaganda, censorship, and political espionage machineries were dismantled. The SDCI, CODICE, the Dynamisation Cabinets, and the Fifth Division were eliminated. The new official discourse warned of the dangers of politicisation of the military and relied on mutual awareness between the civilian and military spheres as a means to achieve military subordination. The media, which had strongly promoted the more radical revolutionary agenda, was sanctioned immediately after the coup but censorship was abandoned later. Freed from the previous military censorship, the media launched information campaigns against the CR and in favour of the complete subordination of the military to civilian rule. After 1976, the information detectors disappeared from the control toolkit. Only after 1982, when the military was integrated into the Defence Ministry, was some oversight mechanisms introduced. Nonetheless, until the creations of the SIED, the SIS, and the SIM in 1984, the government lacked any reliable information system that could assess military threats.

5.3 Authority

The governing bodies used their *authority* to create incentives and rewards (appointments and promotions, high autonomy, special powers, and amnesty laws) as well as sanctions and constraints (punishments for conspirators, restrictions to the power of institutions, and bans on political activities) to keep the military under control. Although after the failed November 1975 coup, some changes can be observed in the strategy, the most important adjustments in the use of *authority* tools took place in 1982 when the constitutional reform and new defence law were enacted. These reforms contributed to redefine the political and military functions by reinforcing the civilian government and military subordination. Afterwards, the use of new *authority* tools as a means of control became less discernible.

5.3.1 Rewards and incentives

After the end of the Estado Novo, the governments used several types of incentives to achieve military satisfaction and support. Military promotions and appointments were granted to reward loyal officers. At the collective level, the ruling bodies granted the military an enormous degree of autonomy, important special powers beyond their typical defence functions and amnesty, laws that benefited most military incarcerated or expelled from the military by previous governments.

The military leaders that had participated in the fall of the regime were rewarded with promotions. The new military and political institutional structures introduced by the MFA created new opportunities for the military to acquire power and carry out functions beyond those customary to their rank. Loyal military were appointed to public administration and to executive bodies such as the government, the JSN, the Higher Council of the MFA, the Armed Forces Assembly, and the CR

(Carrilho 1994). The process of 'democratic institutionalisation' of the MFA elicited a parallel political hierarchy with representative bodies at all military levels, which collided with the traditional military hierarchy (Sánchez Cervelló 1993). This new structure, with ramifications in all military branches, divisions, and units, created an incentive to endorse and promote the revolutionary programme of the MFA. Those loyal to the MFA could become more powerful and influential in the military than many officers of higher rank.

After the November 1975 coup, many officers that had opposed the coup were promoted and appointed to lead strategic units and military regions (Rato 2000:148–9). For instance, three 'moderate' brigadiers were appointed by the government as commanders of the military regions in the north, centre, and south (Sánchez Cervelló 1993:229) and military from the northern regions, traditionally less revolutionary, occupied the positions of those involved in the coup (Carrilho 1994:89). However, after 1976, the utilisation of military promotions and appointments decreased. The MFA's parallel political hierarchy had created disorder and unrest amongst the ranks (Graham 1979:237). Further, the separation of the military and political spheres was decreed and the 'democratic institutions' of the MFA in the military were abolished diminishing the opportunities for political appointments of loyal officers. Moreover, although the CR (until 1982) and the government (after 1982) had the capacity to validate or reject the promotions of senior rank officers,[59] in reality political interferences in the system of promotions and appointments were rare. In most cases the CR and the government were very respectful with the seniority principle (Santos 1980; Ferreira 1994:231).

The extraordinary degree of autonomy was another important collective incentive. The autonomy that the military enjoyed in Portugal until 1982 had no match in any other Western democracy (Graham 1993; Ferreira 1994). In May 1975, the MFA decreed the autonomy of the military from the government.[60] The military was led by the CEMGFA, who had a rank equivalent to that of the prime minister and was subordinated to the president of the republic.[61] The chiefs of staff of the branches were also autonomous from the government, hierarchically linked to the CEMGFA and had a rank equivalent to that of a minister. Moreover, the CEMGFA General Costa Gomes was appointed president in September 1974. The accumulation of both positions continued during the mandate of Ramalho Eanes until 1981.[62]

The 1976 Constitution reduced the prerogatives of the military but preserved their autonomy (Santos 1980). Until 1982, their legislative and administrative autonomy remained intact.[63] Governments did not have hierarchical authority over the military and were not responsible for the military aspects of defence. Portugal can be considered as a diarchic system because, unlike the rest of Western Europe, the military was independent of civilian power (Júdice 1978:27).

In 1982, the constitutional reform, the law of national defence, and the military set a new framework for civil–military relations and tackled several issues related to military subordination such as the extensive powers of the president, the insufficient competences of the defence minister, and the excessive autonomy of the military. The Defence Ministry was then charged with the preparation and execution of defence policy and the military formally integrated into the ministry. Therefore, these laws subordinated the military to the civilian power both in legislative and administrative terms (Balsemão 1986:202). The goal was to reproduce the system of civil-military relations in most NATO countries where military autonomy was much more limited (Amaral 2000:182–3).

Not only was the military granted autonomy but it was also entrusted with special powers. From 1974 to 1976, the military controlled the government and all major state institutions. During this period, the president and the provisional governments were not democratically elected but appointed by the military ruling bodies. The CR was an autonomous body with far-reaching powers to oversee the transitional process.[64] The members of the CR received honours equivalent to those of the ministers.[65] The political power of the CR was such that in some organisation charts, the government appeared hierarchically subordinated to the CR.[66]

In addition to the political functions that the military was assigned, many other functions related to internal affairs strengthened their influence and pride. The military continued leading the main security forces such as the GNR, the PSP, and the Fiscal Guard. The COPCON had far-reaching powers regarding internal security.[67] The military had the capacity to intervene directly in civilian affairs in order to guarantee the provision of essential public services, economic activity,[68] and electoral processes.[69] They were in charge of the very important process of the demise of the PIDE/DGS and the Legion.[70] In sum, the military fulfilled many tasks and were implicated in decision-making at many levels so that they were expected to feel empowered and to endorse the regime.

The 1976 Constitution tried to merge both the Western model of civil-military relations in which military subordination was a principle with a socialist approach that gave room to a certain level of military participation in politics. The 1976 Constitution granted the military many important functions in the new democratic system and confirmed the CR as a fundamental political institution.[71] The military was expected to ensure the equilibrium of the political system and provide guidance during crises (Pires 1976). The constitution also reserved legislative powers to the CR concerning the organisation, functioning, and discipline of the military (Article 148.1) and military justice (Articles 167, 218, 293.2). The government's laws and decrees had to be then approved by the president of the republic and ultimately by the CR.[72] In sum, no other Western constitution recognised a higher level of military autonomy and involvement in the political system (Miranda 1978). According to the constitution, the military were guardians not only against external but also internal threats (Seixas 1978). These prerogatives can be construed as a truce amongst the rival political and military groups that had disputed the military's supremacy during the transition (Maxwell 1989:135; Ferreira 1994:219; Rato 2000:142–3).

However, the ambiguity and overlapping in functions that this system generated became problematic for civil-military relations and defence purposes (Santos 1978; Moreira 1980:136). In 1982, the constitutional reform, the law of national defence, and the military made profound changes in the formal distribution of power by eliminating the CR and laregely reducing the powers of the Portuguese military.

Finally, the series of amnesties launched during the transition were important *authority* incentives applied to some specific groups of military. From 1974 to 1982, up to 13 different amnesties concerning political and indiscipline crimes were decreed by the authorities. These amnesties responded to corporatist claims and had a positive impact on the motivation and loyalty beyond those who directly benefited from them. The officers that had been purged due to political reasons during the Estado Novo and those who had been punished for having surrendered in Goa in 1961 were readmitted to the military. Many of the crimes committed by the military during the revolutionary period, such as acts of public disorder and indiscipline, were also exonerated.[73]

5.3.2   Sanctions and constraints

The governing bodies also used their authority to control the military by punishing or restraining its actions. First, individuals that had endorsed the previous regime or revolted against the government were expelled or demoted. Second, the institutions that could threaten the ruling bodies were abolished or saw their powers limited. Finally, legal constraints and prohibitions were introduced to achieve depoliticisation and professionalisation of the military.

There is evidence of purges, 'saneamentos', associated to each of the major civil-military crises in the period analysed. After the 25 April coup, hundreds of officers were sacked or forced to the reserve or retirement due to their support of the previous regime including President Tomás and all of the military in Caetano's government.[74] After the incidents of September 1974 in which the political centre and right tried to support Spínola's political programme through mass mobilisations, many renowned senior officers that were involved were sanctioned. General Spínola was forced to resign as president and the Generals Galvão de Melo, Diogo Neto, and Silverio Marques were forced to quit the Junta. More severe punishments were applied to those involved in the counter-revolutionary coup of 11 March 1975. Those who had participated were expelled from the military and lost their political rights for 20 years.[75] Some even saw their properties and bank accounts confiscated.[76]

Whereas initially the military linked to the Estado Novo and the right-wing movements were targeted, after November 1975 those associated with the far-left were punished too. General Otelo was dismissed as Lisbon's military governor on 20 November 1975, and after the 25 November coup, many MFA officers that had held important positions during the revolutionary period were demoted. For instance, Vasco Gonçalves was removed from the High Military Studies Institute and then forced into retirement; the Army Chief of Staff (CEME) Carlos Fabião was relegated to administrative tasks and replaced by Eanes; in 1978, the CEME Vasco Rocha Viera and Lisbon's military governor, Vasco Lourenço, were also discharged (Rato 2000:148, 155). MFA-Moderates and some centrist military filled the positions left by the MFA-Radicals and MFA-Populists. The utilisation of *authority* sanctions for the depoliticisation of the military became very important for the success of the transition into a pluralist democracy (Santos 2000:167). After the 1982 defence law, which transferred the power to demote senior officers from the CR to the government, there are not many examples of this type of sanctions. The most prominent one was the demotion of the CEME General Garcia dos Santos in 1983 for criticising the political system (Ferreira 1994:238).

Authority was also used to eliminate institutions or kerb their power whenever they were considered negative to military satisfaction and subordination. After the Carnations Revolution, the JSN decreed the liquidation of the organisations that had contributed to the control of the military during the Estado Novo such as the PIDE/DGS and the Portuguese Legion[77] as well the High Staff Corps.[78] These were very unpopular institutions amongst the military that had opposed the regime. After the 25 November 1975 coup, the government wanted to send the message of change and moderation and approved the elimination of many of the MFA institutions of political control. On 26 November, the COPCON was dissolved and some restrictions imposed to its members.[79] Additionally, the MFA Assembly and all of the political-military assemblies in the military were dismantled. All the political organisations that had inspired acts of indiscipline within the ranks during the revolutionary period, such as the 'Soldados Unidos Vencerão', 'Acção Revolucionária das Praças do Exército', and 'Forças Armadas Democráticas', were dissolved.[80]

The constitutional reform and defence law in 1982 can be construed as the *authority* tools that completed the legal process of political neutralisation and subordination of the military (Vieira 1995:71–2). These laws reduced the autonomy of the military, eliminated their capacity to intervene in politics, and circumscribed their functions to the defence against external threats. The legislative powers of the CR were transferred to the Portuguese Assembly. The government acquired the capacity to appoint the CEMGFA and the chiefs of staff of the branches. Legal mechanisms for the civilian control of the military through the Defence Ministry were introduced (Rato 2000:160–1). Thus, these *authority* constraints set the basis for normalisation of civil-military relations and civilian supremacy.[81]

Lastly, *authority* was used to set legal boundaries to political activity and reduce the size of the military to increase professionalism. Some regulation was enacted to clarify the concept of discipline and limit insubordination.[82] The Decree-Law 17/75 (26 December 1975), which launched the reorganisation of the military, aimed at the military's professionalisation and subordination to civilian authority and can be construed as an *authority*-based constraint. It prohibited political partisanship in the military and specified the necessity of a 'conscious discipline' and the unity of the chain of command. Moreover, the limitation of the size of the armies aimed at enabling some improvement of salaries and working conditions. The numbers in the military were reduced from 217,000 in 1975 to 59,800 in 1976 (CESEDEN 1988:197). The 1976 Constitution and the new Military Disciplinary Regulations also confirmed the prohibition of political membership and participation in political activities for all of the military on active duty or in the reserve.[83] On 11 August 1976, the CR approved the prohibition of the accumulation of functions for the military. Members of the CR had to resign from their command functions. This prohibition also contributed to reducing the power of the CR over the military sphere (Ferreira 1992:315–16; Rato 2000:154).

Moreover, any appointment outside the military for public or private office had to be approved by the chief of staff of that branch and in some cases by the CR.[84] Finally, the defence law of 1982 eliminated the right of union membership for the military (Article 31).

5.3.3 First purges and autonomy, then amnesties and legal control

Authority rewards and incentives became extremely important after the Carnations Revolution but then saw their salience decrease. Appointments to senior positions in the military, public administration, the MFA organisation, and government rewarded and empowered loyal officers, especially from 1974 to 1976. An extraordinary degree of autonomy and many functions concerning political and internal affairs were granted to the military as a means to reinforce collective military satisfaction and support for the regime. Although some military prerogatives were reduced after the coup of November 1975, the 1976 Constitution still recognised its higher degree of autonomy than in any other Western democratic country. Additionally, numerous amnesty laws were approved to satisfy military corporatist claims from 1974 to 1981. After 1982, *authority*-based incentives and rewards almost disappeared from the control toolkit.

Authority-based sanctions and constraints were also important. Purges were conducted aiming initially at military officers identified with the Estado Novo and later with anti-government insurrections. Similarly, some institutions were abolished for having contributed to the Salazarist control machinery, such as the PIDE/DGS, the Legion, and the High Staff Corps, and later for their involvement with the failed revolutionary experience, such as the COPCON, the MFA assemblies and committees, and finally the CR. Finally a series of prohibitions and constraints were introduced in the military after the events of November 1975 in order to ensure depoliticisation and professionalisation. These regulations included a ban on political activities and unionism as well as restrictions on employment outside the ranks and the accumulation of functions for the military on active duty.

Thus, the *authority*-based rewards and sanctions were intertwined. The expulsions and demotions were linked with the appointments and amnesties. Incentives such as wide degree of autonomy and special powers were annulled through *authority*-based constraints. In general, the periods of higher instability and change in government were associated with a more intensive use of *authority* tokens. The constitutional reform and new defence law of 1982 contributed to consolidate a Western style legal framework of civil-military relations. This new arrangement restricted the autonomy and other incentives and rewards previously enjoyed by the military and confined them to the defence functions.

5.4   Treasure

The utilisation of financial resources as a tool of control over the military continued to be very limited during the transition to democracy. Portugal's economic problems had been aggravated by the colonial conflict. The deficiencies in terms of social services convinced the governments to concentrate their economic efforts on non-defence sectors. This section analyses military budgets by linking them to the general evolution of the Portuguese economy, then it explains military staff expenditures as a tool of control, and finally, the military expenditure on equipment.

5.4.1   Evolution of military budgets

From 1974 to 1977, budgets drastically decreased and then remained stable until 1986 both in real terms and as percentage of GDP (Figures 5.1, 5.2, and 5.3). The drastic initial decline can be associated with the end of the colonial conflict, the policy of de-mobilisation of the troops initiated by the MFA (Barros and Santos 1997:204–5), as well as with the economic problems that the transitional governments faced. The provisional governments inherited from the Estado Novo a high trade deficit (17,000 million escudos in 1974), high unemployment (8 per cent), and

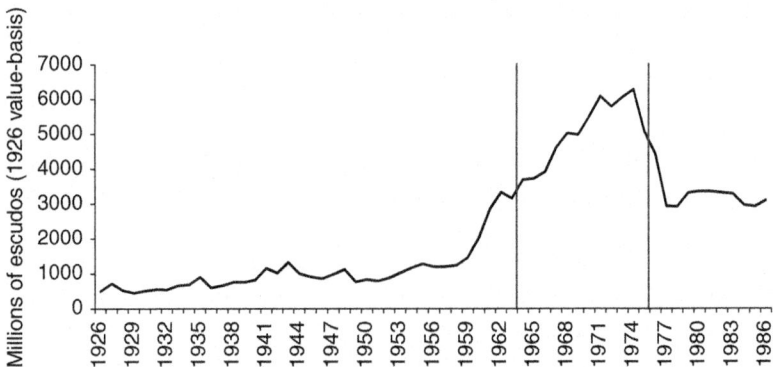

Figure 5.1   Total expenditure in defence (in constant escudos of 1926). Colonial Wars period marked by vertical bars†

Note: †Data include the expenditure in the overseas territories.

Source: Based on Mata and Valerio (1994:253–4, 270–1).

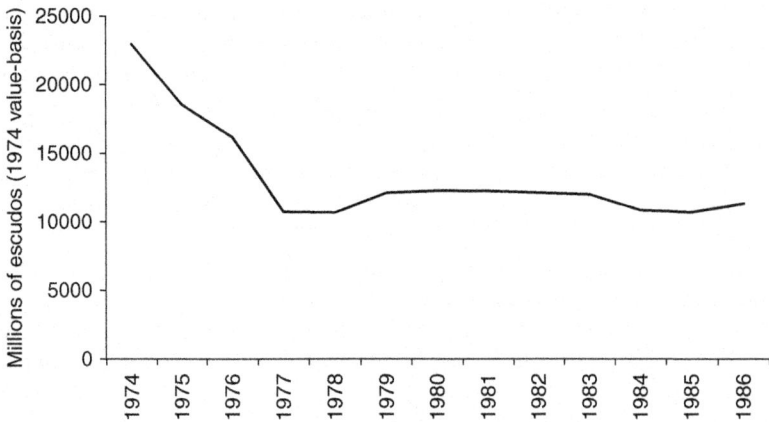

Figure 5.2 Total defence expenditure (1974–86) in constant escudos of 1974
Source: Based on Mata and Valerio (1994:253–4, 270–1).

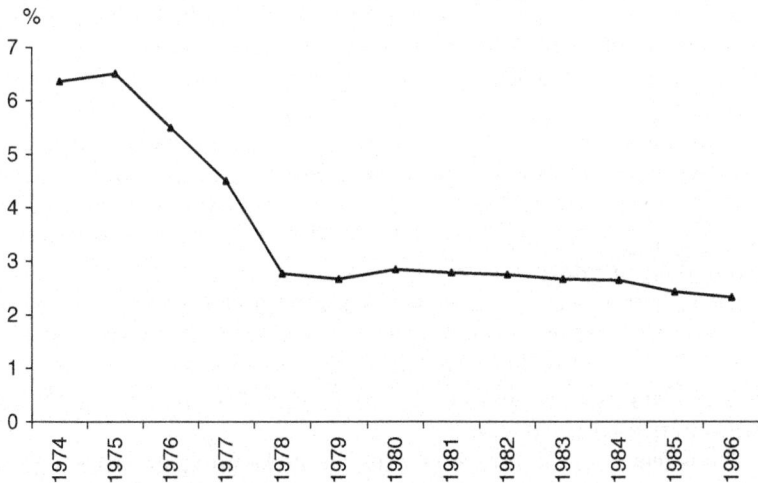

Figure 5.3 Defence expenditure as a percentage of GDP in Portugal
Sources: Based on Mata and Valerio (1994:253–4, 270–1).

a fall in GDP (–6 per cent).[85] The fast economic growth that the country experienced in the early 1970s was interrupted as a result of the socio-political agitation and decolonisation. During the revolutionary period, numerous nationalisations of companies and land seizures took place but they did not solve the serious economic problems, such as large budget deficits, high rates of inflation and unemployment, shrinking commercial relations with the former colonies, high costs associated with the estimated 500,000 people returning from the colonies ('retornados'),[86] as well as the fall of tourists inflows and emigrants' remittances (Robinson 1979:261–4; Mata and Valerio 1994:219–23). These problems, especially unemployment, contributed to the fall of Gonçalves' revolutionary government in September 1975 (Maxwell 1995:142).

After 1976, the revolutionary agenda was abandoned and instability reduced. However, the efforts to address the economic problems limited the capacity to increase military budgets. The governments undertook a fundamental reorganisation of the administration, public corporations, and the agricultural sector. The expansionary policies to stimulate growth and absorb the 'retornados' increased the deficit, debt, and inflation. From 1980 to 1983, the economic situation worsened as a consequence of the second oil shock and the appreciation of the escudo of the escudo which harmed Portuguese exports. The stand-by agreements with the IMF in 1978 and 1984 portrayed the complicated financial situation. The austerity policies introduced in 1984 had some positive effects after 1985 but did not solve the problem of inflation.[87]

The economic setbacks diverted spending preferences away from defence. Other sectors, fundamentally linked to social expenditure were prioritised and absorbed most budget increases (Amaral 2000:184). Moreover, the number of civil servants grew faster than the military staff (Mesquita 1986:48–9). While total public expenditure continued to grow in real terms, military expenditures shrank in the 1970s and in the 1980s as a percentage of total public expenditure. The downward trend in the weight of defence expenditures in government spending can also be observed in other European countries, including Spain. In Portugal, this reduction can be linked to the growth of the state and the correction of some traditional social problems inherited from the previous authoritarian regime (Figure 5.4).

The salience of *treasure* tools was very limited. Portuguese spending on military and defence was low in comparison to other European countries (Figure 5.5). While military expenditure in most NATO countries experienced double digit growth, Portugal's military expenditure decreased by 20 per cent from 1975 to 1982 (IISS 1986:138). From 1977 to 1986, only Turkey had lower per capita military expenditures in NATO (CESEDEN 1988:135; IISS 1986:140, 1988:212). Portugal's military expenditures were so low that the basic defence functions and commitments with NATO could not be guaranteed. As former prime minister, Amaral acknowledged, the funding for the military during this period decreased

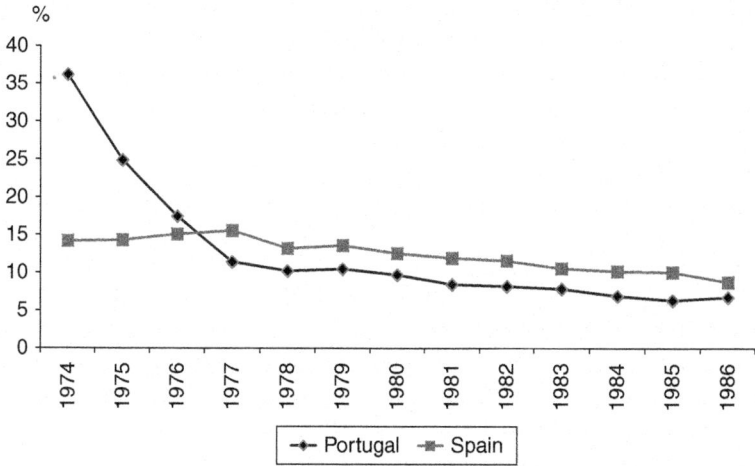

Figure 5.4   Defence budget as a percentage of total public expenditure in Portugal and Spain (1974–86)

Sources: Based on Mata and Valerio (1994:253–4, 270–1) and Pérez Muinelo (2009:84).

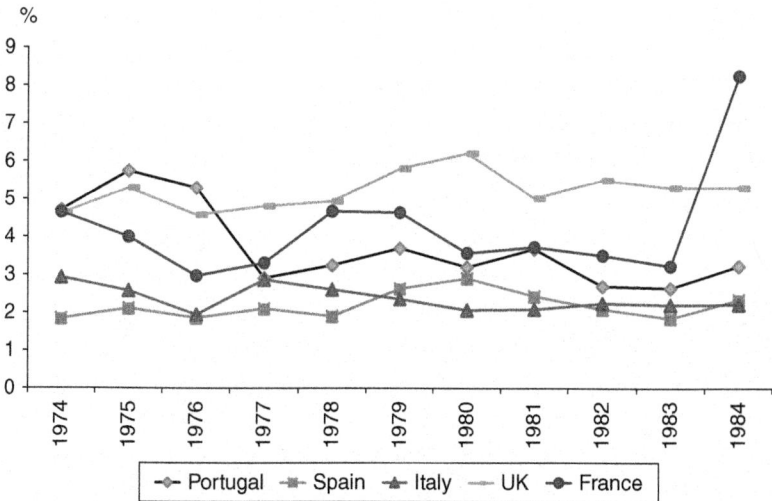

Figure 5.5   Defence expenditure as a percentage of GNP

Source: Based on CESEDEN (1988:120).

below the 'acceptable minimums' (Amaral 2000:184). The fact that by 1986, a modern process of planning and budgeting to rationalise military expenditures was still not an official requirement also points at the low relevance of *treasure* in the strategy of the governments.[88]

5.4.2   Staff expenditure

Although in Portugal, military expenditures were fundamentally devoted to salaries, pensions, and staff-related costs (Figure 5.6), salaries and pensions remained very low. Military budgets were shrinking and an important share was dedicated to the demobilisation process that followed the Colonial Wars. Salary increases merely attempted to compensate inflation that was severely reducing military purchasing power. The large size of the military, designed to maintain the occupation of the large colonial territories, ruled out sufficient salary raises. The initial downsizing of the military after the Colonial Wars reduced the staff from 217,000 in 1975 to 59,800 in 1976. However, the numbers in the military grew again after 1978 reaching 73,400 in 1985 (CESEDEN 1988:197). The share of expenditure per member of the military remained very low in comparison with other European militaries (Figure 5.7).

There were several general salary increases during the period but rather than improving the living conditions of the military and their families, they served to compensate for the effects of inflation on their

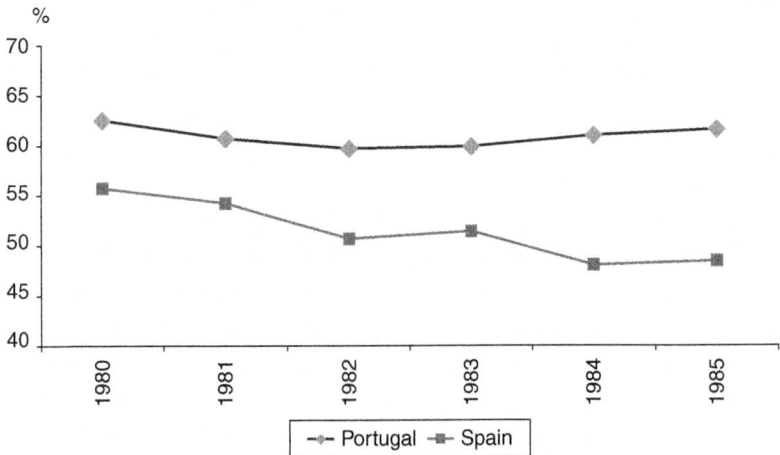

Figure 5.6   Percentage of defence budget allocated to staff expenditure in Portugal and Spain

Sources: Based on MDN (1986:154) and Pérez Muinelo (2009:93).

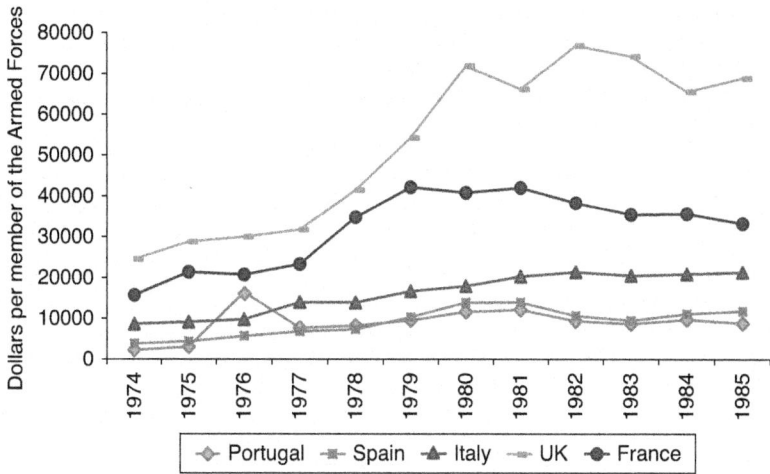

Figure 5.7 Defence budget per member of the armed forces in current dollars
Source: Based on CESEDEN (1988:123).

purchasing power. The economic situation of the military staff was so precarious for the military and their families that many deserted the ranks to take up other jobs.[89] The Decree-Laws 498-E/74, 75-V/77, 251-A/78, 209-A/79, 354/80, 164-A/81, 141/83 were *treasure* tools that updated salaries and pensions usually following previous similar adjustments in the civil service. However, these raises did not fully compensate the loss of purchasing power. The financial situation was so constrained that some economic prerogatives were eliminated, such as some gratuities associated with the accumulation of functions and to special tasks as well as the discrimination of salaries according to different placements in continental Portugal.[90] The military continued to rely on the Social Services of the Armed Forces to compensate for their low salaries.

5.4.3 Equipment expenditure

The greatest part of the defence budgets was earmarked for staff expenditures and for covering the exceptional cost of the repatriation and downsizing of the military. This reduced the flexibility of the governments with regard to the expenditure on equipment. The efforts to modernise weapons and materials were motivated by NATO membership and were enabled thanks to the military aid from NATO. However, overall these efforts were insufficient and they were not instrumental in the military control strategy.

Thirteen years of Colonial Wars had created a distortion in the struc-ture and equipment of the military, which suffered from being over-sized and reliant on obsolete material. In order to adapt to the new context and to the new NATO defence doctrine launched in 1968, the Portuguese military required a fundamental process of modernisation (Pereira 1986:63–4). This modernisation was not undertaken during the transition and early democratic period. These were 'survival' budgets not adapted to ensure the missions of the military including the compromises acquired with NATO (Mesquita 1986). Arguably, the Portuguese governments adopted a sort of free-rider attitude by relying on NATO to guarantee the defence of the country (Barros and Santos 1997).

Since modernising all of the military was not possible it was decided to concentrate efforts on the Independent Mixed Brigade of the Army (BMI). After 1976, the BMI was the flagship unit that channelled Portuguese participation in NATO and became the first unit to be modernised, fundamentally thanks to the arrival of armoured vehicles from the German and US armies. The brigade was increasingly involved with NATO and became a model and a source of pride for the rest of the military in terms of preparation and professionalism.

In the 1980s, the resources remained very scarce. Even Prime Minister Cavaco Silva (1986:18) recognised the shortages in terms of equipment and the need to increase budgets. The government tried to compensate for the deficient material conditions by introducing in 1985 the NATO military planning process to rationalise investments and procurement[91] and by launching a rearmament programme in 1986.[92] These measures also contributed to increasing civilian budgetary control of the military since they established that all investment programmes required the approval of the assembly (Almeida 1986:31–4).

The government also tried to increase external aid and cooperation, in particular from NATO allies, and the development of the Portuguese defence industry (Silva 1986:18–19; Lopes 1986). The contacts with the more advanced militaries of NATO was considered to be the starting point for the reorganisation and modernisation (Pereira 1986:70). The United States was the main contributor through subsidies and credits for re-equipment. Yet this aid was considerably lower than that received by Greece, Turkey, or Spain (IISS 1988:223). Germany and France provided financial aid for the acquisition of equipment. Canada, the United Kingdom, Netherlands, Norway, Italy, and Belgium provided some material assistance too. Thanks to the support of its allies, Portugal received tanks and other armoured vehicles for the army, A-7 and C-130 planes for the air force, as well as components for the new programme of frigates in the navy (Mesquita 1986:53–4; Pereira 1986:71). NATO also provided technical support for the manufacture of weapons and military materials in Portuguese factories. Finally, the government introduced new more flexible regulation for the defence industry to facilitate the rearmament (Almeida 1986:35).

5.4.4 Economic hardship and inherited deficiencies

The evolution of military expenditure during the transition and early democratic stages can be explained by the economic hardship that the governments faced: the need to absorb the 'retornados' and to downsize the military as well as the higher priority that the governments conceded to social spending and civilian infrastructures. Comparatively speaking, the resources allocated to the military were scarce. Overall the use of *treasure* tools as a means to increase military satisfaction and adherence to the governments was not salient in this period.

Although the majority of *treasure* resources were destined to staff expenditure, the impact on military satisfaction was not considerable. Staff expenditure was constrained by the size of the army and the compensations associated with the process of demobilisations of the troops after the colonial conflict. Very often salaries and pensions were revised, but these served merely to partially balance the loss of purchase power suffered due to inflation. No significant changes can be observed in the utilisation pattern of staff expenditure vis-à-vis the authoritarian period.

Equipment expenditure was also extremely stretched. The overall situation of the Portuguese military was very precarious in terms of weaponry, ammunitions, and materials. The BMI was the only well-equipped military unit, became a model for the rest of the military, and was the main Portuguese contribution to NATO Forces. The material modernisation was highly dependent on foreign financial, material, and technical support and did not receive a definitive response until the mid-1980s. Then, the government launched a new military planning process to rationalise acquisitions and a general programme of re-equipment to improve the working conditions and defence capabilities.

5.5 Conclusions

Two different periods in the utilisation of basic resources to control the military can be oulined. The first one corresponds to the provisional governments' period and its zenith can be found around the November

1975 coup attempt. The control strategy was very different during the period of constitutional governments and especially after 1982.

Paradoxically, the approach to control developed by the provisional governments was to a great extent similar to that of the Estado Novo. Salazarist coercive *organisation* tools were abolished but replaced by a series of similar ones. The special military unit COPCON, in charge of fighting insurgency, was the most representative but not the sole coercive tool. Other military units, the security forces, tribunals, prisons, and even civilians acted as deterrent instruments against military disobedience too. As during the last years of the Estado Novo, military education and training were neglected and the provision of services, goods, and jobs continued as a means to compensate for poor salaries. The MFA created a series of institutions and a parallel hierarchy that worked for the politicisation and subordination of both civilians and the military. The reliance on politicisation as a mechanism of control was also evident in the use of *nodality*. New organisations such as the Fifth Division, CODICE, and the SDCI collaborated on an intensive propaganda campaign and the collection of information concerning political affiliation and adherence to the MFA principles. The extraordinary degree of autonomy and the extensive functions granted to the military in this period were important collective incentives to endorse the MFA-controlled governments. Amnesty laws, promotions, and political appointments also contributed to reward the military. Initially, sanctions were imposed on the military officers and organisations identified with the Estado Novo and later with anti-government activities. Finally, the availability of *treasure* for control purposes was seriously compromised not only by the economic crises but also due to the funds committed to the process of demobilisation that followed the end of the Colonial Wars. Salaries were not significantly increased in real terms and equipment was not modernised.

Deep transformations in the control toolkit were initiated after the 1975 November coup, the underlying principles being the depoliticisation and professionalisation of the military. For instance, the abolition of the COPCON marked the end of the coercive use of *organisation*. Organisational design continued to be an important non-coercive mechanism of control but with an opposite purpose. After 1976, the reorganisation efforts served to depoliticise the military and demilitarise politics. Political and military power was gradually centralised. Education and military training were reinforced through the actions of the IDN, military academies and institutes, as well as through joint exercises with NATO. The *nodality* tools of political control, CODICE, SDCI, and the Fifth Division, were abolished and propaganda and censorship abandoned. The free media monitored the military, contributing to their extrication from politics. Governments promoted mutual awareness between the military and civilian spheres, and a new doctrine of national defence sought to persuade the military of the virtues of subordination to civilian rule. In terms of *authority* tools, the fundamental changes were: the elimination of most non-defence functions attributed to the military, the limitation of its degree of autonomy, and the introduction of legal sanctions and constraints to prevent politicisation and encourage professionalism in the ranks. In 1982, the CR was abolished and the constitutional reform and the defence law defined a new legal framework for civil-military relations, formalising for the first time the principle of civilian supremacy. Lastly, although *treasure* remained marginal in the control strategy, there was a growing concern about the deficient material conditions. For instance, the government created the BMI, tried to stimulate foreign military cooperation and the Portuguese defence industry, and finally in 1986, launched a general programme of rearmament and modernisation.

Part 3
Spain

6
History of Contemporary Civil-Military Relations in Spain

The military uprising that initiated the Civil War in 1936 was by no means the first example of military intervention in politics in Spanish contemporary history. As in the Portuguese case, the Spanish problem of military interventionism can be easily traced back to the period of the Napoleonic invasions (Ballbé 1983; Seco Serrano 1984; Alonso Baquer 1983, 1988). The 'pronunciamientos' and other forms of military pressure on the governments were very common. Since 1814, more than fifty 'pronunciamientos' and coups have been documented (Busquets 1982). The army held extraordinary political power in Spain and was prone to act in order to defend its corporate interests whenever these were threatened (Boyd 1979:274).

This chapter examines the main features of the Spanish political and military history during two periods: Franco's dictatorship (1936–75) and the transition and early stages of democracy (1976–86). The analysis covers the Civil War and the implications of the Second World War. It also outlines the regime's political institutional setting and the functions and attitudes developed by the military during Franco's regime. Further, this chapter explains the sources of the military's dissatisfaction and its plots during the period of Suárez's governments and the impact of the first socialist government on the military's subordination.

6.1 Franco's regime

6.1.1 The Civil War and the Second World War

On 17 July 1936 and in response to the electoral victory of the left coalition 'Frente Popular', an important part of the military, with the support of conservative political parties and the Church, launched a coup d'état against the Second Republic. The rebels claimed that the country was in serious danger of social and political disintegration (Cardona 1983:197–247). This coup initiated the Spanish Civil War (1936–9), the implications of which conditioned the life of Spain for the next four decades, including the strategy and tools its governments employed to control the military. General Francisco Franco Bahamonde reached power after a series of hazardous events and strategic manoeuvres that eliminated senior generals from the race to the rebel camp's supreme command, such as Sanjurjo, Cabanellas, Queipo de Llano, Fanjul and Mola, and political leaders, such as José Antonio Primo de Rivera and Manuel Hedilla. On 1 October 1936, Franco was proclaimed 'Generalísimo' of the Nationalist Armies in Burgos, a position that he was supposed to occupy provisionally but that he maintained until his death 39 years later (Preston 1993; Cardona 2001:19–38).

Hundreds of thousands of Spaniards lost their lives as a result of the Civil War (Beevor 2006; Preston 2006 [1986], 2011). The country was divided into two camps, the loyalist Republicans and the rebel Nationalists. In addition to the battlefield casualties many civilian and military were executed, imprisoned, or forced into exile during and after the war.[1] As a result of the war, the military was confronted with important challenges such as the reconstruction and integration of the structures that during the war had been decimated and duplicated, as well as the absorption of many militia fighters, 'alfereces provisionales', who had fought for the rebels. The war also altered the basic recruitment principles of the military cadres. Formal military education was suspended. Political ascription and combat experience became the driving principles until the restoration of formal military education after the end of the war. The war nonetheless allowed Franco to consolidate personal power unparalleled among other fascist leaders or Spanish rulers (Payne 1987:245; Jerez Mir 2009). The Civil War left a very important and durable legacy not only on Spanish politics and society but also on the military and civil-military relations.

Starting in 1936, Italy and Germany helped Franco to win the war and influenced him ideologically. Franco dissolved all unions and political parties and unified the Carlist and Falangist militias by creating the single party, 'Falange Española y Tradicionalista de la JONS'.[2] On 8 May 1939, Spain pulled out of the League of Nations and pro-Axis right-wing propaganda became pervasive in the press. The infiltration of Falange militants into the military, the appointment of military to top positions in Falange, and the use of paramilitary symbolism among civilians were inspired by these totalitarian regimes. The result was a certain level of politicisation of the military and the militarisation of politics. The confusion between military and political values hindered the advancement of military professionalism (Bañón and Olmeda 1985:274–82).

The Civil War and the popularity of totalitarian views in Europe until the decline of the Axis temporarily legitimised Franco's initial aggressive stance on control. Some control tools persisted throughout the dictatorship, such as the intensive use of propaganda, censorship, military speeches, and parades. However others, such as the use of armed militias or the penetration of the military by the party, were soon abandoned. Fascism was weaker in Spain and the Spanish military were less subservient than in the case of Germany and Italy (Preston 1990:7). Although initially the regime expressed its wish to build a totalitarian state and used control tools similar to those employed by Nazi Germany or Fascist Italy, overall Franco's dictatorship should not necessarily be considered a totalitarian regime but as a conservative civilianised authoritarian one (Linz 1970 [1964]; Tusell 1988:272–305).[3]

The regime was ideologically aligned with the Berlin-Rome Axis but avoided direct involvement in the war. Several reasons precluded Spain's direct participation. Francoist Armies were large, but they were not suitable for the new type of warfare triggered by Germany;[4] aircrafts and mechanised forces were too scarce, and the men were poorly equipped. The military high command did not support the entrance of Spain into the Second World War (Preston 1990:51; Cardona 2001:83–4).[5] The dreadful socioeconomic situation of post-war Spain, the expectation of a long conflict, and the British and Portuguese diplomatic efforts also discouraged Spanish participation (Preston 1990:84; Palacios 1999:264–6). Finally, Hitler did not agree to provide the military equipment, food, and the industrial goods needed nor did he guarantee the concession to Spain of French Morocco requested by Franco for joining the Axis (Serrano Suñer 1977:299).

Despite its official non-belligerent stance, in Spain, unlike in Portugal, the Nazis had won the propaganda war during the Second World War (Stone 2005:213). Franco's regime organised the expeditionary units the Blue Division and the Blue Legion that fought alongside the Germans on the Russian front. Around 45,500 Spanish voluntary fighters joined these units (Moreno Juliá 2004). The Blue Division and the Blue Legion were compensation for German support during the Civil War and a means to appease pro-Axis sympathisers within Spain. This enterprise was less expensive than a full scale involvement in the war to which Spain was not ready in terms of equipment and arms and which was less disturbing for the monarchic generals.

6.1.2   The international insulation of the regime

After the Second World War, the Francoist regime was insulated from the international arena due to the defeat of the Axis and the adoption of an autarchic economic model. The regime secluded itself from external influence and employed its strong propaganda machinery to conceal a situation of deep socioeconomic crisis and problems such as hunger, droughts, anti-Francoist guerrillas, and the international boycott. Among the international community, Spain was a pseudo-fascist state that had collaborated with the Axis.

The United Nations' (UN) resolution 39(I) of 12 December 1946 condemned the regime, advised the withdrawal of ambassadors, and established sanctions. Spanish membership to the UN was rejected. For the next four years, most countries kept their diplomatic relations with Spain at minimal levels. The international insulation and the sanctions imposed by the UN worsened the Spanish socioeconomic situation. Salazarist Portugal and Peronist Argentina were among the few sources of external support. Spain had lost the opportunity to receive Marshall Plan aid and later was not invited to join NATO, the Council of Europe, or the European Communities. Franco used the UN boycott, the menace of the communist intervention, and the nationalistic feelings to strenghen internal support. Even the critical monarchist generals stopped opposing Franco (Liedtke 1999:231; Portero 1999:218–24).

In the 1950s, new ties with the Western world were gradually created. Franco sought international recognition. Spain's strategic location and Franco's anti-communism made the regime an acceptable ally.[6] In 1953, Spain signed the Madrid Pact with the United States which approved the creation of four US military bases on Spanish soil in exchange for economic and military support. The United States facilitated Spanish integration into the UN (1956) and Bretton Woods institutions (1958). Spain also strengthened its commercial relations within Europe, becoming a member of the Organisation for European Economic Cooperation (1958). In the 1960s, Spain undertook a semi-liberalisation of the economy that transformed the economic structure of the country and further integrated Spain into Europe. The influence of fascism in Spain had been largely substituted in the 1960s by the 'developmentalism' ('desarrollismo') of the Opus Dei technocrats (Bañón 1978; Preston 1990:14; Rodrigo 1992:64–5). This gradual socioeconomic evolution in Spain was also reflected in the military and in the control toolkit, especially after the late 1950s.

6.1.3 The malleable political institutional setting

The Civil War profoundly shaped the institutional configuration of the regime (Jerez Mir 2009). The new political structure was basically an instrument designed by Franco to strengthen his personal power. Erasing the legacy of the Second Republic became a priority for Francoist governments. The single party 'Falange' included a variety of ideological streams such as traditionalist Carlists, fascists, authoritarian Catholics, and aristocratic monarchists (Preston 1990:2). All traditional labour unions were suppressed, and the new 'vertical unions' were controlled by the Falange. Moreover, the Law of Political Responsibilities in 1939 paved the way for massive purges in all state institutions (Richards 2006:13). This law meant the elimination of the majority of the potential veto actors in Spanish institutions, which helped Franco to impose his own personal preferences in terms of policy.

In the Francoist authoritarian regime, the executive, legislative, and the civil service were indissolubly entangled. Spanish political institutions were a combination of highly legalistic procedures with a certain military hierarchical style (Linz 1970 [1964]; Comas and Mandeville 1986:52). The political system he designed was based on the principles of hierarchy and discipline.[7] The Francoist parliament, 'Cortes', was created in 1942 as a council body to assist Franco in the legislative tasks but did not approve laws. As in Portugal, corporatism was the only form of limited pluralism allowed by the regime. Officially, the term of 'organic democracy' was used and the Cortes did not represent citizens but the 'natural organisations'; that is, the local councils, the vertical unions, the corporations, the universities, the Church, and the military. All members were appointed until 1967, when the introduction of 108 elected seats slightly increased the pluralism and independence of the Cortes (Alba 1981:261).

After the defeat of the Axis, the Falange was relegated to a secondary role and became mainly a patronage dispensing machine in the service of Franco (Preston 1990:11, 112–13). Franco even referred to the Falange as the 'claque'; a professional body of professional applauders.[8] Moreover, there were no serious checks to Franco's powers outside the state apparatus. The only strong independent organisation was the Catholic Church that from the beginning firmly supported the regime. Franco's administration was extremely centralised and relatively small.[9] There was a profusion of administrative norms that tried to regulate every aspect of the state and society, although many of them were not observed (Olmeda 1988:150). Bureaucratic entrenchment in general did not affect important decisions concerning the military. The formal legalism could be easily curbed by the government whenever required. Franco was the sovereign and as such he could quite freely choose the types of policies and tools without major constraints.

Power struggles among different political factions or 'familias' within Francoism were common.[10] Changes in the administration's personnel and ministerial reshuffles were made with the objective of the survival of the regime and in accordance with changes in the international context. Despite the influence of these 'familias', Franco always maintained absolute control. Like Salazar, Franco never clearly endorsed one single faction, but his personal power was much greater than that of Salazar in Portugal. He was heads of state, the military, the Falange, and head of the governments. Franco held absolute authority and was not to be held accountable for his actions. A common quote by the dictator and his followers that captures this aura was: 'Franco only answered to God and History' (Aguilar Olivencia 1999:38–9).

Many in the military occupied top positions in the political and administrative apparatus. Around a third of the ministers during the regime were military officers.[11] The military maintained its strength in the public administration until the early 1960s when it was replaced by the Opus Dei technocrats as the most influencial political pressure group (de Miguel 1975; Bañón 1978; Jerez Mir 1982). At the end of the regime, the military continued to enjoy exclusive competences in military and defence issues and important participation in the areas of policy and state-owned companies.

In sum, the institutional setting provided Franco with absolute control of the regime and its resources. There was no clear division of powers. His decisions and actions, including those regarding the military and the tools of control, were not contested. The military actively participated at different levels in the political-administrative Francoist system and, as next section shows, developed important functions in the regime.

6.1.4   Guardians against the internal enemy

Although the Francoist was a civilianised regime (Ballbé 1983:iii; Danopoulos 1991:28), the military played a central role in the dictatorship. In addition to their traditional defence function, they became guardians against the 'internal enemy' and key to the post-war reconstruction and social integration of Spain. Franco used many different policy instruments to promote these special functions and thus, the sense of responsibility and their engagement with the regime.

The Spanish military traditionally felt a strong sense of mission according to which they had the power and obligation to defend and reconstruct Spain (Fontana 1986/ed.:13). They considered themselves guardians of traditions and national values (Blanco Ande 1987:212). The military intervention that overthrew the Second Republic and established Franco's dictatorship was justified as a fight against an internal enemy. Franco fuelled this sense of mission by constantly promoting a mythic image of the military, which he even called 'apostles of the Fatherland', and of the Civil War as a crusade (Aguilar Olivencia 1999:53). The military became inquisitors and repressors. Military courts maintained wide competences and were in charge of the fight against communism and masonry (Olmeda 1988:110).[12] Moreover, army officers were appointed to lead the security forces, police and civil guard, in their fight against the anti-Francoist militias known as 'maquis'.[13]

The military had an important function in the reconstruction of Spain after the Civil War. It contributed to re-activate the economy by consuming great quantities of fuel, textiles, food and clothing, and creating a significant military industrial complex. The military also had the logistics and organisational expertise necessary to re-build the destroyed infrastructures and state apparatus. Finally, the military, alongside the Catholic Church, became the most powerful tools for social integration. Mandatory military service was instituted after the Civil War on 8 August 1940. One of the main tasks assigned to the military was the integration and homogenisation of Spanish society through the use of the Castilian language, favouring interregional mobility and the indoctrination in the values of the Francoist regime (Bañón and Olmeda 1985:281; Olmeda 1988:106–7, 132).

Franco was more concerned with the internal threats and establishing mechanisms of political control to guarantee loyalty to the regime than with external threats. The organisation and equipment of the military were outdated, which hampered professionalism (Bañón and Olmeda 1985:280; Payne 1986). The Second World War revolutionised warfare not only at the material but also at the tactical and organisational levels. However, the Spanish military, especially the army, considered themselves as experienced fighters who had prevailed in the Civil War. Thus, they did not have a sense of urgency for deep transformations in the military. Officers were permitted to take other parallel jobs in private business or the public administration to compensate the very low salaries which negatively affected professional preparation.[14] Moreover, Franco divided the War Ministry into three independent ministries and reserved for himself the role of coordinator, strengthening his authority.

This division made the emergence of military leaders that could have broad support across branches and challenge his personal rule more difficult but also lowered the level of coordination against a potential external threat.

Many of the pitfalls of the Spanish military were evidenced during the Sidi Ifni War (1957–8). In addition to the logistics and coordination problems, the scarcity and inadequacy of material means was obvious. The weapons dated from the Second World War; there were scarcities of fuel, vehicles, food, and boots. Even the most basic military training exercises, such as shooting practice, were rare. Only the support of the French military, which was much better prepared for guerrilla warfare saved Spain from disaster (Azcona et al. 1994; Fernández-Aceytuno 2001:560–1; Segura Valero 2006:218–20, 246–51, 311–12). The army had become a mechanism for guaranteeing the survival of his regime rather than an instrument of national defence (Preston 1990:39).

6.1.5 Military subordination

The military never seriously threatened Franco's position. The victory in the Civil War and the central position that they occupied in the regime enhanced military pride and maintained military contestation at the lowest levels. This was an important difference from the Portuguese military which was far less cohesive and more docile than the Spanish military.

Only a small minority of officers dared to express their discontent with some aspects of Franco's rule. From 1943 to 1948, there were several manifestations of unrest among monarchist sectors which became the only menaces to Franco's supreme authority.[15] On 8 September 1943, Generals Orgaz, Dávila, Varela, Solchaga, Kindelán, Saliquet, Monasterio, and Ponte co-signed a letter requesting Franco to restore the monarchy (Bravo Morata 1978:319–1; Palacios 1999:436–52). Several senior officers and other personalities also maintained contacts with the exiled heir of the Spanish monarchy, Don Juan, in order to plan his return. Franco used honours, promotions, economic incentives, relocations, and one-to-one meetings to silence this contestation from the monarchic generals. The symbolic enactment of the Law of Succession in 1947 that declared Spain a Catholic monarchy also contributed to appease the monarchic sectors. Overall, Franco enjoyed the loyalty of the middle-rank and militia officers (Payne 1967:445; Preston 1990:103–4), and by the early 1950s, most of the senior generals with legitimacy to contest Franco's leadership had already died.[16]

Loyalty to the regime was reinforced by an extreme sense of discipline inculcated in the Spanish military (Allendesalazar Urbina 1977:84–98). Francoist military doctrine conceded an exaggerated value to discipline.[17] Religious and military values were to a great extent interpenetrated during Francoism (Oltra and de Miguel 1978). Obedience, abnegation, honour, and religious belief were exacerbated by the official discourse as a means to guarantee military discipline. The military was led to believe that discipline was intertwined with their Christian feelings; obedience was considered an act of faith or expression of religiosity (Vigón 1956 [1950]:149). The notion of discipline was so entrenched in the military's imagery that even those trying to promote disobedience to Franco justified their claims in terms of discipline.[18]

The strong conservatism and cohesion of the Spanish military also contributed to prevent deviant attitudes against the dictator (Aguilar Olivencia 1999). The Spanish military surpassed the usual levels of conservatism due to the purges of republican and liberal officers; the incorporation into the ranks of thousands of militia fighters whose ideology was often pro-fascist; and the recurrent anti-communist, anti-liberal, pro-authoritarian rhetoric fomented by the regime apparatus and the reactionary press (Preston 1990:179–80). The active role played by the military in Francoist indoctrination and propaganda campaigns made them especially vulnerable and acquiescent to these types of control tools. The new generation of officers that in the 1960s took over senior positions had always been subordinated to Franco and had never considered him as 'a primus inter pares' as some of the older generals had. For these new generals, Franco had always been the supreme leader (Cardona 2001:213).

The ideological military cohesion was fostered by their gradual divorce from society at large. There was little ideological evolution in the Francoist army, which became more insulated in a changing society (Preston 1990:134). Several factors had favoured this isolation: their elitism, social endogamy, self-recruitment, military housing, separation of education and work from civilians, a ritualised system of values, and territorial uprooting (Busquets 1984 [1971]). According to social origin, the Francoist Military were the most, or at least among the most, elitist in the world (Olmeda 1988:290–2). The provision of housing for military families reinforced the esprit de corps and endogamy. From 1961 to 1963, 70 per cent of the new cadets were sons of military officers, a higher percentage than in any other Western country (Payne 1967:448). Fifty per cent of the officers married the daughters of other officers (Preston 1990:179–80). Peer pressure was very strong and reinforced unity in support of the regime.

6.1.6   New views at the end of the regime

Despite the great degree of cohesiveness and support for Franco, during the last years of the regime, two different groups of military began to stand out. On the one hand, there was a reactionary group, the 'bunker', which favoured a praetorian view of the state and was preoccupied with the prolongation of the dictatorial regime after the death of Franco. This was the most powerful group and dominated the senior ranks through the former Blue Division combatants, 'Generales Azules', and the secret services (Preston 1990:153–8). On the other hand, military cooperation with the United States and NATO[19] convinced some officers that change in the level of professionalisation and the modernisation of military methods and doctrine were necessary (Puell de la Villa 1997; Fernández López 1998). This group was called 'liberal' or 'reformist'.[20]

In parallel to the moderate liberalising socioeconomic reforms in the 1960s and early 1970s, some changes were introduced in the military. However, these were not as fundamental as the liberal military had expected. The unification of the three branches that had become a request from military scholars and from within the higher education system was not undertaken (Salas López 1974:250–1). In the 1970s, the military, especially the army, continued to have poor salaries and equipment, and many officers were confined to administrative tasks (Olmeda 1988:251). Although in the government the military ministries had fought against the reduction of the military budgets, the more influential technocrats managed to convince Franco of the opposite. The army did not benefit from the economic boom the Spanish economy experienced during the 1960s.

This scenario did not considerably reduce the support for the regime. The 'Matesa' corruption scandal in 1969 tainted the reputation of the technocrats in the government, and the increasing ETA terrorist attacks whose most important action was the assassination of the Prime Minister Almiral Carrero Blanco in 1973, contributed to the radicalisation of the hardliners who publicly expressed the need to reinforce authority in Spain. The extreme right exerted pressures to secure the dominance of the reactionaries among the top tiers of the administration and questioned the attempts to modernise the political system.[21]

Finally, the Carnations Revolution in Portugal in 1974 inspired the Democratic Military Union (UMD) which was a clandestine group of officers that sought for a reorganisation of the military and the end of the authoritarian regime. The UMD wanted to provoke a 'pronunciamiento' similar to the contemporary military rebellions of Portugal, Greece, and Abyssinia or to those in nineteenth-century Spain in order to force a transition to democracy (Fortes and Otero 1983:236–8). Although UMD reveals the existence of liberal ideology within the ranks, its neutralisation in 1975 and the severe punishment suffered by its members indicates the supremacy of the reactionary views in the Spanish military that after the death of Franco complicated the transition to democracy.

6.2 Transition and democracy

6.2.1 Suárez's governments

The socioeconomic modernisation in the 1960s and early 1970s can be considered the main accomplishment of the Francoist regime but also an important factor in its demise. Spain had become an urbanised and industrialised country that attracted tourists and foreign capital. By the time of Franco's death, there was a majoritarian belief in Spanish civil society of the necessity of a democratic political system. The Spanish transition was basically a civilian-led process, initiated by pressures from inside the regime and its apparatus (Fishman 1990; Linz et al. 1995). Spanish political elites, including the clandestine opposition parties and the members of the Francoist administration, with the support of intellectual and economic elites launched a transition into a Western-type pluralistic democratic system (Viñas 1999:246–7).

Franco died on 20 November 1975 leaving King Juan Carlos as his heir and head of state and Carlos Arias Navarro as prime minister. Social and political contestation and the inability to conduct the reforms forced Arias Navarro's resignation.[22] In July 1976, the king appointed Adolfo Suárez as prime minister. Suárez, a former general secretary of the Spanish single party, became a key figure who launched and conducted the main political reforms that led Spain into democracy. His party, the Democratic Centre Union (UCD) won the first two democratic general elections since 1936, in June 1977 and March 1979.

The military who continued to be loyal to Francoist principles did not fully endorse the reforms nor participated in the core decisions during the transition. They were persuaded that Franco's appointed successor, Juan Carlos, was the safeguard for the continuity of the regime and initially accepted a secondary role in the reforms (Agüero 1995:43, 61–2). Once the king and Suárez's government showed commitment to a profound democratisation process, military discontent grew and subordination weakened.

Several factors contributed to military unrest. Some of the structural problems were inherited from Francoism. For instance, officers were insufficiently qualified, badly paid, and subject to a system of promotion based almost exclusively on seniority. There was an abnormal abundance of high ranking officers, a scarcity of material means, a territorial distribution similar to that of an army of occupation, and a strong isolation within Spanish society.[23] Nonetheless, the military did not blame the dictatorship for their problems. Most of them, even the reformists, continued to feel admiration for Franco (Gutiérrez Mellado and Picatoste 1983:49–58). The tolerance displayed for the structural problems during the dictatorship disappeared during the UCD's governments.

A series of decisions and incidents throughout the transition complicated civil-military relations. First, the evacuation of the Spanish Sahara protectorate that concluded in February 1976 was a setback for the military's pride (Alonso Baquer 1978:170–2). Second, the Political Reform Act meant the legal self-dissolution of the regime, to the extent that it was termed the political 'harakiri' of Francoism. Although half of the military representatives in the Cortes voted against the Political Reform Act (Sánchez Navarro 1990:23), it obtained a landslide majority in the Cortes (November 1976) and in the subsequent referendum (December 1976).[24] Most of the military considered Francoist principles and laws as immutable. The approval of the act put some generals in a state of 'total dissonance' with the reforms launched by the UCD's governments.[25]

Third, legalisation of the Spanish Communist Party (PCE) during Easter 1977 was considered as a betrayal by many senior generals. The formal objection of the Higher Council of the army and the protest memorandum addressed to the king co-signed by several lieutenant-generals (Játiva conspiracy) were evidence of military discontent.[26] Fourth, the restoration of the Catalan regional government 'Generalitat' in September 1977 and the decentralisation process, initiated with the approval of the autonomy statutes of the Basque Country, Catalonia, Galicia, and Andalusia in referenda between 1979 and 1981, was seen by the military as a threat to the unity of Spain. Finally, after the death of Franco, the growing spiral of terrorist violence by ETA, GRAPO, and other groups reached its peak in 1980 with 91 attacks and 124 persons assassinated (Reinares 1990:272–95; Sánchez Cuenca and Aguilar 2009). The military were priority targets. For instance, of those killed by the ETA between 1976 and 1986, 89.7 per cent were professional military or policemen (Agüero 1995:143).

Suárez, aware of the risks that some military represented, had appointed the liberal General Gutiérrez Mellado as deputy prime minister (1976–81). Gutiérrez Mellado, who also became the first defence minister in the democracy (1977–9), launched a series of reforms that aimed at the modernisation and professionalisation of the military as a means to counter the influence of the reactionary 'bunker' and to consolidate the military's subordination.[27] These reforms included the creation of the Joint Chiefs of Staff (JUJEM); the Defence Ministry (1977); and a new legal framework for national defence, military organisation, and military justice (Ballbé 1983; Rodrigo 1992:69, Chapter 8)

The reforms introduced by the UCD government proved to be insufficient to consolidate civilian supremacy (Serra 1986:175; Navajas Zubeldía 1995:183–8). Due to the strong military opposition, these reforms were not as decisive as Suárez government had initially wanted. The new legal framework left room for an ambiguous interpretation concerning the chain of command (Puell de la Villa 2005:236). Honour Trials or the Francoist formula of oath to the flag were not abolished, conscientious objection was not regulated, and the promotion of reactionary officers opposed to the government continued (Busquets and Losada 2003:135–44). In addition, the problems with the implementation of some of the norms had a negative impact on the military's subordination. The practice often did not follow the formal principles (Ballbé 1983:469–88). Although the Constitution of 1978 established that military justice was limited to strict martial matters, the military courts often exceeded their functions by judging civilians. Military courts also imposed soft sentences on those responsible for aggressive police repression or anti-democratic actions. The UCD governments failed to persuade the military of the necessity of reforms and were too permissive with anti-democratic attitudes (Busquets and Losada 2003:138).

Finally, the socioeconomic and political problems that Suárez's government encountered became an additional source of military discontent and an alibi for potential intervention. The second oil crisis in 1979 affected the manufacturing industry and the banking system, increased unemployment and the public deficit, and constrained military budgets (Powell 2001:259, 268). Suárez's government ruled in the minority and had to face strong opposition, not only from rival parties but also from within the UCD (Hopkin 1999:225–31). The the political pressure of growing discontent in Spanish society and the militaryresulted in Suárez's resignation in January 1981.

6.2.2 Anti-government plots

Initially, Suárez underestimated the threat posed by the military (Fernández López 2000:17). Suárez's government carefully launched the major political reforms scrupulously respecting the framework of Francoist legality so that the military could not question them.[28] However, most of the military rejected the advent of democracy and adopted an attitude of passive resistance towards liberalisation.[29] The dominance of the reactionary generals opposed to the reforms and the discrepancies between the more liberal ones weakened civilian supremacy.[30] The high degree of military autonomy and the permissiveness vis-à-vis the reactionary propaganda and acts of indiscipline instilled anti-government activity.[31] During the transition and early years of democracy several conspiracies and military plots took place.

After Franco's death, the bunker had begun to organise large-scale strategic actions to sabotage the political reforms and to promote a military intervention. Extreme right newspapers such as 'El Alcazar', 'El Imparcial', and 'Reconquista' and magazines such as 'Fuerza Nueva' or 'Servicio' fuelled military discontent. These publications projected a pessimistic vision of Spain: denouncing the dissolution of the unity of Spain, terrorist impunity, degradation of moral values, and the planned destruction of the military establishment. The government underestimated the impact of the bunker propaganda among the ranks (Preston 1990:194).

The extreme right also committed acts of violence against left-wing students, workers, bookstores, and even clergymen and moderate conservatives[32] often trying to provoke a spiral of the violence to legitimise a military intervention. The terrorist attacks of ETA and GRAPO were instrumental to reactionary groups. Funerals of civil guards or military officers assassinated by terrorist groups were used to hail radical positions (Gutiérrez Mellado and Picatoste 1983:107–14). The acts of military indiscipline against the government became recurrent.[33] Moreover, after the bad results of the extreme right in the first elections in June 1977, the military bunker realised that maintaining the regime would only be possible through non-democratic means.

The government miscalculated the level of discontent within the military and the capacity of the bunker to organise a military coup. The lack of sanctions on overt anti-democratic attitudes within the ranks had reinforced the bunker's conviction of the likelihood of success of a military intervention (Preston 1990:161). According to the foreign affairs minister Areilza, during the transition there was a state 'permanent military conspiracy'.[34] The first important coup attempt was the 'Operación Galaxia',[35] which was planned for 17 November 1978 in order to prevent the Constitutional Referendum in December. However, the secret services informed the government of the attempt and the leaders of the plot, lieutenant-colonel of the civil guard Tejero and captain of police Ynestrillas, were arrested. The fact that many officers were aware of the plot and did not denounce it meant that the military's loyalty to the government was not assured anymore (Ballbé 1983:472–3; Busquets and Losada 2003:139).

Another attempt was aborted in 1979. The Armoured Division (DAC) located in Madrid was the key to control of the capital. The DAC had become a bastion of reactionary ideas due to the influence of Generals Milans del Bosch and Torres Rojas. In 1979, under the command of the latter some unauthorised manoeuvres simulated the seizure of Madrid. Apparently, Torres Rojas was plotting to take control of the Presidential Palace of Moncloa with the help of the Parachutist Brigade stationed in Torrejón and then use the DAC to control the city. The coup was delayed due to insufficient supplies of ammunition and fuel (Preston 1990:200).

The 23-F coup on 23 February 1981 was the most important one. A group of civil guards hijacked the congress during the investiture session of the new prime minister Leopoldo Calvo Sotelo following Suárez's resignation. Some of the implicated officers, General Milans del Bosch and Colonels Tejero and San Martín, had planned a Turkish or Chilean-style coup followed by draconian measures. On the other hand, General Alfonso Armada preferred a coup along the lines of De Gaulle's. Armada sought to take advantage of the situation resulting from the Milans and Tejero violent coup in order to force the king to approve the introduction of a Government of National Salvation that would be headed by Armada himself. However, due to the actions of the king, the royal military household, the political parties, and some loyal military, the coup failed and the plotters were incarcerated (Preston 1986, 1990:176–7; Medina 2006).

The failure of the 23-F had a great impact on civil-military relations. The coup attempt shocked Spanish civil society which for the most part was unaware of the extent of the military threat. Moreover the coup was broadcasted live by radio and TV, which amplified its impact. Spanish society reacted strongly against the plot. The behaviour of the plotters during the coup and their trials embarrassed most of the military and became a tipping point in the political influence of the bunker and its ascendency within the ranks (Preston 2004:498). Calvo Sotelo's new government undertook some important measures concerning military subordination. It was the first government not to include any military members and to appoint civilians to top positions in the Defence Ministry.[36] It reinforced the intelligence services, CESID, appealed against the 'soft' sentences initially imposed on the conspirators by a military court, and most importantly, signed NATO membership on 30 May 1982 (Agüero 1995:176). However, the consolidation of the military's subordination continued to be an issue during Calvo Sotelo's mandate.

The 'Manifesto of the Hundred' on December 1981 in defence of the 23-F plotters and against the military's subordination to civilian rule was a new sign of contestation. Conspiracy groups such as the 'Union Militar Española' (UME) continued to operate. Finally, a hard-line coup seeking to prevent the elections of October 1982, 'Operación Cervantes', was aborted (Bañón 1988:342; Busquets and Losada 2003:145–66). Although some of the plotters' claims and fears were shared by the majority of the military, overall the military had stopped endorsing insurgency. The memories of the Civil War and the fear of new bloodshed during the transition were present in the ranks (Barrachina 2002:389). The socialist party, PSOE, won the general elections and took over government without any further military interference. This peaceful transfer of power can be considered as the end of the military threat and the culmination of the transitional process (Linz and Stepan 1996:108).

6.2.3   The first socialist government

The landslide victory of Felipe González in the October 1982 elections granted his government the legitimacy and a solid parliamentary majority to conduct deep reforms. The government restructured and liberalised the economy, developed the autonomous communities' territorial model, negotiated the membership to the EEC, and most importantly, introduced profound transformations in the defence and military policies. This was the first left-wing government in more than four decades, and paradoxically it suffered much lower contestation to its reforms than the previous centre-right UCD governments. The growing popular support for democracy reinforced the military's subordination to the government (Danopoulos 1991:36). Even among conservative voters, those supporting democracy were a majority.[37] This new context enabled the government to implement the necessary in-depth changes in military policy to ensure subordination.

Narcís Serra, an economist and former mayor of Barcelona, was appointed defence minister.[38] Serra spent his first year in office analysing the ministry and the military and designing a plan to increase centralisation and strengthen the power of the government vis-à-vis the military as a requisite for further reform and modernisation (Agüero 1995:188). González and Serra, conscious that ideological change within the ranks was not achievable in the short term, concentrated their efforts on obtaining material obedience and on developing a regulatory framework aimed at profound transformations in the long term (Comas and Mandeville 1986:148).

The reforms launched by the first socialist government were far-reaching and served to consolidate civilian supremacy.[39] The Organic Law of Defence 1/1984 unambiguously stated the supremacy of the prime minister and centralised powers in the hands of the defence minister (Serra 2008:107–8). The role of the king as chief of the armies became mostly symbolic. In order to improve coordination, the position of Chief of the Joint Staff (JEMAD) was created and hierarchically subordinated to the defence minister. The reforms also tackled the 'brutal excess of personnel' that compromised most of the defence budgets and hindered military modernisation.[40] Other important measures were the regulation of the military service (Law 19/1984), the introduction of conscientious objection (Law 48/1984), the homologation of benefits with those of the civil administration (Laws 20/1984 and 40/1984), and the separation of the military from the state security forces, national police, and civil guard (Law 2/1986).

The consolidation of civilian supremacy was facilitated by Spain's integration into NATO. The navy, which collaborated closely with NATO, was especially keen on Spanish membership, but the support for NATO was also majoritarian in the air force and the army.[41] González, who as leader of the opposition had previously been opposed to NATO, understood its importance with regard to the military's subordination and changed his discourse to the extent that, in 1986, PSOE was the main defender of the 'yes' in the referendum that confirmed NATO membership. NATO doctrine justified changes in the territorial organisation and strategic planning of the military, a growing presence of civilian personnel in the Defence Ministry, and increases in defence budgets.

Overall, the reforms by the first socialist government meant a reinforcement of the Defence Ministry and a centralisation and modernisation of the processes of defence management (Agüero 1995:190–203). These reforms were inspired by NATO templates and involved all categories and subcategories of control tools. They were more profound than those attempted by UCD governments.[42] The military cooperated with these reforms because it was concerned with its future and individual prerogatives rather than because it fully endorsed democratic values (O'Donnell and Schmitter 1986:24–5). Probably the clearest expression of the success of the PSOE government was the changing nature of military discontent (Agüero 1995:214). Protests now came from specific problems such as promotions and career patterns, shortages in budgets, bureaucratic excess, or preferential treatment of some units. With the exception of a plot by a small group of hardliners to assassinate the king and some members of the government during a military parade in

La Coruña in 1985, quickly unveiled by the secret services, no further serious challenge was posed to civilian supremacy. By 1986, most of the military realised that the catastrophic predictions of the defenders of authoritarianism had proved exaggerated and that Spain was better off under democracy.

6.3   Conclusions

Spain experienced processes of political transformations during the twentieth century that were similar and parallel to those of Portugal. Nonetheless, the evolution of Spanish civil-military relations was very different. The Spanish military was more cohesive and submissive to the dictator than the Portuguese military. During the Civil War, the Spanish military was purged. For the rest of the dictatorship, the military became strong supporters of Franco and his regime. He concentrated more power in his hands than Salazar and never saw his authority seriously threatened internally. The regime suffered an embargo and insulation from the international arena until the early 1950s; however, it never faced an external challenge of the scale of the Portuguese Colonial Wars.

After the death of Franco the situation changed drastically. The military, very critical of the political democratic reforms undertaken by the Suárez's government, withdrew their support and became a growing threat. The UCD governments faced several different socioeconomic and political problems, which limited their resources and capacity to undertake action. However, the defeat of the military plots, in particular the 23-F coup in 1981, and the landslide PSOE victory in 1982 again changed the civil-military relations in Spain. The reactionary military plotters were discredited, and the military understood that the democratisation process was irreversible. Moreover, the electoral results and the socioeconomic and political reforms granted the first Gonzalez government legitimacy and the capacity to undertake the actions required for the consolidation of the military's subordination.

7
Francoist Tools of Government

This chapter analyses the tools that the Francoist regime utilised to keep the military subordinated. Many of these tools were similar to those observed during the Estado Novo. However, there are some fundamental discrepancies concerning the intensity or salience of some types of tools that contribute to rejecting the hypothesis of a common 'authoritarian' style of control in both countries.

Table 7.1 summarises the fundamental features of the Francoist control toolkit developed in this chapter. It suggests that the first period of the regime (1936–45) was characterised by a very intensive use of coercive *organisation* (Section 7.1.1) and inquisitorial *nodality* detectors (Section 7.2.1). Repression was much stronger than in Portugal. However, after the thorough purges in the military and coinciding with the fall of the Axis in Europe, Franco changed his stance on the military's subordination. The use of courts-martial, imprisonments, and executions decreased. Moreover, unlike in the Estado Novo, the paramilitary militias were banned and the use of the secret services to spy on the military was kept at low levels. Franco trusted 'his' military and adopted a softer control approach. The scarcity of *treasure* (Section 7.4) was compensated with *organisation, nodality,* and *authority* rewards. For instance, the regime provided services, jobs, and goods to the military and their families (Section 7.1.2); ideological gratifications through propaganda, laudatory speeches, and censorship (Section 7.2.1); promotions, special functions in the regime apparatus, and a high degree of lenience with the military (Section 7.3.1). Franco's governments utilised organisation to prevent the emergence of any figure or group with the capacity to defy his power. Military education and training were never a central concern and the impulse to professionalisation and modernisation of skills and procedures reached Spain late, in the 1960s (Section 7.1.2). The recourse

Table 7.1 Summary of tools of government during Francoism (1936–75)

	Tools	Trajectory
Organisation	*Coercive* (Section 7.1.1): Summary executions, courts-martial, prisons until mid-1940s. Paramilitary militias were not allowed and the security forces were controlled by the army and not used as a check on the military	Very intensive utilisation from 1936 to 1945, then essentially abandoned
	Non-coercive (Section 7.1.2): Formal military education and training. Exchanges with the US Armed Forces	Reintroduced in 1940. Until late 1950s military exercises were rare and the military education served to instil Francoist values
		Emphasis on professionalism and development of modern skills fostered from the 1960s
	Organisational design following a 'divide-and-rule' logic	Stable
	Provision of services and goods to the military and their families. Provision of jobs in the public administration	Very important during the post-war period. Declining from the 1960s
Nodality	*Information effectors* (Section 7.2.1): Propaganda and censorship. Intensive use of public speeches, media, and specialised publications praising Franco, increasing the status of the military, and diverting the attention away from the scarcity of resources	Very intensive throughout the regime
	Information detectors (Section 7.2.2): Many different intelligence services collected information about the military (such as SIPM, 'Tercera del Alto', Brigade for Social Investigation, SIP, and SECED).	Very important during the war and decreased afterwards. The information services were fragmented and intensive espionage of the military was avoided. Centralisation and increase in salience in the 1970s
	Friendship networks within the military	Important throughout the regime

Category	Mechanism	Salience / Status
Authority	*Rewards and incentives* (Section 7.3.1): Appointments of loyal officers to high responsibility positions in the state apparatus and armed forces	Very important throughout the regime, especially at the end of the Civil War
	Special powers granted to the military related to the maintenance of public order (judiciary and security forces)	The powers of the military in the justice system decreased after the mid-1940s
	Tolerance with secondary employment and abuses of privileges	Decreased after the 1960s
	Integration of militia fighters as permanent officers in the military	Very important at the end of the Civil War and after the Sidi-Ifni War.
	Sanctions and constraints (Section 7.3.2): Reduction of retirement age and limitations to the size of the military	Basically in the 1950s.
	Prohibitions in order to enhance a distinct esprit de corps. Honour Trials	Stable
	Relocations and demotions to those holding critical view	Important after the monarchic plots in the 1940s
	Indirect: prohibitions to carry arms for civilian, anti-liberal and repressive laws on society at large	Stable
Treasure	*Staff expenditure* (Section 7.4.1): Salary rises (often through extraordinary budget allocations) to compensate for inflation and special circumstances that could provoke military unrest	Low salience in the overall control strategy
	High salaries and benefits to reward loyalty of top-rank officers	Stable
	Equipment expenditure (Section 7.4.2): Acquisition (and production) of modern weapons and other material means. Military materials ceded by the United States	Low. The scarcity of equipment and military materials. From 1953, new equipment was introduced. However not in-depth modernisation efforts, the economic growth of the country was not matched by a similar increase in military expenditure Increasing in the 1970s

to *treasure* was minimal. Military salaries were low in general, and until the 1970s, the equipment was scarce and obsolete (Section 7.4).

7.1 Organisation

The utilisation of coercive means such as imprisonments, summary trials, and executions was central from the outbreak of the Civil War until the mid-1940s. Once the military had been thoroughly purged, Franco drastically reduced the use of coercive *organisation* means to control the military. Among the non-coercive control tools, education, and training were not central but increased their salience after the 1960s. Franco also used the institutional design of the military through a 'divide-and-rule logic' and the provision of goods, services, and jobs, especially in the aftermath of the Civil War when the complete state apparatus had to be reconstructed.

7.1.1 Coercive organisation

From 1936 to 1945, *organisation* was intensively used in a repressive manner by Franco's government on both civilians and the military. During the war, martial law was imposed and summary executions conducted frequently. Tens of thousands were executed; the goal was to eliminate the opposition to the regime within and outside the ranks (Payne 1967:409–20). There is no agreement on the exact number of people executed, partly because the official records were often destroyed. The latest research by local historians calculates about 130,000 judiciary executions. To that, about 50,000 more people should be added that were executed without even a trial (Preston 2006 [1986]:302). Beevor (2006:405) estimates 200,000 deaths, including the official executions, the random killings during the war, and the deaths in prison. These figures exclude the killings in the Republican camp.

Unlike other authoritarian regimes in the twentieth century, such as Salazar's, Tito's or Mussolini's, Franco's government did not use the civilian paramilitary forces to control the military. The paramilitary militias Falangist (fascist) and Carlist (conservative traditionalist) that had played an important role during the war were unified and placed under military command in April 1937 and disarmed in July 1944. Even during the war, military officers were used to control the militia battalions rather than the other way around. Many military officers disliked the Falange's pro-Axis and anti-monarchic views. The defence and security forces were the sole ones authorised to carry arms, and most of the officers came from the army. There is no evidence showing that the paramilitary or police forces played any role which countervailed the coercive power of the military.

The judiciary and penitentiary systems were the real coercive *organisation* tools at the service of the government during and after the war. The High Court of Military Justice, after 1936, and later the Supreme Council of Military Justice, after 1939, undertook continuous ordinary and summary inquisitorial processes (González Padilla 2002:156–8). The Law of Political Responsibilities (9 February 1939) remained as a mechanism for repression after the war. After Franco's victory, around 20,000 people were executed (Preston 2011:17).

The military that had served in the Republican camp were court martialed or when found innocent were normally expelled from the military (Cardona 2001:56). Military courts counted on the complicity of important segments of the population (Anderson 2009). Many former members of the Republican army were sentenced to forced labour.[1] At the end of the war, 300,000 soldiers were kept in concentration camps (Puell de la Villa 2005:212). Moreover, about 5,000 officers were purged (executed, imprison, or exiled) after the war (Preston 1990:179–80; Fernández López 1998:48). General Varela, army minister from 1939 to 1942, was especially central to the purges. He organised 'Honour Trials', expelled military, forced retirements and relocations, and other means of administrative repression to cleanse the army of any suspected Masonic, liberal, or Republican officer (Losada 1990:13; Cardona 2001:52). Through these purges, Franco managed to shape the military to the extent that ever since they were considered the 'Francoist Armies': a new institution almost completely disconnected from its immediate past as the Armies of the Second Republic.[2]

Nonetheless, by 1942, the coercive instruments of control in the regime began to show signs of overstretch.[3] From 1939 to 1941, the Regional Courts of Political Responsibilities tried 38,055 cases but they still had 188,671 cases pending. Similarly, the military courts also had over 30,000 open cases. Moreover, the number of prisoners greatly exceeded the normal capacity of the Spanish penitentiary system (Beevor 2006:404–5). At the beginning of the Second Republic, Spain had 12,574 prisoners. This number reached 270,710 prisoners in 1939. The number of prisoners decreased after the war but in 1942 there were still 124,423 inmates (Jordana and Ramió 2005:1023).

The government was forced to drop many cases and to reduce the severity of the punishments. The Law of Political Responsibilities was reformed and softened in 1942. The judiciary reform of 1942 reduced both the presence of the military in the courts and the general levels of repression (Dueñas 1990:150–5). However, executions and long prison sentences continued until 1944 (Delgado 2005:31). A series of laws were launched to reduce the prison population (González Padilla 2002:160). The number of inmates dropped to 43,812 in 1945 and then continued to decrease gradually so that in the 1960s, Spain reached levels similar to those at the beginning of the Second Republic (Jordana and Ramió 2005:1023). The Law of Political Responsibilities was finally revoked in 1945 but only in 1966 were the people condemned under this law amnestied and liberated (Dueñas 1990:158).

In brief, neither armed militias nor security forces were used as coercive *organisation* tools against the military. The utilisation of the coercive *organisation* capacity was channelled through the judiciary and penitentiary systems. Franco stretched these tools to their limits during the war and post-war. Once the purges in military were completed and the judiciary and penitentiary system gave strong signs of saturation, the regime quickly reduced their utilisation.

7.1.2   Non-coercive organisation

The most important non-coercive *organisation* tools in the Francoist regime were: formal military education which was used until the late 1950s primarily as a means of indoctrination; organisational design which followed a 'divide-and-rule' logic; and the provision of services, goods, and jobs in the administration.

Franco, who was a former director of the General Military Academy of Zaragoza, was aware of the impact of education in shaping military beliefs and attitudes. In 1940, the General Military Academy was re-opened and in 1943 the Navy Academy was transferred from San Fernando to Marín and the Air Force Academy was founded in San Javier. Military education gave prevalence to indoctrination of the regime's religious, moral, and social values rather than to technology or strategy (Preston 1990:39). The Army Ministers Generals Varela (1939–42), Asensio (1942–5), Davila (1945–51), and Muñoz Grandes (1951–7) strongly contributed to the indoctrination process and to the prioritisation of ideology in military education.

After 1953, some military officers spent long periods training and doing courses in the United States and other Western countries, such as Germany, France, and Italy. This education helped introduce new ideas and a growing concern for military professionalism. On average, 200 officers were trained by the United States each year. The US military became the doctrinal, tactical, and organisational reference for the Spanish military, in particular for the navy (Platón 2001:109–23;

Barrachina 2002:229–58). The exchanges with these more modern and better organised armies, as well as, the Sidi-Ifni War (1957–8) served to highlight the severe deficiencies of the Spanish military. The Army Minister General Barroso's reforms from 1958 were the first steps towards professionalisation. The size of the officers' corps was reduced, barracks were built away from cities, and there was a much stronger effort to organise military manoeuvres (Payne 1967:446–7).

This initial impulse was followed by further reforms in military education in 1964 and 1973. The fundamental goal was to increase coordination among the different branches and to unify doctrine and procedures.[4] In 1964, the Centre of National Defence High Studies (CESEDEN) was created to coordinate the military academies and to develop a joint military doctrine and the education of military cadres.[5] The CESEDEN contributed to the process of convergence with Western standards and to the shift from a doctrine of national security into that of national defence. The logic of the internal enemy lost prominence in military education (Agüero 1995:111–12). Following this growing concern about military education, the Higher School for Army Generals and the High Staff School for chiefs and officers were merged (1964), the Service of Operational Military Research (1965) and the Spanish Institute of Strategic Studies (1973) were established, and the military curriculum was reformed to introduce academic standards in an effort to bring the military closer to society (1973) (Salas López 1974:209–14; Olmeda 1988:236).

In brief, the reforms in military education aimed to create institutions that served the government as non-coercive *organisation* instruments, initially to indoctrinate the military in Francoist values, but later also to professionalise and modernise the military.

Franco also relied on organisational design to reinforce the subordination of the military. He had the capacity to shape the structure of the state apparatus, including the defence institutions, at his will. The division of the military into three different ministries and that of the territory into many different military regions for each of the branches[6] can be seen as an exercise in 'divide-and-rule' (Wheeler 1979:199; Preston 1990:135). The Law of Re-organisation of the Central Administration of the State in 1939 produced the fragmentation of the National Defence Ministry into three different ministries directly subordinated to Franco. Moreover, the scarce budgetary allocation to the inter-branch coordination body, the High General Staff, usually less than 1 per cent of the military expenditure, shows that coordination was not a priority (Olmeda 1988:236). Franco never wanted to create any organ or position concentrating too much power nor did he want to eliminate the rivalries and jealousies among ministers (Puell de la Villa 2005:188, 231–2). He employed the organisational design as a control tool reinforcing his central power and preventing the rise of any alternative source of military leadership (Olmeda 1988:109).

Additionally, Franco also used the machinery of the state to appease the military. The provision of services and goods for the military and their families compensated low salaries. Housing, transportation, education, health, food, and medicine were provided for free or at reduced prices.[7] This was an especially important privilege during the Spanish Civil War period which was characterised by the extreme poverty and high numbers of disabled veterans. Although most of these benefits were maintained until the end of the regime, the priority given by the technocratic governments to economic development restrained military budgets that heavily affected the provision of services and goods after the 1960s (Puell de la Villa 2008:198–243).

The provision of jobs in the public sector was another crucial tool for the cooptation of the military. Through the provision of jobs, the regime rewarded loyalty while enabling the military alternative sources of remuneration, influence, and prestige. It also helped improve control on the administration through strategic postings of loyal military. The annihilation of the Republican Administration created an opportunity for the government. In 1937, 50 per cent of the new civil service positions were reserved to those that fought in the Francoist Military[8] and in 1939, that quota was increased to 80 per cent.[9] From 1936 to 1945, 31 per cent of the jobs in politics were occupied by military (Viver Pi-Sunyer 1978). Moreover, Spanish security forces also became an important job destination for the military.[10] The reforms aiming to reduce the size of the army in the 1950s meant the absorption of many reserve military officers by the central and local administrations (Busquets 1984[1971]:172–5). Finally, the development of a signficant defence industry under the umbrella of the National Institute of Industry (INI) meant new job opportunities for many military and ex-military.[11] Although after the 1960s, it became gradually less acceptable for the military on active duty to undertake second jobs in the administration and to appoint military to the public sector, this practice persisted until the transition.

7.1.3   Purges; internal competition; and state provision of goods, services, and jobs

During the Francoist regime there was an evolution of the type of *organisation* tools used by the government to control the military. It initially favoured coercive means on the military such as courts-martial, imprisonments, and summary executions. In Spain, there was a more intensive coercive component of control than in Portugal but its use quickly declined after the military had been purged and the repression tools showed signs of saturation in the mid-1940s. Unlike Salazar and Caetano, Franco did not grant the security or paramilitary forces the function of controlling the military.

With regard to the non-coercive use of *organisation* tools, the government used military education; the design of the military organisation; and the capacity of the state to supply services, goods, and jobs. Until the late 1950s, military education was mainly used as a control device prioritising the indoctrination of Francoist values and the preparation of the military to the new modern requirements of warfare. After the contacts with the US military and the Sidi-Ifni War, there was a gradual change aiming to modernise the education and develop professionalism and increase operational capacity. Organisational design was used according to a 'divide-and-rule' logic. The idea was to maintain internal competition and to preclude the concentration of power in any military figure that could challenge Franco's authority. Finally, the government provided goods, services, and jobs to improve the well-being of the military and their families. The utilisation of the state organisational capacity for these provisions was very important to increase the military's satisfaction with the regime. Although this supply function had its peak during the post-Civil War and later gradually declined, it never stopped being important for the government's control strategy.

7.2 Nodality

The Francoist regime relied heavily on information manipulation tools such as propaganda and censorship to maintain the military under control. *Nodality* effectors were employed to indoctrinate the military in Francoist values and make them rationalise the poor material conditions in which it worked, overstate the threats Spain faced, and hide inconvenient news that could have undermined Franco's rule. *Nodality* detectors were important during and after the war to control civil society. However, they were not as intensively used to control the military. There were many different information services during the regime, but Franco, aware of the unrest that their use would create, avoided intensive espionage on the military. On the other hand, Franco's continuous personal interaction with the military constituted a valuable source of information and a means to influence the military.

7.2.1   Information effectors

All the media were controlled by the regime including the radio, the press, military publications, and later the official cinema news report No-Do. Propaganda became a fundamental weapon in the Spanish Civil War, which is claimed to be the first war to have been photographed for a mass audience (Brothers 1997:2) and to have been instrumentalised by competing international powers (Wingate Pike 1968; Barrera 2006:3). The military were continuously exposed to it. Not only political parties and unions produced pamphlets and newspapers, most army corps, divisions or brigades also produced their own publications.[12] Franco took advantage of this context to consolidate his leadership. The media, the nationalist administration, the Falange, and even the Church excessively praised him as a military and political genius. Any comment against him could be considered as treason (Cardona 2001:39).

After the war, governmental propaganda acclaimed the institutional values of the Spanish military such as discipline and courage, and stressed their past glories as imperial armies and the Civil War victors.[13] Annual military parades such as those of the 'Pascua Militar' (6 January), Day of the Victory (1 April), Day of the Uprising (18 July), and Day of the Caudillo (1 October) became ideological gratifications. The continuous displays of public recognition had an important impact on the morale of the troops. The military felt that their status under Francoism was high (Cardona 2001).

The propaganda machinery was also very important in diverting attention away from the penury and professional problems suffered by the military. Due to financial constraints, the necessity of more modern and ample material supplies was questioned by government propaganda. For instance, General Mendoza wrote in 'Ejército' that having secured a minimum of military material, the only important things in war were 'morale, drill and discipline'.[14] The government conveyed the idea that Franco won the war thanks to his moral principles not to superior material means.[15] During the Second World War, the propaganda overemphasised the relevance of any war action in which traditional cavalry was involved while minimising the importance of mechnised cavalry.[16] The influential military ideologist Jorge Vigón refused to acknowledge that the diet had any impact on troops' efficiency. He argued that these were arguments 'lacking spiritual sense'.[17] Franco in a military speech in 1951 emphasised that in warfare the man, the tactics, and the spiritual and moral values continue to have primacy over the material means.[18]

Nodality effectors were also used to call for military unity against internal threats. For instance, Franco and the ministers blamed communists and Masons for Spain's problems (López Rodó 1977:39–41) and justified the return of the troops following Morocco's independence in 1965 as a means to concentrate on the 'internal front' (Cardona 2001:171). The military speeches of Vice-President Admiral Carrero Blanco on 24 April 1968 (Carrero Blanco 1974:212–15), that of the Captain-General of the Canary Islands Pérez Luna, on 24 October 1972 (Celhay 1976:112, 118), as well as the several speeches made by the government after the Carnations Revolution in 1974 show that the threat of the internal enemy was a recurrent element in Franco's propaganda.

In addition to manufacturing and diffusing information in favour of the regime, the government also censored information deemed dangerous. The Press Law, inspired by Italian fascism and enacted in April 1938, was very restrictive and remained in effect for many years (Martín de la Guardia 2008:18). The Falange was initially in charge of censorship until the establishment of the Ministry or Information and Tourism in 1951. The government controlled the production of news, appointed editors, restricted the number of newspapers and journalist licences, and exerted an intense censorship (Barrera 2006). The goal was to suffocate and prevent any opinion that could jeopardise the stability and continuity of Francoism.

Francoist censorship was a crucial device to maintain the morale of the troops during the Civil War and post-war, limit the monarchic ideas in the barracks, and keep the military unaware of many of the international political developments. For instance, after the defeat of the Axis, Don Juan the heir in exile published a Manifesto in Lausanne, requesting Franco to abandon power and reinstitute the monarchy. The Francoist censorship prevented the document from being spread throughout the barracks (Cardona 2001). Censorship was employed to minimise the information available about the Sidi-Ifni War, which had revealed the lack of operational and logistical capacity of the Spanish military fighting against a comparatively very weak adversary (Segura Valero 2006). The new Press Law in 1966, which replaced that of 1938, aimed at a relaxation of the censorship in Spain. However, its effects were not very profound. It was quickly countered by the Law of Official Secrets in 1968 that brought the suppression and withdrawal of many publications and censored themes such as the decolonisation of Equatorial Guinea, the Matesa corruption scandal, and some cases of terrorism (Martín de la Guardia 2008:17–45).

In brief, propaganda and censorship tools became fundamental to the governmental's control strategy. The strong use of propaganda and censorship during the Civil War paved the way for the continuation of the manipulative use of information during peace time. *Nodality* effectors were important to create symbolic rewards and enhance the military's prestige, to drive the attention away from the material and organisation deficiencies of the Spanish military, to reinforce the sense of unity against the internal threats, and to limit the exposure of the military to certain developments that otherwise would have created unrest.

7.2.2   Information detectors

The regime's intelligence services were fundamental control tools for the subordination of the military during the Civil War but they lost prominence afterwards. Informal information networks developed by Franco and his entourage replaced a more formal surveillance of the military's attitudes. Only in the final years of the dictatorship did intelligence services again acquire salience in the military subordination strategy.

During the war, the Francoist camp had several different small information structures that aided his war effort; some linked to the civil administration, others to generals, and even businessmen (Mola 1940:320–1). The most important organisations were: the Fifth Column, which was a decentralised organisation that operated in the Republican zone with acts of sabotage, propaganda, and disinformation; the Military Police of Vanguard, which paradoxically acted as a counter-information and anti-infiltration organisation; and the Service of Information of the North-East Frontier (SIFNE), founded by the politician Francesc Cambó and the businessman Juan March, which connected the rebels with foreign powers. The SIFNE was transformed in 1938 into the Service of Information and Military Police (SIPM), which had military and political control functions and was directly controlled by Franco's headquarters.

New information detectors were created in 1939 to ensure the military's subordination. Following the 'divide-and-rule' logic, Franco avoided intelligence functions that were concentrated in a single organisation. For example, the Service of Personal Information (SIP) aimed to identify subversive tendencies within the military but quickly became a merely bureaucratic body that compiled data about the new recruits. The defence information service of the High Joint Staff, the 'Tercera del Alto', had precarious means and ended up investigating civilian subversive groups in Spain. From 1944, it was in charge of military counter-espionage functions. The Brigade of Social Investigation[19] was an information service linked to the staff offices of the three branches and aimed at eliminating any trace of Republicanism in the ranks. However, its control capacity was also very limited. The 'Brigadilla' of the civil guard, the information systems of the Ministry of Foreign Affairs, the police, the Falange, the 'Hermandad de Alfereces Provisionales', and the 'Servicio de Informacion de Presidencia' were other intelligence services operating during the regime. These sometimes monitored the military but mainly focused on civilian affairs (Ros Agudo 2002; Díaz Fernández 2005). The lack of resources and coordination of the information services constrained their effectiveness as control tools. Moreover, Franco was aware of the unrest that the information services created among the ranks.[20] Thus, once the war was over and the military had been purged, these types of information detectors were not very intensively or intrusively applied within the ranks.

After the agreements with the United States regarding the use of military bases, the intelligence services began to develop again, but fundamentally for defence and civilian control purposes. Only in the 1970s did the intelligence services again acquire salience in the government's toolkit. The Central Documentation Service (SECED) established in 1972 and composed of army officers but hierarchically linked to the prime minister, was the first step towards the organisation of a powerful service concentrating different intelligence functions including counter-subversive action.[21] By 1975, there were still 11 different intelligence services, most of them controlled by the military (Ynfante 1976:24–31) but relatively weak and focused on countering subversion within civil society. The sole well-known example of the utilisation of an intelligence service against the military was the detection and arrest of the UMD members by the Brigade for Social Investigation (Díaz Fernández 2005).

Finally, the lack of strong formal surveillance on the military in Spain was compensated for by informal networks. Over the years, Franco built a far-reaching social network within the military. His privileged position allowed him to receive and spread information as a non-intrusive *nodality* detector and effector. He used the phone, letters, and his official office. The salience of Franco's personal involvement as an information detector in the military is indicated by the extremely abundant private audiences he held with the military. For instance, in 1951 alone, Franco granted personal audiences in his official office to more than 184 military men.[22]

Franco invested personal efforts as a government tool to win the favour and convince some of the critical generals, sometimes dividing them and pitting them against each other (Preston 1990:102–4). For instance, following a letter signed by eight generals requesting the restoration of the monarchy in September 1943, Franco spoke to each of them separately and convinced them that the country was not ready for a monarchy yet (Payne 1967:433–4). To counter the effects of Don Juan's Manifesto in March 1945, Franco immediately organised a seminar with the highest ranking generals in which he personally argued in favour of his regime.[23] In 1948, when some generals proposed again the restoration of the king, Franco spoke personally with each of them and applied different sanctions and rewards to ensure their subordination. Some generals were threatened, some arrested, some promoted, and others simply flattered to dismantle the conspiracy.[24] The fact that Juan Carlos was sent to the three military academies to study was part of a plan devised by the government to build a social network similar to that previously enjoyed by Franco around the future King. Later, Juan Carlos's personal ties proved useful in appeasing the military during the 23-F coup.

7.2.3 Propaganda, censorship, and Franco's personal involvement

Nodality instruments were very important means of control of the military, especially during and right after the Civil War and in the 1970s. The government fundamentally promoted manipulative information effectors that spread the regime's propaganda and censored inconvenient news and ideas. Military speeches, specialised publications, and the mass media were used to raise the morale of the military and to divert the attention away from their professional problems. Thus, *nodality* was used to overstate Franco's leadership skills, the supremacy of moral values over material means, the glorious past of the Spanish military, and the internal threats as means to reinforce unity. With regard to information detectors, the intelligence services, although very important during the war, lost prominence and did not play as central a function as in Portugal. Franco knew the military disliked being spied on and minimised the utilisation of this type of tool. Moreover, he feared the concentration of power and decided to maintain multiple smaller intelligence services. Franco's friendship networks, built before the war, and the constant meetings he held with many military served as a less intrusive but equally effective means to assess the levels of satisfaction and to counter contestation within the ranks.

7.3 Authority

Authority-based rewards and incentives were very important to the government's strategy to control the military. The main *authority*-based rewards used were: appointments of military to top positions in the state apparatus, the special functions as guardians against the internal enemy, a high degree of permissiveness with nonprofessional practices, and finally the integration and recognition of militia fighters as officers. *Authority*-based sanctions and constraints were also used as a means of control among which the most important were: the regulations determining the size of the army; the constraints imposed to the military, in an attempt to reinforce their distinct esprit de corps and conservative values; the sanctions imposed on those that did not fully endorse Franco's decisions; and the legal restrictions imposed on the civilian sphere aiming to attract the support of the most conservative of the military.

7.3.1 Rewards and incentives

Franco, who had been promoted to the rank of general at a very young age thanks to the merit system of the Republic, re-established the seniority principle after the Civil War. The merit-based system of promotions that operated during the Republic had been strongly criticised in the ranks, and Franco decided to abolish it. Nonetheless, in such a centralised regime, Franco and his government enjoyed the authority necessary to reward the loyal military by granting them key positions in the state apparatus. Under normal circumstances, a captain would only be promoted to the rank of major according to his seniority but could aspire to be appointed civil governor or union leader on the basis of merit or allegiance to the regime (Cardona 2001:57). The appointment of the military to senior political/administrative positions was extremely important to ensure loyalty throughout the regime (Viver Pi-Sunyer 1978:70–2; Jerez Mir 1982) (Tables 7.2 and 7.3).

Table 7.2 Percentage of military 'procuradores' (MPs) in Spanish Francoist Cortes

Session	Years	Percentage of military procuradores
I	1943–1946	19.1
II	1946–1949	19.2
III	1949–1952	19.9
IV	1952–1955	20.2
V	1955–1958	22.9
VI	1958–1961	22.8
VII	1961–1964	22
VIII	1964–1967	18
IX	1967–1971	14.9
X	1971–1976	11.3

Source: Agüero (1995:49).

Table 7.3 Military presence in the senior positions in the administration (%)

	Ministers	Undersecretaries	General Directors	Total
Jan.1935–Jul.1945	45.9	42.3	34.1	36.8
Jul.1945–Jul.1952	37.8	37.8	32.1	34.9
Jul.1951–Feb.1957	51.2	51.2	33.3	36.6

Source: Aguilar Olivencia (1999:27).

Although seniority was the general rule, there were special circumstances in which military promotions and distinctions were used to reward allegiance to the regime. Suspicious of a monarchist military conspiracy in 1943, Franco reacted by promoting 26 generals to the rank of lieutenant-general and awarded the Medal of Military Merit to 26 generals and admirals. In March 1945, Franco repeated the tactic by making appointments in order to prevent a new monarchist plot. Muñoz Grandes was appointed Captain-General of Madrid, Moscardó Chief of the Military House, and Solchaga Captain-General of Barcelona (Payne 1987:346–7). In April 1945, Franco, aiming to divide the monarchist camp, bought the allegiance of some of their most prominent figures. He appointed the monarchists José Monasterio and Juan Bautista Sánchez as captain-generals (Cardona 2001:116). At the end of 1959, in order to counter the malaise of the military due to the decolonisation of Morocco, the incidents in the Sahara, and the bottleneck in the promotion system, the government decided to promote 1,075 captains to majors in one week (Busquets 1984 [1971]:109–10; Cardona 2001:202). Finally, Franco even created nobility titles to reward loyal officers: Moscardó was named 'Conde del Alcazar de Toledo' and Juan Antonio Suanzes 'Conde de Fenosa'.[25]

The Francoist government also granted the military some special functions to make them feel empowered and in control. Although the army was not directly involved in the maintenance of public order as during Primo de Rivera's dictatorship, military officers were in charge of leading the security forces (Delgado 2005:60–2). The Law of Police in 1941 established that the cadres of the armed police were military officers, and the statutes of the civil guard in 1942 established its integration into the military structure and its military character (Blanco Valdés 1999:54–5). The security forces were purged after the war. Thousands of positions were filled by ex-combatants from the nationalist camp (Delgado 2005:35–6).

The military also played an important role in the judicial system. They had the capacity to judge civilians and political crimes while they reserved the right to be judged exclusively by military courts. For instance, the Special Tribunal for the Repression of the Freemasonry and Communism established in 1940 was led for several years by General Saliquet. The Law of Political Responsibilities in 1939 provided that the regional courts for political crimes always had to include military judges (Dueñas 1990:149–50). In addition, the powers of the ordinary military courts were far reaching: 270,719 people were court martialed in 1940 (Olmeda 1988:279–80). After 1943, offences against the public order were equated to military rebellion and subject to military jurisdiction (Ballbé 1985:412–3). Equally, the Code of Military Justice of 1945 provided that any information jeopardising national defence could be prosecuted by military courts. Although the far-reaching scope of the military justice was gradually reduced,[26] military courts continued to judge civilians until the end of the regime. In 1971 and 1972, military courts handed down sentences for 277 'political crimes', mainly due to verbal offences directed at the military (Oneto 1975:63–7).

In addition to the political appointments and special functions in internal affairs, the level of tolerance with some unprofessional practices can be considered as a tool for subordinating the military. Spanish officers were permitted to take second jobs or take long-term leave in order to work in private business or the administration to compensate for their very low salaries.[27] It seemed that in the late 1950s, two thirds of the officers in Madrid and one third of those in the provinces had a secondary civil job (Puell de la Villa 2005:207). This practice extended to all levels. For instance, General Gabeiras maintained a secondary job until he became brigadier; General Gutiérrez Mellado took a leave of several years to work in the private sector due to financial problems; even General Barroso, after launching army reforms aimed at professionalisation, requested Franco in a private letter to recommend him for a position on the board of Tabacalera, the national tobacco company.[28]

Moreover, the government often turned a blind eye to army corruption as a means to keep the military under control, especially in the post-war period. Senior officers with business interests used troops and even prisoners of war as cheap labour; they used official cars for private business, and conscripts as handymen or baby-sitters (Preston 1990:105–6). In order to control the generals, Franco gave them a great deal of leeway and often tolerated their abuses of their positions of power (Cardona 2001:119). It was common for officers to resell the goods and materials destined to the military on the black market (Payne 1967:435). Even physical abuses by officers were permitted by the Code of Military Justice supposedly as a means to maintain the discipline of the troops (Cardona 2001:55). In sum, the inaction in these cases were positive *authority* tools that enabled many in the military to enjoy some unofficial benefits.

Finally, the incorporation of militia fighters in the officers' corps of the military was another example of the use of *authority* as a control instrument. This recognition aimed to reinforce loyalty for Francoist principles within the ranks while counterbalancing the monarchist aspiration of many career officers (Preston 1990:139). Out of the 29,033 'alféreces provisionales' that fought in the Francoist camp, 9,758 remained in the army after the conflict (Busquets 1984 [1971]:106–8). The government granted these militia fighters the rank of officer after an eight-month period in a military academy that was created *ad hoc*. The favours to the 'alféreces provisionales' continued throughout the regime, in 1959 out of the 1,075 officers the government decided to promote through an extraordinary procedure, 976 were 'provisionales' (Cardona 2001:202). For Franco, their political loyalty compensated for their lack of military training and the eventual bottleneck this abrupt influx of officers created in the system of promotions.

7.3.2 Sanctions and constraints

The Francoist dictatorship used authority sanctions and constraints in several ways to reinforce military subordination. It limited the military retirement age to reduce the size of the armies; established legal constrains to enhance the esprit de corps; discharged and relocated the military suspected of not endorsing the government; and imposed prohibitions on other actors in Spanish society in order to please the military.

Franco believed that given limited financial resources, a smaller army could be better paid and equipped, and thus more satisfied. Franco used regulation to reduce the size of the army. The two-year reduction in the retirement age in 1952 and the laws stimulating an early passage to the reserve (with generous economic compensations) in 1953 and 1958 were the most significant examples.[29] Nonetheless, in the long run, the success of these instruments was limited; especially the Law of 1958 that did not result in a significant reduction of the number of officers. The problem of oversize persisted after the end of the dictatorship.[30]

Legal constraints were used to reinforce the conservative principles of Francoism within the ranks and to maintain a separate and homogeneous esprit de corps. Secret societies were forbidden and prosecuted, officers suspected of being Masons were placed under surveillance;[31] the military could only marry Catholic Spanish, Latin American, and Filipino women; officers were banned from participating in sports teams; and, until 1941, to dress as civilians. Most importantly, the Code of Military Justice of 1945 introduced the notion of crimes against military honour such as cowardice, unjustified surrender, or homosexuality and imposed severe punishments for them. The military's 'Honour Trials' acted as an *authority* tool based on peer control. Officers could be tried and punished by their peers for any behaviour deemed deviant even in their private lives outside the barracks.

Any displays of the military's insubordination or criticism against the regime or Franco was reprimanded or sanctioned with demotions and relocations (Comas and Mandeville 1986:36). After the monarchic plots in the 1940s, many generals were relocated or sacked. Orgaz went from being high commissioner in Morocco to being Central Chief of Staff, Saliquet was appointed head of the Supreme Council of Military Justice, both positions without command of troops. Varela was sent to Morocco and therefore far from Madrid, and Kindelán was sacked from the Army Higher School and confined in Tenerife. General Aranda was temporarily exiled to Portugal in 1943; and after demanding political asylum in the US embassy, he was arrested for two months and sent to Mallorca in 1946 (Cardona 2001:118, 127). Generals Beigbeder and Kindelán were arrested in 1948. In 1957, Juan Bautista Sánchez, the Captain-General of Barcelona, died when he was about to be discharged for his possible participation in a new monarchic plot, and two colonels close to him were fired (Busquets 1982:141).

The 'liberal' military were also sanctioned by the regime. The government decreed the dissolution of 'Forja' in 1959. Forja, created in 1951, was a group of military officers seeking to develop professional and religious values within the military. Although Forja members were never subversive, they criticised the lack of professionalism in the military. Some of the ideas first promoted by Forja were later embraced by the UMD (Busquets 1982:142–5). In 1970, the reformist Chief of the Joint Staff General Manuel Díez-Alegría was dismissed for holding an interview with the exiled leader of the PCE, Santiago Carrillo. These sanctions satisfied many conservative officers.

Finally, some of the restrictive laws and norms directed at other social actors were very often requested by the military and can be construed as tools to increase military satisfaction: the prohibition on carrying arms for the Falangist and Carlist militias after the war; the prosecution of dissidents by the Tribunal for the Repression of Freemasonry and Communism from 1940 onwards; the Law of Security of the State in 1941 that made strikes and spreading rumours against the regime and the military illegal; the Law of Repression of Banditry and Terrorism in 1947, which reduced individual liberties; the Law of Official Secrets in 1968; and the suppression of the habeas corpus for six months in 1970 are examples of the use of *authority* aimed indirectly at fostering military satisfaction and therefore having a positive impact on its subordination. The Francoist military was very conservative and liked the repressive measures that the regime imposed on society.[32]

7.3.3   Special public order functions and selective permissiveness

Franco enjoyed high levels of support from the military, which granted him the capacity to effectively use *authority* as a source of power. The authority rewards and incentives were crucial control tools. Unlike the Estado Novo which used the 'escolha' as an ordinary mechanism for promotions to the senior ranks, the Francoist government reintroduced the seniority principle. Nonetheless, Franco still had the capacity to reward loyal officers through military distinctions and appointments not only to especially prestigious positions in the military but also in the political-administrative apparatus. The special functions conceded to the military related to the control of internal public order, the general tolerance towards vis-à-vis secondary jobs, and the favourable treatment of 'alfereces provisionales' became salient tools for the military's subordination specific to Spain.

The *authority*-based sanctions and constraints were for the most part similar to those in the Estado Novo. Some regulation was launched to downsize the military to alleviate the scarcity of material means and to enhance the distinct conservative esprit de corps of the military. Although there was a great permissiveness concerning the abuse of power and unprofessional practices, Franco did not tolerate any criticisms against the regime. Sanctions were imposed on those in the military who were critical of the regime. The 'Honours Trials' established by Franco, through which the military had the capacity and obligation to control their peers and the utilisation of more constraining laws on Spanish society in order to increase military satisfaction, differentiate his from the Portuguese regime.

Overall, there were no major changes in the use of *authority* tools throughout the regime.

7.4 Treasure

In Spain, as in Portugal, the poor economic conditions during the regime precluded the utilisation of treasure tools. In the 1960s, when the economy grew and therefore more financial resources were available, the government prioritised social expenditure and investment in the infrastructure over defence or military expenditures. Nonetheless, there is still evidence of the utilisation of some *treasure* tools; fundamentally salary raises. This section briefly analyses the evolution of defence budgets explaining whether these changes were linked to efforts to impact the military's subordination.

7.4.1 Evolution of military budgets

The disastrous socioeconomic situation and the oversized army inherited from the Civil War limited the leeway of the government. The economic situation of the country after the Civil War was extremely dire (Jiménez Jiménez 1987). The Second World War aggravated the crisis. This is evidenced by the fact that against the official pro-Axis discourse and with the mediation of Portugal, Spain secretly accepted the provision of thousands of tonnes of food products funded by the UK government in 1940,[33] phosphates by the French government in 1941,[34] and diesel fuel from the United States in 1942.[35] Nonetheless, after the end of the Second World War, the United States did not offer Marshall Plan aid to Spain, which continued the autarchic economic policy adopted in 1939. It is estimated that not until 1950 did Spain recover the per capita level of income and industrial activity of 1935 (Pérez Muinelo 2009:111). Military expenditure remained high during the Second World War; some years, it accounted for more than half of the total budget of the state. After the Second World War, budgets declined, both as a percentage of the GNP and of the total public expenditure (Figures 7.1 and 7.2).

After 1953, the economic aid received from the United States through cheap raw materials, food, and credits as well as the liberalisation of the economy through the Stabilisation Plan (1959–61) and the Economic Development Plan (1964–7) reinforced economic growth in Spain (Pérez Muinelo 2009:113). However, the general improvement in the economy did not translate into military budgets. During the 1950s and 1960s, the economy and total public expenditures constantly grew; but there was a decline in the weight of military expenditures due to the strong increases in other budgets, especially those of public infrastructure, education, and agriculture (Comín and Diaz 2005:929–34). The technocrats that had controlled the Francoist government since 1957 prioritised

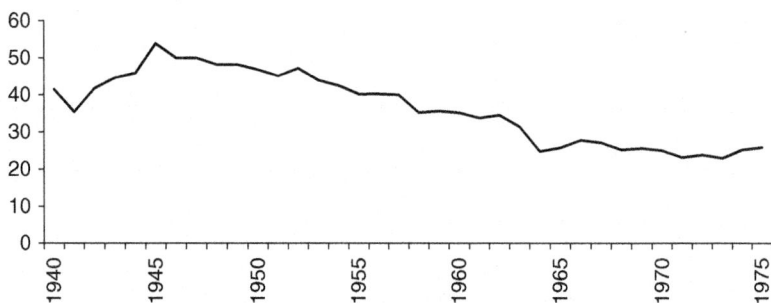

Figure 7.1 Spanish military budget as a percentage of the total budget (1940–75)*

Note: * Figures include Military Administration, Military Security and Public Order Forces (Guardia Civil and Dirección General de la Seguridad). See detail in Olmeda (1988:200–3).

Source: Based on Olmeda (1988:204).

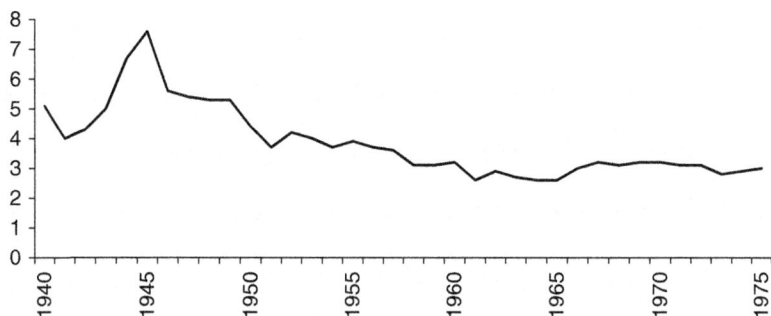

Figure 7.2 Spanish military budget as a percentage of GDP (1940–75)

Source: Based on Olmeda (1988:204).

economic development over military and defence problems (Aguilar Olivencia 1999:111). Despite the nominal increases in the budget of the three branches (Figure 7.3) there was a continuous decline in military expenditures as percentage of total public expenditure (Figure 7.1).

Overall, budgets were low as a percentage of the GDP (see comparison with NATO countries in Chapter 4, Table 4.4) and per soldier. For instance, in 1966 the military expenditure in Spain was 1,783 dollars per soldier, similar to that of Portugal (1,660) and far below other Western European countries, such as the United Kingdom (12,763), France (12,087), and Italy (5,315) (de Miguel 1975:161). In 1975, the military expenditures in Spain were 4,538 dollars per soldier, more than that of

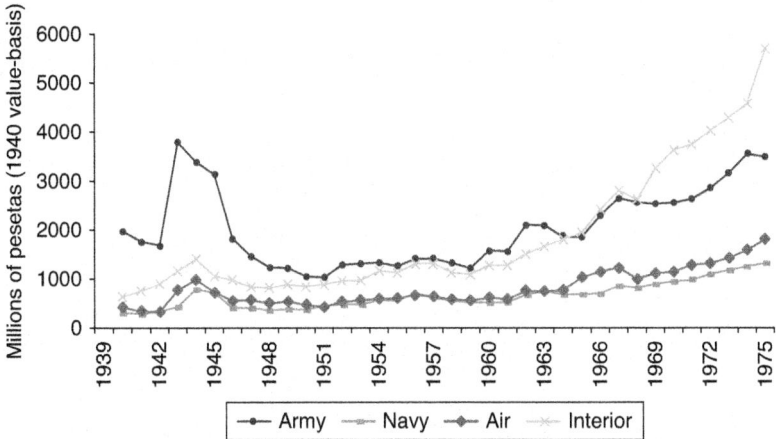

Figure 7.3 Spanish military budgets in constant pesetas of 1940 (including extraordinary allocations)

Sources: Inflation from Maluquer de Motes (2005:1292). Military budgets and extraordinary budget allocations in Comín and Diaz (2005:929, 947).

Portugal (3,230) but still far below the United Kingdom (28,901), France (21,440), and Italy (9,242) (CESEDEN 1988:113).

7.4.2 Staff expenditures

Franco's government saw its capacity to use staff expenditure as a means to control the military constrained. In the military, as in the rest the public administration, the evolution of staff expenditures was determined by law. Budgetary incrementalism and the repetition of the allocations was a general practice during the regime (Gunther 1980:293–6; Olmeda 1988:217–34). Although the share of the total military budgets devoted to the staff was very high (Figure 7.4), most of the financial resources were allocated to officers' salaries and the general living costs of the troops. The expenditure on military salaries was determined by the size of the army (nearly 300,000 men) and, as in Portugal, by the disproportionately high level of senior officers whose salaries were very high (Tables 7.4 and 7.5).

However, Francoist governments still had some flexibility to use treasure tools. During the 1940s, the government utilised important extraordinary budgetary allocations for the military ministries. These allocations were treasure tools to offset the high inflation of the 1940s (344 per cent over the decade) which also damaged the purchasing power

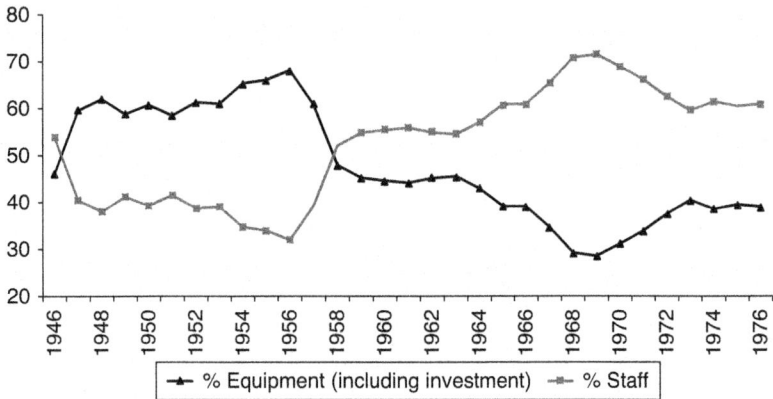

Figure 7.4   Defence budget distribution of expenditures in percentage (1946–76)
Source: Based on Pérez Muinelo (2009:93).

Table 7.4   Percentage of generals among total officers in active duty in Spain, Portugal, and the United States

	Spain		Portugal		US	
	Year	Generals/ Officers (%)	Year	Generals/ Officers (%)	Year	Generals/ Officers (%)
Army	1930	1.3	1930	0.5	1920	0.4
	1968	1.3	1965	1.8	1950	0.8
	1975	1.5	1970	1.8		
Navy	1930	1.4	1930	1.9	1920	1.3
	1968	2.3	1965	3	1950	0.8
	1975	2.2	1974	2.1		
Air Force	1968	1.7	1965	2	1950	0.5
	1975	1.5	1973	3		

Sources: Based on Jordana and Ramió (2005:1015–18), Carrilho (1985:442), and Janowitz (1960:67).

of the military (Maluquer de Motes 2005:1292). Thus, salary raises kept discontent under control. For instance, in 1940, Franco increased the salaries of military officers: 15 per cent for colonels, 26 for captains, and 40 for first lieutenants. Another 40 per cent general pay raise took place in 1949 (Payne 1967:527–32). The next significant general pay raise took place in 1956 to counter military discontent resulting from the loss of

Table 7.5   Military annual salaries and annual per capita consumption in Spain (in pesetas)*

Ranks	1936–1939	1940	1949	1956
Captain General	30,000	50,000	70,000	–
Lieutenant General	27,000	30,000	42,000	68,000
Major General	22,000	25,000	35,000	57,700
Brigadier General	17,000	20,000	28,000	48,500
Colonel	13,000	15,000	21,000	41,500
Lieutenant Colonel	11,000	13,000	18,200	37,100
Major	9,500	11,000	15,400	31,300
Captain	7,500	9,500	13,300	25,000
First Lieutenant	5,000	7,000	10,500	19,000
Second Lieutenant	4,000	6,000	9,100	16,150
Average per capita annual consumption	1,111	1,484	3,858	9,753

Notes: *Total per capita consumption includes food and tobacco, clothing, rent and utilities, hygiene and personal care, transportation, leisure, and others.

Sources: Based on Payne (1967:527–532), Nicolau (2005:125–6), and Maluquer de Motes (2005:1286)

Morocco: 104 per cent for majors and lieutenant-colonels, 81 for first lieutenants, and 62 for generals (Cardona 2001:1973).

The government was more concerned with the loyalty of senior officers than with that of junior officers. Junior officers' salaries, despite the nominal pay raises, were not enough to cover the expenditures of a family, which in the case of the military tended to be very large. They relied heavily on secondary jobs and on the services and goods provided by the regime. Top ranking officers, in addition to higher salaries, enjoyed other benefits and subsidies that increased their income over 50 per cent. For instance, in 1953 about 2,000 senior officers retired with their full salary (Payne 1967:439–43, 532–4).

In sum, despite the rigidity of the budgeting process linked to regulations and structural features, the government used some extraordinary salary raises, essentially as palliative measures, attempting to counterbalance the degradation of purchasing power and to limit military discontent. The clear bias in favour of senior officers can also be considered as a *treasure* control tool.

7.4.3   Equipment expenditure

As the government's financial resources were extremely constrained the living conditions of the military were prioritised over the expenditure on weaponry and material means. After the Second World War, the external threats and the emphasis on improving military capabilities dwindled and the government largely relied on American military aid to partially modernise equipment. The use of *treasure* for equipment expenditure remained very low until the 1970s, when new programmes for material acquisitions were launched.

Although the part of the defence budget in equipment was higher that that on staff until the late 1950s this was to a great extent due to the investment and expenditure in military housing, hospitals, food stores and pharmacies, highly appreciated especially during the period of extreme economic deprivation that followed the Civil War. For instance at the end of the 1940s the military managed 21 hospitals and 23 health centres compared to 34 hospitals, and 28 health centres in the early 1960s (Massons 1994:549–53).

Overall, the Spanish Military were poorly equipped. The large quantities of weapons acquired during the Civil War became technologically obsolete and there was a lack of spare parts (Preston 1990:136–40). The gold reserves of the Bank of Spain had been depleted due to the military effort of the Republican government. The Second World War limited the capacity to import weapons and even the availability of basic resources for their manufacture. Before the agreements with the US in 1953 the equipment of Spanish Military was even older and more inadequate than that of the Portuguese ones. In 1953 Spain, with a larger army, had only 950 trucks, 20 modern tanks and 548 pieces of artillery while Portugal had 3698 military trucks, 193 modern tanks and 619 pieces of artillery (Telo 1996:221, 357).

Later, Spain became a valuable ally for the US thanks to its geographical location, its resources in terms of raw materials and its relatively large army (Liedtke 1999:229–35). The Madrid Pact signed in 1953 allowed the US to establish Air Forces and navy bases on Spanish soil in exchange for help in rebuilding and modernising Franco's military. The financial aid received from the US was very important for the morale of the Spanish military. The impact of this support was particularly positive for the Air Force that until 1953 was using airplanes from the Civil War.[36] From 1954 to 1964, Spain received military aid of 600 million dollars value and extra economic aid of 500 million. In addition, Spain obtained one billion dollars from American private institutions and 500 million from the US Export-Import

Bank (Payne 1967:446; Liedtke 1999). The value of the materials received from the US was higher than the ordinary allocations for investment in materials in the defence budgets (Pérez Muinelo 2009:114). The agreements with the US had also paved the way for the restoration of military cooperation with France, Germany, Italy and the UK. In addition to the purchase of weapons, Spain produced in its military industrial complex equipment that had been patented by its European allies.

Still, the funds received by Spain from 1953 to 1963 were very low compared to those received by the European beneficiary countries of the Marshall Plan (Barciela Escolá 2000). For instance, France and the United Kingdom, received six times as much from the United States; Italy four times; Germany three times; Greece and Turkey twice as much (Cardona 2001:211). Moreover, financial aid decreased. In 1963 Franco obtained a 100 million dollars loan from the US Export-Import Bank, 100 million dollars in military equipment and the permission to buy 50 million dollars worth of materials. The financial aid obtained by the renegotiation of the pacts in 1970 was reduced to 50 million dollars of military aid and 25 million dollars in loans (Salas López 1974:301–3; Liedtke 1999:240–1).

The agreements of mutual defence with the US and the cooperation with other Western countries injected significant quantities of military materiel and were very positively perceived by the military, but they also entailed some important downsides. First, the concessions of sovereignty in return for the financial support created unease in the ranks.[37] Second, the military industry became gradually more dependent from the US and other Western European powers (Daguzan 1982:107–12). Investment in military research was reduced.[38] Finally, American military aid led the government to believe that they could rely exclusively on foreign aid to modernise equipment. In the successive years, governmental funds that should have been normally destined to the military ministries were diverted to other ministries.[39] Figure 7.4 in p.152 shows the drastic reduction of the percentage of equipment expenditure in military budgets after Spain started receiving US military aid.

Little attention was paid to the equipment of the military and military working conditions remained poor (Gutiérrez Mellado and Picatoste 1983:56). Only in the 1970s did the modernisation of the equipment become a priority for the government. The Law 32/1971 sought to launch a new programme of investment and renewal of equipment of the Military during the period 1972–6 and in 1975 the Council of Ministers declared the national defence a priority (Pérez Muinelo 2009:116). This

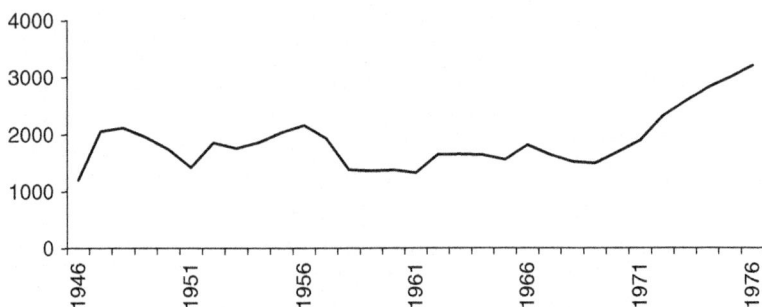

Figure 7.5   Defence equipment expenditure (including investments) in constant million euros of 2009 (1946–76)

Source: Based on Pérez Muinelo (2009:93).

more important utilisation of *treasure* to improve military material conditions can be observed in Figure 7.5.

7.4.4   Scarcity of resources and external dependence

Treasure was a scarce resource for Francoist government and its utilisation vis-à-vis the military was constrained by the size of the army and also the excessive proportion of senior officers. *Treasure* was a resource that had been depleted due to the Civil War. When the economic situation improved, the government preferred to invest in the industrial and social development of the country rather than in the military and defence. Most of the resources of the regular military budget were devoted to salaries and other living expenses for the army, such as housing, hospitals, pharmacies and food stores. Salary raises and economic benefits were subject to regulations and there was little flexibility in the use of salary expenditure to ensure military obedience.

Nonetheless, Franco used extraordinary budget allocations and salary raises, but these were fundamentally designed to compensate the impact of inflation and loss of purchasing power of the military. The high salaries and economic benefits received by top rank officers shows the government was more concerned with the subordination of senior officers. The purchase of equipment and weapons was not central to the strategy of military subordination. No modernisation was conducted after the Civil War and the situation remained dramatic until 1953. After the defence agreements of 1953, thanks to the US military aid, Franco's government acquired equipment and materials which improved the defence capacity of the military and the morale of the military. However, overall, the government did not pay attention to the quantity and the adequacy of the material means of the military until the 1970s when equipment expenditure was prioritised and grew steadily.

7.5 Conclusions

During the Civil War and the early 1940s the utilisation of coercive *organisation* power was very intense. Franco's initial totalitarian repressive strategy served to cleanse the military (and civil society) but also overstretched the Spanish judiciary and prison systems. Coinciding with the demise of the Axis and totalitarianism in Western Europe, the government decided to reduce drastically the use of coercive *organisation* tools vis-à-vis the military. The non-coercive uses of *organisation* became more important than the coercive ones. For instance, indoctrination through the military education system, an organisational design based on a 'divide-and-rule' strategy and the capacity of the state to supply services, goods and jobs were used for control purposes. Overall, the organisational power of the state was used not so much to improve the military professional skills or enhance Spanish defence capabilities but to reward loyalty. This shows a discrepancy with Portugal where from 1950, due to NATO membership, important reforms had been introduced in organisational design, military education and training aiming at improving defence coordination and professionalisation. In the 1960s, the Estado Novo abandoned these reforms due the Colonial Wars. Conversely, the Sidi-Ifni War (1957–8) and the cooperation with other Western military triggered some gradual changes in military education in Spain during the 1960s.

The utilisation of *nodality* effectors to keep the military away from politics and loyal to the regime was very similar to that in Portugal. Propaganda and censorship were pervasive. In Spain, the intensity was higher especially due to the importance that information control had acquired during the Civil War and to the longer insulation of the regime and of the Spanish military. Franco disliked the idea of spying on the military. He largely trusted them (after the purges), felt close enough to them to obtain information through informal networks and knew they would feel harassed if spied upon by other state institutions.

Franco had centralised the executive and legislative powers and shaped state institutions to his convenience, acquiring an extensive capacity to use his legal *authority* as a means of control. As in Portugal, *authority* incentives and rewards were extremely important. The military enjoyed important powers in the Francoist regime. They controlled the security forces and held broad judiciary powers. Nontheless a fundamental difference with the Estado Novo can be found in the system of military promotions. Salazar introduced the 'escolha' merit-based system. Franco restored the seniority principle for military promotions but used his power to appoint loyal officers to important positions in the government and the political-administrative apparatus of the state. Franco's government also enacted laws to allow militia fighters to integrate into the permanent structure of the army. This was a means to reward those who had fought in his camp and to introduce in the army men that strongly endorsed the values of the new regime and that would later act as an internal check on dissent within the ranks. To a lesser extent, *authority* was also used in a constraining fashion to reinforce the 'esprit de corps', reduce the size of the armies and to sanction those suspected disloyal to the regime. Moreover, repressive or action constraining tools applied on society usually had a positive effect on the satisfaction of the very conservative Spanish military. Franco's regime did not tolerate any type of criticism from the ranks. Nonetheless, overall Franco opted for a 'carrot' approach to *authority* with the military.

Finally, the utilisation to *treasure* tools in Spain was constrained by a lack of resources. Three years of Civil War had a devastating impact on the Spanish economy. Simultaneously, the international context of instability and the wars pushed the governments to maintain a large army that, due to the profusion of senior rank officers, limited the flexibility in terms of the allocation of financial resources. Although there is evidence of the utilisation of direct treasure tools, general salary raises and generous financial compensations for the senior officers, the impact on subordination was mild. Despite the fact that most defence budgets were spent on salaries, these remained low, especially for lower rank officers. *Organisation, authority* and *nodality* instruments became necessary to compensate for the frustration that could have emerged for the poorly paid services of the military. The utilisation of equipment expenditure was even less relevant. The resources devoted to the acquisition of materials and equipment were minimal. Some ideas and perceptions underpin these choices. Franco, like Salazar, believed the main threat came from the internal enemy. Therefore a modernisation of the weaponry and equipment necessary for conventional warfare was not a top priority. Moreover, the military became used to the outdated and meagre equipment and ended up, thanks to government propaganda, believing than moral values were more important than the material. From 1953 onwards, the US began to supply foreign military aid that enabled a relative modernisation of the equipment and pushed new defence doctrines. Nonetheless, in the approach to *treasure* remained largely unchanged. In Spain the economic paradigm embraced by the technocratic governments channelled the funds available thanks to the economic boom in the 1960s to other non-military expenditures. *Treasure* tools continued to be used until the 1970s when some efforts were made to improve the material conditions of the military.

8
Tools of Government in the Spanish Transition to Democracy

The Spanish transitional governments deeply transformed their mix of control tools to face the new challenges that the military posed and to enhance professionalism in the ranks. The role and attitude of the military in the Spanish transition and early stages of democracy was completely different than that of Portugal's. While in Portugal the military defined and controlled the political transformations, in Spain the military was excluded from the most important political decisions. Whereas in Portugal, the left-wing military dominated the ranks, in Spain extreme right-wing officers were the most influential. While in Portugal the military pushed for thorough reforms, in Spain the military wanted to keep an authoritarian regime and resisted most changes that the governments launched. These different circumstances had a strong impact on the choice of control tools, in particular during the period of the UCD governments (1976–82). Suárez enjoyed great legitimacy only in the eyes of civil society, not the military. Afraid that some control tools could generate more discontent in the military, he adopted a somewhat laissez-faire approach to the military's subordination. This strategy was proven inadequate by the military's growing disloyalty and various anti-government plots. The first PSOE government (1982–6) undertook many changes in its control strategy in order to consolidate the military's subordination. González had wider social support and did not have to face as serious military challenges as Suárez.

Table 8.1 summarises this chapter. Coercive *organisation* tools were marginal before the 23-F coup and inexistent afterwards (Section 8.1.1). There were important changes in the use of non-coercive *organisation*, in particular after 1982. Military education was reformed to stimulate professionalism and emphasise technical skills over indoctrination. Military training was also reinforced thanks to the closer collaboration

Table 8.1 Summary of tools of government in Spain (1976–86)

	Tools	Trajectory
Organisation	*Coercive* (Section 8.1.1): The army acted as a self-control device. Civil guard and police forces were minimally used	Very low utilisation (none after the 23-F events)
	Non-coercive (Section 8.1.2): Military education abandoned the emphasis on moral indoctrination. Training was reinforced alongside the process of modernisation of the equipment and incorporation into NATO	Education and training grew especially after 1982
	Provision of services was reinforced (ISFAS)	Provision of services grew from 1978
	Provision of jobs in the public administration	Abandoned during transition
	Organisational design employed to increase coordination centralise power in the hands of the government	Extremely important. It salience grew with the PSOE governments
Nodality	*Information effectors* (Section 8.2.1): Media were used to gain support for the democratic reforms: Public TV and mainstream private press. Lack of control on the reactionary press	Lower utilisation than during Francoism. The government dismantled the propaganda and censorship machinery. Free press law and elimination of the state-owned press
	Use of formal and informal meetings, visits, public speeches to convince the military and in particular the senior ranks of the advantages of the new political system and democratic values. Personal involvement of Suárez, defence ministers, and the king	Decreasing importance during the PSOE government which focused on achieving material obedience rather than on changing the ideology
	Information detectors (Section 8.2.2): The secret services spied on the military and neutralised some military plots	The use of secret services increased. First centralisation of functions into CESID and after the 23-F coup reorganisation of CESID
	The personal network of the defence ministers	Stable
	The independent media, academics, and politicians were used as a source of information	Growing salience

Continued

Table 8.1 Continued

	Tools	Trajectory
Authority	*Rewards and incentives* (Section 8.3.1): Appointments and promotions sometimes decided by the government circumventing the seniority principle	The interference of the government in promotions decreased in practice during the socialist period
	Symbolic rewards: centrality of the armed forces in the Constitution, new military statutes and the figure of the king as (honorary) supreme commander	Mostly during UCD governments
	Degree of autonomy of the military. Ambiguity in the line of command	Very high until the PSOE government then drastically reduced
	NATO membership pleased many officers and created incentives to maintain subordination	Growing salience since 1982
	Sanctions and constraints (Section 8.3.2): Legal constrains aiming to enhance professionalism (prohibition to political activities or expressing political views, elimination of multi-job situation, reduction of size of the army and retirement age)	The regulation aiming to increase professionalism and reduce non-defence functions were initiated by UCD but reinforced under the socialists
	Punishment to officers responsible for acts of indiscipline or anti-government plots	Very abundant but soft sanctions during UCD governments. Severe sanctions to the few acts of insubordination under PSOE's rule
	Limitations to the power held by the military. Their power within the defence sphere was reduced and the functions as guardians of internal order (police and justice) eliminated	The process was initiated by the UCD but the PSOE government gave a strong impulse making it a priority
Treasure	*Staff expenditure* (Section 8.4.1): General salary raises to prevent protests, compensate inflation and achieve exclusive dedication (professionalism). In parallel with the effort of reduction of the size of the army. Pensions were increased to stimulate early retirement	More frequent utilisation than during Francoism. The weight of staff expenditure decreased during Suárez's governments and remained stable during González's first mandate
	Equipment expenditure (Section 8.4.2): Modernisation of weaponry and materials. Expenditure in equipment was prioritised and some flexibility introduced in the budgetary	Increasing concern for military material means until 1985. Prioritised over staff

with NATO. Very important changes were conducted in the organisational design to centralise power under the defence and prime ministers. The provision of services grew but that of jobs was abandoned for being considered counterproductive for military professionalism (Section 8.1.2). As for *nodality*, information detectors gained relevance to the detriment of information effectors. The government dismantled the Francoist propaganda and censorship machinery but reinforced the secret services (especially after the 23-F coup) (Section 8.2). *Authority* incentives and rewards were more intensively used during the UCD period. The liberal military was promoted to important positions. Symbolic rewards and high levels of autonomy were granted to the military (Section 8.3.1). From 1982, the socialist government intensified sanctions and constraints in order to enhance professionalism and limit military autonomy and power (Section 8.3.2). Although *treasure* remained the least salient category in the toolkit, its relative weight increased, in particular that of equipment expenditures (Section 8.4).

8.1   Organisation

Non-coercive *organisation* continued to be preferred over coercive *organisation* tools. Although there were a few examples of the utilisation of coercive power, in Spain only the military could effectively control the military by violent means. Moreover, the memories of the Civil War made coercive *organisation* tools undesirable. Conversely, non-coercive *organisation* tools were extremely important for the military's subordination. The provision of services replaced the provision of jobs in the public administration. Military education and training and, more importantly, the organisational design sought to improve the defence capacity of the Spanish military and its professionalism so that they could concentrate on their duties and not challenge the government.

8.1.1   Coercive organisation

Coercive *organisation* tools were uncommon during this period. Nonetheless, they were employed on at least two occasions. First the state's organisational capacity was used as a deterrent tool during an illegal demonstration of members of the armed police and civil guard, which had military status, in Madrid on 17 December 1976. The armed police and the Brunete Armoured Division of the army (DAC) were deployed to control the demonstrators. Eventually, the demonstration was dissolved and a violent intervention was not necessary (Fernández López 2000:24). Two-hundred and eighty policemen and civil guards were arrested and kept in custody in the prison of Soria, 240 were sanctioned, amongst which 14 were dismissed (Delgado 2005:296–300).

The second and best-known case of utilisation of coercive organisation tools occurred during the 23-F coup attempt in 1981. The deterrent capacity of the DAC and the police forces was important for the neutralisation of the 23-F coup. Although initially the insurgent officers deployed some of the DAC units to control strategic targets, such as TV and radio stations and the congress, the intervention of the Captain-General of Madrid Quintana Lacaci and the JEME General Sáez de Tejada reversed the situation. They persuaded the heads of the DAC units to return to their quarters and to use their coercive power to neutralise the insurgents. The plotters had lost the coercive superiority and their chances to succeed militarily (Fernández López 2000:136–54). Moreover, the national police, following the orders of General Sáez de Santamaría, surrounded the congress to prevent any type of support to the group of 200 civil guards that kept the members of the parliament hostage. The special operations units from civil guard and the national police had a plan to free the congressmen by force. In the end, the use of force was not necessary (Prego 1999:619). The plotters were convinced to follow the orders of the military's hierarchy and the king and surrendered without offering resistance.

Despite these examples, the use of coercive *organisation* tools to control the military remained marginal, no state organisation had the power to deter the army and moreover the government did not want to challenge the military. The approach was to show confidence in the obedience and self-control of the military. The memories of the Spanish Civil War were very strong amongst political leaders and the society at large and ruled out the use of violence as a control device during transition (Pérez Díaz 1993; Aguilar 1997).

8.1.2 Non-coercive organisation

The non-coercive use of organisation continued to be important for governments after the death of Franco, although some evolution can be identified. Military education was used to introduce democratic values, enhance cooperation amongst branches, and stimulate professionalism. The UCD introduced changes in the curricula of the military academies, including the study of the constitution (Rodríguez Sahagún 1986:193). The need for inter-branch coordination was emphasised.[1] Later, the PSOE government tried to shape the process of socialisation in the military and make the military accept the new political system. The responsibilities for military education were transferred to the coordination body of the Defence Ministry and the autonomy of the branches was reduced.[2] The CESEDEN and the Institute of Strategic Studies were two fundamental tools in promoting professional training over indoctrination and moral values (Agüero 1995; Barrachina 2002). From 1982, the General Directorate of Information and Social Relations of Defence (DRISDE) served to promote wider and more professional information about defence, workshops, cultural activities, and collaboration with universities and research centres (Ministerio de Defensa 1986:393–405). Moreover, military training improved. The membership in NATO introduced a series of joint military exercises and courses with other militaries which provided the Spanish military with a benchmark in terms of professionalism that promoted a change in their views.[3]

Despite all these efforts a gap in terms of values and preoccupations between Spanish and other militaries from Western countries persisted. In Spain, there was a paternalistic conception of education that prioritised the instruction of values over that of skills. The gap and lack of exchanges between civil and military education persisted.[4] The most of the military rejected the plots against the new democratic system. However, this was not due to a change in their values and political ideas but to their sense of discipline and loyalty to the king and the senior officers that supported the government.

The provision of services to the military was also enhanced by the early transition in the democratic governments. The goals and financial efforts linked to the developmentalism of the 1960s undermined military salaries and social services (Aguilar Olivencia 1999:117). The fundamental instrument to correct this trend during transition was the Social Institute of the Armed Forces (ISFAS). The institute was created in 1975 and began to deliver its services in 1978 (Puell de la Villa 1997:212–13, 2008:225–43). The ISFAS provided health and economic services to over 300,000 members. The ISFAS also organised cultural and leisure activities, supported retired officers and, particularly, promoted the construction of military housing (Rodríguez Sahagún 1986:193). For instance, up to 50 per cent of the military enjoyed military housing in 1984 (Bañón 1985).

On the other hand, the provision of jobs in the administration, crucial during the dictatorship, was severely reduced. Having more than one job became incompatible with the standards of professionalism. The traditional positions reserved for the military in the administration or public companies were eliminated.[5] The government believed that to improve their efficiency and reach civilian supremacy the military had to be disentangled from the political-administrative apparatus and concentrated exclusively on military duties.

Most important, the government used its capacity to modify the organisational design of the defence and military institutions as a tool of control. The logic was the opposite to that of 'divide-and-rule' that Franco has imposed. The military reforms initiated by General Gutiérrez Mellado and the UCD governments aimed to gradually centralise power in civilian hands while regrouping and adapting the structures that were scattered amongst the military ministries to increase coordination. The reorganisation was very ambitious and affected 440,000 people. The goal was to improve the operational capacity and efficiency of the military[6] but also to consolidate civilian supremacy (Rodríguez Sahagún 1986:190–2).

This process of re-designing the defence organisation was gradual and followed several steps. On 8 February 1977, the reorganisation of the military was launched with the creation of a Joint Chiefs of Staff (JUJEM) hierarchically linked to the prime minister.[7] This new institution worked to create a unified doctrine, integrate plans of defence, and to advise the National Defence Board (Junta) on military policy. This tool was an intermediate step to establish a unitary Defence Ministry because it started separating operational from administrative tasks previous to the reunification of the three ministries.[8] The second important step by Suárez's governments was the regulation of the functions and organisation of the Defence Ministry[9] and the redefinition of the functions of the higher defence institutions including the JUJEM, the National Defence Board, and the Chiefs of Staff of the military branches.[10]

However the new configuration of these defence bodies can still be characterised as a dual stucture due to the separation of political-administrative and military affairs and due to the fact that the general headquarters of the army, navy and air force were integrated in this new structure but not the three branches as such (Navajas Zubeldía 1995:181; Serra 2008:149). This ambiguity was mainly introduced because most of the military did not want to give up their autonomy in military affairs, did not share the ideal of civilian supremacy in defence issues, and wanted two different hierarchical chains for civilians and the military.

The same concern and ambiguity was reflected in the new Organic Law 6/1980 that regulated the basic criteria of national defence and military organisation. The law did not make explicit the subordination of the JUJEM and the newly created Chief of Defence Staff (JEMAD) to the government. Although the JUJEM and JEMAD were created following the American model for which civilian supremacy was a basic principle,[11] most of the military continued to think that the defence minister and the government remained merely administrators of military budgets (Puell de la Villa 2005:236).

The organisation of the Defence Ministry was more deeply reformed by the PSOE government, mainly through Organic Law 1/1984 and Royal Decree 135/1984. These reforms concentrated power in civilian hands and limited the autonomy of the military. The central coordination body of the Defence Ministry was restructured into three sections,[12] two of them led by civilians. Its personnel grew steadily and many competences were absorbed from the three branches, which lost much of their autonomy (Table 8.2).[13] The defence minister became responsible for the elaboration and implementation of military policy and, by delegation from the prime minister, of the command, coordination, and leadership of the military (Ministerio de Defensa 1986:63). Civilians saw their participation in the ministry grow and their influence gradually surpassed that of the military (Agüero 1995:192–6).

The JUJEM passed from being the supreme collegiate body in the chain of command to being merely an advisory board for the defence minister. The unified command of the military was placed under the direct authority of the minister in contrast to the UCD period when the head of the JUJEM played that role (Powell 2001:374). With Law 1/1984, the JEMAD became the main assistant to the minister in the planning and execution of operative aspects of military policy and represented the minister and the military in international organisations (Ministerio de Defensa 1986:63). The new unified intelligence service (CESID) and the civil guard were directly subordinated to the defence minister, although the former was functionally dependent on the prime minister and the latter on the interior minister. In 1984, the territorial organisation of the military was simplified. Spain was divided in six military regions and two military zones for the Canary and Balearic Islands.[14] Finally, in 1985, the relationships within the Defence Ministry were regulated with the purpose of overcoming red tape and to facilitate information flows.[15]

In sum, the reorganisation launched by the socialist government intended to reduce the frictions between the branches and increased the contacts and collaboration amongst them.[16] Most changes in the design of the defence organisations aimed to enhance the coordination and centralisation of decisions into civilian hands.

Table 8.2 Percentage of the total defence budget allocated to the central coordination bodies

1975	1976	1977	1978	1979	1980	1981	1982	1983	1984	1985	1986
0.42	0.41	0.38	5.46	5.75	6.85	8.6	11.93	14.3	12.81	13.97	16.85

Source: Based on Pérez Muinelo (2009:91).

8.1.3   Professionalisation and centralisation

During the Spanish transition, the use of the *organisation* capacity as a control tool evolved. The changes can be mostly spotted in the non-coercive tools. The use of the coercive *organisation* instruments on the military such as the armed police or civil guard continued to be marginal. The fighting capacity of some army units could not be challenged by violent means. The memories of the Civil War and the fear to the repetition of any type of armed conflict disqualified coercive tools as valid control methods.

The government preferred non-coercive *organisation* tools. Amongst them, the institutional and organisational design was the most salient for the subordination of the military. Franco had shaped the organisation of the military with a divide-and-rule logic to eliminate any concentration of power and potential challenge to his personal leadership. On the other hand, the transition governments aimed to improve coordination amongst the branches and efficiency as well as to gradually concentrate decision-making power in the hands of the civilians in the Defence Ministry. Gradually, military education switched from indoctrination of values to development of skills and training, especially after NATO membership in 1982. The development of professionalism was expected to reduce military interventionism. Following the same logic, the government stopped providing jobs for the military in the public administration because these diverted the attention away from purely military duties. In parallel, the government increased the provision of services for the military, mainly through the ISFAS, as a means to increase their well-being and to compensate for low salaries.

8.2   Nodality

The use of *nodality* by the governments changed drastically after the death of Franco. The propaganda and censorship machinery that Franco had used to indoctrinate the military and society was dismantled. Suárez's governments used formal and informal channels of communication to persuade the military of the virtues of the political and military reforms. However, fuelled by the reactionary media, anti-democratic attitudes persisted in the military. The socialist government reduced its reliance on information effectors prioritising material subordination over ideological endorsement. Additionally, information detectors gained importance, especially after the 23-F coup. The independent media and the new centralised secret services became a check on the military.

8.2.1 Information effectors

Propaganda and censorship had been identified with the authoritarian rule and the democratic government tried to avoid them. Rather than eliminating or imposing manufactured information, Suárez's governments used the media, meetings, speeches, and official communications to convince the military, and society at large, of the advantages of the political and military reforms. After the mild results of Suárez's information strategy, the socialist government reduced the utilisation of effectors and concentrated on strengthening detectors.

Suárez's will to break with the information control of the authoritarian period is revealed by the Royal Decree 24/1977, which established the freedom of expression and information, which was later also enshrined in the 1978 Constitution. The propaganda machinery was also dismantled. The official cinema news report NO-DO disappeared in May 1978 and most state-owned newspapers were closed in June 1979 (Martín de la Guardia 2008:250–65).

However, the media continued to be used in the military's subordination. The Office for Information, Diffusion and Public Relations was established in order to improve the image of the Defence Ministry and the military in the media. The government needed to counter the effects of the extreme right-wing newspapers, such as 'El Alcazar' and 'El Imparcial', which launched a smear campaign against the government.[17] The privately owned mainstream press, such as 'ABC', 'Diario 16', and 'El País', built a consensus in favour of the political reforms and provided nuanced opinions on the military (Cayón García 1995:465–77), thus, playing a stabilising role between the military and society at large (Busquets and Losada 2003:166; Preston 2004:498). Suárez also used his oratory skills and influence on the Spanish national television to consolidate his image in public opinion, the support of which served to shield the government from attacks from the extreme right and facilitated the reforms (Preston 1986; Morán 2009). Notwithstanding, Suárez's media strategy was overall too permissive with anti-democratic attitudes (Busquets and Losada 2003:138) and failed to persuade the military of the necessity of reforms (Osorio 1980:183–9).

In addition to the media, Suárez's governments used other *nodality* effectors such as personal communications with top officers, military speeches, and official reports. Many formal and informal meetings were conducted between members of the governments and senior military leaders, although with mixed results on the military's subordination. A landmark of *nodality* use was the meeting that Suárez held with the top ranking generals on 8 September 1976 to convince them to support the upcoming Law of Political Reform. However, it ended up being counterproductive. During the meeting, Suárez insinuated that he would not legalise the communist party, which he did the next year during Easter break by creating serious unrest amongst the ranks. For instance, the Higher Council of the army issued a formal objection, the Marine Minister Admiral Pita da Veiga resigned and several generals sent a protest memorandum to the king.[18]

Some individuals also became important information effectors. The Deputy Prime Minister Gutiérrez Mellado often visited military quarters addressing officers and troops, for example, when he undertook a campaign to explain the Constitution. The effectiveness of this approach was unclear since Gutiérrez Mellado often encountered displays of indiscipline and insults in his visits, as in the Cartagena quarter and the funerals of military assassinated by terrorists. The first civilian defence minister, Rodríguez Sahagún, also tried to develop a close personal relation with the military in order to earn their trust, even playing cards or going to restaurants with them.[19] Despite these efforts, the government struggled to penetrate certain sectors of the military where anti-democratic values were deeply rooted. King Juan Carlos was a much more successful nodal effector. Through his visits to military institutions and speeches, he highlighted the need for reforms and to keep the military away from politics (Agüero 1995:213). He maintained very good personal relations with many senior officers, partially due to his education in the three military academies (Bernecker 1998). They recognised him as the rightful successor of Franco and respected him as their supreme commander (Tusell 1995:633). His intervention was fundamental to discourage a military putsch after the legalisation of the communist party by the UCD government in 1977.[20] During the 23-F events, he personally called every top ranking general to announce his opposition to the coup and to command them to capture the insurgents (Preston 1986; Tusell 1995; Powell 1996).[21]

Military speeches and official communications were also important information tools. They aimed to inculcate the political neutrality and respect of the government's reforms and to counter the growing number of episodes of military indiscipline. For instance, military speeches and communications emphasised the need to preserve discipline, hierarchy, and loyalty;[22] the degree of the military's autonomy;[23] the rehabilitation of the image of liberal officers;[24] to stress the apolitical character of the military;[25] and to try to calm the military.[26]

Nodal effectors lost salience during the PSOE government, which preferred information detectors. The military held an ideological position even more distant from that of the PSOE. Informal negotiations, visits, and speeches lost prominence. On both sides, unexpected political reforms and secret plots had generated suspicion. The government continued to use some nodal effectors to gain the confidence and respect of the military but gave up on the goal of convincing the military to change their values and wholeheartedly embrace the reforms (Cardona 1990:206). The government emphasised the most appealing aspects of its military policy to justify many of the reforms, such as the non-intervention in the promotion system or the virtues of NATO membership (Rodrigo 1985:369, 1992:73). Moreover, the PSOE government also enjoyed favourable support from the mainstream media that wanted to avoid a return to authoritarianism.

In sum, the Spanish government abandoned the Francoist *nodality* strategy that had been grounded in intensive propaganda and censorship. Suárez's governments tried to persuade the military to support the political and military reforms through press releases, appearances in the media, meetings and informal negotiations with senior officers, and public speeches. Notwithstanding, the deeply rooted anti-democratic values in the ranks and the pressures form the bunker limited the success of these tools. The socialists were aware of the poor results that the *nodality* strategy had for their predecessors and of the ideological gap that separated them from the military, and accordingly their reliance on *nodality* effectors decreased.

8.2.2   Information detectors

During the transition, the intelligence services were concentrated. 'Tercera del Alto' and SECED merged in 1977 into the Higher Centre of Defence Information, CESID. The Brigade for Social Investigation was dissolved in 1978 and its functions passed to CESID. This consolidation meant a change from the authoritarian regime during which the information services were scattered so that none of them had much power. The CESID collected all internal affairs information and became very powerful in the military. From then on, the intelligence services were progressively civilianised (Díaz Fernández 2003:234–89). Although the secret services served to prevent some military plots, including the 'Operación Galaxia' in 1978, their overall attitude towards military insurgence remained ambiguous. They were dominated by conservative officers and had been accused of passivity and even participation in the 23-F coup (Fernández López 2000:214–18; Díaz Fernández 2005;

Palacios 2009). Colonel San Martín, one of the plotters sentenced for his participation in the 23-F coup was the head of SECED until 1974.

After the events of the 23-F, the CESID was reorganised and fighting reactionary military coups became its priority (Serra 2009:85–6). The new director of CESID, Colonel Alonso Manglano Manglano, created a network to spy on the military.[27] The CESID reported directly to the prime minister.[28] Amongst other contributions, the CESID exposed the 'Operación Cervantes' in October 1982 and the assassination attempt on the king and several members of the government in La Coruña in 1985 (Díaz Fernández 2005:221–35). After 1985, military conspiracy was no longer the main priority of the secret services.

The nodal location of some important figures in the government served to obtain first-hand information valuable to assess the situation in the barracks and to inform decisions. For instance, many of the top-ranking officers during the transition were old colleagues of Gutiérrez Mellado, from the time of the General Academy and the High Staff School (Puell de la Villa 1997:55, 178). As mentioned earlier, Rodríguez Sahagún and, in particular, Juan Carlos also used friendship as a means to collect relevant information. Narcís Serra spent his first year as defence minister analysing the ministry and the military, with the support by military aides; studying other European countries; and meeting weekly with the president of the government (Agüero 1988:44). This process of information collection was fundamental to establish the new defence policy and the reforms that ended up consolidating the military's subordination.

Finally, the function of oversight developed by journalists, academics, and politicians was made possible by the new rights concerning freedom of speech and the effective limitation of the jurisdiction of military justice. The moderate media not only supported most democratic political and military reforms but also acted as a detector and deterrent against the military's insubordination. They reproduced and criticised any military declaration against the reforms. The government could easily monitor the acts of indiscipline and subversion and take disciplinary measures with greater legitimacy. The media paid an enormous attention to military affairs.[29] One of the clearest examples of the detection function occurred in 1980. The director of 'Diario 16', Miguel Ángel Aguilar, accused General Torres Rojas of preparing a plot against democracy and the government quickly removed him from the command of the powerful DAC.[30] The role of the media was especially important during the 23-F coup and its aftermath. Equally, the academic and political elites became more concerned about the military's subordination. Research and publications proliferated and in the parliament, defence commissions acquired more relevance. The DRISDE and CESEDEN also assisted the government's monitoring of the military and establishing links with the media, universities, and research centres (Ministerio de Defensa 1986).

8.2.3   Freedom of information, personal networks, and intelligence

With the advent of democracy, the Francoist approach to *nodality* tools became discredited. Guided by democratic ideas, Suárez's governments dismantled the propaganda and censorship machinery and guaranteed freedom of information and opinion. His governments used the media, formal and informal meetings, visits to the quarters, and public speeches to convince the military of the necessity of reforming the political system and its subordination to civilian authority. The political instability and lack of information control was opportunistically used by anti-democratic elements to undermine the image of the government. The number of acts of indiscipline and military plots indicates the limited success of the information campaign of the government within the ranks. González's government learnt the lesson and shifting efforts from information effectors to information detectors. If convincing the military was not possible, then the priority became to monitor the military's behaviour and to punish any deviance. The new powerful information services, CESID, the personal networks of the members of the government, the king, the media, as well as academics and politicians became useful sources of information for the government in the endeavour of controlling the military.

8.3   Authority

Authority was used to change some behaviours and practices that were not compatible with the new democratic model. Suárez's governments placed liberal military and civilians in key positions and granted great autonomy and special functions to the military. The PSOE government relied less on military promotions and symbolic rewards and reduced the military's autonomy. Membership in NATO became a tool in their control strategy. A series of constraints were imposed on the military in order to increase professionalism. Sanctions for indiscipline and anti-democratic behaviour as well as the legal restrictions imposed on the scope of military justice had been timid until the advent of the PSOE government. After 1983, the socialists perfected the legal framework that established the boundaries of military functions and imposed punishments for indiscipline. Overall, there was a gradual shift from rewards and incentives, preferred during the UCD period, towards sanctions and constraints during the PSOE period.

8.3.1 Rewards and incentives

The transitional and democratic governments continued to use *authority* tokens to provide incentives for the military's subordination, although this decreased over time. Franco had used his authority to appoint the military to key positions in his administration. After his death, this practice was reduced and completely abandoned during the PSOE government. The transitional government used promotions within the military to reward loyalty and to ensure endorsement of the upcoming reforms. Seniority was not strictly respected in the promotion of senior officers. Political loyalty or other merits were considered. For instance, Arias Navarro promoted Vega Rodríguez to captain-general of Madrid and Gutiérrez Mellado to the rank of lieutenant-general and the Central Joint Staff. During Suárez's rule, the appointment of Gutiérrez Mellado as vice-president (1977–81) and defence minister (1977–9) aimed to avoid the military's opposition to the reforms.

Gutiérrez Mellado also used strategic posting to consolidate his power. He relied on graduates of the prestigious High Staff courses that had experience working with foreign armies to implement the reforms (Puell de la Villa 1997:189, 203–4). The appointment of Generals Ibáñez Freire and José Timón de Lara as heads of the civil guard and armed police in 1976, the promotion of Ibáñez Freire as captain-general of the IV Military Region in 1978, and the appointment of General Gabeiras Montero as JEME in 1979 were some of the most important, albeit controversial, measures aimed at replacing reactionary generals by more moderate ones.[31] In 1977, the appointments of the civilians Eduardo Serra as undersecretary of defence and Jesús Palacios as secretary general of economic affairs in the Defence Ministry and later that of Rodriguez Sahagún as defence minister in 1979 held a symbolic importance, too (Preston 1990:195–8).

Calvo Sotelo passed the Law 48/1981 (24 December 1981) that established that the generals had to be promoted by the government. This law, together with the Law 20/1981 of Active Reserve (6 July 1981) regulating early retirement from active duties were intended to renew the conservative top tier of the military. Nonetheless, these laws created unrest in the ranks.[32] Finally, the socialist government, although keeping the capacity to appoint senior officers, decided to follow a policy of non-interference. They made clear that any act of disobedience or public declaration related to politics would result in expulsion but also that the government trusted the capacity of the military to select its own elite.[33]

Authority tokens were also used as symbolic rewards aiming to increase the military's status and self-esteem by emphasising the salience of its functions. For instance, the military was dignified by the 1978 Constitution (Blanco Valdés 1999) whose Article 8.1 established that their mission 'is to guarantee the sovereignty and independence of Spain and to defend its territorial integrity and the constitutional order'. The idea was to make the military feel important as participants in the fight against regional separatism that was one of the main concerns they expressed during the transition.[34] The fact that the constitution recognised the king, a military, as supreme commander of the military was also as a symbolic reward for the military who acknowledged him as the rightful successor to Franco.[35] The enactment of new military statutes, 'Reales Ordenanzas'[36] was also used as a symbolic reward. These statutes, which substituted the previous 'Ordenanzas de Carlos III' of 1768, were not very restrictive and recognised many rights of the military. The statues also set limits to the obedience principle. The Article 34 of the 'Reales Ordenanzas' established that the military was not obliged to follow orders from its commanders when it was in conflict with the constitution. Thus, the military was given the capacity to reject orders from superiors attempting to attack the regime.

Moreover, the UCD governments granted a great degree of autonomy to the military, expecting to reinforce their allegiance. The military took most day-to-day decisions without any interference or control from the Defence Ministry. For the military, there was a difference between 'authority', held by the government, and 'command' held by the military's top ranks.[37] The sense of autonomy was reinforced by the fact that the military occupied most of the positions in the Defence Ministry too. However, the PSOE government put an end to the military's autonomy. The Organic Law of Defence 1/1984 (5 January 1984) was the fundamental *authority* tool that set the pillars for the new military organisation and unmade the ambiguity of the military's subordination to the government. The law also eliminated the requirement of being an officer to occupy certain positions in the Defence Ministry, accelerating the process of civilianisation (Puell de la Villa 1997:210). The military's autonomy, although it had been initially positively perceived amongst the ranks, also fuelled anti-democratic attitudes.

Finally, the adhesion to NATO can be considered an *authority*-based incentive for the military. The Spanish government signed the North Atlantic Treaty in 1982 and ratified it after a referendum in 1986. Many

Spanish political leaders campaigned for the alliance (Arenal and Aldecoa 1986:213–32). The majority of the military were also in favour of the integration, in particular the navy.[38] Membership in NATO diverted the military's attention away from domestic politics (Gillespie 1989:425); exposed them to the company of new allies with more democratic values (Fernández López 2000:189); and provided a new powerful enemy, the Eastern Bloc (Aguilar 1985:51). NATO contributed to improve civilian expertise on military affairs and helped the government to justify many of its reforms by arguing that these were membership requirements (Rodrigo 1992:73). Even the PSOE, previously opposed, once in power decided to support NATO membership as a means for increasing professionalism and reducing reactionary attitudes. This shift in the stance of the PSOE leadership was welcomed by the military and helped dissipate some of their fears.

8.3.2   Sanctions and constraints

The governments after Francoism also used their legal authority to establish limitations and sanctions in order to prevent and punish non-compliant behaviour. First, the government imposed a series of legal constraints to military life and rights in order to enhance professionalism and subordination. The Royal Decree 10/1977 (8 February 1977) prohibited political and union activities from members of the military. It banned the military from the expression of political views in public and holding political positions until retirement. In 1978, Gutiérrez Mellado, as a means to enhance professionalism, extended the regular working hours until 5p.m. This extension was intended to prevent the military from undertaking second jobs in the afternoon, which until then had been a common practice. Extra funds were allocated to compensate for their loss of purchasing power. Secondments in the administration or public companies were also eliminated.[39]

Law 20/1981 (6 July 1981), regulating the passage to the reserve, also served as a mechanism to reinforce professionalism through the reduction of the size of the military and the rejuvenation of its cadres. A younger and smaller military could be better paid and equipped, be more open to change, and be more professional. This law also limited the capacity of the military to decide on the promotions to the top ranks. Notwithstanding, the oversize and the excess of officers persisted.[40] The reforms initiated by the PSOE government were more successful when it came to reducing the size and rejuvenating the military. Law 19/1984 (8 June 1984) reduced the length of mandatory military service to 12 months; Law 40/1984 (1 December 1984) defined the maximum number of officers in active duty per rank in the rmy; and Law 48/1984 (26 December 1984) introduced the possibility of conscientious objection. These authority tokens contributed to improve professionalism and indirectly the military's subordination.

Moreover, the government dismissed the senior officers acting or speaking against the government. For instance, Deputy Prime Minister General de Santiago was obliged to resign due to his disagreements with Suárez in September 1976. In October 1976, Suárez's government decreed the passage to the military reserve of the Generals De Santiago and Iniesta Cano.[41] General Félix Álvarez-Arenas was sacked on 1976 as director of the Army Higher School due to the mishandling of a breach in discipline. General Prieto López was also discharged from the command of the sixth zone of the civil guard due to his criticism of the government in a funeral speech (Fernández López 1998:117–19). General Campano was substituted by General Ibañez Freire as head of the civil guard and General Aguilar by General Timón de Lara in the armed police after the illegal demonstrations of police and civil guard agents in Madrid in 1976 (Gomáriz 1979:72–3).

Although sanctions for insubordination were common, they were not severe. In many cases, the sanctions were simply reassignments to different positions, usually of a similar level. For instance, in 1977, the reactionary General Milans del Bosch was removed from the DAC but appointed captain-general of the Third Military Region. General Armada was sacked from the secretariat of the king's military household for urging people to vote for the right-wing party Alianza Popular during the 1977 elections but then put in charge of the Army Higher School.[42] Minor disciplinary sanctions were taken against seven officers who participated in an illegal meeting with the extreme-right leader Blas Piñar in Ceuta in March 1978.[43] General Atarés Peña, who, during a visit of Gutiérrez Mellado to Cartagena in November 1978, had insulted and attacked the government, was acquitted without any charges from a court-martial.[44] During the funerals of two officers of the armed police and a civil guard assassinated by the GRAPO in January 1977 and that of General Ortín, assassinated by the ETA in January 1979, some officers insulted Gutiérrez Mellado and the government. Only some of them received (minor) sanctions (Gutiérrez Mellado and Picatoste 1983:107–14). The prestige that the outspoken military earned from its reactionary colleagues compensated the minimal punishments imposed (Fernández López 1998:130–2).

Contrary to the severe punishment against the clandestine liberal group UMD,[45] the sanctions against the reactionary military that attempted to

overthrow the democratic system were very soft during the UCD governments. For instance, the sanctions against 'Operación Galaxia' plotters in November 1978 were minimal. Captain Sáenz de Ynestrillas was
sentenced to only six months of preventive arrest and was soon after
promoted to the rank of major. Tejero was imprisoned for seven months
and soon given a post as head of a transport unit. General Luis Torres
Rojas, commander of the DAC that had been involved in a plot in January
1980, became military governor of La Coruña (Ballbé 1983:472–3; Preston
1990:177–8). After the 23-F coup, only 33 plotters were tried of which
22 were sentenced to prison. The infrequent sanctions to overt anti-
democratic attitudes within the military had ended up reinforcing the
ultras' conviction of the likelihood of success of a military intervention.

The PSOE government, aware of the failure of the soft policy in terms
of punishments, started a non-tolerance policy. After 1983, the ministry
began to regularly use sanctions against anti-constitutional attitudes as
a sign of firmness and control. For example, Captain-General Soteras
was sacked for trivialising the importance of the 1981 coup, General
Fernández Tejeiro for a laudatory speech on Franco, and Vice Admiral
Moreno de Alborán for circulating a memo criticising the government
(Agüero 1995:212). Serra also appealed against the reduction of the
sentence for the authors of the 'Operación Cervantes' decided by a military court (Busquets and Losada 2003:183).

As part of the control strategy, Spanish governments gradually
constrained the powers of the military, reducing their capacity to interfere with other institutions of the new democratic regime. Royal Decree
2723/1977 that created the Defence Ministry, the 1978 Constitution,
the Organic Laws of Defence 6/1980 and 1/1984, as well as the other
regulations that accompanied them meant a transfer of functions and
powers away from the military. Through these legal reforms, the coordination and control of the military, the command in case of war, the
definition of the strategic goals, and the approval of military policies
were assumed by the prime minister. The defence minister exercised
the management of defence policy and of the military. All collective
decision-making bodies in the military were transformed into advisory
bodies as a means to reinforce discipline and effectiveness in the chain
of command and to clarify individual responsibilities (Serra 2008:97).
Some of the military's prerogatives were eliminated, such as the exclusive capacity over promotions, logistics, infrastructures, and military
education, which were transferred from the military branches to the
Defence Ministry. All companies controlled by the military became part
of the state holding INI.

Formal constraints were introduced gradually to limit police and judicial functions of the military. The process restricting the powers of the military was initiated in 1976 with the elimination of the Public Order Tribunals in which the military had played an important role.[46] In 1978, the constitution established a clear separation between the military and the security forces (Articles 8 and 104) and limited the scope of military justice (Article 117). In 1980, the Code of Military Justice was reformed.[47]

However, the 'Honour Trials' were not abolished (Busquets 1999:271) and the implementation the new formal principles met with many obstacles (Ballbé 1983:469–88). Some of the limitations imposed on the military were not effective. They were always judged by other military officers and often suffered minimal or no punishment for their actions. Moreover, the military continued to use their powers on civil society. For instance, in 1978 a military court tried and sentenced some actors of the theatre group 'Els Joglars' for offending the military institutions in the play 'La Torna'. The film director Pilar Miró was tried in 1980, because her film 'El Crimen de Cuenca' 'offended' the civil guard (Cardona 2001:286). In 1981, the journalist Miguel Angel Aguilar was tried for denouncing a military putsch (Ballbé 1983:474–5) and the union leader Romualdo Irujoa for insults against the military.[48]

Aware of these problems, in 1985, the PSOE government launched further reforms circumscribing the scope of military justice and further separating the police and military (Valenciano Almoyna 1986:147–52). Military offences and their sanctions were redefined in a new disciplinary regime.[49] A new military penal code specified which could be considered crimes against the military institution and the limits of military jurisdiction.[50] Some crimes, such as military sedition during peace time or espionage, were integrated into the ordinary penal code.[51] Ultimately, the government also incorporated military justice into the civilian justice system by replacing the Supreme Military Council by a Military Chamber within the Spanish Supreme Court[52] Moreover, the military nature of the police forces was eliminated.[53] Only the civil guards kept a military status but became independent from the army and were jointly administered by the Defence and Interior Ministries. Troops were redeployed away from the main urban areas. The Brigades of Operative Defence of the Territory were eliminated and their functions assumed by the civil guard (Payne 1986:186). Thus, after 1986, the preservation of internal public order was exclusively assigned to the security forces independent from the military branches.

8.3.3   From incentives and rewards to legal constraints and non-tolerance policy

The utilisation of *authority* tools evolved greatly during this period. Overall, during the UCD governments, *authority* was primarily used through incentives and rewards. Conversely, the PSOE government introduced many legal constraints to limit the military's autonomy and power. In general, loyalty was not rewarded by appointments to the public administration or state-owned companies but by military promotions. The government promoted 'liberal' generals and civilians to key positions in the Defence Ministry to facilitate the reforms. The prominence and autonomy that the new legal framework granted to the military sought to motivate it and to attract its support for the democratic reforms. The military occupied a privileged position in the constitutional text which established them as defenders of Spain's territorial integrity and of the constitutional order. They were also initially entrusted with great autonomy and decision-making powers, although later the PSOE government drastically reduced them. Membership in NATO after 1982 can be seen as a fundamental political instrument for civilian supremacy creating many incentives for the military to accept its subordination and the political reforms.

On the other hand, *authority* tokens were also used to establish constraints on the capacity of the military to interfere with the political system and society beyond their strict functions as well as to punish disobedience. The prohibition of political activity and secondary jobs as well as the laws limiting retirement age and the size of the military were the most salient. They helped address some of the problems that had hindered professionalism during the dictatorship, such as a lack of dedication, politicisation, excess of officers, and opposition to change and modernisation. The evidence shows that the sanctions on deviant behaviour were soft and not systematic and that the reforms limiting the reach of military justice were insufficient during the period of the UCD governments. *Authority*-based sanctions and constraints increased their salience during the PSOE government. Punishment of deviant behaviour became more severe. The power of the military concerning defence, military education, and the armament industry was limited. The reform and subordination of military justice to civilian justice as well as the effective separation of the military from the security forces was achieved. In brief, through a series of regulations, the PSOE government managed to redefine the boundaries of military functions and to consolidate the principle of civilian supremacy.

8.4   Treasure

After the death of Franco, Spanish governments tried to increase the amount of financial resources devoted to defence and to change the structure of military expenditures to restore the balance between staff and equipment expenses. The goal was not simply to increase the defence capacity but also to motivate the military and contribute to its depoliticisation and professionalisation. This section, first, analyses the evolution of the military budget and its distribution between staff and equipment expenses and investments. Second, it shows that the successive governments wanted to modernise equipment and increase salaries as a means to increase professionalism. Military budget allocations grew, especially those spent on equipment. However, military expenditures remained low in comparative terms and the excess of staff in the army hindered not only the increase of salaries but also investments in weapons and materials.

8.4.1   Evolution of the defence budget

Military expenditures grew during the transition and during most of the first socialist government. The admiration and extreme loyalty to Franco had served to keep down the criticism directed at the poor economic and material conditions of the military. After his death, the military became less willing to accept poor working conditions under a government that was dismantling the regime they had served for several decades. The government understood that the symbolic rewards were not sufficient anymore and that in a situation of instability and discontent the military's loyalty had to be, at least partially, bought. The utilisation of treasure that was intensified at the end of Francoism (Figure 8.1)

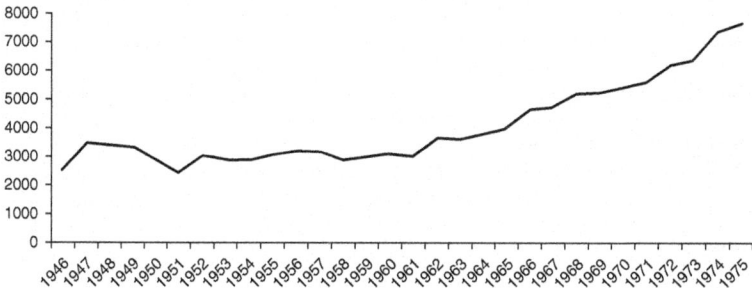

Figure 8.1   Total defence budget in constant million euros of 2009 during Francoism

Source: Based on Pérez Muinelo (2009:85).

received a new push after the end of the regime. *Treasure* gained salience in the democratic governments' control strategy. In order to improve the efficiency of *treasure* as a tool of control the distribution of expenses was adjusted and the budgeting and investment processes centralised and modernised. Nonetheless, defence budgets grew less than other budgets in the public administration and in comparison with other countries they remained low.

Defence budgets grew in nominal and real terms, as well as a percentage of Spanish GDP from 1975 to 1985 (Figures 8.2 and 8.3). The most important increases coincided with the years of higher political instability. Thus, right after the death of Franco, the 1976 and 1977 defence budgets grew 8.18 and 8.95 per cent. In 1982, the year of the general elections and one year after the 23-F coup attempt the budget rose by 8 per cent (Pérez Muinelo 2009:85). The new impetus in the utilisation of *treasure* tools during the first democratic governments was possible due to the success of the far-reaching economic plans launched following the Moncloa Pacts.[54] The pacts created a social climate of stability necessary to tackle the structural economic problems inherited from the rapid development of the previous decade and the oil crisis (Tarrow 1995; García Díez 2000).

As during Francoism, the defence budgets grew slower than other public budgets. Public expenditures grew 136 per cent from 1975 to 1986. Spain, as well as Portugal, was still far behind most European countries in terms of economic development and social welfare, and other investments and expenses were prioritised (Comín and Diaz 2005). Although the weight of defence budgets increased, from 12.25 per cent in 1972 to

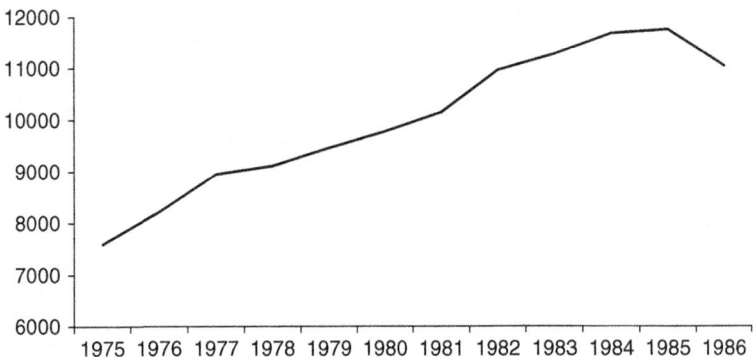

Figure 8.2 Total defence budget in constant million euros of 2009 (1975–86)
Source: Based on Pérez Muinelo (2009:85).

%

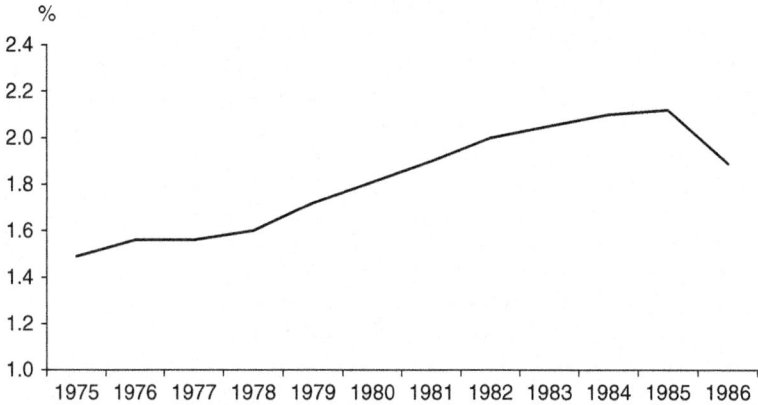

Figure 8.3   Defence budget as a percentage of GDP in Spain (1975–86)
Source: Based on Pérez Muinelo (2009:84).

%

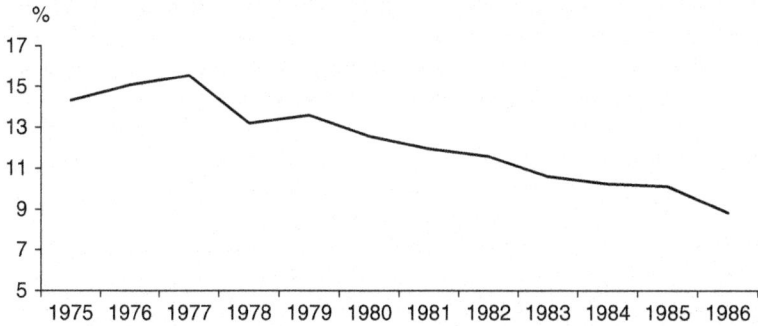

Figure 8.4   Defence budget as a percentage of the total public expenditure in Spain (1975–86)
Source: Based on Pérez Muinelo (2009:84).

15.54 in 1976, later their share of the total public expenditures gradually shrank to 8.81 per cent in 1986 (Figure 8.4). In 1986, the defence budget in real terms decreased by 6 per cent.

The governments also adjusted the distribution of financial resources and the budgeting and investment procedures to enhance the professionalisation of the military. The UCD government increased investments and acquisitions of weapons and materials so that equipment passed from 39 per cent of the total defence budget in 1976 to 49 per cent in 1982 (Pérez Muinelo 2009:93). Calvo Sotelo also aimed to further change the structure of the consumption of financial resources by reducing staff expenses to 40 per cent of the total defence budget.[55] However, this target was never achieved. During the first PSOE government the balance between staff and equipment remained basically unchanged (Figure 8.5).

Aware of the problems of coordination amongst the three branches, the governments developed a centralisation strategy for the military economic policy. The Defence Undersecretariat was created in 1982[56] to coordinate the allocation of financial resources and the acquisition of equipment. After 1984, the State Secretariat of Defence[57] was in charge of budget planning and incontrol of the financial resources. An Economic Affairs General Directorate was introduced to improve the budgeting process. The government aimed to coordinate and rationalise military expenditures and investments. The responsibilities for procurement were transferred to the Defence Ministry, and the branches had to plan and justify their staff and equipment demands and compete for the allocation of economic resources.[58] Overall the process of evaluating needs and planning military expenditures greatly improved.[59]

Notwithstanding, military expenditures were considerably lower when compared to other Western democracies and Mediterranean countries as a percentage of GNP (CESEDEN 1988). For instance, from 1980 to 1984, the average military expenditures in Spain were 2.3 per cent of the GNP

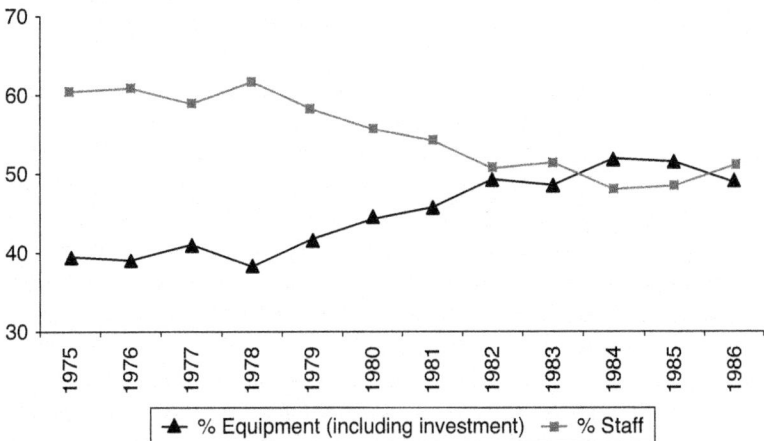

Figure 8.5   Defence budget distribution of expenditure in percentage (1975–86)
Source: Based on Pérez Muinelo (2009:93).

while the average of European NATO members were 3.6 per cent (Cosidó Gutiérrez 1994:182).

8.4.2 Staff expenditure

As during the dictatorship, salaries were periodically raised to counter inflation and to reduce military unrest. Higher salaries were considered essential to achieve professionalisation and exclusive dedication by the UCD government (Gutiérrez Mellado 1981:216). The goal was to increase military salaries to the level of civil service salaries, which at the time were 30 per cent higher. In 1976, there was a general increase of 3,000 pesetas and in 1977 a reform in the salary regulation to equate military conditions to those of Spanish civil servants.[60] Next, in 1978, the government announced new raises; salaries grew 14 per cent for the top ranks and 25 for the lower ranks and pensions increased between 20 and 40 per cent. These overall raises were accompanied with a change in the salary structure that largely benefited lower rank officers, and with the introduction of a salary supplement for exclusive dedication to gradually eradicate secondary jobs (Bañón 1988:342–3; Puell de la Villa 1997:210–11).

Although salaries increased more by than 20 per cent on average, they did not noticeably reduce the pressures against liberalisation within the ranks (Preston 1990:196). The most reactionary military and political leaders interpreted these concessions to the military simply as signs of weaknesses in the government. Moreover, salaries continued to be lower than those in the civil service and other Western militaries.

Calvo Sotelo's government intended to protect salaries while reducing staff expenses by diminishing the size of the officers' corps.[61] The reduction particularly affected the senior ranks.[62] However, as officers continued to earn their salaries in the reserve, expenditures in staff remained almost constant in the following years (Figure 8.6, p. 184). The PSOE government followed a similar logic, trying to increase salaries while reducing the cost of staff and attempting to strengthen professionalism. Law 19/1984 reduced the length of the mandatory military service to 12 months, and Law 20/1984 again raised salaries to make them equivalent to those of civil servants. This law simplified the benefit system and introduced new remuneration for technical abilities, level of responsibility, productivity, and extraordinary services (Ministerio de Defensa 1986:173–9).

8.4.3 Equipment expenditure

Expenditures and investments in equipment were prioritised to achieve not only a stronger but also a more professional and obedient military.

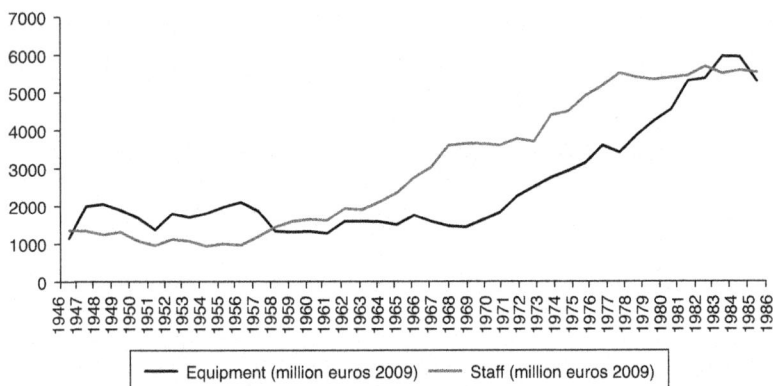

Figure 8.6   Distribution of defence budget (equipment – including investments – and staff) in constant million euros of 2009

Source: Based on from Pérez Muinelo (2009:93).

The UCD and PSOE governments were aware of the poor material conditions of the Spanish military and committed themselves to modernisation. Fund allocations were increased (until 1985), and budgeting and investment procedures improved. The development of a defence industry and cooperation with other Western countries contributed to the rearmament and modernisation, which were, however, slowed down by the needs in terms of staff spending.

Following that initial boost from Law 32/1971 the expenditure in materials continued to grow during the transitional period (Figure 8.6).[63] The salience of American direct aid was greatly decreased by the beginning of the transitional period down to only 2 per cent between 1972 and 1976. The government aimed to expand and update defence budgetary resources in order to fulfil the plan of modernisation of materials and weaponry for the period (1976–9).[64] In 1977, the government granted 686,948 million pesetas for the modernisation of materials to make credible the commitment to professionalisation in the military (Rodrigo 1989:229–31). Moreover, the governments also facilitated defence acquisition programmes by condoning the pending debts of the defence ministries in 1976 and by financing the interests of some of their credits (Pérez Muinelo 2009:116–18).

From 1977 to 1982, UCD governments made an effort to renew and modernise military equipment that had been neglected during the dictatorship.[65] During this period, the running costs and investments in new equipment and materials increased from 39 to more than 49 per cent of the total defence budget (Figure 8.6). The US aid continued to decrease to 1.4 per cent although American loans accounted for 13.5 per cent of the supplementary funds for equipment acquisitions (Pérez Muinelo 2009:118). The first Strategic Global Plan of Defence (PEC) (1979–80) aimed to help the Spanish defence industry and reduce its dependency on external suppliers. Spain acquired technology and agreements for joint production with other countries such as Germany, France, Italy and the United Kingdom (Rodríguez Sahagún 1986:191). Nonetheless this plan suffered several delays and was not fully implemented until the advent of the PSOE government.[66]

The PSOE government continued to promote the acquisition of equipment. Law 44/1982 established that budgets for acquisition and running costs of equipment and weapons would be at least increased on average by 4.43 per cent annually in real terms from 1983 to 1990. The Spain's defence industry, military research, and development as well as the cooperation with supranational organisations were reinforced. The government exempted the import of equipment from taxation. Furthermore, the government obtained 1,582 million dollars in loans from the Federal Financing Bank from 1983 to 1986. The acquisition of F-18s and the plan for naval modernisation can be considered amongst the most relevant investment programmes.

However, the targeted increase in equipment expenditure was not achieved because the government also established a ceiling to the maximum average increase of the defence budget.[67] In the end, the cost of early retirement policies, combined with the salary increases impeded cutting staff expenses sufficiently and thwarted the goal for material and investment expenditures (Powell 2001:377). Another problem was that sometimes the needs in the running costs were underestimated in the budgets which made later reallocations necessary. In fact, in real terms in 1986, equipment expenditures (including investments) was slightly lower than in 1982 (Pérez Muinelo 2009:93, 120–3).

8.4.4 Better salaries but limited modernisation of equipment

Treasure gained salience in the government control strategy after the death of Franco. Many military questioned the authority of the government and were not willing to continue operating with the same conditions of penury as during the dictatorship. Many of the symbolic and material rewards they had been receiving during Francoism were abandoned. The government embraced the idea, widespread in the NATO area, that a better paid and equipped military would develop a more professional dedication and abstain from interfering in politics. Military expenditures grew continuously until 1985, but not as fast as other social and infrastructure expenditures. The procedures for budgeting and investments were modernised and centralised in order to increase the impact of treasure tools.

Although both staff and equipment expenditures were used to control the military, Spanish governments tried to enlarge the share devoted to equipment. Thus, in order to increase salaries while reducing the proportion of staff expenditures, the size of the army was reduced. Four salary raises were decided on in 1976, 1977, 1978, and 1984; and in parallel, pensions were increased to stimulate early retirement. These measures served to bridge the economic gap between civil servants and the military while countering the unrest created by the political instability. The UCD government revitalised the modernisation plan initiated in 1971. Acquisitions of equipment and materials were facilitated by the cancellation of previous debts, the reduction of import taxation, the support of the Spanish defence industry, and the acquisition of foreign technology. The three branches had to plan their needs and compete for funds. Equipment expenditures were increased to the level of staff expenditure. The latter, nonetheless, remained high due to the extraordinary payments and pensions inherited from the policy of reducting personnel. Overall, the growth of military spending slowed down during the PSOE government when the military threat had vanished and Spanish defence budgets were still one of the lowest in the Western developed countries.

8.5   Conclusions

After Franco's death, there were deep transformations in the patterns of utilisation of control tools. The underlying principle was that a more professional, better prepared, and equipped military would concentrate on their duties and not interfere in politics. Many of the prerogatives they had enjoyed during the dictatorship had to be sacrificed. The changes were for the most part gradual and can be observed in each of the four types of tools of government.

Coercive *organisation* tools were minimally used but non-coercive tools acquired new salience. Military education and training were intensified, especially after NATO membership in 1982. Gradually, the attention shifted from inculcating distinct moral values to introducing technical skills and moving the military closer to society. The state organisation's capacity replaced the provision of jobs by the provision of social services. Organisational design became the most important mechanism of control. The UCD and PSOE governments introduced far-reaching reforms abandoning the Francoist 'divide-and-rule' logic. They created a unified Defence Ministry and shaped the military to improve coordination and to centralise decision-making powers under civilian authority. During the UCD governments, the incipient administrative machinery of the ministry was fragile and the laws and regulations that established it were ambiguous and incomplete, leaving room for interpretations incompatible with the Western democratic principle of civilian supremacy. During the PSOE government, the bureaucracy and legislation grew, steadily achieving a transfer of competences to the ministry and a reduction in the autonomy of the three branches. Moreover, the new organisational design demarcated the functional boundaries of the military making explicit the civilian supremacy.

Franco's approach to *nodality* was also reversed. Information effectors saw their relevance reduced. The propaganda and censorship apparatus was dismantled. Rather than indoctrination and limited access to information, the democratic approach favoured persuasion and freedom of information. Public speeches, meetings, and the media were used to convince the military of the need for political reforms and civilian supremacy during the Suárez's rule. González's government was not convinced of the effectiveness of information effectors in changing the military's mentality and put emphasis on detecting threats from the ranks and learning from them. Information detectors grew in importance. The information services were strengthened. Academics, politicians, and in particular the media contributed to the monitoring of the military's insubordination.

While some of the traditional rewards were abandoned, *authority*-based sanctions and constraints grew in salience. While the UCD promoted loyal liberal generals, the PSOE opted for a minimal interference stance. The special treatment that the military received in the constitution, the honorary role of the king as supreme commander, the new military statutes, and in particular the high degree of autonomy of the military intended to foster military support for the new political system. However, these formal recognitions were not comparable to all of the prerogatives and symbolic rewards received during the dictatorship and did not serve to ensure loyalty. The decision to join NATO became an effective *authority*-based incentive that encouraged professionalism and subordination. The limitations to the military's autonomy and to their prerogatives became crucial mechanisms of control, in particular under the PSOE government. The regulations launched after 1984 clarified that the military was completely subordinated to the government, imposed a new disciplinary regime, and completed the process of limitation to their judicial and police powers. Moreover, the sanctions applied for insubordination that during Suárez's government had been very soft were toughened.

Finally, the approach to *treasure* tools also evolved in this period. They became more salient in the control strategy. The contact with the Western allies had made evident that the Spanish armies were badly paid and armed. Salary raises for the military took place to bring them closer to the level of the civil service. The modernisation of equipment and rearmament became a top priority to enhance professionalism. Military investments and acquisitions were stimulated, and the budgeting process was modernised and centralised. Equipment expenditures reached the level of staff expenditures during the initial years of the PSOE government. Notwithstanding, the growth of defence budgets was slower than that of other ministries, and the extra costs derived from the early retirement policy constrained the modernisation of the military. Once the danger of military intervention declined, the budgets shrank, especially those dedicated to equipment.

In sum, during this period many important changes were introduced to the control strategy. Two broad different trends in control can be observed. First, Suárez's government, afraid of the reactions of the most conservative sectors in the military, adopted a somewhat laissez-faire approach with low interference in military affairs and great levels of tolerance towards the acts of indiscipline. Second, after the 23-F coup attempt and in particular during the first PSOE government (1982–6), more decisive actions were taken to restrain the autonomy and powers of the military.

Part 4
Comparisons and Explanations

9
Comparisons and Explanations

This chapter compares the basic trajectories in tool choice and civil-military relations from a country perspective and contrasts two types of neo-institutionalist explanations: one based on the legacies of past macro-historical events and the other on the ongoing impact of environmental factors. The chapter shows that the most significant changes in the trajectories of tool choice coincided with important historical junctures. The Spanish Civil War, the Second World War, the creation of NATO, the colonial conflicts, the fall of the authoritarian regimes, as well as the military coup attempts in Portugal in 1975 and in Spain in 1981 concurred with the points of departure and/or closing stages for distinct trajectories. Nonetheless, this chapter also reveals that although history matters, 'orthodox' path-dependence interpretations need to be qualified. Environmental factors such as ideas, political-institutional structures, and international actors acted as 'constant causes' shaping trajectories in civil-military relations and tool choice too.

9.1 Comparing general trends in Portuguese and Spanish civil-military relations

As illustrated in previous chapters, there were periods in which the trajectories of civil-military relations and the tools of government in the Iberian countries were divergent and periods when they converged. Portugal and Spain developed different patterns of tool choice during their dictatorships. The rise of fascism in the 1930s and the Spanish Civil War shaped the paths of civil-military relations and control policies in both countries, although more profoundly in Spain. They created a window of opportunity and incentive for repressive action manifested in the intensive utilisation of coercive *organisation* instruments as well as intrusive *nodality* detectors and effectors.

The Civil War allowed Franco to purge the military of anyone suspected of being critical of his regime. Moreover, Franco's legitimacy as a ruler was built on his military victory against the Second Republic (Aguilar Olivencia 1999). He managed to transform the Spanish military to the extent that ever since they have been considered the 'Francoist Armies'; a new institution virtually disconnected from its past as the Armies of the Second Republic. Franco's military was cohesive and professed fervent admiration for the dictator. The levels of contestation in the ranks were very low after the purges.

In Portugal, the military appointed Salazar as prime minister. His legitimacy was not based on a military victory but on his capacity to lead the government. The Portuguese military was not purged and homogenised, the allegiance to the figure of the dictator in Portugal was not near as strong as in Spain (Duarte 2010). Often the government's decisions were contested from the ranks, and military coup attempts occurred periodically. Civil-military relations were less stable and more susceptible to crises. Salazar had to maintain a more active strategy of control vis-à-vis the military.

During the 1940s, a relative convergence in tool choice and civil-military relations can be observed. In Spain, the repressive approach to control of the military was gradually reduced. The military had already been thoroughly purged and the defeat of the Axis had contributed to the discredit of the control mechanisms associated with totalitarianism. At the same time that Franco softened his control approach on the military, Salazar managed to use the threat of the Second World War to consolidate his political leadership and reinforce his authority on the military.

NATO membership (1949) brought about some changes in the tools of control and within the Portuguese military, putting Portugal's civil-military relations again on a path divergent from that of Spain. At the level of tool choice, Portugal's NATO membership triggered an increase in the intensity of education and training and changes in organisational design (non-coercive *organisation*). It is also associated, albeit to a lesser extent, with the modernisation of weaponry and materials (*treasure*), and a gradual decline in information manipulation (*nodality* effectors). The goal was to keep the military concentrated on their professional tasks and to improve their coordination and operational capacity vis-à-vis external threats.

Whereas Franco's military became self-complacent and did not question the dictator, the Portuguese military's mentality was strongly affected by their participation in the alliance. The Spanish military continued to be isolated, concentrating on internal threats and recalling their past glory. The control toolkit remained stable. On the other hand, many in the Portuguese military went to study abroad and participated in NATO bodies and activities. This 'NATO generation' developed awareness of the deficiencies of the Portuguese military and the political system. These officers became influential and later spread critical thinking within the ranks, which was one of the main factors for the fall of the Estado Novo (Carrilho 1992; Telo 1996).

The path of civil-military relations that NATO had initiated in Portugal was, nonetheless, truncated by the Colonial Wars. These conflicts forced Portugal to change its military policy and priorities. During the Colonial Wars, the changes made to the control toolkit throughout the 1950s were reversed. Moreover, the wars drained the government's resources and legitimacy. Quickly, it became evident that Portugal had little chances to reach a definitive victory and retain the colonies for long. Military dissatisfaction grew steadily. After the replacement of Salazar by Caetano in 1968, the government's position vis-à-vis the military weakened, and the military put an end to the regime in 1974. In sum, the Colonial Wars provoked a process of regression in terms of civil-military relations and ultimately caused the regime's downfall (Ferreira 2006:60).

Conversely, in Spain from the late 1950s, there were signs of evolution in some aspects of military policy. Franco reshuffled the cabinet in 1957, and the new technocratic ministers pushed for the abandonment of the previous autarchic ideas which initiated a moderated liberalisation that made Spain more permeable to ideas and normative pressures from international actors. In this context, the contacts with the US and French armies and the experience in the Sidi-Ifni War made the government and the military realise that the reality of the Spanish military was far from the optimistic image projected by the official propaganda. In order to overcome some of the serious deficiencies limiting defence capabilities, reforms in military education and training (non-coercive *organisation* tools) and a modernisation of equipment were launched.

Finally, the end of the dictatorial regimes led to deep but very distinct changes in civil-military relations in both countries. In Portugal, the military subverted the traditional relation of power. The government was subordinated to military executive bodies such as the JSN and later the CR. Although the MFA's revolutionary model meant to be a response against the previous regime and its military policies, the tools of military control employed ended up being to a great extent similar to those used during the Estado Novo, especially in terms of coercive *organisation*, intrusive *nodality* effectors and detectors, and low intensity *treasure*. Moreover, the military's supremacy in politics did not contribute to the military's subordination in the barracks. Ideologically, the military were very fragmented and posed constant challenges to the governments during 1974 and 1975.

The continuous political instability discredited the government led by Gonçalves and the MFA-Radicals. The MFA-Moderates stepped into power and after the left-wing November 1975 coup, abrupt changes were adopted in the control toolkit. Coercive *organisation*, propaganda, and censorship were abandoned. The special functions granted to the military in internal affairs were eliminated. Non-coercive *organisation* tools and *authority* constraints gained more salience. Professionalisation replaced politicisation as a guiding principle. Nonetheless, the 1976 Constitution prolonged the situation in which the military held important political powers and had complete autonomy from the civilian government. The 1982 constitutional reform and the new defence law put Portugal on a civil-military relations path similar to that of most of its Western allies, including Spain.

The Spanish transition also showed an important degree of political contestation in the military but overall, the trajectory of civil-military relations was very different. The military lost agenda-setting power and did not participate in the core political decisions. While in Portugal the approach to control was initially similar to that of the previous regime (followed by a drastic reversal after late 1975), Spanish transitional governments gradually introduced a new toolkit after the death of Franco. The re-design of the defence organisation became a fundamental tool of control. Franco's logic of 'divide-and-rule' was replaced by the coordination and centralisation of decision-making power under the defence minister. Information effectors and *authority* rewards were less intensively used; at the same time, *nodal* detectors and *authority* constraints gained relevance. The modernisation of equipment initiated at the end of the dictatorship was further developed as a means to facilitate professional dedication and divert the military's attention away from politics. Finally, after the 1981 coup attempt and the ascent to power of the socialist party in 1982, far reaching reforms in military and defence policy opened a new trajectory in civil-military relations consolidating civilian supremacy.

In sum, the many divergences between the two countries originate from the Spanish Civil War, which enabled a more repressive approach to control. Later, during the 1940s, both countries converged: Franco softened his grip on the military and Salazar gained legitimacy by capitalising on his management of the Second World War crisis. Next, NATO membership in 1949 marked the beginning of a new direction in Portuguese civil-military relations. However, this direction was truncated by the Portuguese Colonial Wars (1961–75). During this period, there was fundamentally a regression in civil-military relations. In the meantime, in Spain after the appointment of the new technocratic cabinet in 1957 and the Sidi-Ifni War (1957–8) some reforms in the Spanish military were launched. These were somewhat similar to those undertaken in Portugal after joining NATO in 1949. Finally, the fall of the regimes initiated in both countries a period of instability in terms of civil-military relations. Spain, embarked on a gradual process of reforms after the death of Franco. After 1982, the socialist government intensified them. In Portugal, after two years of revolutionary experience, the government implemented drastic changes. This process received a final impedious in 1982 putting Portugal on a path similar to that of Spain.

9.2 Path dependence: the legacies of macro-historical events

Many authors in the sphere of historical neo-institutionalism interpret institutional change as a path-dependent course of action in which dynamics triggered by a past event or process reproduce themselves even in the absence of the initial event or process. As demonstrated earlier in this monograph, the beginning and end of certain patterns in tool choice coincided with some non-controllable overarching historical events, such as the Spanish Civil War, the Second World War, the Colonial Wars, and transitional political processes. This section argues that the macro-historical events acted as catalysts creating 'critical junctures' and change in the control toolkit. It shows that there were periods of relative stability followed by periods of change (sometimes gradual and sometimes more abrupt) in the control toolkit. Moreover, it illustrates the action of some self-reinforcing mechanisms and how temporal sequence affected choices and outcomes. However, the analysis reveals some important limitations in path-dependence explanations, which overall fail to completely capture the evolution observed in Portuguese and Spanish civil-military relations.

9.2.1 Legacy of the Spanish Civil War

In Spain, the Civil War 'legitimised' to a great extent the use of violence (coercive *organisation*), manipulation of information (*nodality* effectors), and the concentration of military and political power in the hands of

Franco. The Civil War also produced the annihilation of the previous state institutions, enabling Franco to provide jobs in the civil service and to appoint military to political positions (non-coercive *organisation* and *authority* tools). It also increased the size of the army, depleted the treasury of the state, and created a long economic crisis that constrained the availability of treasure severely.

Beyond the direct impact on the basic resources, the Civil War entailed some other deeper and more durable implications. The victory in the war cemented Franco's political and military leadership. Franco's image was mythicised thanks to the support of the propaganda machinery (Blanco Escolá 2000; Cardona 2001:213), to the extent that even the 'liberal' military men who guided the reforms after his death continued to admit being admirers of Franco. The systematic purges and the influx of heavily indoctrinated militia officers produced an extremely ideo-logically homogeneous and obedient military. Moreover, the scarcity of material means made military education prioritise moral indoctrination over technical preparation. The official discourse portrayed the war as a crusade. Discipline was emphasised as a moral and religious virtue.

Due to the atrocities committed during and immediately after the war and the association with the Italian Fascists and German Nazis, Franco's regime was isolated by the international community. This isolation limited economic exchanges and obstructed the influx of new ideas and had long-term consequences in civil-military relations. The isolation also aggravated the already dire economic situation of post-war Spain and negatively affected military salaries and equipment. The wide gap in terms of material conditions between Spain and most West European armies and the lack of resources to bridge it pushed the government to accentuate ideological indoctrination and isolation as a means to shield the military from a sad reality. Later, self-recruitment as well as the education and socialisation of the military also acted as a self-reinforcement mechanism perpetuating a frozen military ideology. In sum, the Civil War deeply changed the military (and the government) and introduced a series of self-perpetuating mechanisms that contrib-uted decisively to an extraordinary degree of obedience to the figure of the dictator and created an ideologically cohesive military (Busquets 1984 [1971]; Cardona 2001).

The positive impact of the Civil War on Franco's control on the mili-tary can be better appreciated when compared to the Portuguese case. The inception of the Estado Novo did not follow the collapse of the previous military regime or a war. It was the result of a peaceful transfer of power from the military to Salazar. However, Salazar and especially

Caetano saw their power over the military limited by the fact that they had been chosen by the military, which retained much power in the institutional arrangement. Many military were not pleased with their appointments and others considered that the dictators were indebted to them. Throughout the regime, there were always large groups within the military that did not support the government or even conspired against it (Rebelo de Sousa 1990:66; Gunther 1995:74). Thus, although both were civilian authoritarian regimes their different inceptions introduced different durable inertias at the level of military allegiance to the respective dictators.

The Spanish Civil War also affected Portugal, but to a lesser extent. Salazar shaped his military and international relations strategy due to the threat that the instability in Spain posed (Ferreira 1989, 2006:60). The army grew to face a potential invasion which slowed down the effort of general modernisation of the military launched in the early 1930s. Salazar took advantage of the war threat to divert the attention away from internal affairs and to personally command the War Ministry after 1936 despite the opposition of the military hierarchy (Telo 1996:149). The conjuncture of the Spanish Civil War also allowed Salazar to launch fundamental reforms for the military's subordination in 1937 (Faria 2000; Duarte 2010).

9.2.2 Legacy of the Second World War

The Second World War forced Portugal to continue increasing the size of its military in order to face an eventual invasion. Salazar's foreign and defence policies managed to maintain Portugal in a delicate balance vis-à-vis the pressures from the international powers while steering the internal tension in the military that was also divided in its support for the Allies and the Axis (Rosas 1988; Telo 1989; Carrilho 1989/ed.). During this period, the external threat seems to have reduced military conspiracy against the regime and legitimised Salazar's direct control over the War Ministry, which he maintained until 1944.

The Second World War also precipitated the creation of NATO in 1949 to which Portugal was invited not only owing to its strategic potential but also as a reward for its cooperation with the Allies during the war, especially through the cession of the Azores military bases. NATO marked a new trend in civil-military relations until the outbreak of the Colonial Wars. It mainly led to an increase in the intensity of education and training, changes in organisational design, a limited modernisation of weaponry and materials, and a gradual decline in the salience of *nodality* effectors. In this case, a temporal separation between the event that triggered the process, the Second World War, and the change in the tool choice trajectory can be observed. This separation confirms that in some cases the manifestation of change in a social pattern can be delayed from its causal mechanism (Pierson 2003, 2004). Following Collier and Collier's critical juncture framework (1991:30), the Second World War can be considered as an antecedent to or condition for Portuguese membership in NATO, which constituted the critical juncture in the control toolkit.

However, these changes can also be interpreted not simply as the result of non-controllable external shocks, as path-dependence explanations often assume, but as the result of a process of policy transfer or lesson-drawing (Rose 1991; Dolowitz and Marsh 2000; Lodge and James 2003) in which the Portuguese government chose to apply a transnational template of military organisation and control (Sahlin-Andersson 2002). Using DiMaggio and Powell's terminology (1983), the adoption of NATO templates fits a process of normative isomorphism. The government was seeking legitimacy and support from the military, who to a large majority advocated the NATO doctrine. The fact that the NATO allies could do little to prevent Portugal from abandoning (or reversing) most of these reforms when the colonial conflict broke out confirms this point.

When the defeat of the Axis became likely, it was advisable for Franco to abandon the tools of control associated to totalitarianism in order to gain the sympathy of the Allies. After 1942, the utilisation of coercive *organisation* was reduced and almost completely abandoned after 1945. However, the saturation of the judiciary and prison systems caused by the repressive control policy and the fact that the armies had already been purged were the fundamental reasons for this change in strategy (Dueñas 1990). Thus, the change in the toolkit in this case seems to be the result of mechanisms of diminishing returns (or self-undermining process) initiated during the Spanish Civil War rather than of a new critical juncture.

The ideological alignment with the Axis provoked the rejection of Spain by the Western allies after the Second World War. The isolation of Spain and its military as well as the lack of resources contributed to creating a stable path of civil-military relations and tool choice until the semi-liberalisation and opening in the late 1950s. The apparent stability in civil-military relations after the Second World War masks what could be described as a sort of 'static process of departure'[1] when considered against the backdrop of the general transformations that occurred in civil-military relations in most countries in the Western sphere, including Portugal. The lack of changes in Spain gradually increased the gap vis-à-vis the model of civil-military relations in the West.

9.2.3 Legacy of the Colonial Wars

The colonial conflicts were the next macro-historical event that shaped Portuguese and Spanish civil-military relations. The Suez crisis in 1956 meant a defeat of the traditional European colonial attitude and marked the beginning of a cascade of nationalist independence movements that expanded throughout Africa (Telo 1996:291–318). This crisis was a direct antecedent to the Sidi-Ifni War in the Spanish North-African possessions (1957–8) and to the longer and more extensive Portuguese Colonial Wars (1961–75).

In Spain, the colonial problem had a limited impact on civil-military relations. Despite the efforts of the regime to hide the information about the Sidi-Ifni War, this conflict highlighted the deficiencies of the military and triggered the first crisis in the it since the Civil War (Losada 1990; Segura Valero 2006). The timid modernisation effort launched by the Army Minister General Barroso in 1958 was linked to the problems of organisation, training, and scarcity of materials that the Sidi-Ifni conflict revealed. Nonetheless, the gradual changes in terms of the control toolkit since the late 1950s seem to be more directly correlated to the opening of the regime and the exchanges with the US military than with the colonial conflict.[2] No major changes in the attitude of the military or the government can be associated with the colonial conflict.

The impact of the colonial conflicts was much stronger in Portugal. Salazar's colonialist stance was very unpopular among most NATO allies and many Portuguese officers. The violence used to suppress a rebellion in Angola in 1957, the likely fraud in the presidential elections of 1958, the steps towards decolonisation by France and the United Kingdom, and John F. Kennedy's presidency marked a change in the international community's stance towards Portugal. Salazar's rigid colonialism often embarrassed its NATO allies (Robinson 1979:93). After 1957, Portugal began to detach itself from NATO and the United States and abandoned the NATO-inspired reforms (Telo 1996:324–8). The change in the military and defence strategies was accentuated in 1961 when Defence Minister Botelho Moniz, who had launched many of the NATO-related reforms, failed his coup against Salazar and was forced to resign (Maxwell 1995:47–51). Salazar was aware of the American collaboration with the plotters and the independence movements in Africa (Mahoney 1983). The inflexible attitude vis-à-vis the military who surrendered Goa to Indian Armies in December 1961 underscores Salazar's firm decision to prioritise the defence of the colonies over all other considerations. Portugal was, thus, locked into a long Colonial War with little chance to secure a durable victory in the long term. This war constrained all basic control resources, limited the effectiveness of many of the control tools, and enormously increased military dissatisfaction.

The impact of the Colonial Wars on Portuguese civil-military relations also reveals what Pierson calls a 'slow-moving causal process' and 'threshold effect' (Pierson 2003, 2004). The long Portuguese Colonial Wars had a cumulative effect on military satisfaction. Many in the military began to feel gradually more detached and dissatisfied with the regime. The enactment of the Decree-Law 353 in 1973, which granted privileges to conscript officers, was a landmark in the deterioration of civil-military relations. The military's discontent reached a critical level and the coup against the Estado Novo was triggered, transforming civil-military relations.[3]

In Portugal, the effect of the Colonial Wars was also amplified by the previous impact of NATO on the Portuguese military. This can be construed as an example of how sequences of events matter and can produce unintended consequences (Mahoney 2000). Through the contacts with other militaries, the Portuguese military had developed a more critical perspective of its professional role and on the policies of the regime. The decisions of the government concerning the colonial conflicts were against many of the ideas introduced by the 'NATO generation'. Gradually, dissatisfaction increased until the military decided to plot against the government. Had Portugal not joined NATO and had not been exposed to different military and political ideas, the effect of the Colonial Wars might have been very different. In Spain, the process of decolonisation did not produce any visible impact on the military's allegiance to Franco. Salazar had previously used the threats of the Spanish Civil War and the Second World War as a means to strengthen his leadership. However, the Colonial Wars became a fundamental cause of the fall of his regime.

9.2.4 Legacy of the political transitions

The transitions into democracy in the two countries were macro-historical events producing critical junctures in civil-military trajectories. In Spain, the political transformations and terrorist violence became a source of discontent in the ranks. The strategy of granting a high degree of autonomy and imposing soft sanctions on insubordination did not seem to generate positive feedback. On the contrary, this strategy reinforced the determination of the military conspirators who interpreted it as a sign of the government's weakness. The failure of the 23-F coup in 1981, Spanish membership to NATO, and the land-slide victory of the socialist party in 1982 created the opportunity for new, deeper changes in the government's toolkit and contributed to the subordination of the military.

In Portugal, the political instability generated throughout 1974 and 1975 delegitimised the revolutionary approach of the Gonçalvist sector of the MFA. As during the military dictatorship from 1926 to 1932, the inability of military-led governments to solve the country's problems convinced most military of the need to hand power back to civilians. The failed coup attempt by the revolutionary left in November 1975 served to consolidate the MFA-Moderates in power and paved the way to depoliticisation of the military and profound changes in the control toolkit.

In both countries, the transitions from authoritarian rule were complex processes that did not directly result in a new stable path of civil-military relations. The control policies launched immediately after the end of the dictatorial regimes did not generate any equilibrium or self-reinforcing dynamics. On the contrary, they contributed to creating a window of opportunity for military plotters to try to overthrow the newly established governments. Yet, in both countries the coup attempts failed, which strengthened civilian authority and legitimised further transformations in the control toolkit.

The coups of 25 November 1975 in Portugal and 23 February 1981 in Spain were not merely the result of non-controllable exogenous shocks but to a great extent endogenously generated by civil-military relations. This is in line with some critiques of pure path-dependence explanations which tend to ignore the endogenously generated turning points in institutional or policy trajectories (Greif and Laitin 2004; Howlett 2009b).

9.2.5 Summing up: path-dependent civil-military relations?

Most concepts associated with path-dependence explanations have been identified in the context of Portuguese and Spanish civil-military relations. The evolution observed somewhat matches path-dependence explanations if considered in a broad sense as what occurred earlier in time affects the outcomes in a sequence of events (Sewell 1996:262–3). Some macro-historical events, such as the Spanish Civil War, the Second World War, the Colonial Wars and the political transitions acted as 'historical causes' that put the control toolkit on a particular path different from that of the other country which shared similar initial conditions.

However, if path dependence is understood in a more restrictive orthodox way (Arthur 1989; Mahoney 2000:507; Rixen and Viola 2009) then it fails to explicate civil-military relations and tool choice in the Iberian Peninsula. Choices were not completely locked into paths or the result of increasing returns or positive feedback mechanisms generated by past external shocks. The empirical evidence also suggests the importance of agency and that some of the critical junctures may have been largely endogenously generated by the system of civil-military relations. Moreover, what seems a path at one level of analysis is not necessarily one at a different level. Finally, path dependence can illustrate why the opportunity for change is created, but it does not help in predicting the direction or specific nature of change in the toolkit.

The evolution of the control toolkit and of civil-military relations in general in the peninsula does not completely fit a model of punctuated equilibria. Portugal and Spain experienced some critical junctures and periods of quick changes but these were not always followed by stable trajectories. Although these critical junctures created new patterns in the utilisation of tools, it is very difficult, at least at the level of the control toolkit to find periods of complete stasis. There were variations between critical junctures not directly linked to the legacies of the events that induced them. Even during the times of relative stability, such as the 1940s in Portugal and from the mid-1940s to the mid-1950s in Spain, if analysed closely enough, it is easy to perceive some changes.

The phenomenon of inertia or institutional reproduction (North 1990; Thelen 1999; Pierson 2000) can be observed at two stages. First, it is portrayed at the level of the military's ideology and attitudes in Spain. All of the officers considered liberal or critical of Franco's regime were purged during and after the Civil War. The military that remained was very conservative and loyal to Franco and groomed the following generations of military. This was a self-reinforcing mechanism that made the Spanish military increasingly homogenous and loyal. Later, the isolation from other militaries that followed the Second World War reinforced this inertia.

Second, the limited availability of *treasure*, an excess of officers and the oversize of the armies, generated by the wars 'locked' Portugal and Spain into a pattern of low utilisation of *treasure* that was compensated for by an important utilisation of 'cheaper' tools such as *authority*-based rewards and incentives and intensive propaganda. Equipment expenditure was very low and the weapons and technical means for the defence of the countries were obsolete for the new type of warfare the Second World War had introduced. In order to preserve military morale, the

Iberian regimes emphasised the relevance of manpower and moral values over material means. Moreover, the Second World War proved that the Portuguese military alone could not defend the country and complicated the acquisition of modern equipment by the Francoist regime. These facts contributed to shift the role of the military from defending against the external enemy to defending against internal threats. This new role was more compatible with the tool mix in place: high utilisation of *authority* incentives and *nodality* effectors and low use of *treasure*.

However, self-reinforcing dynamics were not all-pervasive. For instance, the significant reduction of the utilisation of coercive *organisation* tools in Spain from 1942 to 1945 was associated with a process of diminishing returns. In the case of Portugal, it is difficult to identify clear patterns of positive feedback that contributed to the stability of the model of civil-military relations. On the contrary, the circumstances surrounding the inception and the institutional arrangement of the Estado Novo facilitated continuous challenges to the civilian supremacy and therefore introduced elements of instability. Despite the absence of apparent mechanisms of reinforcement, sometimes the control toolkit remained stable, for instance in Portugal after the overthrow of Caetano. This stability suggests that other types of forces (beyond the initial 'historical causes') and the existence of a certain degree of agency were at play (Hall and Taylor 1996; Hay and Wincott 1998; Peters et al. 2005). In this case, the stability in civil-military relations and the reproduction of the toolkit is explained by the active involvement of some political actors which were influenced not only by past legacies but also by the current cognitive and institutional context in which they took decisions.

Orthodox path-dependence explanations attribute the initial impulse for change to forces exogenous to the systems of civil-military relations. However, the evidence suggests that individuals and institutions within the system had the capacity to effect changes and shape policy outputs. Moreover, some of the macro-historical events that triggered critical junctures, if analysed with the sufficient historical distance, can be considered as endogenously generated by the system of civil-military relations. This is the case for the Spanish Civil War, the collapse of the Estado Novo, and the coups of November 1975 in Portugal and February 1981 in Spain. These historical events were, to a great extent, brought about by past decisions from within the system of civil-military relations.

Thus, at different levels of analysis the patterns of evolution observed may vary. The inertias or paths observed at one level may not be considered such from a different level of analysis. Probably the most interesting illustration of this can be found in the case of Portugal from the Colonial Wars until the end of 1975. In this period from the macro-perspective of civil-military relations there was a clear break, especially manifested in the Carnations Revolution. However, if this period is analysed from the meso-perspective of the control toolkit, it can be concluded that there were no fundamental changes, that the logic of control remained to a great extent similar, and that the governments continued to rely on a similar mix of basic resources. Further, at the micro-level, when examining the specific tool choices it needs to be stressed that the stability in the meso-level did not imply a complete stasis. After the fall of Caetano, the provisional governments replaced many of the tools they were using by similar ones. For instance, the PIDE/DGS, Legion, Mocidade, and the Estado Novo's propaganda machinery were replaced by the SDCI, COPCOM, the Fifth Division, and CODICE which performed similar control tasks. Therefore, different patterns and types of explanation can be identified according to the levels of analysis adopted. The impact of macro-historical events, and probably also that of other contextual factors and individual actions, can be asymmetric at different institutional and policy levels.

Although the external shocks explain why previous courses of action were truncated and new windows of opportunity for action were opened at the level of civil-military relations, they are less effective in explaining the specific nature of change or the direction at the level of the tool mix. Path-dependence explanations fit some of the choices of specific tools but overall the explanatory value of the macro-historical events decreases when descending the ladder of abstraction and looking into the specific choices (Table 9.1).

In sum, all four overarching contextual events examined generated critical junctures in the control toolkit and in civil-military relations and produced distinct legacies or trajectories. Path dependence provides an interesting way to conceptualise ex post the evolution of civil-military relations and partly that of the tools of government. History matters but it does not explain the whole picture. In order to capture all of the choices and major changes observed in this book, alternative explanations need to be explored.

9.3 Environmental factors: the continuing action of context

Neo-institutionalist theory provides other analytical concepts that are rooted in the ideational and institutional context that can serve to

Table 9.1 Summary of the evaluation of path-dependence explanations

Analytical concepts	Theoretical claims fitting path dependence	Theoretical claims *not* fitting path-dependence
Critical junctures	All macro-historical events observed produced critical junctures and deep changes in civil-military relations	Did not always produce stable paths in civil-military relations. Moreover its impact can be asymmetric at different levels of analysis
Exogenous Shocks	All change observed has been directly or indirectly associated with external shocks	In the long-term, some of the macro-historical events were partially endogenously generated
Punctuated equilibria	There were periods of stability and periods of drastic changes	During some periods, changes were gradual and did not follow a clear stable path
Self-reinforcing mechanisms	Some events produced long-term legacies on civil military-relations through self-reinforcing (and self-undermining) dynamics	Choices of tools do not seem completely locked-in by self-reproducing mechanisms
Sequence and timing	Some events saw their effects amplified due to the specific timing or sequence in which they took place. Many choices were shaped by earlier choices, outcomes, and events	Some choices do not seem directly correlated to or constrained by past events and choices but fundamentally to the current circumstances

refine the explanations about the evolution of tool choice and civil-military relations. This section examines three sets of environmental factors, ideas, the political-institutional structure, and the international environment, and provides examples that illustrate how the ongoing action of context shaped civil-military relations and tool choice.

9.3.1 Ideas

The cognitive dimension of the context shapes the toolkit in several ways. Decision-makers operate within an interpretive framework of ideas or policy paradigm that specifies not only the problems and goals but also the tools that can be used to solve a problem (Hall 1993:279–80). The shared ideologies of government and control, the economic and technocratic ideas, and the personal past experiences and individual perceptions of decision-makers, help explain some of the trends portrayed in the previous chapters.

Shared ideologies of government and control doctrines affected civil-military relations and tool choice. The origins of these regimes were saturated with the fascist autocratic ideologies that emerged in Europe in the 1920s and 1930s and that legitimised an intrusive approach to control and the military's participation in the state apparatus (Campinos 1975; Payne 1999). Indoctrination and a partial politicisation of the military were carried out through intensive censorship, propaganda, and a significant participation of the military in the state apparatus. Other features of the control toolkit that are associated with these ideologies are the utilisation of paramilitary forces, such as the Carlist and Falangist militias during the Civil War and the Portuguese Legion; the secret political police PVDE/PIDE/DGS; the political purges conducted in the Spanish military until 1945; and the concentration of power in the hands of the dictators (Preston 1990; Medina 2000).

Salazar's and Franco's initial admiration for the fascist governments and their partial imitation is well-documented (Ferro 1933; Salazar 1935; Preston 1993; Loff 2008). The adoption of these approaches to control can be interpreted as a process of mimetic isomorphism (DiMaggio and Powell 1983) in the context of a very unstable and changing national and international environments. Thus, uncertainty made the dictators imitate some of the control mechanisms implemented by Mussolini and Hitler. Imitation was also a way to acquire legitimacy and support from these regimes. Later, with the fall of the Axis and in the context of the Cold War, authoritarian and totalitarian views became discredited in the eyes of the West. The easing of repression in Spain after 1942 as well as the gradual decrease in the intensity of propaganda and censorship were, to a great extent, the result of new normative external pressures and the search for legitimacy and international recognition.

Second, economic ideas also affected the control toolkit. The austerity approach to public spending that Salazar strongly advocated in the 1930s seriously constrained salaries and the modernisation of equipment (Faria 2000). Although the impact of the great depression had not been very strong in Portugal, Salazar was convinced that austerity was the best way to reduce trade imbalances. The initial success of his economic measures reinforced his conviction and austerity remained a driving principle throughout his mandate; only the advent of the

Colonial Wars made him soften the grip on military expenditures (Mata and Valerio 1994:190–3).

In Spain, the 'developmentalist' economic ideas implemented by the technocratic governments from 1957 to 1973 also severely constrained the availability of *treasure* for military purposes. Defence expenditures were not a priority for the technocrats, to the extent that Finance Minister Navarro Rubio considered the military budget was an 'unproductive drain on the economy'.[4] The economic boom of the 1960s served to increase expenditures on public infrastructures, education, and agriculture (considered priorities for the development of the country), but not to noticeably increase military expenditures (Preston 1990:14; Comín and Diaz 2005:929–34). Equally, technocratic ideas during the 1960s made officers' appointments to jobs in the administration and government less acceptable (de Miguel 1975:69).

Third, the ideas and perceptions of decision-makers, including personal inclinations, experiences or interests, had an impact on the choice of instruments. This impact was especially obvious during the dictatorships. Franco's and Salazar's personal preferences were reflected in their governments' policy choices. For instance, their paternalistic view of the regime can be linked to the use of the state apparatus as a means to dispense services, goods, and jobs to the military as well as a justification for information control and censorship (Crollen 1973:51; Bañón 1985:279–80; Medina 2000:42).

Franco's experience as a field officer during the Rif War (1909–27), during which he led several repression campaigns against the local rebels and took harsh disciplinary measures on his troops, had hardened him (Balfour 2002). This experience can be understood as an antecedent for the repressive control measures he adopted during the Civil War (Preston 1993). Franco always considered himself a officer and maintained close contact with them. He constantly granted private audiences to officers, often gave military speeches, and used his network of acquaintances in the military as a *nodality* tool. Franco, as many other officers, believed the military should have an important degree of autonomy and develop their own internal mechanisms of self-control. He avoided the utilisation of paramilitary or police forces and civilian intelligence services as a check on the military and restored seniority as a principle for promotions.

Salazar was a reserved man, he maintained more distant relationships with the military and did not enjoy public acts of glorification (Ferro 2003 [1932–8]:55–6). Salazar's past as a law professor also shaped his somewhat legalistic approach to government and control.[5] For example, Salazar managed to completely renew the top tier of the Portuguese military and to stimulate adherence to the regime, almost exclusively using a set of decrees enacted in 1937. He did not trust the military as much as Franco and relied on espionage and external paramilitary bodies to control them.

The personal experiences of the Portuguese officers in the Colonial Wars also influenced the control toolkit during transition. The counter-insurgency techniques that were intensively used in Africa profoundly marked the strategic thinking of the military (Teixeira 2004:80). The intensive utilisation of *nodality*, the politicisation of the military, and the implication of the civilian population in anti-insurgent actions are the clearest examples of this thinking. The use of propaganda stemmed from the military's exposure to the propaganda techniques used among the pro-independence movements and counter-insurgency in the 1960s and 1970s. The military was also exposed to socialist and communist ideas during their fight, to the extent that many of the officers embraced them. The creation of a parallel structure of political control imitated to a great extent the organisation of some contemporary leftist parties and organisations. Finally, the use of loyal civilians to counter military insurgency, as in November 1975, could have been inspired by the utilisation of paramilitary groups of settlers in the African conflict.

During the Spanish transition, most members of the transitional governments had been involved in the previous regime apparatus and were averse to drastic changes. This aversion explains the insufficient military reforms and high degree of the military's autonomy during Suárez's governments (Barrachina 2002:386–99; Busquets and Losada 2003:138). The majority of the military continued to think that the defence minister and the government remained merely administrators of military budgets (Puell de la Villa 2005:236). Moreover, the traumatic memories of the Civil War made decision-makers behave very cautiously and avoid measures that could disturb hardliners and provoke their intervention in politics.

9.3.2   Political-institutional structure

The political setting influenced tool choice by making available and constraining basic resources and their utilisation. Dictatorial political arrangements facilitated the implementation of the rulers' preferences in the control toolkit. The political transformations which resulted in a distribution of power among diverse actors and institutions were also reflected in the tool choice dynamics. Political conflict and bargaining initially hindered the adoption and implementation of some reforms, but later contributed to stability in civil-military relations and tool choice.

Salazar and Franco designed their new political and administrative institutional orders. The state apparatus became a malleable instrument in the hands of the dictators, especially in Spain where the previous institutions had been completely dismantled during and after the war (Richards 2006:13). The new political system was conceived to avoid checks to Franco's actions. He held the absolute authority and was not to be held accountable for his decisions. Rather than to the strength and supreme authority imposed by the dictator, the longevity of the Estado Novo was more due to Salazar's management of equilibria among the elites (Rosas 1986, 1989). Thus, although in the Estado Novo there was no real scrutiny or political opposition, there were more actors with a capacity to influence or oppose decisions from the government than in Spain.

Equally, the high degree of centralisation of decisions and information flows strengthened *nodality* as a control resource. Salazar and Franco held the executive and legislative powers and no judge would rule against their decisions, the use of *authority* instruments was fully at their discretion. Salazar and Franco also controlled budgets and if they had deemed it necessary, they could have used *treasure* more intensively as well. Overall, the institutional characteristics of the regime stimulated the availability of the four basic resources for the dictators and did not constitute any relevant hindrance for their flexible utilisation.

Caetano faced stronger political opposition and pressures from the military (Graham 1993; Fernandes 2006). The veto power of the military created some rigidity and contributed to the continuation of certain policies and tools despite the preferences of the government. Moreover, during Caetano's rule the changes in the military strategy were constrained by the highly legalistic and bureaucratic institutional framework that slowed down reforms and precluded more energetic actions to counter upheavals (Maxwell 1995:44).

Executive and legislative powers were much more fragmented after the end of the dictatorships. The supremacy of governments was reduced, and new actors acquired the capacity to shape or obstruct policy choices. In Spain, during Suárez's minority governments, the military gained autonomy. The newly created Defence Ministry was in a weak position vis-à-vis the branches of the military (Rodrigo 1989:307). The formal legal subordination of the military to civilian rule remained ambiguous (Puell de la Villa 2005:236). The veto power of the military became evident. Some of the reforms were slowed down by the military ministers and other top ranking officers, the practice often did not follow formal principles and regulations (Ballbé 1983:469–88). For instance, three years were necessary to launch the ISFAS after its legal inception in 1975 (Puell de la Villa 1997:212–13). The socialist government, having a comfortable majority in the parliament and wide public support, managed to kerb the autonomy and veto power of the military and to introduce fundamental reforms.

Compared to Spain, the fragmentation of power and institutional volatility marked more profoundly the civil-military relations in the Portuguese transition. During the period of provisional governments, the continuous reshufflings of cabinets, the multiplicity of bodies sharing governmental functions, and the decisions to link the military hierarchically to the president and not to the Defence Ministry undermined the capacity of the government to reform civil-military relations. The middle management in the public administration that had served during the previous regime was removed, accelerating the process of fragmentation. The public sector grew and political appointments increased (Graham 1983:228–43). The over-bureaucratisation of the administrative apparatus hindered the consolidation of strong independent political parties (Opello 1983:216). In this scenario characterised by reversals in policy choices, bureaucratic barriers, and internal grievances, governments held on to a control strategy that was basically a continuation of that of the Estado Novo. Inertia and red-tape prevailed and the control mix remained essentially unchanged until 1976.

From 1976 to 1982, veto actors such as the CR, the president of the republic, political parties, and the military can be considered responsible for slowing down and hindering some of the reforms in civil-military relations. The best example can be found in the Law for Constitutional Reform that faced intense institutional opposition during its drafting process from the CR, PCP, and President Eanes. The reform was finally approved by the assembly in 1982 and contributed to Portugal's approach to the Western model of civil-military relations by abolishing the CR and therefore the formal veto power that the military had held since the fall of the Estado Novo (Graham 1993). The consolidation of a Western democratic type of regime characterised by a division of powers among different political institutions and several legal checks contributed to the stability in the path of convergence observed in these countries after 1982.

In sum, the political-institutional structure acted as a 'constant cause' facilitating or hindering tool choices and institutional change in civil-military relations.

9.3.3 International environment

Some international actors, countries, and organisations influenced choices and civil-military relations though normative pressures and by stimulating the availability of some resources. As shown in Section 9.2, sometimes these international actors acted as 'historical causes' creating critical junctures and durable paths that outlived their initial action. However, in other cases they merely operated as 'constant causes' in the absence of which the effects on tool choice and civil-military relations disappeared.

The origins of the Estado Novo and that of Francoism were intertwined with the rise of fascism and political instability in Europe (Pinto 1995; Saz Campos 2004). Portugal became one of the targets of the Nazi propaganda machinery in the second half of the 1930s. Germany put pressure on Portugal, assisted Portuguese secret services, and cultivated institutions such as the Legion and the Mocidade (Stone 2005:208). Italy and Germany became the source of inspiration for some of the control choices in Spain and through their military participation in the Civil War they also contributed to the creation of the Francoist regime. Normative pressures from these international actors can be construed as fundamental reasons for the adoption of some *nodality* and *organisation* tools such as modern propaganda, censorship, emphasis on mass speeches, public displays of power, paramilitary and youth movements and political purges in the military.

These international actors can be interpreted as 'constant causes' because after their collapse, many of the effects that they were producing on Portuguese and Spanish civil-military relations vanished. For instance, the process of rearmament and modernisation (*treasure*) was interrupted as soon as Germany and Italy stopped supplying equipment. Additionally, German and Italian political support increased the legitimacy of the dictators in the eyes of the military, which for the most part were pro-Axis. The repressive model of control exerted by the fascist regimes also served as an excuse for the purges committed in Spain during and immediately after the Civil War. The fall of the Axis meant the loss of important political support for the Iberian dictatorships and it contributed to reducing the intensity of the tools they had inspired. The grip on the information control was gradually softened and in Spain executions and imprisonments were reduced.

The Iberian countries continued to be exposed to foreign influence after the Second World War. In 1948, Portugal was invited to join NATO and signed defence agreements with the United States (Beirôco

2003:72–3). The action of NATO and the United States produced important changes in civil-military relations and in the tools for control of the military during the 1950s (Rosas 1994; Telo 1996). Many NATO-led reforms were implemented throughout the 1950s despite the reluctance of the regime (Duarte 2010:244; Telo 1996:211). This is an example of how international normative pressures shaped tool choice and civil-military relations by their constant action. Spain, thanks to its geographical location, its resources in terms of raw materials, and its relatively large army, also became a valuable ally for US government in the context of the Cold War. The Pact of Madrid signed in 1953 allowed the United States to establish military bases on Spanish soil in exchange for material and logistical support and rebuilding and modernising the Spanish military (Liedtke 1999). The Spanish and Portuguese militaries were underequipped and poorly trained. The United States and its allies facilitated the acquisitions of material and supported the education and training of Portuguese and Spanish officers.

The evolution of tool choice in Portugal and Spain suggests that the United States and other NATO allies acted as 'constant causes'. The relations between Portugal and its NATO allies were drastically reduced due to their opposition to the colonial conflict (Porch 1977:37). Many of the reforms promoted by NATO were then abandoned and the control toolkit became again similar to that of the 1940s. Rather than endogenous self-reinforcing mechanisms (as a path dependence explanation might argue), what contributed most to the new trajectory in the control toolkit during the 1950s was the continuing pressure from NATO. Arguably, the reversal of this trajectory could have been caused not only by the absence of forces maintaining it but also by the emergence of new pressures in a different direction. For instance, the United States blocked the sale of equipment to Portugal during the conflict, contributing to the dearth of materials and unrest among the military on the African fronts. Spain gradually integrated into the Western bloc due to the defence agreements with the United States in the 1950s and the liberalisation of the economy in the 1960s. Spain became more prone to the ongoing influence of international actors and gradually adopted many of the *organisation* tools and templates that NATO proposed (Salas López 1974).

During their transitions Portugal and Spain became countries searching for legitimacy and recognition. The international community maintained direct contacts with the Portuguese political and military leaders after the 25 April coup but the ideological fragmentation of the MFA impeded a coherent strategy concerning foreign affairs. For instance, Vasco Gonçalves sought international support in the Eastern bloc, Otelo

Saraiva de Carvalho in Cuba, and Rosa Coutinho in Velasco's Peru. The USSR kept good relations with the MFA; however, the Soviet influence and participation was limited. Both German states were actively involved in the process, East Germany supported the communist approach and West Germany the Western democratic model (Ferreira 1994:72–86). The United States initially maintained a distant approach that can be captured by Kissinger's reference to the Portuguese revolution as a 'vaccine' against future communist revolutions. NATO put pressure on the MFA governments (Ferreira 2006:135–8; Gomes and Moreira de Sá 2008). Once the MFA-Moderates gained control, Portugal was gradually integrated into the Western sphere again. The influence of NATO allies became stronger and was used by the political leadership to legitimise many changes in the control toolkit to consolidate the military's subordination.

In 1976, Spain signed a new treaty of cooperation with the United States and applied for NATO membership. Spain became member of the Council of Europe in November 1977. In 1979, the negotiations for the accession to the ECC started. After the 23-F coup in 1981, the idea of joining NATO became a priority. Politicians considered this as a means of diverting the attention of the military away from domestic politics. The adhesion was made official in 1982. The normative pressures from NATO and the more frequent exchanges with other Western militaries contributed to the convergence of military policies in the peninsula.

In sum, throughout the period analysed it is clear that the international actors affected tool choices and civil-military relations through normative pressures and templates and also by constraining and stimulating the availability of some resources. Section 9.2 suggested that the international actors sometimes created critical junctures, triggering new paths in civil-military relations. This section has shown that the international environment is not only responsible for the initiation of new trajectories but also for sustaining them through its continuing effect.

9.4 Explaining the change in tool choice

This chapter has illustrated how both history and context contribute to shaping civil-military relations and controlling tool choices. Path-dependence accounts based on external shocks, timing, and self-reinforcing mechanisms need to be qualified. In addition to the 'historical causes', there are environmental factors acting as 'constant causes' intervening along the trajectories in civil-military relations and shaping tool choices.

Macro-historical events and environmental factors are linked in many ways: First, often the impact of macro-historical events can only be explained by referring to environmental factors. The environmental factors acted as intermediaries, channelling the effects of macro-historical events into tool choices. For instance, the Spanish Civil War can be considered as a macro-historical event that influenced tool choice through the transmission of certain control ideas and the replacement of the political-institutional structure; the outcome of the Second World War is associated with the normative pressures on civil-military relations by NATO and the United States during the Cold War; and the Colonial Wars transformed the personal experiences and perceptions of the MFA leaders that left an imprint on the control toolkit during the Portuguese transition.

Second, the macro-historical events created critical junctures not only in the control policy but also in the environmental factors. The Civil War and the Second World War, for instance, shattered existing institutional settings and transformed the system of international relations. The evolution of the interpretive frameworks of decision-makers is also linked to history and conjunctures. For example, the ideologies that inspired some of the choices of the dictators shaped and were shaped by macro-historical events. Under exceptional circumstances, usually associated with crises, the framework of ideas changes; a new paradigm involving policy problems, goals, and instruments replace the previous one (Kuhn 1962; Hall 1993). Thus, macro-historical events not only opened windows of opportunity for change and left legacies in the control toolkit but sometimes also influenced the broader context which, in turn, induced tool choices too. The legacy of past events sometimes did not manifest itself directly through the creation of (endogenous) self-reinforcing mechanisms in the system of civil-military relations, but indirectly through the continuing action of environmental factors which sometimes had been locked in paths at previous critical junctures.

Third, the interaction of some environmental factors and previous tool choices was at the origin of some of the macro-historical events studied. In particular, the Spanish Civil War and the Carnations Revolution were the result of: new waves of ideas (fascist, revolutionary and liberation ideologies); the crisis of the existing political-institutional structures (Spanish Republican and Estado Novo political models); the action of international actors (Italy, Germany, independentist forces in the Portuguese colonies); and previous tool choices (creating military dissatisfaction and making them more likely to intervene). Tool choices and civil-military relations were not simply the result of individuals' strategic decisions or the mere reflection of exogenous environmental forces (March and Olsen 1984:741). Therefore a 'chicken and egg' problem without a clear solution emerges: what came first? Environmental factors and tool choices or macro-historical events?

Finally, the impact of past events and that of the current context is asymmetrical across levels of analysis. So, at some levels, the trajectories can be better explained by the action of endogenous self-reinforcing mechanisms caused by past exogenous shocks. At other levels of analysis the evolution seems to be more closely linked to the ongoing impact of the context. Furthermore, sometimes what at a meso- or macro-level is considered an endogenous self-reinforcing dynamic triggered by a 'historical cause' may turn into an exogenous 'constant cause' when the analysis is conducted at the micro-level.

The four reasons above illustrate the interplay between different factors and levels of analysis. 'Orthodox' accounts based exclusively on a single approach (path dependence or environmental factors) will miss important aspects. As this book has demonstrated, policy-makers confronting complex policy problems, such as the military's subordination, usually choose a combination of different policy instruments. Similarly, why should social scientists facing the study of complex policy problems rely on a single theoretical framework or perspective? This chapter has shown how neo-institutionalism helps providing alternative albeit complementary explanatory narratives for civil-military relations and tool choice. In doing so, it builds on the social science tradition that considers important the dialogue across theoretical schools or streams of thoughts (Immergut 1998; Hay 2006; Sil and Katzenstein 2010).

10
Conclusions

The Portuguese and Spanish governments adopted different approaches to the military's subordination through the authoritarian, transitional, and early democratic periods. This monograph has identified and compared the combinations of tools and their evolution, paying special attention to the impact of some past macro-historical events and environmental factors. For that endeavour, this book has relied on historical research of multiple primary and secondary sources, on a comparative framework borrowed from the field of public policy (Hood's NATO scheme), and on neo-institutionalist theory. This final chapter recapitulates the contribution of this book.

10.1 Civil-military relations and government styles in Portugal and Spain

This monograph seeks a better understanding about *what* is done to control the military and *why*. Instead of developing a general explanation of the degree of the military's subordination, it has focused on the tools of control. This focus meant moving the focal point backwards in the causal chain that aimed at contributing to a less divisive common ground of knowledge and a more stable basis for further social enquiry.

Through the analysis of wide-ranging empirical evidence and its classification and comparison according to Hood's four basic resources (*organisation*, *nodality*, *authority*, and *treasure*) important findings about the control strategy in both countries have been revealed. Governments has always used combinations of multiple tools.[1] Tools were not completely unrelated to each other or purely the outcome of random selection. The evidence shows that most tool choices were purposefully taken and that governments followed some patterns in their choices.

The existence of some underlying Iberian ethos and a common political culture is often assumed in social sciences. Could the same be said about the style of control? Is it accurate to speak about an 'Iberian style' of control or model of civil-military relations? The answer is no, as the different trends identified in Portugal and Spain in this book refute the existence of a unique distinctive Iberian style of control or a common system of civil-military relations. Portugal and Spain, despite having experienced similar political regimes and sociopolitical transformations, developed very different civil-military relations. The analysis of the trends in the control toolkit also disproves the existence of a stable 'Portuguese' or 'Spanish style of control'. The degree of utilisation of control tools (in particular *organisation* and *nodality* tools) varied significantly both across country and across time.

The rejection of an 'Iberian style' needs to be qualified. In fact, the utilisation of *authority* and *treasure* tools was very similar in both countries. Moreover, this rejection should not be extended beyond the military sphere and the period analysed. A preliminary analysis of civil-military relations in the nineteenth and early twentieth centuries points to numerous similarities in both countries (Ballbé 1983; Ferreira 1992; Seco Serrano 1984; Caeiro 1997). Equally, after 1982, there was a convergence between Portugal and Spain. Nonetheless, it would be necessary to confirm that this convergence continued beyond 1986 and extend the analysis to other countries in order to verify that such a shared style is unique or specific to the Iberian Peninsula.

Is it possible to establish, at least, common patterns associated to the type of regime? Again the evidence discards the existence of cross-country 'authoritarian' and 'transitional' styles of control on the military. Many differences in the control toolkit during the authoritarian periods (Chapters 4 and 7) and in the case of the transition to democracy (Chapters 5 and 8) have been unveiled in this book. These discrepancies go beyond tool choice and reach other aspects of civil-military relations.

In Portugal there was no total support for the authoritarian government within the ranks. The fact that Salazar, and especially Caetano, had been appointed by military men limited their authority (Rebelo de Sousa 1990:66). Franco was a military leader before he became a ruler and enjoyed higher levels of support in the armed forces. Franco and Salazar had different personalities as well as different preferences and priorities concerning military and defence policies (Medina 2000). The political institutional structure of the regimes also varied. Much more power was concentrated in the hands of Franco for whom the military were never a serious threat, but strong supporters. On the other hand, Salazar and Caetano had to share their power and face challenges from the military (Fernandes 2006; Duarte 2010).

The Estado Novo was more exposed to the international actors and events. The traditional English-Portuguese Alliance, the Spanish Civil War, the (First and) Second World War, NATO, and the Colonial Wars strongly affected Portuguese civil-military relations. The relative seclusion of Spain in the first decades of the twentieth century was aggravated due to the repression during and after the Civil War and the alignment with the Axis powers. Only after the defence agreements, the establishment of US military bases in the 1950s, and the liberalisation of the economy in the 1960s, did Spain very gradually integrate into the Western bloc and become more susceptible to the influence of international actors (Salas López 1974).

All of these differences contributed to different patterns in the utilisation of the tools of government in both authoritarian regimes. For instance, Franco used thoroughly coercive *organisation* (executions, imprisonments) until 1945 in order to purge the military and then abandoned its utilisation. On the other hand, coercive *organisation* (basically paramilitary forces) was used in a less intensive manner in Portugal but without interruption during the Estato Novo. Another difference is that Salazar spied more intensively on the military while Franco preferred to detect threats through his personal relations in the ranks. In both regimes, there were diverging approaches to *authority*, in particular concerning military promotions and the integration of militia officers. Franco restored seniority as the driving principle and integrated the 'alfereces provisionales' as officers in the military in order to reinforce loyalty and conservative ideology within the ranks. Conversely, Salazar combined political appointments, 'escolha', with the limitations to the retirement age to renew the top tier of the military and reward loyalty. Salazar de-mobilised the 'milicianos' recruited during the war period, many of which did not share the ideas of the regime.[2]

During the transition to democracy the discrepancies were accentuated. Although both countries shared the problem of the military's insubordination, many of the features of their civil-military relations diverged. The Portuguese transition originated from a military coup and a revolutionary movement. The Spanish transition was not rooted in the collapse of the former system and a military intervention, but, among other factors, by pressures from inside the existing regime (Fishman 1990). The composition of the Portuguese military was much more ideologically and socially heterogeneous, in part due to the massive recruitment for the Colonial Wars (Carrilho 1985). While in Portugal the military provided the impulse for democratisation, in Spain they largely opposed the process. In Portugal, the MFA military occupied the main posts in the government and advisory bodies. In Spain, the military lost its agenda-setting power and remained reluctant spectators of the reforms (Agüero 1995). In both cases the principle of civilian supremacy was threatened; the revolutionary military controlled the civilian governments in Portugal and the reactionary military did not accept their subordination to those in Spain.

The tools of control used immediately after the end of the dictatorships differ in important aspects. The Portuguese governments used *coercive* organisation to deter insurrections as well as intensive propaganda, censorship, and political surveillance (*nodality*) to indoctrinate the military. In Spain, on the other hand, intrusive means of control were avoided, and the focus was on gradually reforming the the military (*non-coercive organization*) and its legal framework (*authority*) to concentrate power within the government.

However, these countries experienced a process of convergence from 1982 onwards, which was also reproduced in the control toolkit. In Portugal, the failed military coup of 25 November 1975 was a turning point in the process of democratic institutionalisation and a first step for the withdrawal of the military from politics, later accomplished with the reforms launched in 1982 (Pinto 2006:64). In Spain, after the 23-F coup attempt in 1981 and NATO membership in 1982, the new socialist government gave a decisive impulse to the process of the military's subordination and consolidation of democracy (Preston 1986; Agüero 1995). Accession to the EEC in 1986 confirmed that Portugal and Spain had developed Western liberal democratic systems. The underlying strategy for the governments to strengthen civilian supremacy was to instill professionalism in the ranks (Danopoulos 1991).

The convergence in political and civil-military dimensions was accompanied by a convergence in the control toolkit. Non-coercive *organisation* tools such as a formal military education and organisational design were used to foster professionalism and coordination; the new independent media and centralised secret services acted as *nodality* detectors to prevent military interference with politics; *Authority* sanctions and constraints were redefined to limit military autonomy; and utilisation of *treasure* aimed primarily at the modernisation of equipment. These common features suggest a common democratic or Western democratic style after 1982.

10.2   Alternative explanations for tool choice: 'history' and 'context'

This book proposes a neo-institutionalist explanatory framework for the evolution of policy instruments. Rather than exploring the causes of specific micro-choices, the analysis has focused on the factors that produced changes in the general patterns of the control tool mix and has shown how history and context decisively shaped most choices.[3] Historical legacies, ideas, institutions, and international actors facilitated and hindered ways of action.

Most of the evidence examined defies 'technical' models of tool choice (March and Olson 1984; Linder and Peter 1998:37–8). Clearly, in the case of Portuguesee and Spanish military politics, tool choices were not mechanical exercises in which decision-makers simply matched the attributes of the problem to those of the instruments available. Different tools were used to tackle similar problems. This book corroborates what some authors had anticipated (Bruijn and Hufen 1998; Howlett 2005:49–50; Bemelmans-Videc et al. 1998/eds; Eliadis et al. 2005/eds); that is, instruments are generally used in combinations or mixes and therefore it is extremely important to move beyond single instrument approaches. Similarly, the evidence challenges pure 'self-interest' and pure 'political' models that, assuming complete technical substitutability between instruments, explain choices based either on the calculated maximisation of individual benefits or by proximity to cultural values and ideology (Howlett and Ramesh 2003:197–8). Neo-institutionalist theory provides a better alternative explanation.

This research has analysed two contending types of interpretations for instrument choice: on the one hand, path-dependence accounts based on external shocks, timing, and self-reinforcing mechanisms (historical causation); and on the other hand, those grounded in the continuing impact of environmental factors (constant causation).

Historical events played an important role in shaping civil-military relations and control tools in these countries. The beginning and end of distinct trajectories in the utilisation of particular mixes of tools coincided with some non-controllable overarching macro-historical events. Chapter 9 takes a closer look at the legacy of the Spanish Civil War, the Second World War, the colonial conflicts, and transitional political processes and shows that these events triggered 'critical junctures' in the control toolkit. These exogenous shocks generated sometimes endogenous self-reinforcing (or self-defeating) dynamics that contributed to the stability (or reversal) of certain patterns in tool choice and civil-military relations. Chapter 9 also illustrates how the temporal sequence influenced choices and outcomes and that formative periods usually conditioned later developments.

However, some limitations in the orthodox path-dependence explanations have also been revealed. The evolutions of the control toolkits and of civil-military relations in the peninsula do not completely fit a model of 'punctuated equilibria'. Portugal and Spain experienced critical junctures and periods of cathartic changes but these were not always followed by stable trajectories. The periods after some critical junctures showed gradual changes not directly associated to the legacies of the macro-historical events analysed. Self-reinforcing dynamics were not pervasive and in some cases the stability of a trajectory should be attributed to the continuous effect of contextual factors that were not directly related to the 'historical causes' that initated the trajectory. Agents (the dictators) had the capacity to alter the trajectories. Moreover some of the events that triggered critical junctures can be considered as endogenously generated by the system of civil-military relations (in particular the Spanish Civil War, the collapse of the Estado Novo, and the coups of November 1975 in Portugal and February 1981 in Spain). These findings contradict the contingency and determinism that the most orthodox path-dependence interpretations suggest.

Although history matters, path-dependence interpretations of the Iberian cases need to be qualified. Accordingly, three categories of environmental factors have been examined: ideas, political institutional structures, and international environments. These factors act as 'constant causes' shaping trajectories in civil-military relations and tool choice: ideologies as well as the personal experiences and preferences of decision-makers (in particular those of Franco and Salazar) influenced tool choices. The political institutional structure affected the availability of some basic resources. For instance, the centralisation of power and the absence of veto actors amplified the capacity of dictators to implement their preferred tools. The political transitions resulted in the redistribution of power among diverse actors and institutions which impacted military policy; political conflict and bargaining initially hindered some reforms but later contributed to stability in civil-military relations and tool choice. Finally, international actors (countries and organisations) shaped tool choices and civil-military relations through normative pressures and by constraining and stimulating the availability of some resources (in particular *treasure* and *organisation*).

The historical and constant causes observed in each of the two cases were deeply intertwined, and therefore it is important to take both of them into consideration to better explain the trajectories. The environmental factors often translated effects of past macro-historical events into tool choice. These events at times created critical junctures in the environmental factors which in turn offset or magnified the trajectories of civil-military relations and tool choice. On the other hand, these overarching events were sometimes the result of the interaction of environmental factors and previous tool choices. Furthermore, the conceptual differences of both alternative types of explanations for the evolution of tool choice and civil-military relations, although initially important, blurred gradually as the focal point of the study travelled through the time dimension and through different levels of analysis. Current contexts become past legacies from a future perspective; stable trajectories may turn into changing paths if the time segment analysed is longer and some endogenous mechanisms of self-reproduction become exogenous environmental factors when looking at an institutional subset.

Thus, it can be concluded that tool choices are the result of complex social processes that do not fit a simple causal model with well-defined independent and dependent variables. There are interactions between different factors and types of explanations. The 'walls' that separate different streams of neo-institutionalism have been helpful to support the 'scaffolding' that permitted the development of many useful (often parsimonious and elegant) theoretical concepts and analytical tools. However, some of the theoretical divides such as 'structure vs. agency', 'culture vs. calculus' and, as this book shows, 'legacy of the past vs. continuing action of the ideational and institutional context' are not Gordian knots that can be cut or unravelled.[4] As the scrutiny of the empirical evidence on government tools of control has shown, these 'walls' are to a great extent artificial. The proponents of different paradigms could potentially fill gaps in their own theoretical developments by exploring alternative approaches.

10.3   Hood's tools of government revisited

Many authors have previously discussed Hood's NATO scheme but there have been very few attempts to apply it systematically to a specific empirical case. Never before have civil-military relations been studied through the lenses of a policy instrument framework. The historical data on civil-military relations in the Iberian Peninisula have offered the opportunity to test the heuristic value of Hood's NATO scheme and substantiate several of its advantages and limitations.

Systematically linking each of Hood's basic resources with specific policy problems or goals is extremely difficult (if at all possible). The wide variety of instruments that each of these generic categories encompasses as well as the impact of history and context (on the nature of the problems, availability of resources, and policy implementation) turn this endeavour into a fool's errand.[5] The evidence reveals that not all of the instruments that integrate each category evolved synchronously, suggesting that analytic associations might be better explored at the instrument level, not at the level of Hood's generic categories.[6] This is consistent with Hood's work which, despite presenting some canons of 'intelligent policy design' or 'good application' of government tools (Hood 1983:132–3; Hood and Margetts 2007:144–5), never clearly links them to the basic resources.

The availability of the basic resources can be directly linked to choices but still this readiness can be seen as just a mechanism mediating the impact of other historical and environmental factors on tool choice. This problem has been avoided by decoupling the comparative from the explanatory framework. This book has restricted the role of the NATO scheme to that of a 'marker' or 'indicator' of change in tool choice and has relied on two approaches to neo-institutionalism as an explanatory framework.[7]

Hood's NATO framework is well suited for the classification and comparison of instrument choice. It is a resource-based scheme that focuses on what governments actually do, not so much on their intentions, and thus, it reduces the level of subjectivity and simplifies the task of classifying tools. Moreover, the NATO framework has proved to be flexible and parsimonious enough to capture and process all the empirical evidence encountered (Chapters 4, 5, 7, 8) and to establish meaningful cross-temporal and cross-country comparisons (Chapter 9). The NATO framework allows the processing of enormous amounts of information from different sources, covering more than 50 years in the history of civil-military relations in Portugal and Spain. All of the tools of control elicited from the scrutiny of the primary and secondary sources have been classified in one of the four categories: *organisation, nodality, authority,* and *treasure*. None of Hood's categories were redundant. The distribution and evolution of these tools within these categories has served to delineate trajectories in the control strategy of the governments.

However, the simplicity and flexibility of this framework also entails some problems. Hood's basic categories are very broad and not always mutually exclusive. They accommodate much variance within and therefore can hide very disparate attitudes towards the military's subordination. In order to counter this shortcoming, this book has introduced two new subcategories in each of the four basic types. These are different from Hood's subcategories and reflect the way in which the basic resources are used. These subcategories have enabled the establishment of a more nuanced, and still balanced, classification of the control tools and helped establish sharper depictions and comparisons of the action of the governments without over-complicating the analysis.

Furthermore, occasionally instruments can be assigned to more than one category. The tools of government can be considered as the building blocks of policies, but they are not indivisible or homogeneous units. The evidence on tools for the military's subordination confirms that often control instruments are bundles of different 'smaller' instruments (Le Galès 2007) or that they rely on more than one basic resource. For instance, the censorship effort, despite being mainly a nodality tool, has an important organisation component (teams of censors scrutinising the information) or even an authority component (since there is a law that prohibits or constrains certain information, people will exert self-censorship not to commit an offense). For the sake of simplicity this book has allocated each tool to only one basic resource. The hybridisation in the context of Hood's basic resources remains a question for future research.

Lastly, it is important to note that the NATO framework is not time, country, or sector specific. Despite the changing nature of security problems and civil-military relations a generic policy instrument framework such as Hood's is useful for the analysis of past, present and future civil-military relations because it does not focus on the specific goals pursued by a government at a particular time but on the tools employed and the resources they draw their power from. The revised NATO framework could be similarly applied to other countries with salient civil-military relations issues (such as Egypt, Libya, Turkey, Thailand, and Pakistan) or to other areas of government action within the same countries (such as public order, fiscal policy, and education). Additional research in this sense could contribute to complete and refine the debate intitiated here about governments' styles.

10.4 Further implications

This book has defined an alternative (more structured and analytical) narrative about military history and a new angle to the complex socio-political developments that Spain and Portugal experienced from the

1930s to 1986. Many of the findings in terms of control tools and civil-military relations here are associated or precede similar patterns in the control mechanisms and relations of the Iberian governments with society at large. Hopefully this monograph can contribute to a better understanding, or at least inspire a new angle to the study, of the socio-political transformations which occurred in Portugal and Spain.

Moreover Iberian civil-military relations can be useful in order to understand and even anticipate obstacles, opportunities, and likely outcomes in transitional processes in other countries. The different trajectories in terms of democratisation and civil-military relations can be used to establish comparisons and draw lessons relevant for countries undergoing similar political transformations such as those belonging to the so-called 'Arab Spring'.

Although the military's subordination became an important challenge for both countries, Portugal and Spain experienced very different models of democratisation which allows the drawing of lessons applicable in diverse contexts. Some of the issues outlined here that deserve further attention are: the different origins of transitional processes (military coup vs. reforms from within the regime); roles undertaken by the military and involvement in the political reforms (drivers of the reforms vs. spectators); social and ideological compositions of the military (heterogeneous with left-wing dominance vs. homogenous conservative); and strategies and tools for the subordination of the military.

Finally, the Portuguese and Spanish experiences illustrate the need to analyse not only the current context but also the history of the countries undergoing transitions. The introduction of democratic ideas and political institutions even with the support from the international community may not guarantee the military's subordination. Past historical events, such as wars and regime transformations, have longstanding consequences that should be taken into account by anyone concerned about the success of any democratisation process.

Appendix

Table A-1   Brief chronology of events

	Portugal	Spain
1926	Coup against the First Portuguese Republic led by General Gomes da Costa. Military Dictatorship is established	Failed Military coup attempt (Sanjuanada) against the dictator General Primo de Rivera
1928	Salazar is appointed Finance Minister	Opus Dei is founded
1929	Stock market crash. The Great Depression. Military Rebellion ('Revolução do Castelo')	International Exposition of Barcelona Coup attempt by artillery officers
1930	National Union movement is set. Portuguese Colonial Act	General Primo de Rivera resigns as head of state
1931	Ambitious plan of the rearmament and modernisation of the armed forces (proposed by Major Barros Rodrigues).	Second Republic is established. King Alfonso XIII goes in exile. Centre-Left governments are elected.
	Military rebellions in Madeira and in Lisbon	War Minister Manuel Azaña's military reforms
1932	Salazar becomes Prime Minister ('Presidente do Concelho')	Failed military coup attempt of General Sanjurjo
1933	Estado Novo Constitution. General Carmona is elected President and appoints Salazar as Prime Minister. PVDE and the SNP are established	Anarchist revolt of Casas Viejas Right wing government elected. Fascist like party Falange Española is founded

Continued

Table A-1 Continued

	Portugal	Spain
1934	Military rebellion of Marinha Grande. The extreme right National-Unionist Party is banned	Leftist revolution in Asturias repressed by the Army
1936	Salazar is (self) appointedWar Minister. Captain Santos Costa is appointed Undersecretary of State. The paramilitary Portuguese Legion and the youth organisation 'Mocidade' are created. Communist Navy revolt in Tagus.	Left wing Popular Front wins the elections. The military with the support of right wing groups attempt a coup but it fails (18 July). Beginning of the Spanish Civil War. Franco is appointed chief of the state by the military Junta
	Germany substitutes the UK as the main weapons supplier	
1937	Military reforms introduces the ministerial approval, 'escolha' in substitution of seniority for promotion and the creation of the elite High Staff Corps. New recruitment laws following the model Nation in Arms and the reduction of the permanent Army	Franco unifies right wing parties into 'FET de las JONS' that is assigned the control of the Press and Propaganda. Battles of Jarama, Brunete, Santander and Belchite. Bombing of Guernica. Santoña Pact between the forces linked to the Basque Nationalists
1938	Military plots in March, April and May	Battles of Teruel and Ebro
1939	Signature of the Iberian Pact of Defence with Spain. Beginning of WWII; Salazar declares Portuguese neutrality	End of the Spanish Civil War. Political repression continues. Purges in the armed forces
1940	Military plot in May. Signature of the Additional Protocol of Defence with Spain. Concordat with the Vatican	Spain adopts a non-belligerent position in WWII.

Continued

Table A-1   Continued

	Portugal	Spain
		General salary raises for officers
		The Blue Division begins its deployment.
1943	Agreement with the UK for the utilization of Azores bases.	The Blue Division begins its withdrawal.
1945	End of WWII. Military reform is launched eliminating some units and undertaking the construction of many new military quarters. The PVDE is refounded and becomes PIDE	Spanish Fueros (Bill of Rights) and the Code of Military Justice are enacted. Some Monarchic Generals consider to plot against Franco
1946	Military rebellion 'revolta da Mealhada'. Portugal membership to the UN is vetoed by the USSR.	The General Assembly of the UN recommends the rejection of Spanish membership
1947	First Army Officers' statutes are enacted. Independence of India from the UK. 'Abrilada' military plot	Law of Succession that establishes Spain as a Monarchy is enacted
1949	Portugal becomes a founding member of NATO. Salazar accepts the Marshall Plan for 1949–1950	General 40% pay raise in the Armed Forces.
1950	National Defence Ministry and the CEMGFA are established	
1951	Defence Agreement with the US. Groups of military officers begin to be sent to the US for education and training.	The Ministry of Information and Tourism is created
	Beginning of decolonisation of Africa (Libya is the first one)	
1953	Law 2066 transforms the colonies in overseas provinces.	Economic and military agreements with the US (military bases in Spain). Concordat with the Vatican
1955	Portugal joins the UN. The Warsaw Pact is established	Spain joins the UN

Continued

Table A-1   Continued

	Portugal	Spain
1956	Suez Crisis	Spain recognizes the independence of Morocco
1957		Sidi-Ifni war in Sahara (1957–1958). Technocrats dominate the government
1958	Rebellion in Angola severely squashed	Spain joins the OECE, IMF and the World Bank.
1959	Portugal is a founder member of the EFTA agreement. Military rebellion of Sé	Economic Stabilization Plan. ETA is founded
1961	Coup attempt by Defence Minister Botelho Moniz. Portugal loses Goa, Damau and Diu to India. Angola claims independence. Portugal joins the IMF and World Bank	Last Spanish troops abandon Morocco
1962	Military Rebellion in Beja. Independence of Algeria	
1963	Guinea and Cabo Verde claim independence	Tribunal of Public Order is established
1964	Mozambique claims independence	CESEDEN is established
1965	Assassination of the opposition leader, General Humberto Delgado in Spain, supposedly by PIDE agents	
1968	Caetano becomes Prime Minister in substitution of Salazar	Independence of Equatorial Guinea from Spain
1973	Oil crisis. Caetano is forced to cancel the Decree-Law 353, benefiting conscrip officers, due to the opposition among academy officers	Carrero Blanco, Prime Minister of the Francoist government is assassinated by ETA. Reform of the military curricula
1974	Military coup attempt in March. Military coup of 25 April (Carnations Revolution). Negotiation for the independence of the colonies. Right wing coup attempt (September)	The clandestine Democratic Military Union is created

Continued

Table A-1 Continued

	Portugal	Spain
1975	Right-wing coup attempt (March). First Pact MFA-Political Parties (April). First democratic elections (April). Left-wing coup attempt (November). Law 5/75 establishes the Council of the Revolution	Last executions of the regime (2 ETA and 3 FRAP members). Spain transferred the sovereignty of the Sahara possessions to Morocco and Mauritania. Death of Franco. UMD is dismantled and its members arrested
1976	Second Pact MFA-Political Parties. MFA apparatus is dismantled. Portuguese Constitution is issued. PS wins the legistative elections. IDN is created	Suárez is appointed PM. Political Reform Act produces the self-dissolution of the Francoist regime
1977		UCD wins the legislative elections. A unified Defence Ministry is established
1978	Stand-by agreements with the IMF	Spanish Constitution is issued. Operación Galaxia plot is neutralised
1979	Centre-right coalition 'Aliança Democrática' wins the legislative elections	UCD wins the legislative elections
1980	PM Sá Carneiro and Defence Minister Amaro da Costa die in a plane crash	National Defence and Military Organisation Law
1981		Suárez resigns. 23F coup attempt is neutralised
1982	Constitutional Reform and National Defence Law. The CR is abolished	Spains becomes a member of NATO. PSOE wins the legislative elections
1983	PS wins the legislative elections	
1984	Stand-by agreements with the IMF. Reunification of the secret services (SIRP)	Organic Law of Defence and creation of the JEMAD
1985	PSD wins the legislative elections	Military coup in La Coruña is neutralised
1986	Portugal becomes member of the EEC	Spain becomes member of the EEC. NATO membership passed a referendum. PSOE wins the legislative elections

Notes

1 Civil-Military Relations and Policy Instruments

1. For instance, Venezuela (2002), Mauritania (2003), Chad (2004), Democratic Republic of Congo (2004), Thailand (2006), Timor (2008), Ecuador (2010), South Sudan (2013), and Libya (2014).
2. Sun Tzu (2003 [c. 500 BC]), Thucydides (1972 [431 BC]), Machiavelli (2002 [1521]), and Clausewitz (1966 [1827]).
3. These waves are based on Feaver (1999).
4. For example, Vagts (1937) and Lasswell (1941).
5. For example, Smith (1951), Mills (1956), and Huntington (1957).
6. For example, Janowitz (1960), Abrahamsson (1972), and Moskos (1977).
7. For exmple, Finer (1988 [1962]), Stepan (1971), Feit (1973), and Nordlinger (1977). Many authors following this line of research delve into specific cases or regions, among others: Horowitz (1980) who writes about Sri Lanka, Pion-Berlin (1992) about Latin America, Welch (1987) about Africa and Latin America, Decalo (1976) about African countries, Danopoulos (1991) about Southern Europe, Herspring (1996) about Russia and Staniland (2008) about India and Pakistan.
8. For example, Avant (1994), Desch (1999), Feaver (1998a, 2003), and Forster (2006).
9. See a similar argument in Olmeda's (2012) meta-analysis based on the scrutiny of *Armed Forces & Society.*
10. See, for instance, Bacevich (1998), Burk's (1998, 2002), Dauber (1998), Desch (1998a, 1998b), Feaver (1998b), and Feaver and Kohn's (2001/eds), Cottey et al. (2002), Cohen (2002), and Murdie (2012)
11. Most works focus almost exclusively on civilian control as a dependent variable (Nielsen 2005) and generally study the degree of professionalism, political institutionalisation, legitimisation of the government, and the existence of internal and/or external threats as explanatory variables (Bland 1999).
12. This book follows Bland's suggestion about the need to dissect civil-military relations into finer categories that can be operationalised across cases and make findings transferable (Bland 1999:9, 22).
13. The degree of control of the military is usually studied as a dependent variable. Nonetheless some scholars have also used control as an independent variable in order to explain other phenomena such as military effectiveness, military technological and doctrine innovation, or military expenditure (Zuk and Thompson 1982; Van Evera 1984; Avant 1994; Rosen 1995; Biddle and Zirkle 1996; Nielsen 2005).
14. In this book the terms 'policy instruments' and 'tools of government' are used as synonyms. Many authors including Hood, use the terms 'tools' and 'instruments' interchangeably.

15. In sum, policy instruments are the manifestation of a government's power. The choices of instruments reflect different government strategies or styles. Since an understanding of governments and the way they exercise their power is important for civil-military relations, taking a closer look at the tools they employ seems a logical endeavour.

16. An increasing number of authors seem to agree that the study of governance is inextricably linked to the study of the sets of instruments used to 'steer' complex networks of actors with a public purpose (Bressers and O'Toole 1998; Commission of the European Communities 2001; Salamon 2002/ed.).

17. See a similar argument in Hood (1983:2).

18. Lasswell (1958 [1936]:204), Dahl and Lindblom (1953), and Lowi (1966) can be considered the inspirations for the study of policy instruments that mainly developed in the field of public policy and administration from the late 1970s to the early 1990s (Anderson 1977; Salamon 1981; Trebilcock et al. 1982; Doern and Phidd 1983; Hood 1983; Woodside 1986; McDonnell and Elmore 1987; Linder and Peters 1989; Salamon and Lund 1989; Schneider and Ingram 1990).

19. For example, Eliadis et al. (2005/eds), Hood and Margetts (2007), Howlett (2011), and Jennings and Lodge (2011) as well as the special issues in *Governance* (2007), *West European Politics* (2010), and *Revue Française de Science Politique* (2011).

20. These combinations are referred to here as the control or government 'toolkit' or 'tool-mix'. This approach is consistent with recent claims in the literature. For instance, Howlett suggests that policy instrument research should be extending the analysis to what he calls 'policy-instruments mixes', 'portfolios', 'governance strategies', 'implementation styles' (Howlett 2005:32–3, 49), or 'governance modes' (Howlett 2009). Bressers and O'Toole (2005:135–6) suggest passing from the study of single instruments to that of 'instrumentation strategies' or 'blends of instruments'.

21. See, for instance, O'Donnell and Schmitter (1986), Chilcote (1990), Huntington (1991), Gunther et al. (1995/eds), Linz and Stepan (1996), Diamandouros and Gunther (2001/eds), and Gunther et al. (2006/eds)

22. The study of other cases in the Mediterranean area such as Greece and Turkey could also be helpful in this regard. See Brown (1980), Kourvetaris and Dobratz (1981), Karabelias (1998), Narli (2000), and Cizre (2004).

23. Different styles of government or control linked to meta-policy preferences have been explored in the subfields of policy instruments (Hood 1983:153–63, 1998; Howlett 2005: 47, 2011:7–11; Ringeling 2005:193–5) and civil–military relations (Huntington 1957; Janowitz 1957; Luckham 1971).

24. Neo-institutionalism provides many varied interpretations for processes of institutional stability and change (March and Olsen 1984; North 1990; Powell and DiMaggio 1991/eds; Thelen 1999; Pierson 2004; Hay 2006).

2 An Interdisciplinary Analytical Framework

1. For instance, Huntington (1957), Stepan (1971), and Herspring (1996).
2. For instance, Finer (1988 [1962]), Decalo (1990) and Forster (2006).

3. Much of the information related to government tools surrounding some critical periods such as the Spanish Civil War, the Portuguese Colonial Wars, and the 23-F coup have been destroyed or remain classified.

4. Some tools draw their power from more than one basic resource; however, for the sake of simplicity, hybrid categories are not considered, and tools are classified according to the predominant resource.

5. *Authority* and *nodality* operate fundamentally at a cognitive level.

6. For instance, Hood (1983:133) suggests four 'canons of good application of government instruments': the examination of alternative possible tools, match to the job, ethical considerations, and economy. Hood and Margetts (2007:145) refer to appraisal criteria for 'intelligent' design: deliberative choice, fitness for purpose, economy, and moral acceptability.

7. Hood also introduces additional subsets within these subcategories; he suggests a third- and fourth-tier subdivisions of the tools (Hood 1983:18, 88; Hood and Margetts 2007:9–10).

8. It is very difficult to empirically distinguish Hood's *nodality* detectors ('*nodality* receivers') from the detectors within the other categories: 'rewards' (*treasure*), 'requisitions' (*authority*), and 'ergonomic detectors' (*organisation*)

9. The level of coerciveness has been a general criterion widely used to discriminate tools of government (Anderson 1977; Doern and Phidd 1983) but it is much better adapted to organisation tools than to any of the other categories.

10. This distinction follows a logic similar to that of Ajzen (1991) and Howlett (2005:37) who draw a distinction between 'positive' and 'negative' instruments, that is, tools that encourage or discourage behaviours which are aligned or incongruent with policy goals. Similarly Vedung (1998:26) refers to 'affirmative' (promoting) and 'negative'(restraining) tools.

11. It seems easier to use Hood's four basic resources than to categorise the observed tools according to other frameworks focusing, for instance, on the behavioural mechanisms that the tools aim to trigger (Schneider and Ingram 1990), the level of state capacity (Howlett 2005), or the degree of legitimate coercion the government is willing to employ (Anderson 1977). Moreover, many of the non-resource approaches classify tools as a continuum which suggests technical substitutability by formalising differences in degree not in nature (Howlett 1991; Landry and Varone 2005:111).

12. This does not exclude the possibility that some instruments may portray characteristics of more than one category.

13. For instance, Anderson's (1977), Doern and Phidd's (1983), and McDonnell and Elmore's (1987) typologies do not comfortably cover instruments of control based on the collection of information in order to prevent deviant behaviour (*nodality* detectors in Hood's terminology). Similarly, Vedung's (1998) classification, as the author admits, does not give room for the utilisation physical resources, such as people, lands, buildings, or equipment (*organisation* tools in Hood's terminology).

14. This is consistent with the more widely accepted definitions of institutions. For instance, Hall states that institutions are 'the formal rules, compliance procedures, and standard operating practices that structure the relationship between individuals in various units of the polity and economy' (Hall 1986:19), and North argues that institutions are 'the humanly devised constraints that shape human interaction' (North 1990:3).

15. Although both approaches have been often associated with 'historical insti-tutionalism'. For further details about historical institutionalism see, for example, Steinmo et al. (1992/eds), Hall and Taylor (1996), Peters (1999), and Sanders (2006). The second type of explanation can also be associated with other streams of neo-institutionalism such as sociological (Hall and Taylor 1996) or constructivist institutionalism (Hay 2006).
16. For instance, Krasner (1984), David (1985, 2000), Thelen (1999), Hacker (1998, 2002), and Pierson (2000, 2003, 2004).
17. This conception of context is broader than that used by some historical neo-institutionalists who focus exclusively on the temporal context and not on the specific circumstances in a given situation (Pierson 2004:172).
18. Alternative categories of factors could be used in a similar analysis. An example of a very influential alternative is the categorisation of factors into 'ideas, interests and institutions' (Goldstein 1993; Garrett and Weingast 1994; Majone 1996; Hall 1997; Hay 2004).
19. See Keynes (1936), Wilson (1980/ed.), Kingdon (1984), Majone (1989), Mashaw and Harfst (1990), Rose (1993), Goldstein and Keohane (1994/eds), Hood and Jackson (1994), and Blyth (1997).
20. For a similar argument, see Blyth (1997:230), Checkel (1998:326), and Wendt (1998:112–13).
21. See, for instance, Goldstein and Keohane (1994/eds), Wendt (1999:113–35), Blyth (2002:39), and Hay (2007:68–73).
22. These mechanisms through which international actors shape policy choice are inspired by Lukes's (1974) three-dimensional approach to power.

3   History of Contemporary Civil-Military Relations in Portugal

1. See an extensive list of internal conflicts in Portugal with the participation of the military (Valério 2001:814–31).
2. The 1933 Constitution together with the Colonial Act of 1930 became the legal foundations of the Estado Novo (Salazar 1939:27).
3. Salazar claimed 'although the Dictatorship ends, the revolution continues'. (Speech, 9 December 1934, Salazar 1935:385). Salazar justified the necessity of the military dictatorship as a means of restoring the 'order' in Portugal, 'imposing silence to some' and ensuring the necessary conditions of 'tran-quillity and security' for public governance (Speech to military officers, 28 May 1930, Salazar 1935:52).
4. For instance, he argued that '[t]he absolute liberty does not exist' and that 'there cannot be liberty against the general interest' (SPN n.d.1:29). In the Congress of National Union (26 May 1934), he claimed that Portugal was a 'national and authoritarian' system, although different from a totalitarian state (Salazar 1935:335–8). Salazar also wrote that 'it is not necessary to believe that authority is to be found in the masses, that justice is ruled by numbers, and that the administration of the law can be carried out by the mob instead of an élite whose duty is to lead and to sacrifice itself for the rest of the community' (Salazar 1939:30).
5. See number III and VIII of the 'Decalogo do Estado Novo' (Salazar 1935:84–7).

6. Salazar defended the notion of organic society in which the basic unit was not the individual but the 'natural groups', among which the family was the basic one (SPN undated 1:29).

7. See, for instance, the Portuguese Estado Novo was not the result of a party or political movement (Schmitter 1979:6). God, Fatherland and Family constituted the basic elements of Salazar's ideological discourse (Medina 2000:55–67). Martins Barata was the artist that best reflected Salazar's conception of Estado Novo. His design 'A lição de Salazar' (in Medina 2000:63) is the most clear example of the 'pax ruris' ideal in the Estado Novo, portraying the ideal life with clear references to religion, nationalism, and family. Salazar's discourse was very nationalistic, but avoided embracing the messianic sebastianism and the radical revolutionary right (Pinto 1994; Medina 2000).

8. The movement, led by Francisco Rolão Preto, reached 50,000 members, while the coetaneous falangista party in Spain did not surpass 10,000 members (Antunes 2000:32). Salazar believed that violence was not a suitable method for Portugal and even labelled the camisas azuis as heretics (Medina 1979:240–3). Salazar's discourse also lacked the anti-semitic and racist references common in other European fascist-like movements (Medina 2000:26).

9. The Finance Ministry could exert veto power on any type of augmentation of expenses in the other ministries and led plans to reduce expenses and increase revenues (Salazar 1935:4–6; Salazar 1939:44). The sessions of the Council of Ministers were replaced by individual meetings with the ministers (Almeida and Pinto 2003:12).

10. The concentration of executive power under Salazar is revealed by the surprise and malaise of President Craveiro Lopes when he learnt in 1958 that he was not nominated for re-election by Salazar (Caetano 2000 [1975]:775–6).

11. See Salazar (1935:81–4, 1939:98–101). Salazar confessed to Ferro that he feared the Parliament: 'O Parlamento assusta-me tanto que chego a ter receio [...] daquele que há-de sair do novo estatuto' (Ferro 1933:162; 2003 [1932–38]:95). Salazar blamed the parliamentary system for the failure of Portuguese democracy (SPN undated 1:25).

12. Letter to Salazar on 25 Augist 1950 (Antunes 1994:266).

13. The National Union acted as the single party in Portugal with the exception of the 1945 legislative and the 1949 presidential elections to which the opposition Democratic Unity Movement also concurred.

14. See, for instance, the PVDE confidential report in 1937 about the Spanish Civil War which denounced that the Spanish Republican Government was already instigating revolution in Portugal (AOS/CO/IN-8A, Folder 3, Page 61). Salazar among his personal documents kept a news clipping of the 'Evening Standard' (16 June 1939) indicating there was a strong movement among Franco's supporters in favour of the annexation of Portugal (AOS/CO/IN-8A, Folder 5, Section 9, Pages 296–8), and another one of the 'Reynolds News' (28 August 1939) arguing that for the United Kingdom, Portugal was rather a liability than an asset because 'her military forces are negligible and her territory might be invaded by Franco' (AOS/CO/IN-8A, Folder 5, Section 26, Pages 425–6).

15. Salazar was so concerned with Spain that the Portuguese National Propaganda Service edited books in Spanish, such as 'Habla Salazar' (SPN undated 1) or 'Portugal ante la guerra civil de España: documentos y notas' (SPN undated 3).

16. For instance, the Corporative Chamber advised Salazar to sign the North Atlantic Treaty without any hesitation but explicitly lamented the exclusion of Spain (report, 20 June 1949, AOS/CO/IN-17-1, Folder 3, Pages 31–2).

17. For instance, up to 70 German civil servants worked permanently on Portuguese territory from 1941 to 1943 producing and distributing pamphlets, publications, radio programs, and films (Telo 1990; Paulo 1994:23–5). A PVDE report to Salazar (16 September 1939), indicates that German professors in Portugal distributed Fichte-Bund pamphlets (AOS/CO/IN-8A, Folder 5, Section 27, Page 440).

18. Despite the fact that the entourage of Salazar was fundamentally Germanophile (especially the Marine Minister). PVDE report in 1939 (AOS/CO/IN-8A, Folder 5, Section 29, Page 458).

19. For instance, Washington barred a Portuguese Army General, who was covering the absence of the Defence Minister, from attending the NATO Defence Committee. The US representatives stressed that the Committee had to be composed of civilian representatives and the Portuguese Ambassador finally replaced him (Confidential memo addressed to Salazar, 29 September 1949, AOS/CO/NE-17-1, Folder 4, Section 41, Pages 181–3 and NATO document, 5 October 1949, AOS/CO/NE-17-1, Folder 5, Section 3, Pages 253–6). A report from the Army Chief of Staff Barros Rodrigues (1 May 1953) refers to the process of introduction through regulations, instructions and handbooks the NATO doctrine. These documents were elaborated in collaboration with the officers that had attended courses abroad (AOS/CO/GR-10, Folder 16, Pages 561–2). NATO suggested improving the education and training of military cadres and specialists (internal report of the Army General Staff, 30 June 1953, AOS/CO/GR-10, Folder 16, Pages 563–82).

20. The Chief of the Joint Staff, the Higher Council of National Defence, the Higher Council of War, and the Higher Military Council were reformed.

21. Salazar declared in 1963: 'I want this country poor but independent' and 'I do not want it colonised by the American capital'. Salazar cited in Franco Nogueira's diaries (Antunes 1985 v.1:23).

22. For instance, the Army report 'The great problems of the Army' (January 1958) makes continuous references to the need of modern equipment and techniques, better integration of the operational capacities of the three branches, and problems of preparation in the Portuguese army. This report set the basis for the reforms from 1958 to 1961 (AHM, divisão 1, secção 39, caixa 1, numero 1, documento 9).

23. See references and comparisons to other NATO countries in the General Programme for the reorganisation of the Army (AHM, divisão 1, secção 39, caixa 1, numero 1, documento 10). This programme or reform was truncated by the colonial conflict and the 1961 coup. See also the secret declassified document of the Army Minister 'Politica Militar Nacional' of April 1959, for comparative tables with the other NATO countries (AHM, divisão 1, secção 39, caixa 1, numero 56).

24. According to Telo (1996:344). NATO pushed Portugal to democracy. See also the 'Chronicle of events of April 1974' by Captain Salgueiro Maia in pointing at NATO membership as one of the antecedents for the Revolution claiming that the more intense contact with the exterior fostered the criticisms about the internal situation (AHM, divisão 1, secção 40, caixa 1, numero 47).

25. For instance, José Norton de Matos (1948), Manuel Quintão Meireles (1951), Humberto Delgado (1958), and Craveiro Lopes (1958–62) (Antunes 2000:59)
26. There is abundant evidence of military protests against the reforms launched in the 1930s in Salazar's personal archives. For instance, Salazar was accused of substituting old officers by the Legion and militia military. Letter to Salazar (undated, probably 1936) (AOS/CO/GR-1A, Folder 13, Document 2, Page 307). In January 1938, General Domigos Oliveira opposing the 1937 reforms posed an ultimatum to Salazar (telegram from Gibraltar, AOS/CO/GR-6, Folder 10, Page 368). There are records of protests usually by officers forced into early retirement, militia officers who saw their rights undermined, and officers who complained about the favouritism showed the High Staff Corps (AOS/CO/GR-6, Folders 9, 12).
27. For instance, an officer, Sebastiano de Sousa Correia in a letter to Salazar criticised the conditions of equipment and food in the Army and the privileges for those serving in the colonies (24 June 1936) (AOS/CO/GR-11, Folder 6, Document 1, Pages 73–9). A confidential report from the Commander of the First Military Region Schiappa de Azevedo to the War Minister in August 1937 showed that the lower rank officers had been badly paid for a long time, which created serious problems of discipline in the region of Porto. The report enclosed a protester's manifesto that called for a revolt and the use of force against Salazar (AOS/CO/GR-1A, Folder 17, Pages 374–7). Several other documents illustrate the unrest among the lower ranks (AOS/CO/GR-1A, Folder 7, Pages 184–229).
28. In 1931, Major Barros Rodrigues presented a plan for the reform of the military, requesting a policy closer to that of the United Kingdom and stressing the need for the demilitarisation of politics. Barros asked for the substitution of all military currently occupying political or administrative positions by civilians, as a means of initiating 'a neutralisation of the War Minister in political terms, absolutely indispensable for the progress and well being of the Nation'. Internal report sent to Salazar (11 July 1931) (AOS/CO/GR-1A, Folder 4, Document 1, Pages 117–18). Barros's proposed reform was never accomplished.
29. For instance, the Governor of Mozambique Rebelo Sousa criticised Kaúlza's ambitions and demeanor since his arrival in Mozambique (letters to Caetano on 23 December 1968 and 4 January 1969) (AMC/12–1549). See also Fernandes (2006:162, 166).
30. After the Second World War, the process of de-mobilisation was aimed specifically at those young officers that did not share the ideas of the regime (Telo 1996:185).
31. For instance, in a letter to the Defence Minister, the undersecretaries of state of the Air Force, Kaulza, and the Army, Almeida Fernandes, warned about the process of 'proletarianisation'. They claimed that the members of the upper and middle classes were attracted to liberal professions due to the higher salaries and only those of the lower classes considered the military as a status improvement. They forecasted that this process would be aggravated in the future, which the Colonial Wars later confirmed (24 June 1958)(AHM, divisão 1, secção 39, caixa 1, numero 16).
32. For instance, the Decree-Law 45661 (14 April 1964) allowed the 'milicianos' to choose their destination when they renewed their engagement. Decree-Law

43101 (2 August 1960) exempted them from the customary requirement of obtaining a permit in order to get married and Decree-Law 48254 (21 February 1968) enabled them to become a career officer (AHM, divisão 1, secção 39, caixa 1, numeros 16, 22, 36).

33. For instance, Brigadier Rezende's letter to Kaúlza (25 July 1961) (AHM, divisão 1, secção 39 caixa 1, numero 1, documento 29).

34. See, for instance, the transcript of the letters that Colonel Costa Gomes sent to the journal 'Diario Popular' and the one Botelho Moniz sent to Salazar in 1961 following the criticisms in the media directed at the military at the onset of the colonial conflict. These letters are part of Captain Ferreira Valença's report 'A Abrilada 1961' (1977) (AHM, divisão 1, secção 39, caixa 1, numero 1, documento 1, 3).

35. For an account on the reasons for the coup attempt see the personal letters from General Albuquerque de Freitas to Brigadier Rezende (16 April 1961) (Declassified document AHM, divisão 1, secção 39, caixa 1, numero 1, documento 23) and from Brigadier Rezende to Colonel Kaúlza in which he questioned that the overseas territories were parts of Portugal similar to the regions such as Minho or Alentejo (2 June 1961) (AHM, divisão 1, secção 39, caixa 1, numero 1, documento 28). See an alternative approach on the report 'The 13 April' by Colonel Kaúlza where he explained his view of the events stressing his differences with Moniz (non dated, AHM, divisão 1, caixa 1, numero 1, documento 25).

36. See, for instance, Rebelo Sousa's letter to Caetano (26 October 1968) (AMC/12–1549) and Caetano's letter to Kaúlza (17 June 1970) (AMC/12–79) which stress the problems between civilians and the military in Mozambique.

37. Salazar suffered a stroke after he fell from a chair in his summer house. Until his death in 1970, Salazar could not speak again and remained in hospital.

38. For instance General Spínola's letter to Caetano stressed the 'absolute impossibility' of success in the military effort in Guinea due to structural deficiencies. (14 March 1972) (AMC/12–1560).

39. Gomes was the military governor in Angola (1970–2) and chief of the Joint Staff (1972–4), and Spínola was the military governor of Guinea-Bissau (1968–73) and vice-chief of the Joint Staff (1974).

40. See the report 'Chronicle of events of April 1974' by Captain Salgueiro Maia (AHM, divisão 1, secção 40, caixa 1, numero 47).

41. This law established that conscript veterans of war could attain a Military Academy degree through an accelerated course of only two semesters and recognised their seniority previous to their attendence at the Academy for the purpose of promotion and pay.

42. See, for instance, complaint letters rejecting the Decree-Laws 353/73 and 409/73 sent to Caetano by army officers from Guinea-Bisau (signed by 45 officers, 28 August 1973) and from Mozambique and Evora (signed by almost 200 officers, 13 September 1973) (AHM, divisão 1, secção 40, caixa 1, numero 4). See also the 'Chronicle of events of April 1974' by Captain Salgueiro Maia (AHM, divisão 1, secção 40, caixa 1, numero 47); a letter from Santos Costa to the new Army Ministry General Sá Viana (1 August 1973) in which he advises to revoke the decree; and a letter from Santos Costa to Caetano on the same subject expressing alarm about the situation in the army (10 October 1973) (AMC/12–425).

43. For instance, General Kaúlza tried to take advantage of the unrest created to plot against the government. Major Carlos Fabião denounced the conspiracy and the coup was prevented in December 1973.

44. Declassified documents from the PIDE/DGS show that Caetano had information about the coup attempt at least one week before 25 April (Porch 1977:80–7; Opello 1985:65–80; Manuel 1995:26–7).

45. Although General Spínola was not a member of the MFA, they selected him following Caetano's demand of surrendering only to an officer of the highest rank.

46. These were not the official designations of the factions but terms coined by Mujal Leon (1978). They are used in this book for clarity purposes.

47. See Carrilho (1994:52) and documents about the first and second MFA-Political Parties Pacts on April 1975 and February 1976 (ACR, MFA/Partidos (84), Pacto MFA-Partidos Parte I, Document 16 and Parte II Document 14).

48. Degree-Law 5/75 (14 Mars 1975). The CR replaced the Junta and the Council of State. See Minutes of the CR reunion, 27/3/1975 and Political Action Plan of the Council of the Revolution, in Annexe B to the Minutes of CR reunion, 20 June 1975 (ACR, Actas Conselho da Revolução – Originais, volume 1 and ACR, Correspondência classificada do secretariado coordenador, volume 8, number 94, document 28).

49. The MFA-Moderates signed the 'Document of the Nine', that denounced the Gonçalves attempt to create an East European style dictatorship and urged for a 'democratic socialism'. The MFA-Populists launched their own critical document, the COPCON Document, against Gonçalves 'Autocrítica Revolucionária do COPCON e Proposta de Trabalho para um Programa Político' (ACR, Correspondência classificada do secretariado coordenador, volume 8, number 94, document 28).

50. According to the minutes of a CR reunion on 7 June 1976, there were more than 200 officers involved in the coup (ACR, Actas Conselho da Revolução – Originais, volume 3). See Sánchez Cervelló (1993:253–8) for an account of the events surrounding the coup.

51. For instance, it introduced the direct universal suffrage for the election of the president abandoning the system of election through a joint session of the MFA and Legislative Assemblies agreed on in the first Pact MFA-Political Parties (Rato 2000:149). This choice meant not only the introduction of a democratic component to the Portuguese political system but also initiated the military disengagement from politics (Ferreira 1983:175–6).

52. For an account of the political parties see Manuel (1996:4–5) and González Hernández (1999:63–84).

53. The winner party PS only received 34.9 per cent and 107 out of 250 seats in the MPs. Different coalitions were explored. The first government of Soares lost a vote of no confidence in December 1977. Soares' coalition government with CDS was dissolved by President Ramalho Eanes a few months later. Eanes appointed successive prime pinisters: Alfredo Nombre da Costa (1978), Carlos Mota Pinto (1978), and Maria de Lourdes Pintasilgo (1979).

54. Democratic Alliance was a coalition formed by the PSD/PPD, CDS, and PPM.

55. Carneiro died in a plane crash in 1980. Diogo Freitas do Amaral led the interim sixth constitutional government. Balsemão led the seventh and eighth constitutional governments (1981–3).

56. Law 1/82 (30 September 1982). See Carrilho (1994), Manuel (1996), and González Hernández (1999).
57. Law 29/82 (11 December 1982). See Balsemão (1986:209).

4   The Estado Novo's Tools of Government

1. PVDE was created by Decree-Law 22992 (29 August 1933), transformed into the PIDE by Decree-Law 35046 (22 October 1945), and finally into the DGS by Decree-Law 49401 (24 December 1969). PIDE's participation was very important to the rebellions in 1946, 1947, 1952, 1959, and 1962 (Pimentel 2007:73, 220–35).
2. The Portuguese Legion ('Legião Portuguesa') was a nationalist and anti-communist voluntary militia created in 1936 (Decree-Law 27058). From 1942, the Legion was in charge of the Civil Defence of the Territory (Decree-Law 31956, 2 April 1942). See Silva (1975) and Rodrigues (1996).
3. These are the three successive acronyms for the Estado Novo secret police (see list of Acronyms)
4. For instance, due to the discontent generated by 1937 reforms the government decided the mobilisation of some Army, GNR and Police units with the assistance of the Legion (Faria 2000:27, 185). The government plans for the Lisbon Military Region in 1941 declared that in case of an eventual coup the GNR, PSP and Legion had to act in a first instance, the Army should only intervene in a second phase if needed (Telo 1996:169–70).
5. In 1939 counted up to 53,000 members (Pinto 1994:291). After the Second World War, the Legion began its decline, the Colonial Wars showed that the Legion had definitively lost any capacity to act as a praetorian guard for the regime (Azevedo 1999:304).
6. For instance, see the report in 1979 of anti-regime involvement of some military officers by Colonel Manuel António Correia (AHM, divisão 1, secção 40, caixa 1, numero 51).
7. In the plot of 1935, among the 40 people arrested, eight were military (Pinto 1994:281).
8. PIDE was often portrayed as the Portuguese Gestapo. See, for instance, (AOS/CO/NE-17-1, Folder 9, Page 578).
9. Allegedly PIDE was responsible of the deaths of Captain Almeida Santos and Lieutenant Colonel Manuel Valente as well as many civilians (Pimentel 2007:387–412).
10. For instance, in January 1936, General Julio Ernesto Moraes Sarmento blamed the lack of efficiency on the absence of military training and field practice activities due to the lack of material means (Report about the situation of the army addressed to Salazar AOS/CO/GR-10, Folder 2, Section 1, Pages 6–8, 18–19). A new report in February of 1937 shows the efforts made in military training in 1936, although it concludes that the situation of the army was still precarious (AOS/CO/GR-10, Folder 2, Section 3, Pages 6–8, 62–116). A PVDE report to Salazar in 1939 explains that the British were disappointed with the lack of preparation of the Portuguese army (AOS/CO/IN-8A, Folder 5, Section 29, Page 458).
11. For instance, see reports for the reform of of High Staff Courses (AOS/CO/GR-1A, Folder 20, Sections 1–8, Pages 412–563).

12. Salazar was involved in the reform of the High Staff Courses and the configuration of the High Military Studies Institute and High Command Courses. See Salazar's handwritten comments and amendments to the project (AOS/CO/GR-1A, Folder 20, Sections 3–7, Pages 463–531). Salazar also supervised the project of reform of the Military College in 1944 (AOS/CO/GR-1C, Folder 23, Pages 355–407).

13. See, for instance, Telo (1996:243) and Matos (2004:170). According to a report to the British Foreign Office (19 June 1950), the Portuguese army was incapable of effectively contributing to any organised force, lacking experience, modern equipment, and training (Telo 1996:205–6). In a letter to the US Ambassador (19 August 1950), Salazar claimed that the reform project of NATO would have to be delayed due to the lack of officers with enough preparation (AOS/CO/NE-17-1, Folder 11, Section 2, Page 616). A document presented by the Portuguese delegation in Ottawa in a NATO conference acknowledges that despite the recent efforts, Portugal was still far from the minimum required number of prepared officers (7 September 1951) (AOS/CO/NE-17-2, Folder 1, Pages 7, 15).

14. There is evidence of important military allocations for training purposes, for instance, in training camps, language courses, training missions abroad, handbooks, publications, and even the translation of NATO publications in Portuguese. See, for instance, Supplementary Defence Budgets 1952–4, 1955–7, 1958, and 1961 (AOS/CO/FI-11T, Folder 1, Pages 2–30; AOS/CO/FI-11T, Folder 5, Pages 373–94; AOS/CO/FI-11T, Folder 8, Pages 605–24; AOS/CO/FI-11T, Folder 11, Pages 677–90).

15. Decree-Law 39053 (26 December 1952)

16. For instance, the reform of the Military Academy by the Decree-Laws 42151 and 42152. See Army Ministry memo (15 December 1959, AHM, divisão 1, secção 39, caixa 1, numero 1, documento 13). See also a list with 17 different reforms most of them organisation based in annexe to an Army Ministry memo (17 November 1960, AHM, divisão 1, secção 39, caixa 1, numero 1, documento 11). In the documentation of reforms, there are continuous references and comparatives to other NATO countries (AHM, divisão 1, secção 39, caixa 1, numero 1, documento 10).

17. See Ferreira (1976:147). The only aspect that was intensified was anti-guerrilla training, fundamentally with the support of the Belgian, Spanish, and French armed forces (Telo 1996:327–8).

18. In 1935, the military demanded a reform with the main goal of rearming and upgrading its equipment. For Salazar, this was the opportunity to introduce organisation changes that could consolidate his control on the military. The rearmament was only partial. However, for Salazar it was a success given that it allowed him to enhance his control over the military thus diminishing the internal risks for the regime.

19. Degree-Laws 1905 and 1906 (22 May 1935). See Carrilho (1985:418–21), Matos (2004:153), Duarte (2010) and project for the reorganisation of the military (May 1936, AOS/CO/GR-10, Folder 3, Section 2, Pages 150–8).

20. Report to the war minister (20 August 1935) (AOS/CO/GR-11, Folder 3, Document 1, Pages 14–22).

21. Passos e Sousa complained about the lack of technical expertise of the Council of Ministers (Letter to Salazar, 11 April 1936, AOS/CO/GR-11, Folder 4, Document

1, Pages 58–9). Salazar replied that these were political decisions not technical ones (17 April 1936, AOS/CO/GR-11, Folder 4, Document 2, Pages 61–3)

22. Degree-Law 1960 (on the organisation of the Army), Law1961 (on recruitment and military service) and Decree-Laws 27627, 28401, 28402, 28403, and 28404. See reports and correspondence about the decrees (December 1937, AOS/CO/GR-6, Folder 3, Sections 1–3, Pages 17–54).

23. Decree-Law 2024 (31 May 1947). See Duarte (2010:235).

24. Decree-Law 37909 (1 August 1950).

25. Decree-Law 2084 (16 August 1956).

26. Decree-Law 42564 (7 October 1959). See Ferreira (1992:255, 282).

27. Memo about the military mission in Angola and Mozambique (December 1937, AOS/CO/GR-11, Folder 8, Section 2, Pages 254–5).

28. Including 149,090 men mobilised in the conflict areas not counting mobilised African regulars and militia forces (Teixeira 2004:79).

29. The Decree-Laws 41559 and 41577 in 1958 changed the military organisation in the overseas territories. The priority was not to provide support for the defence of the metropole but of the colonies, and the troops were not obliged to remain in the capitals of the provinces (Telo 1996:327). New military regions were created in Angola and Mozambique. Guinea, Cabo Verde, São Tomé, Principe, Macao, and Timor also became autonomous military territories (Teixeira 2004:77).

30. There is little evidence on the provision of services or goods for the families of the officers in the early stages of the regime. See, for instance, the detailed reports about military procurement of the war minister in 1937 (AOS/CO/GR-1C, Folder 5, Pages 149–230).

31. Decree-Law 42072 (31 December 1958).

32. Including support for education of the sons of the military (Decree-law 358/70) and for disabled veterans (Decree-law 201/73). See internal Army Ministry memo (13 September 1973) (AHM, divisão 1, secção 40, caixa 1, numero 4).

33. For instance, SPN (1934, 1940, 1942, 1943), Galvão (1938), Ferro (1938), Moniz (1939), and Freyre (1940). Some were published in other languages, for instance, SNP (undated 1, undated 2, undated 3 and undated 4). See also Salazar's own books of speeches and political ideas (Salazar 1935, 1939, and 1951).

34. The Portuguese Youth or 'Mocidade Portuguesa' was created by Decree-Law 26611 (19 May 1936). 'Mocidade' was a patriotic youth movement that also collaborated with the military thanks to the provision of a pre-military training. In this organisation, young Portuguese were taught to praise Salazar, as exemplified by their motto: 'Who rules? ... Salazar! ' (Arriaga 1976; Caetano 2000 [1975]:224).

35. See Salazar (1935:144) and Faria (2000:56–9).

36. For instance, Salazar's speeches to army and navy officers (6 July 1937) and to the National Assembly (22 May 1939) (Salazar 1939:322–34, 378–93).

37. For example, 'Revista Militar', 'Defesa Nacional', 'Revista do Ar', 'Infantaria', 'Revista da Marinha', 'Revista de Cavalaria', 'Revista de Artilharia', and 'Revista de Engenheria Militar'.

38. For instance, Salazar's speech (28 April 1948) (Salazar 1951).

39. For instance, speeches of the Defence Minister Santos Costa (16 May 1958 and 6 June 1958) (Ferreira 1992:244–5).

40. See abundant correspondence from the journalist Jorge Tavares Rodrigues related to propaganda in Caetano's archive (also in Antunes 1985, vol. 2:47–114).
41. Decree-Law 22469 (11 April 1933).
42. Decree-Law 22756 (29 April 1933).
43. For instance, Generals Norton de Matos, Humberto Delgado, Vassalo e Silva, and Spínola suffered the action of the censorhip (Antunes 1985, vol. 1:155; Ferreira 2006).
44. See Azevedo (1999:455–6). When Caetano was appointed, Portuguese journalists expected the abolition of the Censorship. Due to the unstable situation and the pressures from the hardliners this was not achieved. See, for instance, Jorge Tavares Rodrigues' letter to Caetano (26 September 1968) (Antunes 1985, vol. 2:47–9).
45. For instance, in May 1947, the Legion informed the government of the circulation of critical document signed by opposition groups within the military (Ferreira 1992:203).
46. For instance, a report from a lawyer called Angelo César, in 1938, assessed the levels of loyalty within different units of the army, GNR, and PSP (AOS/CO/GR-11, Folder 11, Document 1, Pages 334–42).
47. The military despised the PIDE/DGS, and Salazar and Caetano did not want them to feel humiliated or feel their autonomy threatened (Pimentel 2007:499, 505–6).
48. There is abundant evidence in Salazar's personal archive. For instance, a secret report from the 3rd Military Region informed about a military officer that was visiting different garrisons to promote a military opposition movement (5 April 1947) (AOS/CO/GR-1D, Folder 3, Section 1, Page 16) and a report from the War Ministry identified ten supposedly subversive officers (18 June 1949) (AOS/CO/GR-1D, Folder 3, Section 9, Pages 59–60). Military intelligence reports also informed about problems of public order outside the barracks. For instance reports from the 1st, 2nd, and 3rd Military Region of 1947 and 1949 (AOS/CO/GR-1D, Folder 3, Sections 1–11, Pages 12–80).
49. See Melo (1983), Antunes (1985, 1994), Oliveira et al. (1996), and the abundant correspondence in Salazar's and Caetano's personal archives. See, for instance, exchanges with Army Minister Abranches Pinto and Defence Minister Santos Costa in 1953 (AOS/CO/GR-11, Folder 21, Pages 398–406). Salazar paid great attention to the letters received from military officers. Salazar highlighted what he considered important in the letters he received from military officers, often these were compliments but also protests. Salazar kept 21 letters addressed to him as a reaction to the 1937 military reforms (AOS/CO/GR-6, Folder 9, Sections 1–21, Pages 305–67).
50. See Salazar's and Military History archives.
51. See extensive documentation about the1961 coup in Captain Fernando Ferreira Valença's report (AHM, divisão 1, secção 39, caixa 1, numero 1, documentos 1–29A) and about the 1974 plots in Captain Salgueiro Maia's report (AHM, divisão 1, secção 40, caixa 1, numero 47).
52. For instance, in 1936, Colonel Tasso Miranda Cabral was promoted to brigadier and charged with the reorganisation of the army, Colonel Raul Esteves

became general and Captain Santos Costa was appointed undersecretary of state (Faria 2000:135, 145–7, 175).

53. Decree-Law 28402 (31 December 1937). the ranks of captain, major, and colonel could be reached by seniority and appointment, the ranks of brigadier and general only by appointment (Article 14). However, in the case of members of the High Staff Corps, the promotion to the level of major and colonel was by appointment of the war minister. See, for instance, the Regulations of the High Military Studies Institute, 1939 (AOS/CO/GR-1A, Folder 20, Section 7, Page 529). Even the professors of the Military School were directly appointed by the war minister. See Project of Decree-Law for the reform of the Army School (November 1940, AOS/CO/GR-1B, Folder 5, Section 14, Pages 301–2).

54. Decree-Law 28401 (31 December 1937). The High Staff Corps was fundamental to Salazar's control strategy (Carrilho 1985:318–9). Salazar personally drafted all documents related to the admission process and requirements for the High Staff Corps. See his handwritten amendments in the reform project (AOS/CO/GR-6, Folder 4, Section 1, Page 223) and in the regulations of the High Military Studies Institute concerning the requisites for the High Staff Course (AOS/CO/GR-1A, Folder 20, Sections 3–7, Pages 484–94).

55. The three presidents were military: General Fragoso Carmona (1928–51), General Craveiro Lopes (1951–58), and Admiral Américo Tomás (1958–74). Salazar did not allow Craveiro Lopes to run for re-election in 1958, and Caetano blocked Spínola's candidacy in 1972, in both cases to prevent tensions among the generals (Fernandes 2006:132–3).

56. See General Kaúlza's letters to Caetano proposing military candidates to some state jobs (and thanking him for some favour concerning Kaúlza's brother in law) (23 December 1968) and undated letter (1968 or 1969) (AMC/12–79).

57. See Article 53 of the 1933 Constitution and Salazar's early speeches and writings (Salazar 1933, 1935, 1939; SPN undated 1).

58. For instance, a secret report from the 1st Military Region denounces that the poor salaries that oblige the military to work in their spare time has a negative impact on their military occupation (AOS/CO/GR-1D, Folder 3, Section 3, Page 30).

59. The Statutes of the three branches were revised to conform to the new guarantees of the navy (1966), army, and air force (1971).

60. See Matos (2004:176). An internal memo in the Army Ministry (25 April 1963) explains that military honours and decorations were going to be made in public ceremonies as a means to elevate the morale of the troops, their families and the population (AHM, divisão 1, secção 39, caixa 1, numero 11).

61. Degree-Law 1960 (1 September 1937) of Organisation of the Army.

62. Degree-Law 1961 (1 September 1937) of Recruitment and Military Service.

63. Decree-Law 28404 (31 December 1937).

64. See amendments to the drafts of Decree 28404 by Salazar (1937, AOS/CO/GR-6, Folder 8, Sections 1–5, Pages 233–304).

65. For instance, see the reintegration of conservative military rebels approved in November and December 1936 (Salazar correspondence AOS/CO/GR-6, Folder 2, Sections 1–6, Pages 7–16). After the failed coup on 14 April 1961, the government merely dismissed some of the conspirators but did not take

any further disciplinary measure (Gallagher 1983:152–3). See also the antecedents to 1974 coup.

66. Decree-Law 1901 (21 May 1935).
67. Project of military reform of December 1937 personally amended by Salazar limited the rank to captain (AOS/CO/GR-6, Folder 5, Section 1, Pages 152–8).
68. Regulation draft of military marriage in Salazar's archive (undated, AOS/CO/GR-1B, Folder 19, Sections 1–2, Pages 605–12).
69. See, for instance, documentation about the reform proposed by Major Barros Rodrigues who resigned due to insufficient funding for the project (11 July 1931) (AOS/CO/GR-1A, Folder 4, Document 1, Pages 117–18).
70. Secret correspondence among the finance, army, and defence ministers about the economic situation of the army in 1966 denounces the budgetary deficit in 1965 of 484 million escudos and serious problems in the provisions of materials. The situation was so bad that the Army Ministry was advised to ask for a loan from private banks (AOS/CO/FI-11X, Folder 7, Sections 1–2, Pages 934–63).
71. Eighteen per cent of the population had emigrated between 1960 and 1971 due to the transformations in the Portuguese economic structure and the unequal distribution of wealth. In 1974, a fourth of the adult male population was in the armed forces and almost 150,000 men were deployed in Africa (Maxwell 1995:20).
72. Decree-law 28403 (31 December 1937). See Salazar correspondence (AOS/CO/GR-1B, Folder 3, Sections 1–2, Pages 17–21) and comments on the project of salary raises (AOS/CO/GR-6, Folders 3–4, Pages 27–35, 55–139).
73. See letter to Salazar explaining that the 15 per cent rise had relieved the military momentarily but that the effects of this measure would not last long (20 Mars 1945, AOS/CO/GR-1C, Folder 24, Page 408).
74. See complaints about the loss of purchasing power in secret memo from Santos Costa (8 Mars 1945, AOS/CO/GR-11, Folder 18, Document 1, Page 392), secret reports from the 3rd Military Region (8 Mars 1945), from the 2nd Military Region (8 April 1945 and 1 April 1947)(AOS/CO/GR-1D, Folder 3, Section 1, Page 13; Section 2, Page 22; Section 3, Page 28).
75. See, for instance, the cancellation of some military promotions due to lack of economic resources. Letter from Caetano to Salazar (Antunes 1994:357–8).
76. Second after Turkey (73.7 per cent) and far ahead of the Netherlands (32.1), UK (40.2), Italy (46.9), and France (57.1) (AHM, divisão 1, secçao 39, caixa 1, numero 1, documento 10).
77. The estimate was made assuming a household of four people. Army Ministry report on military salaries (AHM, divisão 1, secçao 39, caixa 1, numero 1, documento 15).
78. 'Cofre de Previdência das Forças Armadas'. Decree-Law 42945 (26 April 1960).
79. On average, 117,000 men were mobilised in Africa between 1961 and 1974, and a total of 1,368,900 men participated in the three main operation theatres (Ferreira 1994:83)
80. See Army reports, August 1933 (AOS/CO/GR-8, Folder 1, Pages 1–156) and June 1934 (AOS/CO/GR-8, Folder 2, Pages 157–192). and Telo (1996:138–9).

81. See Telo (1996:148) and internal government reports about equipment acquisition in 1935. For instance, 68 million escudos spent for maritime defence (AOS/CO/GR-8, Folder 5, Pages 264–6), over 91 million on planes and equipment for training (AOS/CO/GR-8, Folder 6, Pages 260–3), and over 23 million investment on weapon factories (AOS/CO/GR-8, Folder 9, Pages 274–301).

82. See Telo (1996:156–9) and negotiations with German Government (November-December 1936, AOS/CO/GR-8, Folder 15, Sections 1–2, Pages 498–520). The rearmament was financed by an increase of exports of products such as wolfram, oils, cork, canned food, and resins to Germany, as well as by a credit of 20 million marks (Faria 2000:132–4)

83. According to the British newspaper 'Reynolds News' (28 August 1939), Portugal was a liability for the UK because 'her military forces are negligible and her territory might be invaded by Franco' (news clipping and translation sent to Salazar by PVDE, AOS/CO/IN-8A, Folder 5, Section 26, Pages 425–6). Army Chief of Staff Miranda Cabral stated that the defence of Portugal from Spain was 'unfeasible and utopian' if they were not helped by the UK (letter to Salazar, 27 July 1940, AHM, Fundo 26, secção 10, caixa 332, documento 167). A military assessment during the Azores negotiations with the UK reaches a similar conclusion (Secret memos from the Portuguese Delegation, 19 July 1943, AOS/CLB/FA-5, Section 1, Pages 135–60).

84. See, for instance, contract of acquisition of bomb shells from Germany (11 May 1943) (AOS/CO/R-1C, Folder 18, Pages 326–34) and Telo (1996:171–2).

85. See secret memo of the British delegation in the Azores negotiations (31/7/1943, AOS/CLB/FA-5, Section 1, Pages 235–6) and secret report from the British Embassy (17 August 1943, AOS/CLB/FA-5, Section 2, Pages 425–36).

86. For instance Porto (Infantry in 1950 and General Quarter of the North Military Region in 1957), Viseu (1951), Caldas da Rainha (1953), Abrantes (1955), Beja (1953), and Braga (1958).

87. For instance, the total amount received by Portugal from 1949 to 1953 was inferior to what was allocated to Spain in 1953. The reason might be the equipment of the Spanish Armed Forces was even older and scarcer (Telo 1996:221, 357). From 1953 to 1972, the US military aid to Portugal continued to be lower than what most European countries received (Barrachina 2002:269).

88. See confidential reports by the Army Minister explaining the precarious situation in terms of materials and weapons (22 November 1963, AOS/CO/GR-10, Folder 17, Section 1, Pages 583–97) and the unsustainable financial penuries of the Army (18 November 1965, AOS/CO/GR-10, Folder 19, Section 2, Pages 681–98).

5 Tools of Government in the Portuguese Transition to Democracy

1. Establishing a clear divide between the government and the military is problematic until 1982 when the Constitutional Reform eliminated the Council of the Revolution. For the purpose of simplicity, this chapter considers as tools of government all those employed by the prime minister, Council of Ministers, president of the republic, Junta of National Salvation

(JSN), MFA Coordinating Committee, MFA Assembly, and Council of the Revolution (CR).

2. Decree-Law 310/74 (8 July 1974).
3. See the project of reorganisation of COPCON (ACR, Actas Conselho da Revolução – Originais, volume 1, Acta 24 April 1975)
4. Minutes of CR reunion (ACR, Actas Conselho da Revolução – Originais, volume 1, Acta 25 September 1975).
5. Confidential internal report of the Army Ministry about the mission of AMI (12 November 1975, AHM, divisão 1, secção 40, caixa 1, numero 29).
6. See minutes of the CR reunion on 20 November 1975 (ACR, Actas Conselho da Revolução – Originais, volume 2, Acta 20 November 1975) and Sánchez Cervelló (1993:254–60).
7. Secret memo from the Justice Ministry requesting the control function to be transferred from the PJM to the military (24 November 1975), and the Interior Ministry requesting the urgent armament and reform of the PSP and GNR (March 1976, ACR, Correspondência classificada do secretariado coordenador, volume 7, number 93, document 17).
8. There is extensive evidence in the correspondence between the CR and the military staffs of the three branches (ACR, Correspondência classificada do secretariado coordenador, volume 14, 17, 18, numbers 100, 103, 104).
9. Decree-Law 425/1975 (12 August 1975). It judged mainly ex-PIDE/DGS agents but also military officers. Minutes of CR reunion (3 April 1975, ACR, Actas Conselho da Revolução – Originais, volume 1). Later abolshed by Decree-Law 13/75 (12 November 1975).
10. ACR, Correspondência classificada do secretariado coordenador, volume 6, number 92, document 23.
11. ACR, Correspondência classificada do secretariado coordenador, volume 8, number 94, documents 1, 3, 4, 8, 10.
12. Minutes of CR reunion (ACR, Actas Conselho da Revolução – Originais, volume 1, Acta 31 March 1975).
13. For instance, the PCP and MFA-Radicals created the para-military Revolutionary Corps of Popular Defense in imitation of the Cuban Committees of Defence of the Revolution. They were dissolved in November (Sánchez Cervelló 1993:239).
14. Sánchez Cervelló (1993:253–60) explains the civilian involvement in the events and points at Costa Gomes as the great strategist that avoided the civil war.
15. Decree-Law 203/74 (15 May 1974).
16. The Council (also known as 'Council of 20') was composed of seven officers from the MFA Coordinating Committee, the seven members of the JSN, and the MFA ministers in the provisional government. Initially called the 'Assembly of 200', it influenced the decisions of the Higher Council (Carrilho 1994:52)
17. Confidential internal Memo of the Army Ministry on the reorganisation of the MFA, signed by CEME General Carlos Fabião (21 November 1974, AHM, divisão 1, secção 40, caixa 1, numero 16).
18. See the minutes of CR reunions in 1975 to appreciate the ideological cleavages (ACR, Actas Conselho da Revolução – Originais, volumes 1 and 2).

Different MFA factions dominated the Higher Council of the MFA, Armed Forces Assembly, and MFA Coordinating Committee (Graham 1979:240).
19. Law 5/1975 (14 March 1975).
20. Decree-Law 184-A (3 April 1975).
21. ACR, MFA/Partidos (84), Pacto MFA-Partidos Parte II, Document 14.
22. The institutionalisation of the CR in the 1976 Constitution was an important step in order to take the political debate out of the barracks and therefore facilitate the consolidation of the democracy (Ferreira 1992:316; Santos 2000).
23. The defence minister was merely in charge of coordinating the action of the other ministers concerning national defence acting as an interface with the armed forces. The military component was explicitly excluded from the functions of the government. See, for instance, the Project of Organisation of National Defence (15 February 1977, ACR, Correspondência classificada do secretariado coordenador, volume 20, number 106, document 10).
24. The CR and Eanes opposed some reforms of the centre-right coalition 'Aliança Democrática' from 1980 to 1982, in particular the constitutional reform and the new Law of National Defence. For instance, Eanes vetoed the former that had to be resubmitted to the National Assembly (Graham 1993:49). Their opposition was such that two members of the CR told the French defence minister that if the law was approved they would overthrow the government. The threat was never carried out (Amaral 2000:179–81).
25. Decree-Law 1/82 (30 September 1982).
26. Decree-Law 29/82 (11 December 1982).
27. Decree-Law 550-D/76 (12 July 1976).
28. Documents on civic education have been provided to recruits by the Army Staff Office since 1976 (ACR, Correspondência classificada do secretariado coordenador, volume 15, number 101, documents 13–14).
29. For instance, railway concessions of up to 75 per cent of the ticket prices. Decree-Law 389/75 (26 June 1976). These were revised in April 1978 (ACR, Correspondência classificada do secretariado coordenador, volume 8, number 94, document 7).
30. Decree-Law 43/76 (20 January 1976).
31. Minutes of CR reunion (29/10/1976, ACR, Actas Conselho da Revolução – Originais, volume 3).
32. Decree-Laws 294/76 (24 April 1976), 819/76 (12 November 1976), 357/77 (31 August 1977), 175/78 (13 July 1978), 362/78 (28 November 1978), 514/79 (28 December 1979), and 23/80 (29 February 1980).
33. For instance, Kaúlza, military governor of Mozambique stressed this idea in his letters to Caetano (1 June 1970, 18 November 1970, AMC/12–79).
34. See documentation on the information campaign in Guinea-Bissau in 1974 (AHM, divisão 1, secção 40, caixa 1, numero 4).
35. For intance, Spínola's speech 'Self-determination and Democracy' (11 June 1974, AHM, divisão 1, secção 40, caixa 1, numero 4) and the MFA Programme (AHM, divisão 1, secção 40, caixa 1, numero 6).
36. The Fifth Division was inspired by the US Army's Fifth Department that during the Second World War had acted as liaison between the military government and the civilian administrations of the territories liberated.
37. The SDCI, created by Decree-Law 250/75 (23 May 1974), was under the direct command of the CR.

38. CODICE was part of the Social Communication Ministry but worked closely with the Fifth Division (ACR, Correspondência classificada do secretariado coordenador, volume 8, number 94, document 26).
39. There were Dynamisation Cabinets at the branch, region, and unit levels. Their goal was the 'non-partisan politicisation of the Armed Forces' (Internal Memo in the Army Ministry, AHM, divisão 1, secção 40, caixa 1, numero 21).
40. Sequestration of ten days for newspapers and 40 days for other publications. According to the CR the media should not broadcast or publish this type of information about military indiscipline (8 September 1975, ACR, Actas Conselho da Revolução – Originais, volume 1, Acta).
41. Decree-Law 281/74 (25 June 1974)
42. Minutes of the MFA Assembly reunion (5 September 1975, ACR, Actas Conselho da Revolução – Originais, volume 1).
43. Letter from the CR to the CEMGFA (16 April 1975, ACR, Correspondência classificada do secretariado coordenador, Assuntos Económicos Sociais-Cartas Particulares- Diversos, volume 83, document 33).
44. Minutes of CR reunion (18 September 1975, ACR, Actas Conselho da Revolução – Originais, volume 1).
45. See the general principles about information policy in annexe to the minutes of CR reunion (30 July 1975, ACR, Actas Conselho da Revolução – Originais, volume 1).
46. Mario Soares threatened that the PS would abandon the government if the PC continued to control the media (Minutes of CR reunion, 30 May 1975, ACR, Actas Conselho da Revolução – Originais, volume 1).
47. See correspondence of CEMGFA (AHM, divisão 1, secção 40, caixa 1, numero 28) and CR (ACR, Correspondência classificada do secretariado coordenador, volume 8, number 94, document 26).
48. The nationalisations approved on 27 November 1975 claim not only the manipulation of information but also financial reasons. Minutes of CR reunion (27 November 1975, ACR, Actas Conselho da Revolução – Originais, volume 2).
49. See news clips in letters from the 'Procuradoria-Geral da República' to the CR on 1976, 1977, and 1978 (ACR, Correspondência classificada do secretariado coordenador, volume 20, number 106, document 12–13, 16–24). See correspondence between the Justice Minister, EMGFA, and CR (November and December 1976, ACR, Correspondência classificada do secretariado coordenador, volume 8, number 94, document 33) and complaint from the EME (27 February 1976, ACR, Correspondência classificada do secretariado coordenador, volume 7, number 93, document 46) about the publication of secret information in breach of national security.
50. 'Sept-sur-sept', a programme of the French channel TF1 in 1982 reported that censorship had disappeared from Portuguese TV, Telegram from the Embassy in Paris to the Foreign Affairs Ministry (19 September 1982, ACR, Correspondência classificada do secretariado coordenador, volume 6, number 92, document 1).
51. The PJM was created by Decree-Law 520/75 (23 September 1975) and later integrated into the military structure by the Decree-Law 186/77 (8 May 1977). There is evidence of the PJM's important function in the coup investigation.

Minutes of the CR reunion (19 January 1976, ACR, Actas Conselho da Revolução – Originais, volume 2).

52. See, for instance, the Fifth Division's confidential report about the Infantry Regiment of Evora to EME (21 July 1976, ACR, Correspondência classificada do secretariado coordenador, volume 16, number 102, document 27) and confidential memos on denouncing the activity of some political parties (especially PRP) that was affecting the cohesion and stability of the military (June and July 1976, ACR, Correspondência classificada do secretariado coordenador, volume 7, number 93, document 35–42).

53. See, for example, internal information produced by the Army Dinamizing Cabinet in 1975 (AHM, divisão 1, secção 40, caixa 1, numeros 24, 31, 32 and 33).

54. See reports about infiltration attempts by the reactionary right in the Castelo Branco garrison in July 1975 (ACR, Correspondência classificada do secretariado coordenador, volume 7, number 93, document 53).

55. For instance, correspondence between the EME and CR about political activities including manifestos, demonstrations, and land seizures during 1975–6 (ACR, Correspondência classificada do secretariado coordenador, volume 15, number 101, documents 50, 49, 56, 57, 62)

56. For instance, an internal memo in the Army Ministry requested all military to urgently report to the Committee for the Control of the Press, Radio, Television, Theatre and Cinema in case of broadcast or publication to the Army (AHM, divisão 1, secção 40, caixa 1, numero 13).

57. For instance, the attorney general's confidential reports in 1976, 1977, and 1978 about information in the media harmful to the interests of the CR (ACR, Correspondência classificada do secretariado coordenador, volume 20, number 106, document 12–25).

58. Decree-Law 30/84 (5 September 1984).

59. See examples of proposals for promotions of generals in confidential reports, from EME, EMFA and EMGFA (1981 and 1982, ACR, Correspondência classificada do secretariado coordenador, volume 10, number 96, documents 1–12 and volume 11, number 97, documents 2–13), equally in EMA reports to the CR for promotions of admirals 1978–81 (ACR, Correspondência classificada do secretariado coordenador volume 14, number 100, documents 1–8).

60. Decree-Law 3/74 (14 May 1974).

61. Decree-Law 400 (29 August 1974).

62. Except from March to November 1975 when the command of the military was transferred to the CR (Ferreira 1994:225–7).

63. Until 1982, the CR passed about 750 rules and regulations concerning the military and the chiefs of staff over 550 (Ferreira 1994:229–30).

64. Decree-Law 5/75 (14 March 1975).

65. Decree-Law 403/76 (27 May 1976).

66. See, for instance, Annexe A to the Minutes of CR reunion (20 June 1975, ACR, ACR, Actas Conselho da Revolução – Originais, volume 1)

67. For example, COPCON documents in 1975 dealing with issues such as treatment of ex-DGS in prisons, ex-DGS informants, military prisoners in Cabo Verde, and even land seizures (ACR, Correspondência classificada do secretariado coordenador, volume 13, number 99, documents 31–44), and evidence that the COPCON commanded the Fiscal Guard to strengthen the control of

the borders (ACR, Correspondência classificada do secretariado coordenador, volume 15, number 101, document 58).

68. Decree-Law 637/74 (20 November 1974).

69. For instance, the CR decreed that the military should arrest everyone altering the normal development of the electoral process (Annexe of the minutes of the CR reunion, 27 March 1975, ACR, Actas Conselho da Revolução – Originais, volume 1).

70. Degree-Law 8/75 (25 July 1975). The liquidation of the PIDE/DGS involved 17,000 cases: 9,000 for its personnel and 8,000 to the informants and collaborators. See correspondence between the CR and the government in 1978 (ACR, Correspondência classificada do secretariado coordenador, volume 20, number 106, document 9), minutes of CR reunion (4 June 1975, ACR, Actas Conselho da Revolução – Originais, volume 1). In 1979, still almost 100 military worked in the coordination service for the liquidation of PIDE/DGS and the Portuguese Legion (EMGFA document 2 September 1979, ACR, Correspondência classificada do secretariado coordenador, volume 9, number 95, document 13).

71. For instance, Article 3.2 established that the MFA was the guarantor of the democratic progress and the revolution and 'participated, in alliance with the people, in the exercise of sovereignty'. Article 10.1 provided that the alliance between the MFA and the political parties and other democratic organisations ensure the peaceful development of the revolution. Article 46 consolidated the exclusive use of force by specifying the prohibition of militarised or paramilitary groups other than those integrated in the State and the armed forces. Article 142 stated that the CR was guarantor of the functioning of democratic institutions and the respect of the Constitution and revolutionary principles. Finally, Article 273.4 specified that they 'have the historical mission to guarantee the conditions that allows a peaceful and plural transition of the Portuguese society towards democracy and socialism'.

72. For instance, see the correspondence about the approval of diverse regulations in 1979 (ACR, Correspondência classificada do secretariado coordenador, volume 6, number 92, documents 4–7).

73. The first amnesty was formalised by Decree-Law 173/74 (26 April 1974). The Decree-Law 17/82 (2 July 1982) was the last important one. See also Vilar (2009) and the secret law project in CR correspondence (16 May 1980, ACR, Correspondência classificada do secretariado coordenador, volume 7, number 93, document 12).

74. These purges were formalised through the Decree-Laws 178/74 (30 April 1974), 309/74 (8 July 1974), and 648/74 (2 December 1974).

75. Decree-Law 147-D/75 (21 March 1975).

76. Decree-Law 256/75 (26 May 1975). 19 officers were retained by this law (ACR, Correspondência classificada do secretariado coordenador, volume 13, number 99, document 18).

77. Decree-Law 171/74 (25 April 1974).

78. Decree-Law 634/74 (20 November 1974).

79. See minutes of CR reunion (ACR, Actas Conselho da Revolução – Originais, volume 2, 27/11/1975).

80. For instance, 'Soldados Unidos Vencerão' was created by the communist PRP in August 1975 and inspired many revolts in October 1975 (Porch 1977:216).

'Acção Revolucionária das Praças do Exército' was launched by the PCP, after the MFA-Moderates consolidated their power in the MFA Assembly in Tancos in September (Sánchez Cervelló 1993:248). 'Forças Armadas Democráticas' was a clandestine group of officers in favour of the Carnations Revolution but that criticised the communist drift of the transition. See the manifesto in a letter from secretary of the CR, Major Loureiro dos Santos, informing the SDCI about the group (16 July 1975, ACR, Correspondência classificada do secretariado coordenador, Assuntos Económicos Sociais- Cartas Particulares-Diversos, volume 82, document 32).

81. See Santos (2000:171). Maxwell argues that many of these limitations and principles formally introduced in 1982 were 'cosmetic' and that until the 1990s the government did not exert effective control of the military (Maxwell 1991:3).

82. See Annexe I to the Minutes of CR reunion (11 December 1975, ACR, Actas Conselho da Revolução – Originais, volume 2).

83. Decree-Law 142/77 (9 April 1977).

84. Annexe to CR reunion (29 October 1976, ACR, ACR, Actas Conselho da Revolução – Originais, volume 3).

85. See CR Political Action Plan (Annexe B to the minutes of CR reunion, 20 June 1975, ACR, Actas Conselho da Revolução – Originais, volume 1).

86. Other figures can be found in the literature but according to the census in 1981 of Portugal there were 505,078 'retornados'. This means more than 5 per cent of the total population. The repatriation and support of such an influx of people consumed significant financial resources (Ferreira 1994:86–91).

87. 20.6 per cent average annual inflation from 1974 to 1986 (Mata and Valerio 1994:225–9, 254–5).

88. See Mesquita (1986:56–8). A modern budgeting process inspired by NATO was introduced in Spain in 1982. The Portuguese civil-military relations literature devotes little attention to the utilisation of financial resources as a means to appease or satisfy the military. The periods of transition and consolidation of democracy confirm this hypothesis. One exception is Ferreira (1994:233) who stresses that Amaro da Costa, the first civilian defence minister, used the 4 per cent increase in military expenditures approved in 1980 to gain support from the highest ranks

89. For instance, a letter to the CR from the Porto Military Region Commander, General Pires Veloso (16 October 1975), explains that there were around 50 cases of desertions opened in the Military Tribunal of Porto fundamentally linked to the precarious economic situation of the military and their families (ACR, Correspondência classificada do secretariado coordenador, volume 15, number 101, documents 39).

90. Decree-Law 59/82 (27 February 1982).

91. Decree-Law 1/85 (23 January 1985).

92. Decree-Law 34/86 (2 September 1986) and Degree-Law 15/87 (30 May 1987).

6   History of Contemporary Civil-Military Relations in Spain

1. There is great controversy around the total number of victims. Recent demographic studies estimate the number of deaths in excess of 540,000 and the fewer births to 576,000 during the war period (Ortega and Silvestre 2005).

2. Decree 255 (19 April 1937).
3. Whether Franco's was an authoritarian or a totalitarian dictatorship is still subject to a contentious debate. However, after the mid-1940s, the regime exhibited very few traits of totalitarianism.
4. After the demobilisation that followed the end of the Civil War, Franco still commanded an army of over 500,000 men (Preston 1990:85).
5. A PVDE report sent to Salazar, claimed that the Falange propaganda office in London considered generals Yague, Solchaga, Aranda, and in particular, Queipo de Llano, as traitors and pro-Allies (26 July 1939)(AOS/CO/IN-8A, Folder 5, Section 20, Page 361).
6. After 1948, the United States started considering that Europe north of the Pyrenees could not be defended from a Soviet invasion and that the Iberian Peninsula (as well as the United Kingdom) had to become the basis for an eventual re-conquest. Daily Telegraph 'U.S. need of Spanish Bases', Daily Mail (4 October 1948), 'U.S. seeking ports and airfields', New York Times 'Western Europe Fears Spain Base', Le Soir (8 October 1948) 'Franco sera-t-il admis dans l'Union Occidentale?' (Press clippings in Franco's Personal Archive, FNFF, document 8893).
7. Franco had a military vision of political power, when he became the head of state he asked to have a 'Chief of Joint Staff of Politics' to assist him (Interview José María de Areilza, FOG, 13 September 1984, cassette J8).
8. Interview with Antonio Garrigues Díaz-Cañabate (FOG, 4 October 1984, cassette J9).
9. In 1966, in Spain, there was a civil servant for each 53 inhabitants compared to 40 in Italy, 26 in France, and 22 in Germany (Feo and Romero 1968:333).
10. Especially important were the frictions between the Falange and non-falangist military that started in the Civil War and were aggravated during the Second World War. See, for instance, complaints from falangist José A. Girón in a report to Franco (13 August 1937) (FNFF, document 26943) and note of Franco's personal secretary on the attitude of the Falange vis-à-vis the military (21 October 1941) (FNFF, document 28).
11. According to de Miguel (1975:35), 32 out of 114 were military and according to Graham 40 out of 114 (Graham 1984:195). The most accurate figure is probably 40 out of 120 (33.3 per cent) (Linz et al. 2003:75)
12. There is abundant evidence of the persecution of masonry in the 1940s found in Franco's personal documentation (FNFF documents 126, 1597, 5064, 10602, 14022, 15234).
13. Between 5,000 and 6,000 anti-Francoist fighters were very active until 1947. The 'maquis' maintained low-intensity insurgent activity until 1956 (Aguado Sánchez 1975)
14. Interview with Lieutenant-General José Gabeiras Montero (FOG, 11 December 1987, cassette J31bis).
15. Abundant evidence on the monarchic contestation within the ranks can be found in Salazar's (AOS/CO/NE-2B1, Folders 11–12) and Franco's personal archives (FNFF documents 11048, 20529).
16. Orgaz died in 1946; Queipo de Llano and Varela in 1951; Yagüe, Monasterio, and Ponte in 1952; and Solchaga in 1953 (Preston 1990).
17. The classical verses from Calderón de la Barca: 'Here the most fundamental exploit is to obey, and the way how it should be is without requesting or refusing...' became the motto of the army.

18. For instance, General Kindelán in 1943 asked the military not to accept a 'passive' approach to discipline but to adopt an 'active discipline' according to which they should wish to receive orders from their superiors. Kindelán, through a rhetorical exercise, was asking for a move against Franco (Kindelán 1981:125).

19. Although Spain was not a member, the country began to collaborate with NATO to the extent that the navy could be considered de facto integrated into the alliance after 1963 (Olmeda 1988:153).

20. For instance, some of the prominent military that later promoted reforms such as Manuel Díaz Alegría, Manuel Gutiérrez Mellado and Sabino Fernández Campo, had participated in the negotiations with the United States in the early 1950s and later in the renewal of the agreements in the late 1960s. See Viñas (1981) and documents on the negotiations conducted by Díaz Alegría with the United States in 1968 and 1969 (FNFF, documents 19413, 19149, 19311,19312, 19313, 19423, 20343).

21. For instance, the campaign against the modernisation attempts of the new Prime Minister Arias Salgado, called the Gironazo (28 April 1974), ended up with the dismissal of some 'progressive' ministers and influential civil servants (Preston 1990:173).

22. See Preston (1986), Powell (1991), and an interview with Antonio Garrigues (FOG, 4 October 1984, cassette J9).

23. See Viñas (1988:153–4) and Bañón (1988:342). The excess of officers can be attributed to the preparation for the Sahara conflict that accelerated the training period for the cadets in 1975 (Fernández López 1998:88–90; Serra 2008:119).

24. The Cortes votes were 425 for, 59 against, and 13 abstentions, 94 per cent in favour in the referendum.

25. Interview with Antonio Garrigues (FOG, 4 October 1984, cassette J9bis).

26. See Bañón (1988:342). Suárez had promised in a meeting with the top generals that this legalisation would never happen under his rule (Iniesta Cano 1986:16; Preston 1986:97, 115). Nonetheless others doubt that this promise was explicitly made (Interview with General José Miguel Vega Rodríguez, FOG 14 October 1986, cassette J19).

27. Interview with former President and Education Minister José Manuel Otero Novas (FOG, 17 January 1985, cassette J1).

28. See Armed Forces and Military Consolidation workshop organised by Powell and Bañón (FOG, 25 April 1988, cassette CF1).

29. Interview with Lieutenant-General José Vega Rodriguez (FOG, 14 October 1986, cassette J19).

30. Although a group of reformist generals held important positions during the transition, such as Generals Díez Alegría, Gutiérrez Mellado, Ibáñez Freire, Saenz de Santamaria, and Fernández Campos, the reactionary generals still predominated; for instance, De Santiago, Iniesta Cano, Campano, Coloma Gallegos, Milans del Bosch, and Pita da Veiga. From the beginning, Juan Carlos feared the military bunker (Interview with José María de Areilza, FOG, 13 September 1984, cassette J8).

31. In contrast severe sanctions were imposed on the UMD, whose members were imprisoned and then expelled (Preston 1990:183–91; Reinlein 2002).

32. For instance, the violent attack during the traditional Carlist pilgrimage to Montejurra (9 May 1976) (Cardona 2001:267–8).

33. See interview with Lieutenant-General José Miguel Vega Rodríguez (FOG, 14 October 1986, cassette J19)
34. Interview with José Maria de Areilza (FOG, 13 September 1984, cassette J8bis).
35. 'Galaxia' was the name of the coffee shop where the plot was planned.
36. Eduardo Serra as Undersecretary of Defence and Jesús Palacios as Secretary General of Economic Affairs.
37. The percentage of people preferring democracy to any other form of government rose from 49 in 1980 to 69 in 1984 (Gunther et al. 2004:163–4).
38. He was the third civilian defence minister after Agustín Rodríguez Sahagún (1979–81) and Aberto Oliart (1981–2).
39. See interviews with General Saez de Tejada (FOG, 17 November 1987, cassette J25bis) and with Admiral Liberal Lucini (FOG, 27 November 1987, cassette J27).
40. Interview with JEME, Lieutenant-General José Gabeiras Montero (FOG, 15 December 1987, cassette J32).
41. For instance, all members of the Council of the Joint Chiefs of Staff were in favour of the incorporation into NATO (Interview with former President of JUJEM Lieutenant-General Ignacio Alfaro Arregui, FOG, 18 December 1987, cassette J33bis). Although, especially in the army, some officers feared that NATO would diminish the traditional weight of the army (Interview with the first JEMAD Admiral Liberal Lucini, FOG, 4 December 1987, cassette J30).
42. Interview with Admiral Liberal Lucini (FOG, 20 November 1987, cassette J27bis).

7 Francoist Tools of Government

1. For instance, 90,000 prisoners were sent to 121 labour battalions and 8,000 to special military workshops (Beevor 2006:404).
2. For instance, Lieutenant-General Sáenz de Tejada in an interview (17 November 1987) speaks of 'an Army born from a military victory in 1939', 'a new Army' or 'the Army of the victory' (FOG, cassette J25).
3. The rhythm of executions considerably decreased after 1941. See, for instance, Solé i Sabaté (1985), Moreno Gómez (1987), and Dueñas (1990).
4. Decree-Laws 69/1964, 70/1964, and 528/1973.
5. The CESEDEN, created by the Decree-Law 70/1964 (16 January 1964), was responsible for prestigious courses such as EMACON and ALEMI.
6. After the Civil War, Spain was divided into eight military regions. A ninth military region was later added (1944). Spanish air space was divided into five air regions and three air zones (1940) and later reorganised into three air regions and one air zone (1968). Spanish territorial waters were divided into four maritime zones (1970) (Guaita Martorell 1986).
7. Some officers resold products in the black market as a source of extra income (Payne 1967:435).
8. Decree-Law 12 March 1937.
9. Decree-Law 25 August 1939.
10. The officers in the civil guard came from the General Military Academy or the Infantry and Cavalry Corps and those of the armed police came from the latter (Olmeda 1988:139).

11. The INI (created in 1941) comprised among others the aeronautic industry CASA (set in 1942); the Shipyards 'Bazán' (1947); the weapon and ammunition company 'Santa Bárbara' (1960); the components industries 'Experiencias Industriales S.A.' and 'Empresa Nacional de Optica' (1960); and the research centre 'Instituto Nacional de Electrónica' (1965) (Daguzan 1982:116).

12. Beevor (2006:248, 475–6) provides more than 30 examples from both camps.

13. For instance, an enormous parade, with 50,000 ex-combatants, commemorated the twenty-fifth anniversary of the uprising against the Republic (18 July 1961). This was accompanied with a campaign in the official army magazine 'Ejército' framing the Civil War as a crusade. ('Ejército' n. 258 July 1961).

14. 'Ejército' n. 24, January 1942: 'Los Ejércitos modernos ante el material'. 'Ejército' appeared in 1940 as 'Revista de las Armas y Servicios del Ejército de Tierra', and was published by the Central Joint Staff. It was the magazine of the army and the navy, and the air force had its own publications.

15. 'Ejército' n. 15, April 1941, 'Con ocasión del 1 de abril'.

16. Monasterio and other important generals opposed to the replacement of horses by armoured vehicles alleged that that was an act of cowardice. Lieutenant Colonel Valero Valderrabano proposed a mixed cavalry with tanks and horses in Ejército n. 60, January 1945 'La caballeria y la mecanización'. The doubts about the mechanisation were not exclusive of the Spanish army (Liddell Hart 1959; Harris 1996); it is nonetheless striking that these doubts persisted in 1945.

17. Vigón (1956 [1950]:140) criticised an article that appeared in 'Military Review' (September 1947) that argued diet had an impact on military efficiency.

18. Ejército n. 132, January 1951, 'Discurso de la Pascua Militar'.

19. Also known as 'Segunda Sección' or 'Segunda Bis'

20. Interview with José María de Areilza (FOG, 13 September 1984, cassette J8).

21. SECED replaced the National Counter-subversive Organisation (OCN) founded in 1969.

22. There are more than 70 documents about military audiences in Franco's personal archive in FNFF.

23. In the presence of Franco, only Kindelán defended the return of the monarchy. No single general dared to challenge Franco's rule (Cardona 2001:116)

24. Interview with José María de Areilza (FOG, 13 September 1984, cassette J8).

25. Fenosa was a public company 'Fuerzas Eléctricas del Noroeste, Sociedad Anónima'.

26. For instance, the Penal Code of 1944, the Spanish Bill of Rights of 1945, and the Decree-Law against Banditry and Terrorism of 1947 removed some crimes from military jurisdiction (Payne 1967:437).

27. From 1952, reserve military officers could take full-time positions in the administration.

28. See, Puell de la Villa (1997:141–2); Interviews with Lieutenant-General José Gabeiras Montero (FOG, 11 December 1987, cassette J31bis) and Lieutenant-General Manuel Gutiérrez Mellado (FOG, 8 September 1987, cassette J20); and the letter signed by Barroso (29 July 1962) (Franco's Personal Archive, FNFF, document 938).

29. Ministerial Order (18 July 1952) and Laws of Reserve (17 July 1953 and 17 July 1958)

30. The number of officers in the military grew from 0.02 per cent of the country's population in 1936 to 0.04 per cent in 1975 (Olmeda 1988:147, 168–9).
31. Franco's Personal Archive, FNFF, documents 14022, 15234, 26892.
32. For instance, on 14 December 1970, a delegation by Captain-Generals Fernández de Córdoba, García Rebull, Pérez Viñeta, and Chamorro asked Franco to suppress habeas corpus; Franco accepted (Preston 1993:753). On 27 September 1975, when Franco was already seriously ill, Prime Minister Arias Navarro ceded to the pressures of military hardliners and ratified the last death sentences of the regime: three members of the FRAP and two of ETA (Cardona 2001:245).
33. A report classified as top secret (23 May 1940) explains the British plans for the provision of 10,000 tons of wheat for Spain in a triangular procedure called 'Anglo-Spanish clearing'. See document of the British government listing vessels and quantities of grain already diverted to Spain (over 50,000 tons); Document from the Foreign Affairs Ministry (4 July 1940) confirming the acceptance of the proposal and the quantities wished by the Spanish delegation; 44,000 tons valued at 600,000 GBP and an amendment to the triangular agreement by Spain requesting an increase in the supplies (up to a value of 726,000 GBP) (5 September 1940) (AOS/CO/NE-2B1, Folder 6, Sections 4, 5, 6, Pages 441–50).
34. See agreement with French Morocco for the supply of phosphates in the document about the emergency aid to Spain (9 March 1941) (AOS/CO/NE-2B1, Folder 6, Section 16, Page 498).
35. See Foreign Ministry note (30 April 1942)(AOS/CO/NE-2B1, Folder 6, Section 33, Page 585). See extensive evidence of this type of triangular agreements with Portugal in Salazar's personal documentation (AOS/CO/NE-2B1, Folders 6–7).
36. Interview with Lieutenant-General Ignacio Alfaro Arregui (FOG, 18 December 1987, cassette J33). See a similar account by his brother General Emiliano José Alfaro Arregui interviewed by Mérida (1979:24).
37. There were five American bases on Spanish soil and the US put pressure on Spain to abandon Morocco (Preston 1990:143).
38. According to Gabriel Peña Aranda, former Director of the Defence Division of the INI (Seminar 'Armed Forces and Democratic Consolidation', 26 April 1988, FOG, cassette CF6).
39. Interview with Almiral Liberal Lucini in FOG, 27 November 1987, cassette J29 and 4 December 1987, cassette J30).

8 Tools of Government in the Spanish Transition to Democracy

1. Interview with Lieutenant-General Ignacio Alfaro Arregui (FOG, 18 December 1987, cassette J33).
2. Interview with General Sáez de Tejada (FOG, 17 November 1987, cassette J25bis).
3. Interview with Admiral Liberal Lucini (FOG, 4 December 1987, cassette J30). He stresses the impact on the Navy and Air Force.
4. See the seminars 'Comparative perspectives on military education' organised by Bañón and Rodrigo in Cangas de Onis in 1987 with the participation of

German, Italian, Argentinian and US experts (FOG, 30 June 1987 and 1 July 1987, cassettes A2–4, A2–5, A2–7 and A2–8).

5. Interview with Lieutenant-General José Gabeiras Montero (FOG, 11 December 1987, cassette J31bis).

6. The JEME, General Gabeiras Montero argues that the situation of the Army was 'disastrous' in terms of organisation (*ibid.*).

7. Law 11/1977. Navajas Zubeldia (1995:179) claims that it initiated the 'military transition'.

8. See Seminar 'Armed Forces and Military Consolidation' (FOG, 25 April 1988, cassette CF2).

9. Royal Decree 2723/1977 (2 November 1977).

10. Law 83/1978 (28 December 1978).

11. See interview with General Sáez de Tejada (FOG, 17 November 1987, cassette J25T).

12. The first, headed by the JEMAD, was in charge of operational military matters. The second, under a secretary of state, dealt with the management of financial resources, procurement, and investment in infrastructure. Finally, the third block was headed by an undersecretary of state and dealt with personnel policy and military education (Viñas 1988:176).

13. See interview with General Sáez de Tejada (FOG, 17 November 1987, cassette J25T and J25bis).

14. Royal Decree 1451/1984 (1 August 1984). See Guaita Martorell (1986:27).

15. Ministerial Order 18/1985 (1 July 1985).

16. See interview with Admiral Liberal Lucini (FOG, 4 December 1987, cassette J30bis).

17. Interview with Admiral Liberal Lucini (FOG, 20 November 1987, cassette J27bis). 'El Alcazar' was the most significant publication promoting military subversion. Tens of thousands of copies of the journal were sent free of charge to all military units. Interview with José Maria de Areilza (FOG, 13 September 1984, cassette J8bis)

18. Bañón (1988:342, 349). There are different accounts about what happened during the meeting. See, for instance, interview with Vega Rodríguez (FOG, 14 October 1986, cassette J19), Osorio (1980), and Fernández López (1998:91–2).

19. Interview with Admiral Liberal Lucini (FOG, 20 November 1987, cassette J27bis).

20. Interview with Alfonso Osorio (FOG, 29 November 1984, cassette J14–3).

21. Juan Carlos's stance against the plot legitimised the monarchy in the eyes of most Spaniards (Preston 2004:519).

22. See, for instance, Fernández López (1998:101), Gutiérrez Mellado (1981:70–87), and El Pais 6 January 1977 'Los militares deben obedecer también al mando político'.

23. For instance, Gutiérrez Mellado's speech in Seville in 1977 and in the Parliament in 1978 claimed that the chiefs of staff were the 'first authority in the military command chain' (Gutiérrez Mellado 1981:75, 206–7).

24. El Pais 6 January 1978 'El general Vega elogió la capacidad militar de Lister y Modesto'.

25. For instance, Gutiérrez Mellado's intervention at a conference at Seville's general headquarters (7 February 1977) and the General Report 1/77

of the Defence Ministry issued in September 1977 (Gutiérrez Mellado 1981:115–45).

26. For instance, the General Reports of the Army 1/76 in September 1976 and the General Report of the Defence Ministry 1/78 issued in October 1978.
27. See interview with General Saez de Tejada (FOG, 17 November 1987, cassette J25bis).
28. Royal Decree 135/84 (25 January 1984).
29. For instance, Barrachina (2002) counts 548 news items in El País related to the military in 1977.
30. Paradoxically, Miguel Angel Aguilar was then tried by a military court for 'insulting' the military (Ballbé 1983:474–5).
31. Interviews with Alfonso Osorio (FOG, 29 November 1984, cassette J14–3) and Gabeiras Montero (FOG, 15 December 1987, cassette J32bis).
32. Interviews with General Séez de Tejada (FOG, 17 November 1987, cassette J25bis) and with Admiral Liberal Lucini (FOG, 27 November 1987, cassette J29).
33. See Rodrigo (1985:368–9) and seminar 'Armed Forces and Military Consolidation' organised by Powell and Bañón (FOG, 25 April 1988, cassette CF1).
34. See interview with Admiral Liberal Lucini (FOG, 20 November 1987, cassette J27bis) and Ballbé (1983).
35. Article 62, section h), that '[i]t is incumbent upon the King (...) [t]o exercise supreme command of the Armed Forces'. Nonetheless his supreme command over the military was limited by Article 64 which requires the actions of the king to be ratified by the government. The Spanish king, similarly to British or Norwegian monarchs, holds a merely honorific mandate (Lafuente Balle 1987:6–12).
36. Law 85/1978 (24 December 1978).
37. See interview with Admiral Liberal Lucini (FOG, 20 November 1987, cassette J27bis) and Gutiérrez Mellado (1981:75, 206–7). Nonetheless, the 1978 Constitution asserted the principle of civilian supremacy (Article 97).
38. Interview with Admiral Liberal Lucini (FOG, 27 November 1987, cassette J29bis).
39. Interview with Lieutenant-General José Gabeiras Montero (FOG, 11 December 1987, cassette J31bis).
40. Between 1975 and 1983, the number of officers rose by almost 40 per cent (Bañón 1988:331). The periods of effective command for senior officers were very short and the average age continued to be higher than that in most Western militaries (Serra 2008:119–20).
41. El País (2 October 1976) 'Pase a la reserva de Iniesta Cano y De Santiago'.
42. El País (21 February 1982) 'Hubo careo Suárez-Armada en el otoño de 1977'.
43. ABC (10 March 1978) 'Expedientados en Ceuta siete militares por una reunión con Blas Piñar'.
44. El Pais (29 May 1979) 'El general Atarés, absuelto'.
45. The exemplary sentence against the UMD aimed to appease the reactionary generals that opposed the reforms (Busquets and Losada 2003:183).
46. The tribunals that prosecuted political crimes had been created after the disso- lution of the Tribunal for the Repression of the Masonry and Communism in 1963.

47. Organic Law 9/1980 (6 November 1980).
48. ABC (22 February 1981) 'Consejo de Guerra contra un dirigente de Comisiones Marineiras'.
49. Organic Law 12/1985 (27 November 1985).
50. Organic Law 13/1985 (9 December 1985).
51. Law 14/1985 (9 December 1985).
52. Organic Law 4/1987 (15 July 1987). The Military Chamber was composed equally of military and civilian judges and limited the competences traditionally held by captain-generals. This law concluded the process of the delimitation of military justice (Agüero 1988:45).
53. Organic Law 2/1986 (13 March 1986).
54. These were multilateral cooperation agreements signed in October 1977 by the political and economic elites.
55. Law 44/1982 (7 July 1982).
56. Royal-Decree 252/1982 (12 February 1982).
57. Royal-Decree 135/1984 (25 January 1984).
58. Interview with Lieutenant-General Sáez de Tejada (FOG, 17 November 1987, cassettes J25T and J25bis).
59. See seminar 'Armed Forces and Military Consolidation' (FOG, 25 April 1988, cassette CF2).
60. Royal Decree-law 22/1977 (30 March 1977) and Decree-law 923/1977 (13 April 1977).
61. Law 20/1981 (6 July 1981). It aimed to retire from active service 4,332 officers between 1982 and 1987 (Comas and Mandeville 1986:152).
62. For instance the number of lieutenant-generals was halved (Interview with General Ignacio Alfaro Arregui, FOG, 18 December 1987, cassette J33bis).
63. See seminar 'Armed Forces and Military Consolidation' (FOG, 25/4/1988, cassette CF2).
64. Decree-Law 5/1977 (25/1/1977).
65. Gutiérrez Mellado and Picatoste (1983:56).
66. Interview with Lieutenant-General José Gabeiras Montero (FOG, 15 December 1987, cassette J32bis).
67. Law 44/1982 (7 July 1982). The limit was 2.5 per cent annual excluding some budget allocations.

9 Comparisons and Explanations

1. A similar argument was used by Paul Pierson, in his lecture 'Welfare State Reform Over the (Very) Long-run' at the LSE (9 November 2010), who argued that the apparent stability of welfare indicators after 1971 was hiding a deep impact on redistribution and social policy when considering all the socio-economic changes that took place after that date.
2. For instance, the article 'El año militar' in ABC (28 December 1958) stresses the important visits of senior officers to the United States, including that of General Barroso to discuss the need for modernisation.
3. See abundant information in AHM, divisão 1, secção 40, caixa 1.
4. Speech delivered in the Francoist Cortes in 1957. Army Minister Barroso proposed to submit Navarro Rubio to a military trial for his remarks. However,

Franco supported Navarro Rubio's plan to cut the military budget (Navarro Rubio 1991:141–8).
5. The Estado Novo was characterised by Unamuno as a 'sort of academic fascism'or as a 'military-academic dictatorship' (Medina 1977:107–17). See also Massis's depiction of Salazar (Massis 1961).

10 Conclusions

1. This confirms what the dominant literature on policy instruments has suggested (Hood 1983:154; Howlett 2005:33; Bemelmans-Videc and Vedung 1998).
2. See Chapters 4 and 7.
3. The policy instrument literature recognises that the main problem is linking instrument choice with the factors that stimulated them (Linder and Peters 1989:48–53; Howlett and Ramesh 2003:91, 194).
4. See similar arguments in Hall and Taylor (1996) and Bieler and Morton (2001).
5. See a similar critique in Linder and Peters (1989:40–1).
6. A similar problem has been found with the subcategories introduced in this book.
7. Lascoumes and Le Galès (2007) also stress the value of policy intruments as indicators of policy change.

References

Books and articles

Abrahamsson, Bengt (1972). *Military Professionalisation and Political Power.* London: Sage Publications.

Adler, Emanuel (1997). 'Seizing the Middle Ground: Constructivism in World Politics', *European Journal of International Relations*, 3(3): 319–63.

Aguado Sánchez, Fernando (1975). *El maquis en España.* Madrid: San Martín.

Agüero, Felipe (1988). 'Democracia en España y supremacía civil', *Revista Española de Investigaciones Sociológicas*, 44: 23–50.

Agüero, Felipe (1995). *Soldiers, Civilians, and Democracy: Post-Franco Spain in Comparative Perspective.* Baltimore: The John Hopkins University Press.

Aguilar Olivencia, Mariano (1999). *El Ejército Español durante el Franquismo.* Madrid: Akal.

Aguilar, Miguel Angel (1985). 'The Spanish Military: Force for Stability or Insecurity?' in Raymond Carr and Joyce Lasky Shub (eds) *Spain: Studies in Political Security.* Washington, DC: Praeger.

Aguilar, Paloma (1997). 'Collective Memory of the Spanish Civil War: The Case of the Political Amnesty in the Spanish Transition to Democracy', *Democratization*, 4(4): 88–109.

Ajzen, Icek (1991). 'The Theory of Planned Behavior', *Organizational Behavior and Human Decision Processes*, 50(2): 179–211.

Alba, Carlos (1981). 'The Organisation of Authoritarian Leadership: Franco's Spain' in Erza Suleiman and Richard Rose (eds) *Presidents and Prime Ministers.* Washington, DC: American Enterprise Institute for Policy Research.

Allendesalazar Urbina, Rafael (1977). 'Tradition et Changement dans le Système Militaire Espagnol' in Lucien Mandeville and Paul Ourliac (1979/ eds) *Reconnaissances du Système Militaire Espagnol.* Toulouse: Institut d'Etudes Politiques, Université de Toulouse I.

Almeida, Leonardo Ribeiro de (1986). 'Discurso Proferido Pelo Ministro da Defesa Nacional em 11 Julho 1986', *Nacão e Defesa*, 13: 21–37.

Almeida, Pedro Tavares de and António Costa Pinto (2003). 'Portuguese Ministers, 1951–1999: Social Background and Paths to Power' in Pedro Tavares de Almeida, Antonio Costa Pinto and Nancy Bermeo (eds) *Who Governs Southern Europe? Regime Change and Ministerial Recruitment, 1850–2000.* London: Frank Cass.

Alonso Baquer, Miguel (1978). 'Les Relations Politico-Militaires depuis la Mort de l'Almiral Carrero Blanco (1974–1978)' in Lucien Mandeville and Paul Ourliac (1979/eds) *Reconnaissances du Système Militaire Espagnol.* Toulouse: Institut d'Etudes Politiques, Université de Toulouse I.

Alonso Baquer, Miguel (1983). *El Modelo Español de Pronunciamiento.* Madrid: Rialp.

Alonso Baquer, Miguel (1988). 'The Age of Pronunciamientos' in Thomas Barker and Rafael Bañón Martínez (eds) *Armed Forces and Society in Spain: Past and Present.* Boulder: Social Science Monographs.

Amaral, Diogo Freitas do (2000). 'Forças Armadas em Regime Democrático', *Nacão e Defesa*, 94: 175–85.
Anderson, Charles W. (1971). 'Comparative Policy Analysis: The Design of Measures', *Comparative Politics*, 4(1): 117–31.
Anderson, Charles W. (1977). *Statecraft: An Introduction to Political Choice and Judgment*. New York: John Wiley & Sons.
Anderson, Peter (2009). *The Francoist Military Trials: Terror and Complicity,1939–1945*. London: Routledge.
Antunes, José Freire (1978). *A desgraça da República: na ponta das baionetas: as Forças Armadas do 28 Maio*. Lisbon: Bertrand.
Antunes, José Freire (1985). *Cartas particulares a Marcello Caetano*, 2 Vols., Lisbon: Dom Quixote.
Antunes, José Freire (1991). *Kennedy e Salazar: o leão e a raposa*. Lisbon: Difusão Cultural.
Antunes, José Freire (1994). *Salazar e Caetano: cartas secretas 1932–1968*. Lisbon: Difusão Cultural.
Antunes, José Freire (2000). 'Introdução, Salazar e Caetano nas encruzilhadas do Estado Novo' in Marcello Caetano (ed.) [1975] *Minhas Memórias de Salazar segunda edição*. Lisboa: Verbo.
Arenal, Celestino del and Fracisco Aldecoa (1986). *España y la Otan: Textos y Documentos*. Madrid: Tecnos.
Arriaga, Lopes (1976). *Mocidade Portuguesa: Breve História de uma Organização Salazarista*. Lisbon: Terra Libre.
Arthur, W. Brian (1989). 'Competing Technologies, Increasing Returns, and Lock-in by Historical Events', *Economic Journal*, 99: 116–31.
Avant, Deborah (1994). *Political Institutions and Military Change*. Ithaca, New York: Cornell University Press.
Azcona, José Manuel, Agustín Rodríquez and Gonzalo Azaola (1994). 'La Guerra de Sidi Ifni-Sáhara (1957–1958)', *Estudios de Ciencias Sociales*, VII: 68–89.
Azevedo, Cândido de (1999). *A Censura de Salazar e Marcelo Caetano*. Lisbon: Caminho.
Bacevich, Andrew J. (1998). 'Absent History: A Comment on Dauber, Desch, and Feaver', *Armed Forces & Society*, 24(3): 447–54.
Balfour, Sebastian (2002). *Deadly Embrace: Morocco and the Road to the Spanish Civil War*. Oxford: Oxford University Press.
Ballbé, Manuel (1983). *Orden Público y militarismo en la España Constitucional (1812–1984)*. Madrid: Alianza.
Balsemão, Francisco Pinto (1986). 'The Constitution and Politics' in Kenneth Maxwell (ed.) *Portugal in the 1980's: Dilemmas of Democratic Consolidation*. London: Greenwood Press.
Bañón Martínez, Rafael (1978). *Poder de la Burocracia y Cortes Franquistas 1943–1971*. Madrid: Instituto Nacional de Administración Pública.
Bañón Martínez, Rafael (1985). 'La racionalidad de las políticas de remuneraciones y el diseño de la organización militar española', *Revista Internacional de Sociología*, 43(2): 269–303.
Bañón Martínez, Rafael (1988). 'The Spanish Armed Forces during the Period of Political Transition, 1975–1985' in Thomas Barker and Rafael Bañón Martínez (eds) *Armed Forces and Society in Spain: Past and Present*. Boulder: Social Science Monographs.

Bañón, Rafael and José Antonio Olmeda (1985). 'Las Fuerzas Armadas en España: Institucionalización y Proceso de Cambio' in Rafael Bañón and José Antonio Olmeda (eds) *La Institución Military en el Estado Contemporáneo*. Madrid: Alianza Universidad.

Barata, Filipe Themudo (1980). 'Indústria Militar Nacional: como e para quê? *Nação e Defesa*, 16: 85–120.

Barrachina Lisón, Carlos (2002). *El regreso a los cuarteles: militares y cambio político en España (1976–1981)*. Doctoral Book. Madrid: Departamento de Ciencias Políticas y de la Administración. Facultad de Ciencias Políticas y Sociología. UNED.

Barrera, Carlos (2006). 'International News and Spanish Newspapers' Struggle for Press Freedom during Franco's Dictatorship (1939–1975)'. Paper prepared for presentation at the International Association for Mass Communication Research, The American University in Cairo, Egypt, 23–29 July 2006. http://www.aucegypt.edu/conferences/iamcr/uploaded/CD_Carlos%2520Barrera.pdf [accessed 24 February 2008].

Barros, Carlos P. and José C. Gomes Santos (1997). 'A despesa militar em Portugal: 1950–1990', *Nação e Defesa*, 82: 203–16.

Beetham, David (1991). *The Legitimation of Power*. London: MacMillan.

Beevor, Antony (2006). *The Battle for Spain: The Spanish Civil War 1936–1939*. London: Weidenfeld & Nicolson.

Beirôco, Luis (2003). *Cinco Homens de Estado*. Lisbon: Livros do Brasil.

Bemelmans-Videc, Marie-Louise, and Evert Vedung (1998). 'Conclusions: Policy Instruments Types, Packages, and Evaluation' in Marie-Louise Bemelmans-Videc, Ray C. Rist, and Evert Vedung (eds) *Carrots, Sticks and Sermons: Policy Instruments & Their Evaluation*. New Brunswick: Transaction Publishers.

Bemelmans-Videc, Marie-Louise, Ray C. Rist, and Evert Vedung (1998/eds) *Carrots, Sticks and Sermons: Policy Instruments & Their Evaluation*. New Brunswick: Transaction Publishers.

Bernecker, Walther L. (1998). 'Monarchy and Democracy: The Political Role of King Juan Carlos in the Spanish Transición', *Journal of Contemporary History*, 33(1): 65–84.

Biddle, Stephen and Robert Zirkle (1996). 'Technology, Civil–Military Relations, and Warfare in the Developing World', *The Journal of Strategic Studies*, 19(2): 171–212.

Bieler, Andreas and Adam David Morton (2001). 'The Gordian Knot of Agency – Structure in International Relations: A Neo-Gramscian Perspective', *European Journal of International Relations*, 7(1): 5–35.

Blanco Ande, Joaquín (1987). *Defensa Nacional y Fuerzas Armadas*. Madrid: Dykinson.

Blanco Escolá, Carlos (2000). *La incompetencia militar de Franco*. Madrid: Alianza.

Blanco Valdés, Roberto L. (1999). *La Ordenación Constitucional de la Defensa*. Madrid: Tecnos.

Bland, Douglas (1999). 'A Unified Theory of Civil–Military Relations', *Armed Forces & Society*, 26(1): 7–25.

Blyth, Mark (1997). 'Any More Bright Ideas? The Ideational Turn of Comparative Political Economy', *Comparative Politics*, 29(1): 229–50.

Blyth, Mark (2002). *Great Transformations: Economic Ideas and Institutional Change in the Twentieth Century.* Cambridge: Cambridge University Press.

Boyd, Carolyne P. (1979). *Praetorian Politics in Liberal Spain.* Chapel Hill: University of North Carolina Press.

Braga da Cruz, Manuel António Garcia (1988). *O Partido e o Estado no Salazarismo.* Lisbon: Editorial Presenta.

Bravo Morata, Federico (1978). *La postguerra, 1939–1945.* Madrid: Fenicia.

Bressers, Hans T. A. and Laurence J. O'Toole, Jr. (1998). 'The Selection of Policy Instruments: A Network-Based Perspective', *Journal of Public Policy*, 18(3): 213–39.

Bressers, Hans T. A. and Laurence J. O'Toole, Jr. (2005). 'Instrument Selection and Implementation' in Pearl Eliadis, Margaret M. Hill, and Michael Howlett (eds) *Designing Government: From Instruments to Governance.* Montreal: Mc-Gill-Queen's University Press.

Brooks, Risa (2013). 'Abandoned at the Palace: Why the Tunisian Military Defected from the Ben Ali Regime in January 2011', *Journal of Strategic Studies*, 36(2): 205–20.

Brothers, Carline (1997). *War and Photography: A Cultural History.* London: Routledge.

Brown, James (1980). 'Greek Civil–Military Relations: A Different Pattern', *Armed Forces & Society*, 6(3): 389–413.

Bruijn, Hans A. de and A. M. Hufen (1998). 'The Traditional Approach to Policy Instruments' in Guy B. Peters and Frans K. M. Van Nispen (eds) *Public Policy Instruments: Evaluating the Tools of Public Administration.* Cheltenham: Edward Elgar.

Bruneau, Thomas C. and Florina Cristiana Matei (2008). 'Towards a New Conceptualization of Democratization and Civil–Military Relations', *Democratization*, 15(5): 909–29.

Burk, James (1998). 'The Logic of Crisis and Civil–Military Relations Theory: A Comment on Desch, Feaver and Dauber', *Armed Forces & Society*, 24(3): 455–62.

Burk, James (2002). 'Theories of Democratic Civil–Military Relations', *Armed Forces & Society*, 29(1): 7–29.

Busquets, Julio (1982). *Pronunciamientos y golpes de Estado en España.* Barcelona: Ariel.

Busquets, Julio (1984 [1971]). *El militar de carrera en España.* Barcelona: Ariel.

Busquets, Julio (1999). *Militares y demócratas.* Barcelona: Plaza & Janés.

Busquets, Julio and Juan C. Losada (2003). *Ruido de Sables: Las conspiraciones militares en la España del siglo XX.* Barcelona: Crítica.

Caeiro, Joaquim Manuel Croca (1997). *Os Militares no Poder: Uma análise histórico-política do liberalismo à revisão constitucional de 1959.* Lisbon: Huguin Editores.

Caetano, Marcello (1957). *A Constituição de 1933: Estudo de Direito Constitucional.* Coimbra: Coimbra Editora.

Caetano, Marcello (2000 [1975]). *Minhas Memórias de Salazar*, 2nd edn. Lisboa: Verbo.

Campinos, Jorge (1975). *Ideología Política do Estado Salazarista.* Lisbon: Portugália.

Campinos, Jorge (1978). *O Presidencialismo do Estado Novo.* Lisbon: Perspectivas & Realidades.

Cardona, Gabriel (1983). *El Poder Militar en la España Contemporánea hasta la Guerra Civil.* Madrid: Siglo XXI.

Cardona, Gabriel (1990). *El Problema Militar en España*. Madrid: Historia, 16.

Cardona, Gabriel (2001). *Franco y sus Generales, la manicura del tigre*. Madrid: Temas de Hoy.

Cardoso, Pedro (1980a). 'Os Serviços de Informações Nacionais e Estrangeiras', *Nação e Defesa*, 15: 143–57.

Cardoso, Pedro (1980b). *As Informaçoes em Portugal*. Lisbon: IDN.

Carrero Blanco, Luis (1974). *Discursos y Escritos, 1943–1973*. Madrid: Instituto de Estudios Políticos.

Carrilho, Maria (1985). *Forças Armadas e mudança política em Portugal no século XX*. Lisbon: Imprensa Nacional.

Carrilho, Maria (1989/ed.). *Portugal na segunda guerra mundial: contributos para uma reavaliação*. Lisbon: Dom Quixote.

Carrilho, Maria (1992). 'Democracy and the Armed Forces in Portugal' in Richard Herr (ed.) *The New Portugal: Democracy and Europe*. Berkeley: University of California Press.

Carrilho, Maria (1994). *Democracia e defesa: sociedade, política e forças armadas em Portugal*. Lisboa: Dom Quixote.

Cayón García, Francisco (1995), 'Prensa y opinión en el período constituyente' in A. Soto, J. M. Marín, J. R. Díaz Gijón, P. Martínez Lillo, and J. Pan-Montojo (eds) *Historia de la transición y consolidación democrática en España (1975–1986)*, Vol. II. Madrid: UNED & UAM.

Celhay, Pierre (1976). *Consejos de guerra en Espana: fascismo contra Euskadi*. Paris: Ruedo Iberico.

CESEDEN (1988). *Estudio Comparativo de la Evolución de los presupuestos de defensa de los países del área mediterranea (1971–1985)*. Madrid: Centro Superior de Estudios de la Defensa Nacional.

Checkel, Jeffrey T. (1998). 'The Constructivist Turn in International Relations Theory', *World Politics*, 50(2): 324–48.

Cheibub, José Antonio (1998). 'Political Regimes and the Extractive Democracies Capacity of Governments: Taxation in and Dictatorships', *World Politics*, 50(3): 349–76.

Chilcote, Ronald H. (1990). 'Southern European Transitions in Comparative Perspective' in Ronald Chilcote H., Stylianos Hadjiyannis, Fred A. III Lopez, Daniel Nataf, and Elizabeth Sammis (eds) *Transitions from Dictatorship to Democracy: Comparative Studies of Spain, Portugal, and Greece*. New York: Taylor & Francis.

Cizre, Umit (2004). 'Problems of Democratic Governance of Civil–Military Relations in Turkey and the European Union Enlargement Zone', *European Journal of Political Research*, 43(1): 107–25.

Clausewitz, Carl von (1966 [1827]). *On War*. London: Routledge and Kegan Paul.

Cohen, Eliot A. (2002). *Supreme Command: Soldiers, Statesmen, and Leadership in Wartime*. NewYork: Free Press.

Collier, Ruth Berins and David Collier (1991). *Shaping the Political Arena: Critical Junctures, the Labor Movement, and Regime Dynamics in Latin America*. Princeton: Princeton University Press.

Comas, José Maria and Lucien Mandeville (1986). *Les militaires et le pouvoir dans l'Espagne contemporaine de Franco a Felipe Gonzalez*. Toulouse: Institute d'Etudes Politiques.

Comín, Francisco and Daniel Díaz (2005). 'Sector publico administrativo y estado del bienestar' in Albert Carreras and Xavier Tafunell (eds) *Estadisticas Historicas de España, Siglos XIX–XX*. Bilbao: Fundación BBVA.

Commission of the European Communities (2001). 'European Governance: A White Paper'. *White Papers.*COM, 428, http://eur-lex.europa.eu/LexUriServ/site/en/com/2001/com2001_0428en01.pdf [accessed 30 May 2013].

Comprido, Baptista (1979). 'Defesa Nacional: Alguns Subsídios para uma Lei', *Nação e Defesa*, 10: 35–48.

Correia, Ángelo (1978). 'Reflexões Doutrinárias acerca duma Lei de Defesa Nacional', *Nação e Defesa*, 6: 10–29.

Cosidó Gutiérrez, Ignacio (1994). *El gasto militar: el presupuesto de defensa en España (1982–1992)*. Madrid: Eudema.

Cottey, A., T. Edmonds, and A. Forster (2002). 'The Second Generation Problematic: Rethinking Democracy and Civil–Military Relations', *Armed Forces & Society*, 29(1): 31–56.

Crollen, Luc (1973). *Portugal, the U.S. and NATO*. Leuven: Leuven University Press.

Daguzan, Jean-François (1982). 'L'expansion de l'Industrie Militaire Espagnole' in Jean-François Daguzan and Bernard Labatut (eds) *Troisièmes Reconnaissances du Système Militaire Espagnol*. Toulouse: Institut d'Etudes Politiques, Université de Toulouse I.

Dahl, Robert A. and Charles E. Lindblom (1953). *Politics, Economics and Welfare: Planning and Politico-economic Systems Resolved into Basic Social Processes*. New York: Harper and Row.

Danopoulos, Constantine (1991). 'Democratising the Military: Lessons from Mediterranean Europe', *West European Politics*, 14(4): 25–41.

Dauber, Cori (1998). 'The Practice of Argument: Reading the Condition of Civil–Military Relations', *Armed Forces & Society*, 24(3): 435–46.

David, Paul A. (1985). 'Clio and the QWERTY', *American Economic Review*, 75: 332–7.

David, Paul A. (2000). 'Path Dependence, Its Critics and the Quest for "Historical Economics"' in Pierre Garrouste and Stavros Ioannides (eds) *Evolution and Path Dependence in Economic Idea: Past and Present*. Cheltenham: Edward Elgar.

Decalo, Samuel (1976). *Coups and Army Rule in Africa: Motivations and Constraints*. New Haven: Yale University Press.

Delgado, Julián (2005). *Los grises: Víctimas y verdugos del franquismo*. Madrid: Temas de Hoy.

Desch, Michael C. (1998a). 'Soldiers, States, and Structures: the End of the Cold War and Weakening US Civilian Control', *Armed Forces & Society*, 24(3): 389–406.

Desch, Michael C. (1998b). 'A Historian's Fallacies: A Reply to Bacevich', *Armed Forces & Society*, 24(3): 587–92.

Desch, Michael C. (1999). *Civilian Control of the Military. The Changing Security Environment*. Baltimore: The Johns Hopkins University Press.

Diamandouros, Nikiforos P. and Richard Gunther (2001/eds). *Parties, Politics, and Democracy in the New Southern Europe*. Baltimore: The John Hopkins University Press.

Díaz Fernández, Antonio Manuel (2003). *Origen, función y control de los servicios de inteligencia de España*. Doctoral Book. Barcelona: Departamento de Derecho

Constitucional y Ciencia Política. Facultad de Derecho, Universidad de Barcelona.

Díaz Fernández, Antonio Manuel (2005). *Los servicios de inteligencia españoles. Desde la guerra civil hasta el 11M. Historia de una transición.* Madrid: Alianza.

DiMaggio, Paul J. and Walter W. Powell (1983). 'The Iron Cage Revisited: Institutional Isomorphism and Collective Rationality in Organizational Fields', *American Sociological Review*, 48: 147–60.

DiMaggio, Paul J. and Walter W. Powell (1991/eds) *The New Institutionalism in Organisational Analysis*, Vol. 17. Chicago: University of Chicago Press.

Doern, G. Bruce and Richard W. Phidd (1983). *Canadian Public Policy: Ideas Structure, Process.* Toronto: Methuen.

Dolowitz, David and David Marsh (2000). 'Learning from Abroad: The role of Policy Transfer in Contemporary Policy-Making', *Governance*, 13(1): 5–24.

Duarte, António Paulo (2010). *A Política de Defesa Nacional 1919–1958.* Lisbon: Impresa de Ciências Sociais.

Dueñas, Manuel Álvaro (1990). 'Los militares en al represión política de la posguerra: La jurisdicción especial de responsabilidades políticas hasta la reforma de 1942', *Revista de estudios políticos*, 69: 141–62.

Eliadis, Pearl, Margaret M. Hill, and Michael Howlett (2005/eds). *Designing Government: From Instruments to Governance.* Montreal: Mc-Gill-Queen's University Press.

Faria, Telmo (1995). 'O Comunismo. Un anátema estado-novista', *Revista de História das Ideias*, 17: 229–61.

Faria, Telmo (1996). 'As tropas de Santos Costa na elite militar do Estado Novo', *História*, 23/24 Agosto–Septembro.

Faria, Telmo (2000). *Debaixo de fogo!: Salazar e as Forças Armadas (1935–41).* Lisboa: Instituto da Defesa Nacional.

Feaver, Peter D. (1998a). 'Crisis as Shirking: An Agency Theory Explanation of the Souring of American Civil–Military Relations', *Armed Forces & Society*, 24(3): 407–34.

Feaver, Peter D. (1998b). 'Modeling Civil–Military Relations: A Replay to Burk and Bacevich', *Armed Forces & Society*, 24(4): 593–600.

Feaver, Peter D. (1999). 'Civil–Military Relations', *Annual Review of Political Science*, 2: 211–41.

Feaver, Peter D. (2003). *Armed Servants: Agency, Oversight and Military Relations.* Cambridge, MA: Harvard University Press.

Feaver, Peter D. and Richard H. Kohn (2001/eds). *Soldiers and Civilians: The Civil–Military Gap and American National Security.* Cambridge, Mass: The MIT Press.

Feit, Edward (1973). *The Armed Bureaucrats: Military-Administrative Regimes and Political Development.* Boston: Houghton Mifflin.

Feo, Julio and José Luis Romero (1968). 'La Administración Publica comparada de tres países continentales: España, Francia y Alemania', *Sociología de la Administración Publica española*, 17: 315–76.

Fernandes, Tiago (2006). *Nem Ditadura, nem Revoluçao: A Ala Liberal e o Marcelismo (1968–1974).* Lisbon: Dom Quixote.

Fernández López, Javier (1998). *El Rey y otros militares: los militares en el cambio de régimen político en España (1969–1982).* Madrid: Trotta.

Fernández López, Javier (2000). *Diecisiete horas y media: el enigma del 23-F.* Madrid: Taurus.

Fernández-Aceytuno, Mariano (2001). *Ifni y Sahara: una encrucijada en la historia de España*. Simancas: Dueñas.

Ferreira, Arnaldo Manuel de Medeiros (1976). 'Factores da Evolução do Ensino Militar Superior', *Nação e Defesa*, 2: 139–52

Ferreira, José Medeiros (1980). 'Espace Stratégique et Défensif Ibérique' in Alain Montech (1982/ed.) *Reconnaissances du Système Militaire Portugais*. Toulouse: Institut d'Etudes Politiques, Université de Toulouse I.

Ferreira, José Medeiros (1983). *Ensaio histórico sobre a Revolução de 25 de Abril O Period Pre-Constitucional: Coedicao*. INCM – SREC da Regiao Autonoma dos Acores.

Ferreira, José Medeiros (1989). *Um Século de Problemas: As Relaçoes Luso-Espanholas da União Ibérica à Comunidade Europeia*. Lisbon: Livros Horizonte.

Ferreira, José Medeiros (1992). *O Comportamento Político dos Militares: Forças Armadas e Regimes Políticos em Portugal durante o Século XX*. Lisbon: Editorial Estampa.

Ferreira, José Medeiros (1994). *História de Portugal, vol. 8: Portugal em transe*. Lisbon: Editorial Estampa.

Ferreira, José Medeiros (2006). *Cinco Regimes na Política Internacional*. Lisbon: Presenta.

Ferreira, Nuno Estêvão (2009). *A Câmara Corporativa no Estado Novo: Composição, Funcionamento e Influêcia. Doutoramento en Ciências Sociais*. Lisbon: Universidade de Lisboa, Instituto de Ciências Sociais.

Ferro, Antonio (1933). *Salazar: o Homem e a sua Obra*. Lisbon: Empresa Nacional de Publicidade.

Ferro, Antonio (1938). *Homens e Multidões*. Lisbon: Livraria Bertrand.

Ferro, Antonio (2003 [1932–8]). *Entrevistas de Antonio Ferro a Salazar*, 2nd edn. Lisbon: Parceira A. M. Pereira.

Finer, Samuel E. (1975). 'State and Nation-Building in Europe: The Role of the Military' in Charles Tilly (ed.) *The Formation of National States in Western Europe*. Princeton: Princeton University Press.

Finer, Samuel E. (1988 [1962]). *The Man on Horseback: The Role of the Military in Politics*, 2nd edn. London: Allen Lane.

Fishman, Robert (1990). 'Rethinking State and Regime: Southern Europe's Transition to Democracy', *World Politics*, 42(3): 422–40.

Fontana, Josep (1986/ed.). *España bajo el franquismo*. Barcelona: Critica.

Forster, Anthony (2006). *Armed Forces and Society in Europe*. Hampshire: Palgrave MacMillan.

Fortes, José and Luis Otero (1983). *Proceso a nueve militares demócratas: las Fuerzas Armadas y la UMD*. Barcelona: Argos-Vergara.

Freire, João (2003). *Homens em fundo azul-marinho. Ensaio de observação sociológica sobre uma corporação nos meados do séc. XX: A Armada Portuguesa*. Oeiras: Celta.

Freire, João Brito (1998). 'O Partido Comunista Português e a Guerra Civil de Espanha' in Fernando Rosas (ed.) *Portugal e a Guerra Civil de Espanha*. Lisbon: Edições Colibri.

Freyre, Gilberto (1940). *O mundo que o português criou: aspectos das relações sociais e de cultura do Brasil com Portugal e as colônias portuguesas*. Rio de Janeiro: José Olympio.

Frisch, Hillel (2013). 'The Egyptian Army and Egypt's "Spring"', *Journal of Strategic Studies*, 36(2): 180–204.

Gallagher, Tom (1983). *Portugal: A Twentieth-Century Interpretation*. Manchester: Manchester University Press.

Galvão, Henrique (1938). *O Imperio*. Lisbon: SPN.

García Díez, Juan A. (2000). 'The Government's Consensual Strategy' in Monica Threlfall (ed.) *Consensus Politics in Spain: Insider Perspectives*. Bristol: Intellect.

Garrett, Geoffrey and Barry Weingast (1994). 'Ideas, Interests, and Institutions: Constructing the European Community's Internal Market' in Judith Goldstein and Robert Keohane (eds) *Ideas and Foreign Policy*. Ithaca: Cornell University Press.

Gaub, Florence (2013). 'The Libyan Armed Forces between Coup-Proofing and Repression', *Journal of Strategic Studies*, 36(2): 221–244.

Geddes, Barbara (1999). 'What Do We Know About Democratization after 20 Years?', *Annual Review of Political Science*, 2: 115–44.

Gillespie, Richard (1989). *The Spanish Socialist Party: A History of Factionalism*. Oxford: Oxford University Press.

Gilmour, David (1985). *The Transformation of Spain: From Franco to the Constitutional Monarchy*. London: Quartet Books.

Goldstein, Judith (1993). *Ideas, Interests and American Trade Policy*. Ithaca: Cornell University Press.

Goldstein, Judith and Robert Keohane (1994/eds). *Ideas and Foreign Policy*. Ithaca: Cornell University Press.

Gomáriz, Enrique (1979). 'Los militares ante la transición. El postfranquismo', *Zona Abierta*, 19: 71–88.

Gomes, Bernardino and Tiago Moreira de Sá (2008). *Carlucci Vs Kissinger: Os EUA e a Sua Revolução Portuguesa*. Lisbon: Dom Quixote.

González Hernández, Juan Carlos (1999). *Desarrollo Político y Consolidación Democrática en Portugal (1974–1998)*. Madrid: CIS/Universidad de Salamanca.

González Padilla, Eusebio (2002). 'La Justicia Militar en el primer Franquismo' in Manuel Gutiérrez Navas and José Rivera Menéndez (eds) *Sociedad y política almeriense durante el régimen de Franco. Actas de las Jornadas celebradas en la UNED durante los días 8 al 12 de Abril de 2002*. Almeria: Instituto de Estudio Almerienses.

Graham, Lawrence S. (1975). *Portugal: The Decline and Collapse of an Authoritarian Order*. London: Sage.

Graham, Lawrence S. (1979). 'The Military in Politics: The Politicization of the Portuguese Armed Forces' in Lawrence S. Graham and Harry M. Makler (eds) *Contemporary Portugal: The Revolution and Its Antecedents*. Austin: University of Texas Press.

Graham, Lawrence S. (1983). 'Bureaucratic Politics and the Problems of Reform of the Apparatus' in Lawrence S. Graham and Douglas L. Wheeler (eds) *In Search of Modern Portugal: The Revolution and Its Consequences*. Madison, Wisconsin: The University of Wisconsin Press.

Graham, Lawrence S. (1993). *The Portuguese Military and the State: Rethinking Transitions in Europe and Latin America*. Boulder: Westview Press.

Graham, Robert (1984). *Spain. Change of a Nation*. London: Michael Joseph.

Greif, Avner and David Laitin (2004). 'A Theory of Endogenous Institutional Change', *American Political Science Review*, 98(4): 14–48.

Guaita Martorell, Aurelio (1986). 'Capitanes y Capitanias Generales', *Revista de Administracion Publica*, 111: 7–50.

Gunther, Richard (1980). *Public Policy in a No-Party State. Spanish Planning and Budgeting in the Twilight of the Franquist Era*. Berkeley: University of California Press.

Gunther, Richard (1995). 'Spain: The Very Model of Elite Settlement' in John Highley and Richard Gunther (eds) *Elites and Democratic Consolidation in Latin America and Southern Europe*. Cambridge: Cambridge University Press.

Gunther, Richard, Nikiforos Diamandouros and Hans-Jürgen Puhle (1995/ eds). *The Politics of Democratisation. Southern Europe in Comparative Perspective*. Baltimore: The John Hopkins University Press.

Gunther, Richard, José Ramón Montero, and Joan Botella (2004). *Democracy in Modern Spain*. New Haven: Yale University Press.

Gunther, Richard, Nikiforos Diamandouros and Dimitri A. Sotiropoulos (2006/ eds). *Democracy and the State in the New Southern Europe*. Oxford: Oxford University Press.

Gutiérrez Mellado, Manuel (1981). *Al servicio de la Corona: palabras de un military*. Madrid: Ibérico Europea de Ediciones.

Gutiérrez Mellado, Manuel and Jesús Picatoste (1983). *Un soldado de España. Conversaciones con Jesús Picatoste*. Barcelona: Argos Vergara.

Hacker, Jacob S. (1998). 'The Historical Logic of National Health Insurance: Structure and Sequence in the Development of British, Canadian, and U.S. Medical Policy', *Studies in American Political Development*, 12: 57–130.

Hacker, Jacob S. (2002). *The Divided Welfare State: The Battle over Public and Private Social Benefits in the United States*. Cambridge: Cambridge University Press.

Hall, Peter A. (1986). *Governing the Economy*. New York: Oxford University Press.

Hall, Peter A. (1993). 'Policy Paradigms, Social Learning and the State: The Case of Economic Policy-Making in Britain', *Comparative Politics*, 25(3): 275–96.

Hall, Peter A. (1997). 'The Role of Interests, Institutions, and Ideas in the Comparative Political Economy of the Industrialized Nations' in Mark I. Linchbach and Alan S. Zuckerman (eds), *Comparative Politics: Rationality, Culture, and Structure*. New York: Cambridge University Press.

Hall, Peter and Rosemary Taylor (1996). 'Political Science and the Three New Institutionalisms', *Political Studies*, 44: 936–57.

Halpern, Charlotte and Patrick Le Galès (2011). 'Pas d'Action Publique Autonome sans Instruments Propres: Analyse Comparée et Longitudinale des Politiques Environnementales et Urbaines de l'Union Européene', *Revue Française de Science Politique*, 61(1): 51–78.

Harris, J. P. (1996). *Men, Ideas and Tanks: British Military Thought and Armoured Forces, 1903–1939*. Manchester: Manchester University Press.

Hay, Colin (2004). 'Ideas, Interests and Institutions in the Comparative Political Economy of Great Transformations', *Review of International Political Economy*, 11(1): 204–26.

Hay, Colin (2006). 'Constructivist Institutionalism' in R. A. W. Rhodes, Sarah E. Binder, and Bert Rockman (eds) *The Oxford Handbook of Political Institutions*. Oxford: Oxford University Press.

Hay, Colin (2007). 'Globalisation and Public Policy' in R. E. Goodin, M. Rein and M. Moran (eds) *The Oxford Handbook of Public Policy*. Oxford: Oxford University Press.

Hay, Colin and Daniel Wincott (1998). 'Structure, Agency and Historical Institutionalism', *Political Studies*, 46(5): 951–7.

Heclo, Hugh (1974). *Modern Social Politics in Britain and Sweden*. New Haven: Yale University Press.

Herspring, Dale Roy (1996). *Russian Civil-military Relations*. Bloomington, IN: Indiana University Press.

Herr, Richard and John Herman Richard Polt (1989/eds). *Iberian Identity: Essays on the Nature of Identity in Portugal and Spain*. Berkeley: Institute of International Studies.

Hood, Christopher C. (1983). *The Tools of Government*. London: McMillan.

Hood, Christopher C. (1998). *The Art of the State*. Oxford: Oxford University Press.

Hood, Christopher C. (2007). 'Intellectual Obsolescence and Intellectual Makeovers', *Governance*, 20(1): 127–44.

Hood, Christopher C. and Helen Z. Margetts (2007). *The Tools of Government in the Digital Age*. London: Palgrave Macmillan.

Hood, Christopher C. and Michael Jackson (1994). 'Keys for Locks in Administrative Argument', *Administration & Society*, 25(4): 467–88.

Hopkin, Jonathan (1999). *Party Formation and Democratic Transition in Spain: The Creation and Collapse of the Union of the Democratic Centre*. New York: St Martin's Press.

Horowitz, Donald (1980). *Coup Theories and Officers' Motives: Sri Lanka in Comparative Perspective*. Princeton: Princeton University Press.

Howlet, Michael and M. Ramesh (1993). 'Patterns of Policy Instrument Choice: Policy Styles, Policy Learning and the Privatization Experience', *Policy Studies Review*, 12(1): 1–24.

Howlett, Michael (1991). 'Policy Instruments, Policy Styles, and Policy Implementation: National Approaches to Theories of Instrument Choice', *Policy Studies Journal*, 19(2): 1–21.

Howlett, Michael (2000). 'Managing the "Hollow State": Procedural Policy Instruments and Modern Governance', *Canadian Public Administration*, 43(4): 412–31.

Howlett, Michael (2005). 'What is a y Instrument?' in Pearl Eliadis, Margaret M. Hill, and Michael Howlett (eds) *Designing Government: From Instruments to Governance*. Montreal: Mc-Gill-Queen's University Press.

Howlett, Michael (2009a). 'Governance Modes, Policy Regimes and Operational Plans: A Multi-level Nested Model of Policy Instrument Choice and Policy Design', *Policy Sciences*, 42(1): 73–88.

Howlett, Michael (2009b). 'Process Sequencing Policy Dynamics: Beyond Homeostasis and Path Dependency', *Journal of Public Policy*, 29(3): 241–62.

Howlett, Michael (2011). *Designing Public Policies: Principles and instruments*. London: Routledge.

Howlett, Michael and M. Ramesh (2003). *Studying Public Policy: Policy Subsystems*, 2nd edn. Don Mills, Ontario: Oxford University Press.

Huber, Evelyne, Charles Ragin, and John Stephens (1993). 'Social Democracy, Christian Democracy, Constitutional Structure, and the Welfare State', *American Journal of Sociology*, 99(3): 711–49.

Huntington, Samuel P. (1957). *The Soldier and the State: The Theory and Politics of Civil–Military Relations*. Cambridge, Massachusetts: Harvard University Press.

Huntington, Samuel P. (1991). *The Third Wave: Democratization in the Late Twentieth Century*. Norman: University of Oklahoma Press.

IISS (1986). *The Military Balance 1984–1985*. London: The International Institute For Strategic Studies.

IISS (1988). *The Military Balance 1986–1987*. London: The International Institute For Strategic Studies.

Immergut, Ellen M. (1992). *Health politics: Interests and institutions in Western Europe*. Cambridge: Cambridge University Press.

Immergut, Ellen M. (1998). 'The Theoretical Core of the New Institutionalism', *Politics & Society*, 26(1): 5–34.

Iniesta Cano, Carlos (1986). 'Las Fuerzas Armadas (1975–1985)' in Rafael Borrás Bertriu (ed.) *España: diez años después de Franco (1975–1985)*. Barcelona: Planeta.

Jackson, Gabriel (1965). *The Spanish Republic and the Civil War, 1931–1939*. Princeton: Princeton University Press.

Janowitz, Morris (1957). 'Military Elites and the Study of War', *Conflict Resolution*, 1(1): 9–18.

Janowitz, Morris (1960). *The Professional Soldier: A Social and Political Portrait*. Glencoe, Illinois: Free Press.

Jennings, Will and Martin Lodge (2011). 'Governing Mega-Events: Tools of Security Risk Management for the FIFA 2006 World Cup in Germany and London 2012 Olympic Games', *Government and Opposition*, 46(2): 192–222.

Jerez Mir, Miguel (1982). *Elites políticas y centros de extracción en España, 1938–1957*. Madrid: Centro de Investigaciones Sociologicas.

Jerez Mir, Miguel (2009). 'Executive, single party and ministers in Franco's regime: 1936–45' in Costa Pinto (ed.) *Ruling Elites and Decision-making in Fascist-era Dictatorships*. Social Science Monographs, Boulder. New York: Columbia University Press.

Jiménez Jiménez, Juan Carlos (1987). 'Las consecuencias económicas de la guerra civil', *Revista de Historia Económica*, 5(1): 121–30.

Jordana, Jacint and Carles Ramió (2005). 'Gobierno y Administracion' in Albert Carreras and Xavier Tafunell (eds) *Estadisticas Historicas de España, Siglos XIX–XX*. Bilbao: Fundación BBVA.

Júdice, José Miguel Alarcão (1978). 'O Artigo 273°, N° 4, da Constituição da República Portuguesa e a Actual Missão Política das Forças Armadas (Apontamento de Teoria Constitucional)', *Nacão e Defesa*, 4: 17–32.

Karabelias, Gerassimos (1998). *Civil–Military Relations: A Comparative Analysis of the Role of the Military in the Political Transformations of Post-war Turkey and Greece (1980–1995)*. Final Report submitted to North Atlantic Treaty Organization in June 1998.

Katznelson, Ian (2003). 'Periodization and Preferences: Reflections on Purposive Action in Comparative Historical Social Science' in James Mahoney and Dietrich Rueschemeyer (eds) *Comparative Historical Analysis in the Social Sciences*. Cambridge: Cambridge University Press.

Keynes, John Maynard (1936). *The General Theory of Employment, Interest and Money*. London: MacMillan.

Kindelán, Alfredo (1981). *La verdad de mis relaciones con Franco*. Barcelona: Planeta.

King, Desmond (1995). *Actively Seeking Work. The Politics of Unemployment and Welfare Policy in the United States*. Chicago: Chicago University Press.

Kingdon, John (1984). *Agendas, Alternatives, and Public Policies.* Boston: Little Brown.

Kourvetaris George A. and Betty A. Dobratz (1981). 'Public Opinion and Civil–Military Relations in Greece Since 1974', *Journal of Strategic Studies*, 4(1): 71–84.

Knill, Christoph (1999). 'Explaining Cross-National Variance in Administrative Reform: Autonomous versus Instrumental Bureaucracies', *Journal of Public Policy*, 19(2): 113–39.

Krasner, Stephen D. (1984). 'Approaches to the State: Alternative Conceptions and Historical Dynamics', *Comparative Politics*, 16(2): 223–246.

Kuhn, Thomas S. (1962). *The Structure of Scientific Revolutions.* Chicago: Chicago University Press.

Lafuente Balle, José M. (1987). *El Rey y las Fuerzas Armadas en la Constitución.* Madrid: Edersa.

Landry, Réjean and Frédéric Varone (2005). 'Choice of Policy Instruments' in Pearl Eliadis, Margaret M. Hill, and Michael Howlett (eds) *Designing Government: From Instruments to Governance.* Montreal: Mc-Gill-Queen's University Press.

Lânhoso, Adriano Coutinho (1985). 'Discurso do Director do IDN Vice-almirante Adriano Coutinho Lanoso na Sessão Solene de Abertura do Curso de Defesa Nacional de 1986, em 11 Novembro 1985', *Nacão e Defesa*, 36: 15–22.

Lascoumes Pierre and Patrick Le Galès (2007). 'Introduction: Understanding Public Policy through Its Instruments – From the Nature of Instruments to the Sociology of Public Policy Instrumentation', *Governance*, 20(1): 1–21.

Lasswell, Harold (1941). 'The Garrison State and Specialist on Violence', *American Journal of Sociology*, 46: 455–68.

Lasswell, Harold D. (1958 [1936]). *Politics: Who Gets What, When, How.* New York: Meridian.

Liddell Hart, Basil (1959). *The Tanks: A History of the Royal Tank Regiment and its Predecessors.* London: Cassell & Co.

Liedtke, Boris (1999). 'Spain and the United Status, 1945–1975' in Sebastian Balfour and Paul Preston (eds) *Spain and the Great Powers in the Twentieth Century.* London: Routledge.

Lijphart, Arend (1999). *Patterns of Democracy: Government Forms and Performance in Thirty-six Countries.* New Haven: Yale University Press.

Linder, Stephen H. and Guy B. Peters (1989). 'Instruments of Government: Perceptions and Contexts', *Journal of Public Policy*, 9(1): 35–58.

Linder, Stephen H. and Guy B. Peters (1998). 'The Study of Policy Instruments: Four Schools of Thought' in Guy B. Peters and Frans K. M. Van Nispen (eds) *Public Policy Instruments: Evaluating the Tools of Public Administration.* Cheltenham: Edward Elgar.

Linz, Juan (1970 [1964]). 'An Authoritarian Regime: Spain' in Erik Allard and Stein Rokkan (1970/eds) *Mass Politics: Studies in Political Sociology.* New York: Free Press.

Linz, Juan (1994). 'Presidential or Parliamentary Democracy: Does It Make a Difference?' in Juan J. Linz and Arturo Valenzuela (eds) *The Failure of Presidential Democracy.* Baltimore: Johns Hopkins University Press.

Linz, Juan (1996). 'La Transición Española en Perspectiva Comparada' in J. Tusell and A. Soto (eds) *Historia de la Transición.* Madrid: Alianza Universidad.

Linz, Juan and Alfred Stepan (1996). *Problems of Democratic Transition and Consolidation: Southern Europe, South America, and Post-Communist Europe.* Baltimore: Johns Hopkins University Press.

Linz, Juan, Alfred Stepan, and Richard Gunther (1995). 'Democratic Transition and Consolidation in Southern Europe, with Reflections on Latin America' in Richard Gunther, Nikiforos Diamandouros, and Hans-Jürgen Puhle (eds) *The Politics of Democratisation. Southern Europe in Comparative Perspective.* Baltimore: The John Hopkins University Press.

Linz Juan, Miguel Jerez Mir, and Susana Corzo (2003). 'Ministers and Regimes in Spain: From the First to the Second Restoration, 1974–2002' in Pedro Tavares de Almeida, Antonio Costa Pinto, and Nancy Bermeo (eds) *Who Governs Southern Europe? Regime Change and Ministerial Recruitment, 1850–2000.* London: Frank Cass.

Lipset, Seymour Martin and Stein Rokkan (1967). *Party Systems and Voter Alignments: Cross-National perspectives.* Toronto: The Free Press.

Lodge, Martin (2002). *On different tracks: designing railway regulation in Britain and Germany.* Westport: Praeger.

Lodge, Martin and Oliver James (2003). 'The Limitations of "Policy Transfer" and "Lesson Drawing" for Public Policy Research', *Political Studies Review,* 1(2): 179–93.

Loff, Manuel (2008). *O Nosso Século é Fascista!: O mundo visto por Salazar e Franco (1936–1945).* Porto: Campo das Letras.

Lopes, António de Figueiredo (1986). 'A Industria de Defesa e a Modernização das Forças Armadas Portuguesas', *Nacão e Defesa,* 38: 93–105.

López Rodó, Laureano (1977). *La larga marcha hacia la monarquía.* Barcelona: Noguer.

Losada, Juan Carlos (1990). *Ideología del Ejército Franquista (1939–1959).* Madrid: Istmo.

Lowi, Theodore J. (1966). 'Distribution, Regulation, Redistribution: The Functions of Government' in Randall B. Ripley (ed.) *Public Policies and Their Politics: Techniques of Government Control.* New York: W.W. Norton.

Lucena, Manuel (1976). *A Evoluçao do Sistema Corporativo Portugués, Vol I: O Salazarismo.* Lisbon: Perspectivas e Realidades.

Lucena, Manuel (1984). 'Interpretações do Salazarismo: Notas de lectura crítica', *Análise Social,* 20: 423–51.

Luckham, Robin (1971). 'A Comparative Typology of Civil–Military Relations', *Government and Opposition,* 6(1): 5–35.

Lukes, Steven (1974). *Power: A Radical View.* London: Macmillan.

Macdonald, A. Roderick (2005). 'The Swiss Army Knife of Governance' in Pearl Eliadis, Margaret M. Hill, and Michael Howlett (eds) *Designing Government: From Instruments to Governance.* Montreal: Mc-Gill-Queen's University Press.

Machiavelli, Niccolò (2002 [1521]). *The Art of War.* Cambridge: Da Capo Press.

Magone, José Maria (1996). *The Changing Architecture of Iberian Politics (1974–92): An Investigation on the Structuring of Democratic Political Systemic Culture in Semiperipheral Southern European Societies.* Lewiston: Mellen University Press.

Mahoney, James (2000). 'Path Dependence in Historical Sociology', *Theory and Society,* 29: 507–48.

Mahoney, James and Dietrich Rueschemeyer (2003). 'Comparative Historical Analysis: Achieivements and Agendas' in James Mahoney and Dietrich

Rueschemeyer (eds) *Comparative Historical Analysis in the Social Sciences.* Cambridge: Cambridge University Press.

Mahoney, Richard D. (1983). *JFK: Ordeal in Africa.* New York: Oxford University Press.

Majone, Giandomenico (1989). *Evidence, Argument and Persuasion in the Policy Process.* New Haven: Yale University Press.

Majone, Giandomenico (1996). 'Ideas, Interests and Institutions' in Robert E. Goodin and Hans-Dieter Klingeman (eds) *A New Handbook of Political Science.* Oxford: Oxford University Press.

Maluquer de Motes, Jordi (2005). 'Consumo y Precios' in Albert Carreras and Xavier Tafunell (eds) *Estadísticas Históricas de España, Siglos XIX–XX.* Bilbao: Fundación BBVA.

Manuel, Paul Christopher (1995). *Uncertain Outcome: The Politics of the Portuguese Transition to Democracy.* Lanham, Maryland: University Press of America.

Manuel, Paul Christopher (1996). *The Challenges of Democratic Consolidation in Portugal: Political, Economic, and Military Issues 1976–1991.* Westport, Conn.: Praeger.

March, James G. and Johan P. Olsen (1989). *Rediscovering Institutions: The Organizational Basis of Politics.* New York: Free Press.

March, James G. and Johan P. Olsen (2006). 'The Logic of Appropriateness' in Robert Goodin, Michael Moran, and Martin Rein (eds) *The Oxford Handbook of Public Policy.* Oxford: Oxford University Press.

March, James G. and Johan P. Olsen (1984). 'The New Institutionalism: Organizational Factors in Political Life', *American Political Science Review*, 78(3): 734–49.

Marques, Isabel Pestana (2004). '1914–1918. Comportamentos de guerra' in Manuel Themudo Barata and Nuno Severiano Teixeira (eds) *Nova História Militar de Portugal*, Vol. 5. Lisbon: Círculo de Lectores.

Martín de la Guardia, Ricardo (2008). *Cuestión de Tijeras: La censura en la transición a la democracia.* Madrid: Síntesis.

Martins, Herminio (1969). 'Opposition in Portugal', *Government and Opposition*, 4(2): 250–63.

Mascarenhas, Domingo (1982). *Portugalidade: Biografia duma Nação.* Lisbon: Edições FP.

Mashaw, Jerry L. and David L. Harfst (1990). *The Struggle for Auto Safety.* Cambridge: Harvard University Press.

Massons, José María (1994). *Historia de la Sanidad Militar española. Tomo II.* Barcelona: Pomares-Corredor.

Massis, Henri (1961). *Salazar face à face: trois dialogues politiques.* Paris: La Palatine.

Mata, Eugénia and Nuno Valerio (1994). *História Económica de Portugal: uma Perspectiva Global.* Lisbon: Fundamentos.

Mateus, Abel (1998). *Economia Portuguesa: Crescimento no contexto internacional (1910–1998).* Lisbon: Editorial Verbo.

Matos, Luís Salgado de (2004). 'A Orgânica das Forças Armadas Portuguesas' in Manuel Themudo Barata and Nuno Severiano Teixeira (eds) *Nova História Militar de Portugal*, Vol. 4. Lisbon: Círculo de Lectores.

Maxwell, Kenneth (1989). 'Regime Overthrow and the Prospects for Democratic Transition in Portugal' in O'Donnell Guillermo, Philippe C. Schmitter, and Laurence Whitehead (eds) *Transitions From Authoritarian Rule: Southern Europe.* Baltimore: The Johns Hopkins University Press.

Maxwell, Kenneth (1991). 'Portuguese Foreign and Defense Policy: A Global Analysis' in Kenneth Maxwell (ed.) *Portuguese Defense and Foreign Policy Since Democratization*. New York: Camões Center.

Maxwell, Kenneth (1995). *The Making of Portuguese Democracy*. Cambridge: Cambridge University Press.

McDonnell, Lorraine M. and Richard F. Elmore (1987). 'Getting the Job done: Alternative Policy Instruments', *Educational Evaluation and Policy Analysis*, 9(2): 133–52.

MDN (1986). *Livro Branco da Defesa Nacional: 1986*. Lisbon: Ministerio da Defesa Nacional.

Medina, Francisco (2006). *23 F: La verdad*. Barcelona: Plaza & Janes.

Medina, João (1977). *Salazar em França*. Lisbon: Atica.

Medina, João (1979). *Salazar e os Fascistas: Salazarismo e Nacional-Sindicalismo. A história de um conflito, 1932–1935*. Lisbon: Livraria Bertrand.

Medina, João (2000). *Salazar, Hitler e Franco: Estudos sobre Salazar e a Ditadura*. Lisbon: Livros Horizonte.

Melo, José Brandão Pereira de (1970). 'A impresa periódica militar', *Jornal do Exército*, 122.

Melo, Manuel José Homem de (1983). *Cartas de Salazar a Craveiro Lopes (1951–1958)*. Lisbon: Edições 70.

Mérida, Maria (1979). *Mis conversaciones con los generales*. Barcelona: Plaza & Janes.

Mesquita, Mota (1986). 'Esforço Financeiro da Defesa', *Nação e Defesa*, 38: 43–58.

Meyer, John W. and Brian Rowan (1977). 'Institutionalized Organizations: Formal Structure as Myth and Ceremony', *American Journal of Sociology*, 83(2): 340–63.

Miguel, Amando de (1975). *Sociología del Franquismo: Análisis ideológico de los Ministros del Régimen*. Editorial Euros: Barcelona.

Mills, C. Wright (1956). *The Power Elite*. Oxford: Oxford University Press.

Ministerio de Defensa (1986). *Memoria Legislatura (1982–1986)*. Madrid: Ministerio de Defensa.

Miranda, Jorge (1978). 'A Participação dos Militares no Exercício da Soberania', *Nacão e Defesa*, 5: 19–30.

Mitnick, Barry M. (1980). *The Political Economy of Regulation: Creating, Designing, and Removing Regulatory Forms*. New York: Columbia University Press.

Mola, Emilio (1940). *Obras Completas*. Valladolid: Librería Santarén.

Moniz, Júlio Botelho (1939). *Nação em guerra. Organização nacional da defesa*. Lisbon: Editorial Império.

Moore, Clement H. (1970). 'The Single Party as Source of Legitimacy' in Samuel Huntington and Clement H. Moore (eds) *Authoritarian Politics in Modern Society: The Dynamics of Established One-Party Systems*. New York: Basic Books.

Morán, Gregorio (2009). *Adolfo Suárez: ambición y destino*. Barcelona: Debate.

Moreira, Adriano (1980). 'Poder Militar – Poder Civil', *Nação e Defesa*, 16: 133–50.

Moreno Gómez, Francisco (1987). *Córdoba en la posguerra. La represión y la guerrilla (1939–1950)*, Cordoba: Francisco Baena D.L.

Moreno Juliá, Xavier (2004). *La division Azul. Sangre Española en Rusia, 1941–1945*. Barcelona: Critica.

Moskos, Charles C. (1977). 'From Institution to Occupation. Trends in Military Organisation', *Armed Forces & Society*, 4(1): 41–50.

Mujal Leon, Eusebio (1978). 'Communism and Revolution in Portugal' in Rudolf L. Tokes (ed.) *Eurocommunism and Détente*. New York: New York University Press.

Murdie, Amanda (2012). 'The Bad, the Good, and the Ugly: The Curvilinear Effects of Civil–Military Conflict on International Crisis Outcome', *Armed Forces & Society*, 39(2): 233–54.

Narli, Nilüfer (2000). 'Civil–Military Relations in Turkey', *Turkish Studies*, 1(1): 107–127.

Nataf, Daniel (1995). *Democratization and Social Settlements: The Politics of Change in Contemporary Portugal*. Albany: State of New York University Press.

Navajas Zubeldía, Carlos (1995). 'La política de defensa durante la transición y consolidación democráticas (1976–1986)' in Javier Tusell and Álvaro Soto (eds) *Historia de la transición y consolidación democrática en España (1975–1986)*, Vol. I. Madrid: UNED & UAM.

Navarro Rubio, Mariano (1991). *Mis Memorias: Testimonio de una Vida Política Truncada por el Caso MATESA*. Barcelona: Plaza y Janés.

Nicolau, Roser (2005). 'Poblacion, salud y actividad' in Albert Carreras and Xavier Tafunell (eds) *Estadisticas Historicas de España, Siglos XIX–XX*. Bilbao: Fundación BBVA.

Nielsen, Suzanne C. (2005). 'Civil–Military Relations Theory and Military Effectiveness', *Public Administration and Management*, 10(2): 61–84.

Nispen, Frans K. M. van and Arthur B. Ringeling (1998). 'On Instruments and Instrumentality: A Critical Assessment' in Guy B. Peters and Frans K. M. Van Nispen (eds) *Public Policy Instruments: Evaluating the Tools of Public Administration*. Cheltenham: Edward Elgar.

Nogueira, Franco (1980). *Salazar Vol. IV: O Ataque (1945–1958)*. Coimbra: Atlântida.

Nogueira, Franco (2000). *O Estado Novo*. Porto: Livraria Civilizaçao.

Nordlinger, Eric (1977). *Soldiers in Politics: Military Coups and Governments*. New York: Prentice Hall.

North, Douglas C. (1990). *Institutions, Institutional Change And Economic Performance*. Cambridge: Cambridge University Press.

Nunes, Leopoldo (1930). *O Ditador das Finanças*. Lisboa: Ottosgráfica.

O'Donnell, Guillermo and Philippe Schmitter (1986). *Transitions from Authoritarian Rule: Tentative Conclusions about Uncertain Democracies*. Baltimore: The Johns Hopkins University Press.

Oliveira, César (1987). *Salazar e a Guerra Civil de Espanha*. Lisbon: O Jornal.

Oliveira, César (1989). 'Oliveira Salazar ea Politica Externa Portuguesa: 1932–1968' in Fernando Rosas and José M. Brandão de Brito (eds) *Salazar e o Salazarismo*. Lisbon: Dom Quixote.

Oliveira, Pedro Aires (2007). *Os Despojos da Aliança: A Grã-Bretanha e a Questão Colonial Portuguesa 1945–1975*. Lisbon: Tinta da China.

Oliveira, Pedro Aires de, Fernando Rosas, and Júlia Leitão Barros (1996/eds). *Armindo Monteiro e Oliveira Salazar: Correspondência política 1926–1955*. Lisbon: Editorial Estampa.

Olmeda, José Antonio (1988). *La fuerzas armadas en el estado franquista: participación política, influencia presupuestaria y profesionalización, 1939–1975*. Madrid: Ediciones El Arquero.

Olmeda, José Antonio (2012). 'Escape from Huntington's Labyrinth? Civil–Military Relations and Comparative Politics' in Thomas C. Bruneau and Florina

Critiana Matei (eds) *The Routledge Handbook of Civil–Military Relations*. London: Routledge.

Olson, Mancur (1993). 'Dictatorship, Democracy and Development', *The American Political Science Review*, 87(3): 567–76.

Oltra, Benjamín and Amando de Miguel (1978). 'Bonapartismo y catolicismo: una hipotesis sobre los origenes ideologicos del franquismo', *Papers*, 8: 53–102.

Oneto, José (1975). *Cien días en la muerte de Francisco Franco*. Madrid: Felmar.

Opello Jr., Walter C. (1983). 'The Continuing Impact of the Old Regime on Portuguese Political Culture' in Lawrence S. Graham and Douglas L. Wheeler (eds) *In Search of Modern Portugal: The Revolution and Its Consequences*. Madison, Wisconsin: The University of Wisconsin Press.

Opello, Water C. Jr. (1985). *Portugal's Political Development: A Comparative Approach*. Boulder: Westview.

Ortega, José Antonio and Javier Silvestre (2005). *Consecuencias Demográficas de la Guerra Civil*. Paper presented on VIII 'Congreso de la Asociación Española de Historia Económica', Santiago de Compostela 13–16 September.

Osorio, Alfonso (1980). *Trayectoria política de un ministro de la Corona*. Barcelona: Planeta.

Palacios, Jesús (1999). *La España Totalitaria. Las Raices del Franquismo, 1934–1946*. Barcelona: Planeta.

Palacios, Jesús (2009). *23-F: El golpe del CESID*. Barcelona: Planeta.

Paulo, Heloisa (1994). *Estado Novo e Propaganda em Portugal e no Brasil: o SPN/SNI e o DIP*. Coimbra: Minerva História.

Payne, Stanley G. (1967). *Politics and the Military in Modern Spain*. Stanford: Stanford University Press.

Payne, Stanley G. (1986). 'Modernization of the Armed Forces' in Stanley Payne (ed.) *The Politics of Democratic Spain*. Chicago: Chicago Council on Foreign Relations.

Payne, Stanley G. (1987). *The Franco Regime: 1936–1975*. Madison: The University of Wisconsin Press.

Payne, Stanley G. (1999). *Fascism in Spain: 1923–1977*. Madison: University of Wisconsin University Press.

Pereira, António Vaz (1986). 'Portugal e a NATO', *Nacão e Defesa*, 39: 59–77.

Pérez Díaz, Victor (1993). *The Return of Civil Society: The Emergence of Democratic Spain*. Cambridge: Harvard University Press.

Pérez Muinelo, Francisco (2009). *El Gasto de Defensa en España: 1946–2009*. Madrid: Ministerio de Defensa.

Peters, Guy B. (1999). *Institutional Theory in Political Science: The 'New Institutionalism'*. London: Pinter.

Peters, Guy B., Jon Pierre, and Desmond S. King (2005). 'The Politics of Path Dependency: Political Conflict in Historical Institutionalism', *The Journal of Politics*, 67(4): 1275–300.

Pierson, Paul (2000). 'Increasing Returns, Path Dependence, and the Study of Politics', *American Political Science Review*, 94(2): 251–68.

Pierson, Paul (2003). 'Big, Slow-Moving, and…Invisible: Macro-Social Processes in the Study of Comparative Politics' in James Mahoney and Dietrich Rueschemeyer (eds) *Comparative Historical Analysis in the Social Sciences*. Cambridge: Cambridge University Press.

Pierson, Paul (2004). *Politics in Time: History, Institutions and Social Analysis*. Princeton: Princeton University Press.

Pimentel, Irene Flunser (2007). *A história da PIDE*. Lisboa: Círculo de Leitores.

Pimlott, Ben and Jean Seaton (1980). 'The Role of the Media in the Portuguese Revolution' in Smith Anthony (ed.) *Newspapers and Democracy: International Essays on a Changing Medium*. Cambridge, MA: MIT Press.

Pimlott, Ben and Jean Seaton (1983). 'Political Power and the Portuguese Media' in Lawrence S. Graham and Douglas L. Wheeler (eds) *In Search of Modern Portugal: The Revolution and Its Consequence*. Madison, WI: The University of Wisconsin Press.

Pinto, António Costa (1994). *Os Camisas Azuis. Ideologia, Elites e Movimentos Fascistas em Portugal, 1914–1945*. Lisbon: Estampa.

Pinto, António Costa (1995). *Salazar's Dictatorship and European Fascism*. Boulder, Colo.: Social Science Monographs.

Pinto, António Costa (2006). 'Portugal's Transition to Democracy in the 1970's: the Double Legacy' in Marietta Minitos (ed.) *Transition to Democracy in Spain, Portugal and Greece Thirty Years After*. Athens: Ekdoseis Pataki.

Pion-Berlin, David (1992). 'Military Autonomy and Emerging Democracies in South America', *Comparative Politics*, 25(1): 83–102.

Pires, Francisco Lucas (1976), 'As Forças Armadas e a Constituição', *Nacão e Defesa*, 2: 31–9.

Platón, Miguel (2001). *Hablan los militares: testimonios para la historia (1339–1996)*. Barcelona: Planeta.

Pollitt, Christopher and Geert Bouckaert (2000). *Public Management Reform: A Comparative Analysis*. Oxford: Oxford University Press.

Porch, Douglas (1977). *The Portuguese Armed Forces and the Revolution*. Stanford: Hoover Institute Press.

Portero, Florentino (1999). 'Spain, Britain and the Cold War' in Sebastian Balfour and Paul Preston (eds) *Spain and the Great Powers in the Twentieth Century*. London: Routledge.

Posner, Richard A. (1974). 'Theories of Economic Regulation', *Bell Journal of Economic and Management Science*, 5(2): 335–58.

Powell, Charles (1991). *El piloto del cambio: el rey, la monarquía y la transición a la democracia*. Barcelona: Planeta.

Powell, Charles (1996). *Juan Carlos: A Self-Made Monarch*. London: Macmillan Press.

Powell, Charles (2001). *España en Democracia, 1975–2000*. Barcelona: Plaza & Janés.

Prego, Victoria (1999). *Diccionario de la transición*. Barcelona: Plaza & Janés Press.

Preston, Paul (1986). *The Triumph of Democracy in Spain*. London: Routledge.

Preston, Paul (1990). *The Politics of Revenge: Fascism and the Military in Twentieth-century Spain*. London: Unwin Hyman.

Preston, Paul (1993). *Franco: A Biography*. London: Harper Collins.

Preston, Paul (2004). *Juan Carlos: A People's King*. London: Harper Collins.

Preston, Paul (2006 [1986]). *The Spanish Civil War: Reaction, Revolution and Revenge*. London: Harper Perennial.

Preston, Paul (2011). *El holocausto español. Odio y exterminio en la Guerra Civil y después*. Barcelona: Debate.

Przeworski, Adam and Fernando Limongi (1993). 'Political Regimes and Economic Growth', *The Journal of Economic Perspectives*, 7(3): 51–69.

Puell de la Villa, Fernando (1997). *Gutiérrez Mellado, un militar del siglo XX (1912–1995)*. Madrid: Biblioteca Nueva. UNED.

Puell de la Villa, Fernando (2005). *Historia del Ejército en España. Segunda Edición*. Madrid: Alianza.

Puell de la Villa, Fernando (2008). *Historia de la Protección Social Militar (1265–1978): de la Ley de Partidas al ISFAS*. Madrid: Instituto Social de las Fuerzas Armadas.

Radaelli, Claudio M. (2000). 'Policy Transfer in the European Union: Institutional Isomorphism as a Source of Legitimacy', *Governance: An International Journal of Policy and Administration*, 13(1): 25–43.

Rato, Vasco (2000). 'As Forças Armadas e Democracia Portuguesa, 1974–1982', *Nação e Defesa*, 94: 123–62.

Ravara, Rui de Faria (1989). 'As Bases Conceptuais do Ensino e da Investigação no Exército', *Nação e Defesa*, 49: 141–74.

Rebelo de Sousa, Marcelo (1990). 'Da Crispaçao Institucional ao Equilibrio Instable de Poderes' in Antonio Reis (ed.) *Portugal Contemporâneo*, Vol. III. Lisbon: Publicaçoes Alfa.

Reinares, Fernando (1990). 'Sociogénesis y evolución del terrorismo en España' in Salvador Giner (ed.) *España, sociedad y política*. Madrid: Espasa-Calpe.

Reinlein, Fernando (2002). *Capitanes Rebeldes*. Madrid: La Esfera Historia.

Richards, Michael (2006). *A Time of Silence: Civil War and the Culture of Repression*. Cambridge: Cambridge University Press.

Ringeling, Arthur B. (2005). 'Instruments in Four' in Pearl Eliadis, Margaret M. Hill, and Michael Howlett (eds) *Designing Government: From Instruments to Governance*. Montreal: Mc-Gill-Queen's University Press.

Rixen, Thomas and Lora Viola (2009). 'Uses and Abuses of the Concept of Path Dependence: Toward a Clearer Theory of Institutional Change'. Paper presented at the *American Political Science Association Annual Meeting*. Toronto, Ontario, Canada, 3–6 September 2009.

Robinson, Richard (1979). *Contemporary Portugal: A History*. London: Allen and Unwin.

Rodrigo, Fernando (1985). 'El papel de las Fuerzas Armadas Españolas durante la transición política: algunas hipótesis básicas', *Revista Internacional de Sociología*, 43(2): 349–69.

Rodrigo, Fernando (1989). *El camino hacia la democracia: militares y política en la transición española*. Madrid: Doctoral Book. Universidad Complutense.

Rodrigo, Fernando (1992). 'A Democratic Strategy towards the Military in Post-Franco Spain' in Constantine Danopoulos (ed.) *From Military to Civilian Rule*. London: Routledge.

Rodrigues, Luís Nuno (1996). *A Legião Portuguesa: a milícia do Estado Novo (1936–1944)*. Lisbon: Editorial Estampa.

Rodríguez Sahagún, Agustín (1986). 'La Reforma Militar en los Gobiernos de Suárez', *Revista Española de Investigaciones Sociológicas*, 36: 189–96.

Rollo, Fernanda (1994). *Portugal e o Plano Marshall*. Lisboa: Estampa.

Ros Agudo, Manuel (2002). *La Guerra Secreta de Franco (1939–1945)*. Barcelona: Crítica.

Rosas, Fernando (1986). *O Estado Novo nos Anos Trinta*. Lisbon: Estampa.

Rosas, Fernando (1988). *O Salazarismo e a alianza Luso-Britânica*. Lisbon: Editorial Fragmentos.

Rosas, Fernando (1989). 'Salazar e o Salazarismo um caso de longevidade política' in Fernando Rosas and José M. Brandao de Brito (eds) *Salazar e o Salazarismo*. Lisbon: Dom Quixote.

Rosas, Fernando (1994). 'Estado Novo (1926–1974)' in José Mattoso (ed.) *História de Portugal*. Lisbon: Círculo de Leitores.

Rosas, Fernando (2000). 'El desarrollo económico en los años 30 y 40: industrialización sin reforma agraria' in Costa Pinto (ed.) *Portugal Contemporáneo*. Madrid: Sequitur.

Rose, Richard (1991). 'What is Lesson Drawing?', *Journal of Public Policy*, 11(1): 3–30.

Rose, Richard (1993). *Lesson Drawing in Public Policy*. Chatham N.J.: Chatham House Publishers.

Rosen, Stephen Peter (1995). 'Military Effectiveness: Why Society Matters', *International Security*, 19(4): 5–31.

Sahlin-Andersson, Kerstin (2002). 'National, International, and Transnational Constructions of New Public Management' in Tom Christensen and Per Lægreid (eds) *New Public Management: The Transformation of Ideas and Practice*. Aldershot: Ashgate.

Salamon, Lester M. (1981). 'Rethinking Public Management: Third Party Government and the Changing Forms of Government Action', *Public Policy*, 29(3): 255–75.

Salamon, Lester M. (2002/ed.). *The Tools of Government: A Guide to the New Governance*. Oxford: Oxford University Press.

Salamon, Lester M. and Michael S. Lund (1989). 'The Tools Approach: Basic Analytics' in Lester Salamon (ed.) *Beyond Privatization: The Tools of Government Action*. Washington, DC: The Urban Institute Press.

Salas López, Fernando de (1974). *España, la OTAN y los organismos militares internacionales*. Madrid: Editora Nacional.

Salazar, Antonio Oliveira (1933). 'Prefacio de Oliveira Salazar' in Antonio Ferro (ed.) *Salazar: o Homem e a sua Obra*. Lisbon: Empresa Nacional de Publicidade.

Salazar, Antonio Oliveira (1935). *Discursos: 1928–1934*. Coimbra: Coimbra Editora.

Salazar, Antonio Oliveira (1939). *Doctrine and Action: Internal and Foreign Policy of the New Portugal 1928–1939*. London: Faber and Faber.

Salazar, Antonio Oliveira (1951). *Discursos e Notas Políticas 1943–1950*, Vol. IV. Coimbra: Coimbra Editora.

Sánchez Cervelló, Josep (1993). *A Revolução Portuguesa e a sua Influência na Transição Espanhola (1961–1976)*. Lisbon: Assirio & Alvim.

Sánchez Cuenca, Ignacio and Paloma Aguilar (2009). 'Terrorist Violence and Popular Mobilization: The Case of the Spanish Transition to Democracy', *Politics & Society*, 37(3): 435.

Sánchez Navarro, Ángel (1990). *La transición política en las Cortes de Franco: hacia la Ley para la Reforma Política*, Centro de Estudios Avanzados en Ciencias Socialesi, Working Paper 11. Madrid: Instituto Juan March.

Sanders, Elisabeth (2006). 'Historical Institutionalism' in R. A. W. Rhodes, Sarah E. Binder and Bert Rockman (eds) *The Oxford Handbook of Political Institutions*. Oxford: Oxford University Press.

Santos, José Loureiro dos (1978). 'Sobre uma possível Lei da Defesa Nacional – Reflexões', *Nacão e Defesa*, 5: 9–18.

Santos, José Loureiro dos (1980). 'Aspectos a Considerar nas Relações nas Forças Armadas com o Poder Político', *Nacão e Defesa*, 13: 75–108.

Santos, José Loureiro dos (2000). 'Forças Armadas e Poder Político em Democracia: A Transição Democrática em Portugal', *Nacão e Defesa*, 94: 163–174.

Saz Campos, Ismael (2004). *Fascismo y Franquismo*. Valencia: Universitat de Valencia.

Schmitter, Philippe C. (1975). *Corporatism and Public Policy in Authoritarian Portugal*. London: Sage.

Schmitter, Philippe C. (1979). 'The "Régime d'Exception"' in Lawrence Graham and Glyn A. Stone (2005). *Spain, Portugal and the Great Powers, 1931–1941*. Basingstoke: Palgrave Macmillan.

Schmitter, Philippe C. (1999). *Portugal: do Autoritarismo à Democracia*. Lisbon: Instituto de Ciências Sociais.

Schneider, Anne L. and Helen Ingram (1990). 'Fundamentals for a Theory of Policy Instruments', *Journal of Politics*, 52(2): 511–29.

Seco Serrano, Carlos (1984). *Militarismo y civilismo en la España contemporánea*. Madrid: Instituto de Estudios Económicos.

Segura Valero, Gastón (2006). *Ifni: la Guerra que silenció Franco*. Madrid: Martínez Roca Ediciones.

Seixas, Artur Sá (1978). 'A Estructuração das Forças Armadas e a suas Funções Constitucionais', *Nacão e Defesa*, 5: 105–14.

Serra, Narcís (1986). 'La Política Española de Defensa', *Revista Española de Investigaciones Sociológicas*, 36: 173–88.

Serra, Narcís (2000). 'La reestructuración de las Fuerzas Armadas Españolas 1976–1989' in Escuela Superior de Guerra/Pontificia Universidad Javeriana (ed.) *El papel de las fuerzas militares en una democracia en Desarrollo. Memorias de la conferencia internacional*. Bogotá.

Serra, Narcís (2008). *La transición militar. Reflexiones en torno a la reforma democrática de las fuerzas armadas*. Barcelona: Debate.

Serra, Narcís (2009). 'Beyond Threats to Democracy form the Armed Forces, Police and Intelligence: The Spanish Case' in Alfred Stepan (ed.) *Democracies in Danger*. Baltimore: The Johns Hopkins University Press.

Serrano Suñer, Ramón (1977). *Entre el silencio y la propaganda. La historia como fue. Memorias*. Barcelona: Planeta.

Sewell, Williams H. (1996). 'Three Temporalities: Toward an Eventful Sociology' in Terrence J. McDonald (ed.) *The Historic Turn in the Human Sciences*. Ann Arbor: University of Michigan Press.

SIED (2010). 'Resenha Histórica', *Serviço de Informações Estratégicas de Defesa*, http://www.sied.pt/reshistorica_sirp.html [accessed 30 May 2013].

Sil, Rudra and Peter J. Katzenstein (2010). *Beyond Paradigms: Analytic Eclecticism in the Study of World Politics*. London: Palgrave Macmillan.

Silva, Aníbal Cavaco (1986). 'Orientações da Política de Defesa', *Nação e Defesa*, 39: 9–20.

Silva, Josué da (1975). *Legião Portuguesa, força represiva do fascismo*. Lisbon: Diabril Editora.

SIS (2010). 'História do SIS'. *Serviço de Informações de Segurança*, http://www.sis.pt/hsis.html [accessed 29 May 2013].

Skocpol, Theda (1992). *Protecting Soldiers and Mothers: The Political Origins of Social Policy in the United States*. Cambridge: Cambridge University Press.

Skocpol, Theda (2003). 'Doubly Engaged Social Science: The Promise of Comparative Historical Analysis' in James Mahoney and Dietrich Rueschemeyer (eds) *Comparative Historical Analysis in the Social Sciences*. Cambridge: Cambridge University Press.

Skocpol, Theda and Margarett Weir (1985). 'State Structures and the Possibilities for "Keynesian" Responses to the Great Depression in Sweden, Britain, and the United States' in Peter B. Evans, Dietrich Rueschemeyer and Theda Skocpol (eds) *Bringing the State Back In*. Cambridge: Cambridge University Press.

Smith, Louis (1951). *American Democracy and Military Power*. Chicago: University of Chicago Press.

Soares, Alberto Ribeiro (1987). 'Comunicação Social e Forças Armadas Numa Perspectiva de Defesa Nacional', *Nação e Defesa*, 41: 159–76.

Solé i Sabaté, Josep M. (1985). *La repressió franquista a Catalunya (1938–1953)*, Barcelona: Edicions 62.

Spínola, António (1974). *Portugal e o Futuro: Análise da Conjuntura Nacional*. Lisbon: Arcádia.

SPN (1934). *Decálogo do Estado Novo*. Lisbon: Secretariado da Propaganda Nacional.

SPN (1940). *O Estado Novo, Principios e Realizacões*. Lisbon: Secretariado da Propaganda Nacional.

SPN (1942). *A obra de Salazar na pasta das Finanças: 27 de Abril de 1928 a 28 de Agosto de 1940*. Lisbon: Secretariado da Propaganda Nacional.

SPN (1943). *A Revolução Continua*. Lisbon: Secretariado da Propaganda Nacional.

SPN (undated1). *Habla Salazar: Algunos Extractos de sus Discursos y Notas Oficiosas*. Lisbon: Secretariado da Propaganda Nacional.

SPN (undated 2). *La pensée de Salazar*. Lisbon: Secretariado da Propaganda Nacional.

SPN (undated 3). *Portugal ante la guerra civil de España: documentos y notas*. Lisbon: Secretariado da Propaganda Nacional.

SPN (undated 4). *Portugal: The New State in Theory and in Practice*. Lisbon: Secretariado da Propaganda Nacional.

Staniland, Paul (2008). 'Explaining Civil–Military Relations in Complex Political Environments: India and Pakistan in Comparative Perspective', *Security Studies*, 17: 322–62.

Steinmo, Sven, Kathelen Thelen, and Frank Longstreth (1992/eds). *Structuring Politics: Historical Institutionalism in Comparative Analysis*. New York: Cambridge University Press.

Stepan, Alfred (1971). *The Military in Politics: Changing Patterns in Brazil*. Princeton: Princeton University Press.

Stinchcombe, Arthur L. (1968). *Constructing Social Theories*. Chicago: The University of Chicago Press.

Stokey, Edith and Richard Zeckhauser (1978). *A Primer for Policy Analysis*. New York: W.W. Norton.

Stone, Glyn A. (2005). *Spain, Portugal and the Great Powers, 1931–1941*. Basingstoke: Palgrave Macmillan.

Sun Tzu (2003 [c. 500 BC]). *The Art of War*. London: Penguin Classics.

Tarrow, Sidney (1995). 'The International Context of Democratic Consolidation: Southern Europe in Comparative Perspective' in Richard Gunther, Nikiforos Diamandouros and Hans-Jürgen Puhle (eds) *The Politics of Democratisation. Southern Europe in Comparative Perspective*. Baltimore: The John Hopkins University Press.

Teixeira, Nuno Severiano (2004). 'Portugal nos Conflitos Internacionais' in Manuel Themudo Barata and Nuno Severiano Teixeira (eds) *Nova História Militar de Portugal*, Vol. 4. Lisbon: Círculo de Leitores.

Telo, António José (1989). *Portugal na Segunda Guerra Mundial*. Lisbon: Doctoral Book Faculdade de Letras, Universidade de Lisboa.

Telo, António José (1990). *Propaganda e Guerra Secreta em Portugal (1939–1945)*. Lisbon: Perspectivas e Realidades.

Telo, António José (1993). 'As Forças Armadas ou República decapitada' in João Medina (ed.) *História de Portugal: Dos Tempos Pré-Históricos aos Nossos Dias, A República*, Vol. II. Amadora: Ediclube.

Telo, António José (1996). *Portugal e a NATO: o Reencontro da Tradição Atlântica*. Lisbon: Cosmos.

Telo, António José (1999). 'Portugal and NATO 1949–1976' in Leandro García (ed.) *Portugal and the Fifty Years of the Atlantic Alliance (1949–1999)*. Lisboa: Ministry of National Defence.

Telo, António José and Hipólito de la Torre (2000). *Portugal e Espanha: nos Sistemas Internacionais Contemporâneos*. Lisbon: Edições Cosmos.

Thelen, Katheleen (1999). 'Historical Institutionalism in Compartive Politics', *The Annual Review of Political Science*, 2: 369–404.

Thelen, Kathleen (2003). 'How Institutions Evolve: Insights from Comparative Historical Analysis', Authoritarianism' in James Mahoney and Dietrich Rueschemeyer (eds) *Comparative Historical Analysis in the Social Sciences*. Cambridge: Cambridge University Press.

Thelen, Kathleen and Steven Steinmo (1992). 'Institutionalism in Comparative Politics' in Franck Longstreth, Kathleen Thelen and Steven Steinmo (eds) *Structuring Politics. Historical Institutionalism in Comparative Analysis*. Cambridge: Cambridge University Press.

Thucydides (1972 [431 BC]). *History of the Peloponnesian War*. London: Penguin Classics.

Trebilcock, Michael (2005). 'The Choice of Governing Instruments' in Pearl Eliadis, Margaret M. Hill, and Michael Howlett (eds) *Designing Government: From Instruments to Governance*. Montreal: Mc-Gill-Queen's University Press.

Trebilcock, Michael, J. R. S. Prichard, Douglas Hartle and Don Dewees (1982). *The Choice of Governing Instrument*. Ottawa: Minister of Supply and Services.

Tusell, Javier (1988). *La Dictadura de Franco*. Madrid: Alianza.

Tusell, Javier (1995). *Juan Carlos I: la restauración de la monarquía*. Madrid: Temas de Hoy.

Tyler, Tom R. (2006). 'Social Motives and Institutional Design' in Christian Schubert and Georg von Wanghenheim (eds) *Evolution and Design of Institutions*. London: Routlegde.

Vagts, Alfred (1937). *A History of Militarism: A Romance and Realities of a Profession*. New York: Norton.

Valenciano Almoyna, Jesús (1986). 'La reforma de la justicia militar en España durante la transición', *Revista Española de Investigaciones Sociológicas*, 36: 141–152.

Valério, Nuno (2001). *Portuguese Historical Statistics*. Lisbon: INE.

Van Evera, Stephen (1984). 'The Cult of the Offensive and the Origins of the First World War', *International Security*, 9(1): 58–107.

Vedung, Evert (1998). 'Typologies and Theories' in Marie-Louise Bemelmans-Videc, Ray C. Rist, and Evert Vedung (eds) *Carrots, Sticks and Sermons: Policy Instruments & their Evaluation*. New Brunswick: Transaction Publishers.

Vicente, António Pedro (1996). 'Portugal e a Nato Face ao Isolamento de Espanha' in António José Telo (ed.) *O fim da segunda guerra mundial e os novos rumos da Europa*. Lisbon: Cosmos.

Vieira, Belchior (1995). 'A Instituição Militar e as Suas Relações com a Sociedade e o Poder Político', *Nação e Defesa*, 74: 65–76.

Vigón, Jorge (1956 [1950]). *El Espíritu Militar Español. Replica a Alfredo de Vigny*, 2nd edn. Madrid: Rialp.

Vilar, Manuel Dória (2009). 'Direito Penal/Amnistia 1974–2009'. Verbalegis.Net: *Portal de Direito*, http://www.verbalegis.net/leisamnistia.html [accessed 30 May 2013].

Viñas, Ángel (1981). *Los pactos secretos de Franco con Estados Unidos. Bases, ayuda económica, recortes de soberanía*. Barcelona: Grijalbo.

Viñas, Ángel (1988). 'Spain and NATO: Internal Debate and External Changes' in John Chipman (ed.) *NATO's Southern Allies*. London: Routledge.

Viñas, Ángel (1999). 'Spanish Foreign Policy from Franco to Felipe González' in Sebastian Balfour and Paul Preston (eds) *Spain and the Great Powers in the Twentieth Century*. London: Routledge.

Viver Pi-Sunyer, Carles (1978). *El personal politico de Franco (1936–1945)*. Barcelona: Vicens Vives.

Weimer, David L. and Aidan R. Vining (1992). *Policy Analysis: Concepts and Practice*, 2nd edn. Englewood Cliffs, NJ: Prentice-Hall.

Wingate Pike, David (1968). *Conjecture, Propaganda, and Deceit and the Spanish Civil War*. Stanford: California Institute of International Studies.

Welch, Claude E. (1987). *No Farewell to Arms? Military Disengagement from Politics in Africa and. Latin America*. Boulder: Westview Press.

Wendt, Alexander (1998). 'On Constitution and Causation in International Relations', *Review of International Studies*, 24: 101–18.

Wendt, Alexander (1999). *Social Theory of International Politics*. New York: Cambridge University Press.

Weyland, Kurt (2008). 'Toward a New Theory of Institutional Change', *World Politics*, 60: 281–314.

Wheeler, Douglas L. (1979). 'The Honor of the Army', in Lawrence S. Graham and Harry M. Makler (eds) *Contemporary Portugal: The Revolution and Its Antecedents*. Austin: University of Texas Press.

Wiarda, Howard J. (1988). *The Transition to Democracy in Spain and Portugal*. Washington, DC: American Enterprise Institute for Public Policy Research.

Wilson, James Q. (1980/ed.) *The Politics of Regulation*. New York: Basic Books.

Wolf, Charles Jr. (1987). 'Markets and non Market failures: Comparison and Assessment', *Journal of Public Policy*, 7(1): 43–70.

Woodside, Kenneth (1986). 'Policy Instruments and the Study of Public Policy', *Canadian Journal of Political Science*, 19(4): 775–97.

Ynfante, Jesus (1976). *El ejército de Franco y de Juan Carlos*. Chatillon-sous-Bagneaux: Ruedo Ibérico.

Zuk, L. Gary and William R. Thompson (1982). 'The Post-coup Military Spending Question: A Pooled Cross-sectional Time Series Analysis', *American Political Science Review*, 76(1): 60–74.

Newspapers and Magazine Articles

ABC (28 December 1958) 'El año militar'.
ABC (10 March 1978) 'Expedientados en Ceuta siete militares por una reunión con Blas Piñar'.
ABC (22 February 1981) 'Consejo de Guerra contra un dirigente de Comisiones Marineiras'.
Daily Mail (4 October 1948) 'U.S. seeking ports and airfields'.
Daily Telegraph (4 October 1948) 'U.S. need of Spanish Bases'.
Ejército n. 15, April 1941, 'Con ocasión del 1 de abril'.
Ejército n. 24, January 1942: 'Los Ejércitos modernos ante el material'.
Ejército n. 60, January 1945 'La caballeria y la mecanización'.
Ejército n. 132, January 1951, 'Discurso de la Pascua Militar'.
Ejército n. 258, July 1961 'Número extraordinario dedicado a nuestra Cruzada'.
El País (2 October 1976) 'Pase a la reserva de Iniesta Cano y De Santiago'.
El Pais (6 January 1977) 'Los militares deben obedecer también al mando político'.
El País (6 January 1978) 'El general Vega elogió la capacidad militar de Lister y Modesto'.
El País (29 May 1979) 'El general Atarés, absuelto'.
El País (21 February 1982) 'Hubo careo Suárez-Armada en el otoño de 1977'.
Le Soir (8 October 1948) 'Franco sera-t-il admis dans l'Union Occidentale?'.
New York Times (8 October 1948) 'Western Europe Fears Spain Base'.

Archives

António Oliveira Salazar Archive, Lisbon

AOS/CLB/FA-5
AOS/CO/FI-11T
AOS/CO/FI-11X
AOS/CO/GR-10
AOS/CO/GR-11
AOS/CO/GR-1A
AOS/CO/GR-1B
AOS/CO/GR-1C
AOS/CO/GR-1D
AOS/CO/GR-6
AOS/CO/IN-8A
AOS/CO/NE-17–1
AOS/CO/NE-17–2
AOS/CO/NE-2B1
AOS/CO/R-1C

Portuguese Military History Archive, Lisbon

AHM, divisão 1, secção 39: Guerra do Ultramar (1961–1974)
AHM, divisão 1, secção 40: MFA – Conselho da Revolução (1974–1982)
AHM, Fundo 26: Arquivo Miranda Cabral

Marcello Caetano Archive, Lisbon

AMC/12–79
AMC/12–1549
AMC/12–425

Council of the Revolution Archive, Lisbon

ACR, Actas Conselho da Revolução – Originais, volumes 1, 2
ACR, Correspondência classificada do secretariado coordenador, Assuntos
    Económicos Sociais – Cartas Particulares – Diversos, volumes 82, 83
ACR, Correspondência classificada do secretariado coordenador, volumes 6, 7, 8,
    9, 13, 14, 15, 16, 17, 18, 20
ACR, MFA/Partidos (84), Pacto MFA-Partidos Parte I
ACR, MFA/Partidos (84), Pacto MFA-Partidos Parte II

Fundación Nacional Francisco Franco (FFNF) Archive, Madrid

Documents 28, 126, 938, 1597, 5064, 8893, 10602, 11048, 14022, 15234, 19413,
    19149, 19311, 19312, 19313, 19423, 20529, 20343, 26892, 26943

Audio Archive Fundación Ortega y Gasset, Madrid

Interview with José Maria de Areilza (13 September 1984, cassettes J8, J8bis)
Interview with Antonio Garrigues Díaz-Cañabate (4 October 1984, cassettes J9,
    J9bis)
Interview with Alfonso Osorio (29 November 1984, cassette J14–3)
Interview with José Manuel Otero Novas (17 January 1985, cassette J1)
Interview with General José Miguel Vega Rodríguez (14 October 1986, cassette J19)
Interview with General Sáez de Tejada (17 November 1987, cassettes J25bis and
    J25T)
Interviews with Admiral Liberal Lucini (20, 27 November, 4 December 1987
    cassettes J27bis, J29bis, J30, J30bis)
Interview with Lieutenant-General José Gabeiras Montero (11, 15 December
    1987, cassettes J31bis, J32, J32bis)
Interview with Lieutenant-General Manuel Gutiérrez Mellado (8 September 1987,
    cassette J20)
Interview with Lieutenant-General Ignacio Alfaro Arregui (18 December 1987,
    cassette J33, J33bis)
Seminars on Armed Forces and Military Consolidation (25, 26 April 1988, cassettes
    CF1, CF2, CF6)
Seminars on Military Education (Cangas de Onis) (30 June 1987, 1 July 1987,
    cassettes A2–4, A2–5, A2–7, A2–8)

Index

CPSIA information can be obtained at www.ICGtesting.com
Printed in the USA
BVOW06*1219090816

R7278600001B/R72786PG457806BVX16B/7/P